MW01625696

GLOBAL BOOSTERS™

Global History & Geography II
ED BOOSTERS SERIES™

R. Hertz,
Chief Boosters Pal

ISBN 978-0-578-62799-1

My Name: ______________________

(Also known as: Future Global Pro)

Copyright

All the super helpful methods and hints are my original ideas. Please do not reproduce them. Thanks!

THIRD EDITION

Table of Contents

Table of Contents

Can't wait to learn all this together. It looks like a lot, but time flies when you're having fun!

Thanks Page – Warning! Boosters Style 

- A special thanks to the Boosters Geeks Party (yes, it's a party!) who contributed to make this book as accurate, magnificent, and valuable as it is. Thank you, history experts S. Sokoloff, E. Saadia, T. Kuluszyner, and J. Devor. Thank you, talented graphics group L. Falk and Splash Graphics for developing the graphic concept and V. Kasirajan for bringing each page to life. Thank you, editors M. Heimowitz and N. Dave for swinging the perfect balance of Professionalism vs. "Teenagerism" (editor vs. Mr. Booster).

- A special shoutout to my beloved students who make each lesson so engaging and keep me on my toes! Thanks for being the best guinea pigs for the out-of-the-box Boosters methods and for your fabulous feedback and encouragement to continue writing new books. (Read: Mrs. Hertz, I know I only asked you 14 times this week, but when are the Global Boosters going to be ready?)

- And no one beats my spunky and supportive family and extended family who are my best cheerleaders and my greatest joy!

- Last but not least, this book has been dedicated to:
  The one who infuses me with care, creativity, and energy to write during insane hours...
  The one who never discourages my zany ideas, just energizes me to forge ahead...
  My dear... Chocolate!

HOW TO USE BOOSTERS™

Flashcards: Complex material is broken down into small chunks of information. The top box on each page is the title; the bottom box contains the info you need to know on the topic. To test yourself, cover the bottom box with the card cover included.

Hints: Intuitive hints are sprinkled throughout the cards to help you remember the material. There are all different types of hints: acronyms (words made from initials), easy sentences based on the material, and many more.

Common Regents Question: Alert to common question

Essay Topic: Alert to info you can use in your essay

How to Use Boosters™

Note: Important detail indicated

Example: Examples are sprinkled throughout to illustrate the concept.

Mr. Boosters: You can depend on him for "peanut gallery" style comments.

Definitions: The vocabulary word is shown in caps lock, followed by a colon and the definition.

Example — ELEMENTS: The smallest part of matter that can't be broken down into smaller substances.

Hints and funny comments can be found on the right side of the card.

What They're Saying About Boosters™

"My students loved the hints and easy-to-learn format of the cards. They were able to learn and retain the required material effectively."
–D. Sprague,
Teacher, Edward R. Murrow High School

"The information is clear-cut, without extra info. If you know the book, you know the course."
–Brian (Student)

"My son with learning disabilities failed his way through the year. We really wanted him to pass the Regents, but were at a loss. We ordered Boosters™ online and... he passed! This is God sent."
–Christine (Parent)

These cards are a lifesaver. They're so unique and the hints make it so amazingly simple to remember the material. This is truly a must-have for anyone who needs an easier way to retain all the info in their brains!! Buying this product is...what can I say.. it's a NO-BRAINER!!
–S.G.N. (Student)

Test Format

This book is designed to align with the New York Regents curriculum as well as most other educational standards.

For our New York readers, here are some important notes tailored just for you.

The Regents committee made some major changes to the new Global History & Geography II Regents, in January 2020. This book will fully prepare you for the new Regents.

GLOBAL II REGENTS FORMAT:

1. **28 multiple-choice questions:** Each multiple-choice question is based on a document (text, map, or political cartoon).
   - You will find plenty of practice multiple-choice questions following each unit.
2. **Two sets of 3 to 4 Constructed Response Questions:** You provide a written response based on the document given.
   - Throughout this book, you will find "cause and effect" and "turning point" ideas pointed out for you. This will help you answer the Constructed Response Questions.
3. **Enduring Issues Essay:** The Regents will give you 5 documents. You get to choose any Enduring Issue you'd like that connects to the documents, and then you write an essay based on the documents and on your own genius knowledge.
   - Throughout the book, you will find this icon: E This will help you know which historical examples fit in to which Enduring Issues.

Flip to the last two units to learn more about the new Regents format.

How the Boosters Will Prepare You for Global Success

1. In this book, we'll teach you all the info you need to know, chapter by chapter.

2. At the end of each unit, actual practice questions are included to help you apply the info you learned. After each question, Mr. Boosters explains how to solve the question.

3. At the end of the book, you'll find a full unit with instructions on how to answer each type of question.

4. The last unit includes full step-by-step instructions on how to write a killer essay.

The Boosters Multiple-Choice Magic Technique

The new Global Regents' multiple-choice questions are a lot of fun. They will always be based on a document, which means we need to learn how to analyze documents.

The Boosters Multiple-Choice Magic Technique trains your brain to take the document apart, look out for clues, and crack the question! Get out your highlighter and colorful pens to gather the clues you're about to find.

Here's how the Boosters Multiple-Choice Magic Technique works:

1. Find the title. This will guide your brain to the main topic.
2. Find the source. This is usually found on the bottom of the document. These tiny letters can be a huge help! The source often states the year, a key name, or location.
3. Now let's look at the question. What do they want to know? This will guide us to what we are looking for.
4. Finally, we look at the actual document. Highlight, circle, sit with it, and try to crack it! What's it trying to show?
5. Now that you cracked all the codes, you can go back to the question and answer it confidently!

Some documents will be missing a title or source. No problem – just look for the clues in other places.

Boosters Multiple-Choice Magic Example

To make Global super clear, the Boosters magic technique uses fun colors and numbers to guide you. Here's a sample question.

1

Atatürk's Fashion Police Boosters title explanation

Boosters doc explanation

Turkey's restrictions on wearing overtly religious-oriented attire are rooted in the founding of the modern, secular Turkish state, when the republic's founding father, Mustafa Kemal Atatürk, introduced a series of clothing regulations designed to keep religious symbolism out of the civil service. The regulations were part of a sweeping series of reforms that altered virtually every aspect of Turkish life—from the civil code to the alphabet to education to social integration of the sexes.

The Western dress code at that time, though, was aimed at men. The fez—the short, conical, red-felt cap that had been in vogue [fashion] in Turkey since the Ottoman Sultan Mahmud II made it part of the official national attire in 1826—was banished. Atatürk himself famously adopted a Panama hat to accent his Western-style gray linen suit, shirt, and tie when he toured the country in the summer of 1925 to sell his new ideas to a deeply conservative population. That autumn, the Hat Law of 1925 was passed, making European-style men's headwear de rigueur [fashionable] and punishing fez-wearers with lengthy sentences of imprisonment at hard labor, and even a few hangings. . . .

4

2

— Roff Smith, "Why Turkey Lifted Its Ban on the Islamic Headscarf," *National Geographic*, October 12, 2013

Boosters source explanation

3

Boosters question explanation

21 According to this article by Roff Smith, the goal of Atatürk's reforms was to

(1) prevent the elimination of the civil service system
(2) implement a legal system based on religious teachings
(3) revive Turkey's interest in Ottoman-era customs
(4) modernize Turkey in the image of European nations

22 The phrases "deeply conservative population," "lengthy sentences of imprisonment," and "a few hangings" suggest that

(1) Atatürk's reforms were eagerly embraced throughout Turkey
(2) tensions existed between reformers and traditionalists in Turkey
(3) the policy of westernization was abandoned by the Turkish government
(4) most Turks preferred punishment to rapid change

First look at the title (1), then at the source (2), then at the question (3), and then at the document (4). Now go back to the question. The blue text is Mr. Boosters speaking out his analysis out loud so that you can hear and be trained to do it yourself. First try the questions yourself, and then you can check yourself using the explanation page.

Enduring Issues Essay Topics

There are 9 Enduring Issues that we will explore in depth at the end of the book. We'll quickly introduce them here so that you'll be able to follow along as they come up in the book.

INEQUALITY/HUMAN RIGHTS VIOLATIONS:

Inequality means that one person or group of people has control or power over another.

Human Rights are rights and freedoms that every person is entitled to. Human Rights Violations happen when those basic human rights are violated.

INNOVATION:

Innovation is a new idea, a change, or a new way of doing things.

SCARCITY:

Scarcity means not having enough of something. When a country lacks important materials, it might trade with other countries or fight wars to gain access to those materials.

POWER:

Power is the ability of people or a nation to control or influence others.

Enduring Issues Essay Topics (continued):

ENVIRONMENTAL IMPACT:
Our environment is the area around us in which we live (the city, mountains, air...). We are affected by the environment, and the environment is affected by us.

CONFLICT:
Conflict means a serious disagreement or argument. Conflict can be between individuals, groups, or nations and can escalate into a war or revolution.

IDEAS AND BELIEFS:
Ideas and beliefs are the way people view government, religion, and society. Ideas and beliefs can be positive or negative.

INTERCONNECTEDNESS:
As society grows, people and countries grow more connected though trade, cultural diffusion, and better communication.

COOPERATION:
Cooperation means working together to reach a common goal. Nations often work together to solve mutual problems.

Hi there!

I love history and I'm eager to share my excitement and love for history with you.

I teach high school kids and I've discovered how much fun learning becomes when we explore the material in an interesting and clear step-by-step way. (For real! Ask my students!) A minor result (yeah, right) is that they ace their tests.

Together with my team of talented Boosters Geeks, we put all that magic into this fun little book. We hope you enjoy reading it (and laughing through it) as much as we enjoyed creating it!

We love your feedback, so please be in touch!
And welcome to the Boosters Club!

R. Hertz, Chief Boosters Pal

UNIT 1

INTRO & GEOGRAPHY

HISTORICAL THINKING SKILLS

Intro & Geography

Here's some random stuff that's good to know.

This unit will give you a good overview, which will help you understand later concepts. And this info will come up in questions. Have fun!

Geography Basics

Each area has different landscapes/physical settings.

The Regents is kind of obsessed with this concept. So you'll find the concept applied in many different historical events throughout this book. The next few pages will illustrate how different countries are affected by their physical settings.

ex Deserts, water (lakes, rivers, oceans, and waterfalls), mountains, and fertile land

The history of an area is greatly affected by these different physical settings.

- Geographic barriers
- Trade
- Travel

R This is a common Regents question.

Tour of Our World – Continents & Oceans

CONTINENTS: Major land masses of the world

- There are 7 continents: North America, South America, Europe, Asia, Africa, Australia, and Antarctica.

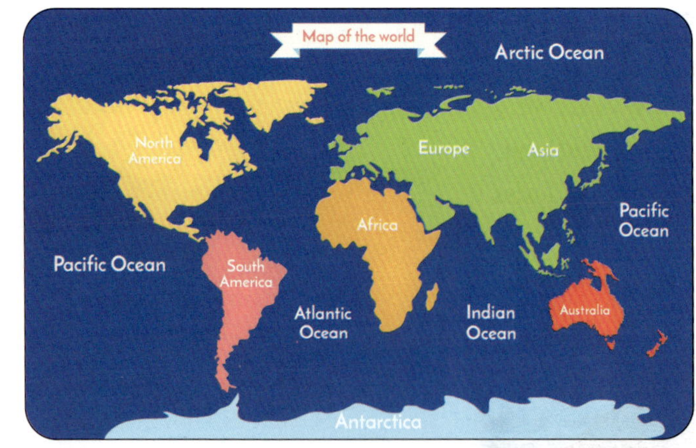

OCEANS: Huge bodies of saltwater

- There are 4 oceans: Pacific Ocean, Atlantic Ocean, Indian Ocean, and Arctic Ocean.

Ⓡ Recognize the 7 continents and 4 oceans on this map.

South America

South America has natural barriers that make it hard to unify the continent:

- Rivers flow from north to south throughout the entire continent.
- The Andes Mountains

These features separate the continent into different parts.

Rivers and Andes Mountains

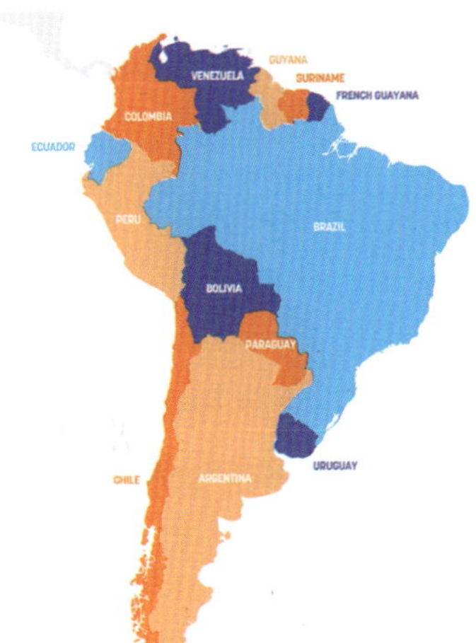

Africa

Africa has many natural barriers that limit cultural diffusion (spread of cultures).

<u>Natural barriers that prevent cultural diffusion:</u>

1. **SAHARA DESERT:** world's largest desert and major natural barrier that separates the north and south of Africa
2. **SAVANNA:** land where wild, tall grass grows. This land is great for growing crops.
3. **TROPICAL RAIN FOREST**
4. **MOUNTAINS**

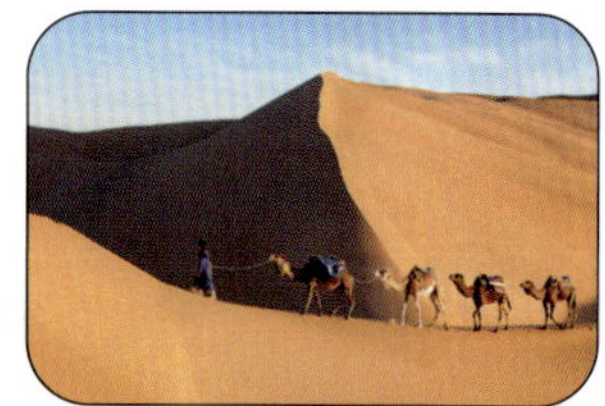

Sahara Desert

Because of these natural barriers, northern and southern Africa have very different cultures, which has led to tribalism (strong loyalty to one's tribe).

- **NORTH AFRICA:** mostly Muslim
- **SUB-SAHARAN AFRICA (south):** mostly non-Muslim

Savanna

Much of Africa remained unexplored by the Europeans because its natural barriers made it difficult to explore.

Europe

Europe has many rivers, which impacted its history in many ways:

- The rivers enabled TRANSPORTATION for trade and travel.
- The water provided NATURAL RESOURCES.
- The water helped countries INDUSTRIALIZE.

<u>Other geography facts about Europe</u>:

- Europe is close to Africa and the Middle East, so it was culturally influenced by these regions.
- Most of Europe's land is flat, fertile plains (like France and Germany), so its frontiers are hard to defend. This made it possible for many wars to occur.
- Europe is densely populated and is home to many different ethnic groups. This, too, led to many wars.
- Great Britain is an island. Therefore, it has harbors for trade, and a navy for defense. Because the British are isolated from the rest of Europe, they weren't busy fighting, and instead they established a stable government.

E Environmental Impact:

- Europe's rivers enabled trade and industrialization.
- Europe's flat plains made it easy for enemy countries to attack and hard for countries to defend themselves in war.

E Scarcity: Europe imperialized weaker countries to gain more natural resources.

Asia

Asia is the world's largest continent!

This massive continent has many diverse cultures.

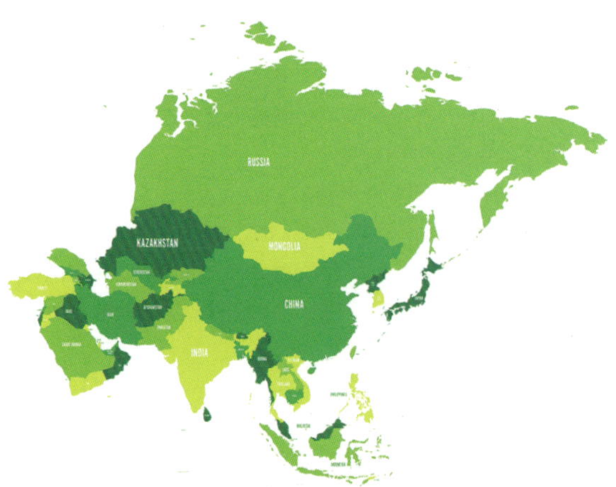

Now let's explore each section of Asia.

Sounds interesting and exciting!

Did you notice that Russia is on Asia's map and on Europe's map? Is Russia part of Europe or Asia? And the answer is... both. It's mainly in Asia, but partially in Europe.

Middle East of Asia ("The Middle East")

- Mostly desert land with 3 major rivers (Nile, Tigris, Euphrates)
- Has a huge oil industry that provides about half the world's oil
- "Crossroads" to 3 continents (Asia, Africa, Europe), so many countries want control over it

The Middle East is a crossroads to many places.

North & Central Asia

North and Central Asia serve as crossroads for trade routes between China, India, the Middle East, and Europe.

Most of RUSSIA is located in Central Asia.

<u>About Russia</u>:

- It has long, cold winters.
- Part of Russia is tundra (frozen ground).
- It has little access to the sea. Russia is always looking for warm water ports, and it wants to expand its territory because of this problem.

> ex Russia fought a lot with Turkey for control over the Baltic Sea.

- Siberia: frigid area that has gas, oil, diamonds, and gold

E Environmental Impact:

- Freezing winters stopped Napoleon and Hitler from invading Russia.
- Russia fought to gain warm water ports.

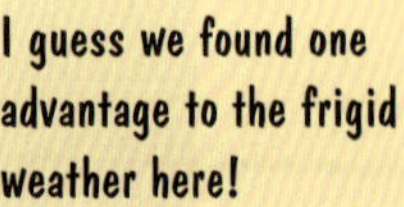

R Cause and effect: Freezing winters in Russia ➲ Napoleon and Hitler couldn't conquer Russia.

Eastern Asia

- China is the most populous country in the world.
  - China is isolated from the rest of the world by mountains (Himalaya mountains), deserts (Gobi desert), and seas.
- Korea is the "bridge" between China and Japan.
- Japan is mostly mountainous, but is densely populated.
  - Japan lacks natural resources, so they need to trade or go to war to get what they need.
  - Japan is an ARCHIPELAGO (group of islands), and at times chose to be isolated from the rest of the world.

China is isolated by mountains, deserts, and seas.

E Environmental Impact: The Chinese population was huge and affecting the environment, so China passed laws to limit its population growth.

E Scarcity: Japan trades or goes to war to gain natural resources.

R Cause and effect: Japan lacks natural resources ➲ Japan trades or fights wars.

South and Southeast Asia

South Asia:
- Himalaya Mountains
- Indus and Ganges Rivers

Southeast Asia:
- Shortest route between the Pacific and Indian Oceans, so these countries were influenced by different people passing through (Arabs, Indians, Chinese, European colonial powers)
- Famous for exporting spices for cooking and preserving
- Southeast Asia gets monsoons (winds that bring heavy rains in the summer). Monsoons cause flooding, damage, and death, but can also be used to help ships sail for trade!

Environmental Impact: Monsoons can cause damage and death.

Types of Maps

There are many different types of maps that show us important info.

- **PHYSICAL MAPS:** Maps that show the physical features of a place, such as mountains and oceans

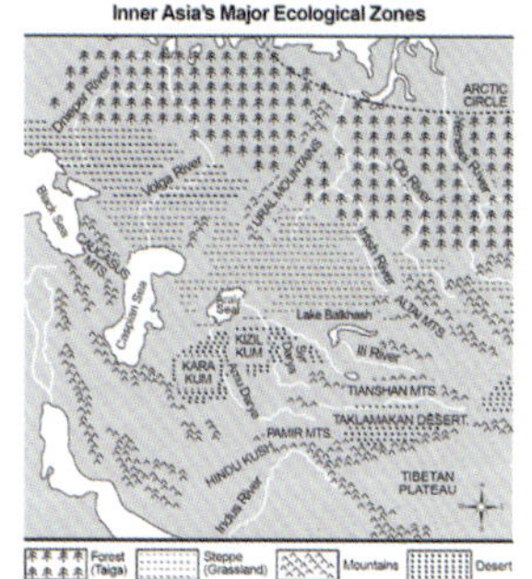

- **POLITICAL MAPS:** Maps that show government boundaries

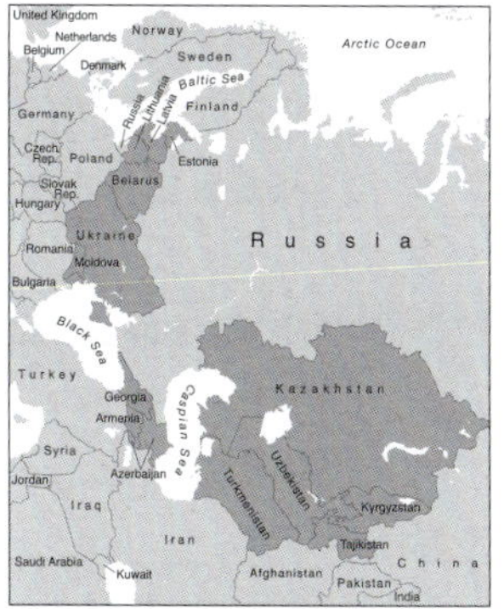

Source: Mountain High Maps, Digital Wisdom (adapted)

EdBoosters™

How to Read a Map

Source: U.S. Holocaust Memorial Museum online (adapted)

A **MAP TITLE:** This tells us what the map is about.

It often gives us a date, which will help us figure out the context.

- Sometimes the title is on the bottom or in the middle of the map.

B **MAP KEY/LEGEND:** Explanation of symbols on a map

- The map key often includes capital cities, trade routes, migration route symbols, etc.

C **MAP SCALE:** The ratio between the distance on the map and the distance in real life

D **COMPASS:** This shows the direction of the map.

Geography Themes

GEOGRAPHY is the study of land and how people use it.

GEOGRAPHY BUZZ WORDS:

- **LOCATION:** Place on earth
- **PLACE:** Each place has unique physical features formed by nature, and human features formed by people.
- **REGION:** An area of land with common features

  ex government, forest, language, etc.

- **HUMAN ENVIRONMENT INTERACTIONS:** The environment causes people to adapt to their surroundings, and humans impact the environment.

MOVEMENT: People around the world are constantly exchanging ideas and products, and are physically moving to other areas.

Key Vocabulary Words

- **TOPOGRAPHY:** surface features
  - ex: mountains, oceans, valleys
- **CLIMATE:** weather conditions over a long period of time
  - ex: hot, cold, rainy

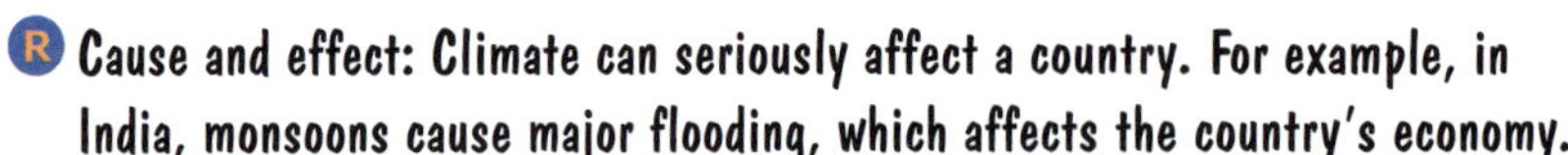

R Cause and effect: Climate can seriously affect a country. For example, in India, monsoons cause major flooding, which affects the country's economy.

- **NATURAL RESOURCES:** a naturally occurring raw material
  - ex: coal, gold, wood
- **DEMOGRAPHY:** the study of human population
  - Demographic patterns (changes in population over a long period) are influenced by geographic features, such as mountains, rainforests, and rivers.
- **CULTURAL DIFFUSION:** exchange of ideas, customs, and goods between different cultures

Cultures are spread through trade, war, and migration, and even the internet!

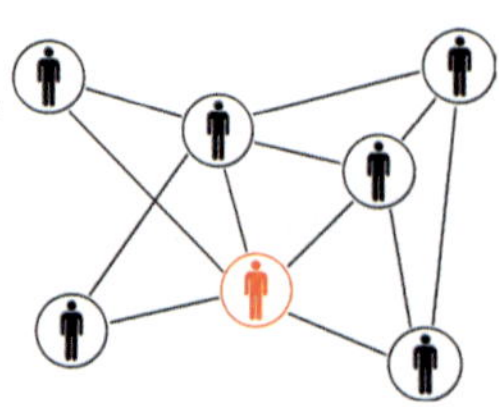

> **HINT:** A <u>top</u>ography graph shows the features seen on the <u>top</u> of the land (mountains, valleys, water).

Sources of History – Primary Source

When you read an article or a book, is it dependable? It depends.
Who wrote it? Were they there when it happened?
There are two types of historical sources – primary and secondary sources.

PRIMARY SOURCE: original records of an event

- Examples of primary sources:
  - Documents
  - Letters
  - Reports written by witnesses or people involved in the event photographs
  - Diaries
  - ARTIFACTS: man-made objects, such as tools, weapons, or ornaments, especially of archaeological or historical interest

Primary sources are usually the most dependable.

R This is a common Regents question.

Is this a primary source?

Look at the writer, the date, and then read the document to see if it's a firsthand account.

> . . .And why do I regard the British rule as a curse?
>
> It has impoverished the dumb millions by a system of progressive exploitation and by a ruinously expensive military and civil administration which the country can never afford.
>
> It has reduced us politically to serfdom. It has sapped the foundations of our culture. And, by the policy of disarmament, it has degraded us spiritually. Lacking the inward strength, we have been reduced, by all but universal disarmament, to a State bordering on cowardly helplessness. . . .

Source: Letter from M.K. Gandhi, Esq. to the Viceroy, Lord Irwin, March 2, 1930

Looks like it's a letter from M.K. Gandhi in 1930 writing about how bad British rule is.
Since it's a firsthand account, this IS a primary source.

Sources of History – Secondary Source

SECONDARY SOURCE: later writings and interpretations of an event

The writer wrote his own interpretation of history based on other sources.

- Types of secondary sources: textbooks and articles based on information from primary sources

Is this a primary or secondary source? Let's look at the author/publisher and the year it was written. When did this even happen? Could the writer have been at this event? Is it a firsthand account?

> . . . The Indian Mutiny [1857] had come as a nasty shock, especially since British rule in India had appeared so secure. In order to prevent such an outbreak again, the authority for governing British India was removed from John Company [the British East India Company] and placed in the hands of the Crown. Queen Victoria became Empress of India, and her personal representative in the country was to be the Viceroy, who replaced the Governor-General, the administration of India being controlled by the India Office in London. The British Army presence in the country, as opposed to what was now called the Indian Army, was increased to 65,000 men, and as a general principle every garrison was now to contain at least one British regiment. . . .

Source: Charles Messenger, *British Army*, Bramley Books, 1997

The book was published in 1997 and the Indian Mutiny happened in 1857. There's no way the author, Charles Messenger, was there at that time! Must be a secondary source.

Guess if Global Boosters is a primary or secondary source? Well, I haven't been around since 1750 and I can't possibly be in every country during every historical event. So I must be a secondary source.

Source Context

The Regents loves supplying us with detective work. They give us a doc and we get to figure stuff out:

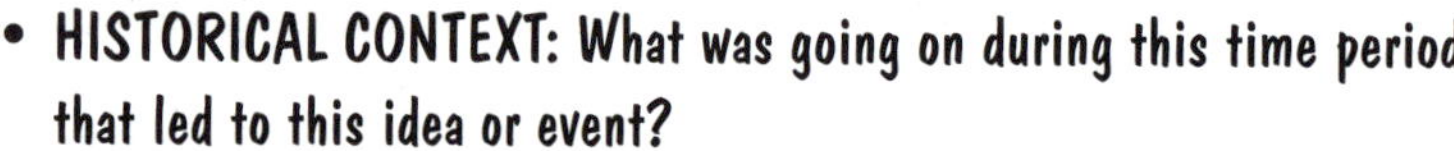

- **HISTORICAL CONTEXT:** What was going on during this time period that led to this idea or event?

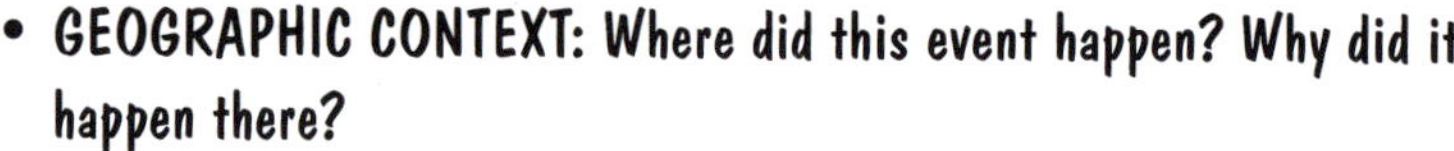

- **GEOGRAPHIC CONTEXT:** Where did this event happen? Why did it happen there?

As we play this detective game, we search for clues in the maps/ documents that offer this info.

Dates, people, places, map location, etc.

We'll discuss this more at the end of the book.

More on Sources

Some sources are more reliable and useful than others.
The reliability of a source depends on:

- **Who** wrote it? Was the author biased?
- **When** and **where** was it written?
- **Why** was it written? What point is it trying to make?
- Who was it written for?

We'll discuss this more at the end of the book.

Quick Review

Check off the boxes beside the topics you know well. Whatever you don't know well (yet!), go back and review now!

- ☐ How physical settings affect the history of a region
- ☐ Names of continents and oceans
- ☐ South America's natural barriers – rivers and mountains
- ☐ Africa's natural barriers – Sahara Desert, savanna, tropical rain forest, mountains
- ☐ Europe has water sources for transportation, natural resources, and energy sources. Europe is flat, which makes it harder to defend.
- ☐ Asia
  - Deserts, mountains, and oceans
  - Crossroads to many parts of the world
  - Middle East oil industry
  - Russia: cold, needs warm water sources
  - China: isolated by rivers and mountains
  - Monsoons in South Asia
- ☐ Maps – physical and political
- ☐ Key words
  - Topography
  - Climate
  - Natural resources
  - Demography
  - Cultural diffusion
- ☐ Primary and secondary sources of history

Enduring Issues Essay Topics That Came Up in This Unit:

For the Enduring Issues Essay, there are 2 geography-related issues that you can write about.

Even before we actually learn history, let's point these issues out and give you a sneak preview of examples that you can be on the lookout for!

Throughout this book, we'll visit lots of places and times in history where you'll see for yourself how geography has a major impact on world events.

ENVIRONMENTAL IMPACT – People are affected by the environment and landscape around them and the environment is affected by people.

- Africa has many natural barriers (Sahara Desert, savanna, tropical rain forest, mountains). Therefore, North Africa and Sub-Saharan Africa have different cultures and religions.
- Europe's rivers helped that continent to be the first to industrialize.
- Europe's land is flat, which makes it difficult to defend. Therefore, many wars were fought in Europe.
- Russia's freezing winters stopped Napoleon and Hitler from conquering it.
- China remained isolated for many years because it's surrounded by mountains and seas.

SCARCITY – when there's not enough of something

- Middle Eastern countries often fight wars to control oil-rich lands.
- Russia fights to gain warm water ports.

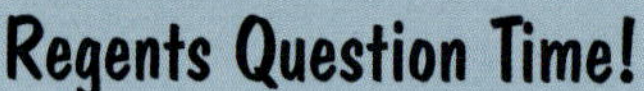

Now it's time to test how well you know your stuff.

Have fun!

Regents Question Time!

Interactions Between the United States of America and the Soviet Union		
1948–49	**1962**	**1979**
In June 1948, the Soviet Union blockades democratic West Berlin. The U.S. and its allies fly in supplies daily to keep the city from starving. The Soviets lift the blockade in May 1949.	U.S. spy planes discover Soviet-built nuclear sites in Cuba. After a tense 13-day standoff with President John F. Kennedy, the Soviets remove the missiles.	Soviet troops invade Afghanistan. Aided by the U.S., Islamic fighters wage a 10-year guerrilla war against the Soviets, who withdraw in 1989.

— Carl Stoffers, "Are We Heading Toward a New Cold War?" *New York Times Upfront*, October 10, 2016 (adapted)

13 Which document would best provide information about the impact these events had on regions other than the United States and the Soviet Union?

(1) Russian textbook published in 2015
(2) television interview with President John F. Kennedy
(3) memoirs of people living in East Germany, Cuba, and Afghanistan
(4) line graph of the Soviet Union's gross domestic product between 1948 and 1968

Answer: ___

1

Interactions Between the United States of America and the Soviet Union

Relationship between USA and Russia

Info about the Cold War

1948–49	1962	1979
In June 1948, the Soviet Union blockades democratic West Berlin. The U.S. and its allies fly in supplies daily to keep the city from starving. The Soviets lift the blockade in May 1949.	U.S. spy planes discover Soviet-built nuclear sites in Cuba. After a tense 13-day standoff with President John F. Kennedy, the Soviets remove the missiles.	Soviet troops invade Afghanistan. Aided by the U.S., Islamic fighters wage a 10-year guerrilla war against the Soviets, who withdraw in 1989.

2

— Carl Stoffers, "Are We Heading Toward a New Cold War?" *New York Times Upfront*, October 10, 2016 (adapted)

2016 newspaper article and reference to the Cold War

3

13 Which document would best provide information about the impact these events had on regions other than the United States and the Soviet Union?

What's the best source for info on the Cold War outside of USA and the Soviet Union?
So we're looking for a source that's dependable (probably a primary source) from a region that was affected by the Cold War.

4

(1) Russian textbook published in 2015
(2) television interview with President John F. Kennedy
(3) memoirs of people living in East Germany, Cuba, and Afghanistan
(4) line graph of the Soviet Union's gross domestic product between 1948 and 1968

Regents Question Time!

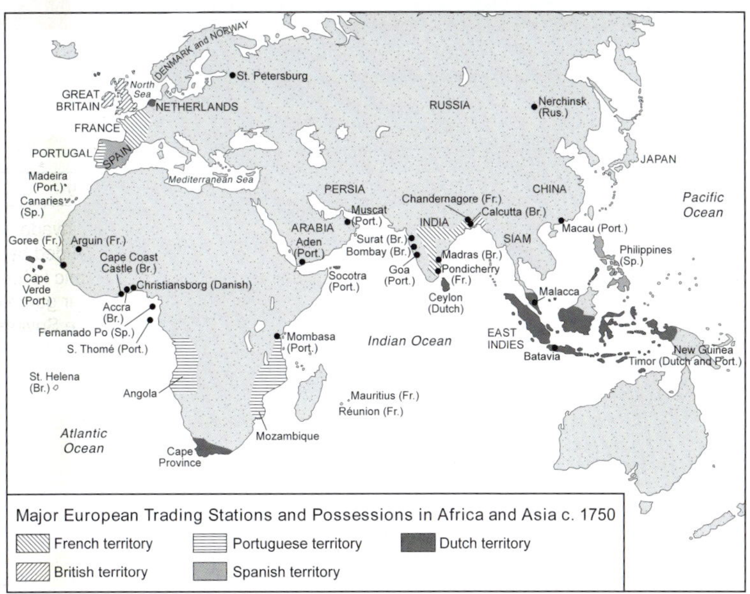

Source: J. M. Roberts, *A History of Europe*, Allen Lane (adapted)

1 What is a valid conclusion based on the information shown on this map?

(1) Russia had the largest number of trading stations in Asia.

(2) Most European trading stations and empires were located along the coast.

(3) France controlled more ports in India than Britain did.

(4) Each European power represented had possessions in the East Indies.

Answer: ___

1

Major European Trading Stations and Possessions in Africa and Asia c. 1750

Note that the title of this doc is on the bottom!

Notice the map key on the bottom representing different European locations whose trading stations you can see on the map.

You're supposed to figure out that the black circles are trading stations (based on the title).

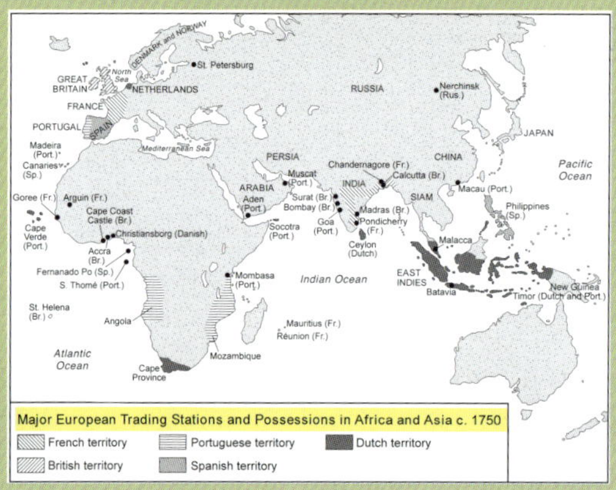

2

Source: J. M. Roberts, *A History of Europe*, Allen Lane (adapted)

3

1 What is a valid conclusion based on the information shown on this map?

(1) Russia had the largest number of trading stations in Asia.
(2) Most European trading stations and empires were located along the coast.
(3) France controlled more ports in India than Britain did.
(4) Each European power represented had possessions in the East Indies.

Info about the map. Go on, read the choices and see which one is correct based on the map.

4

Coast means land that's near the sea. We see that most of the black dots (representing the trading stations) are located on the coast.

FYI: Choice 3 was tricky! You had to look at the key and then the map to see what France controlled and what Britain controlled. Although France controlled more territory in India, if you look closely, you'll see that France controlled only 2 trading stations. Britain controlled a smaller area of India, but also controlled 2 trading stations.

Regents Question Time!

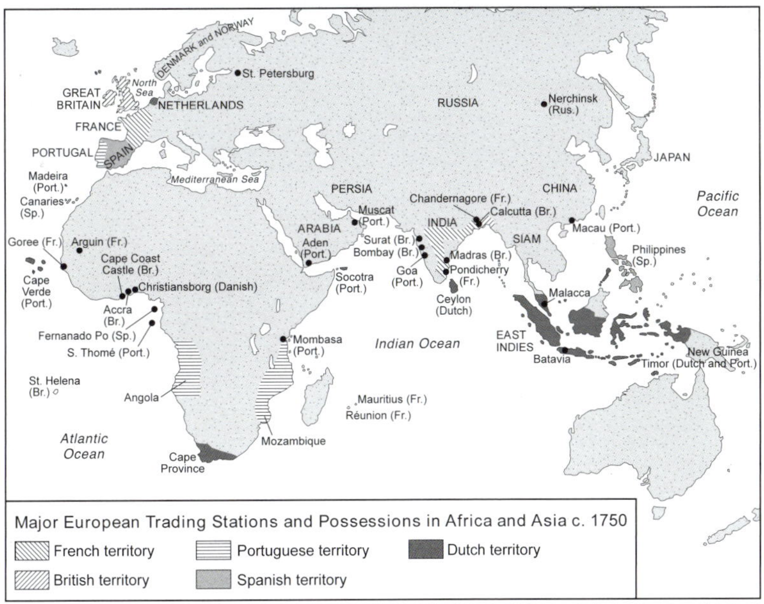

Source: J. M. Roberts, *A History of Europe*, Allen Lane (adapted)

2 Which Europeans controlled the waterways connecting the Indian Ocean to the Pacific Ocean?

(1) Spanish (3) Dutch
(2) Portuguese (4) French

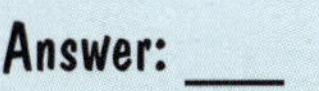

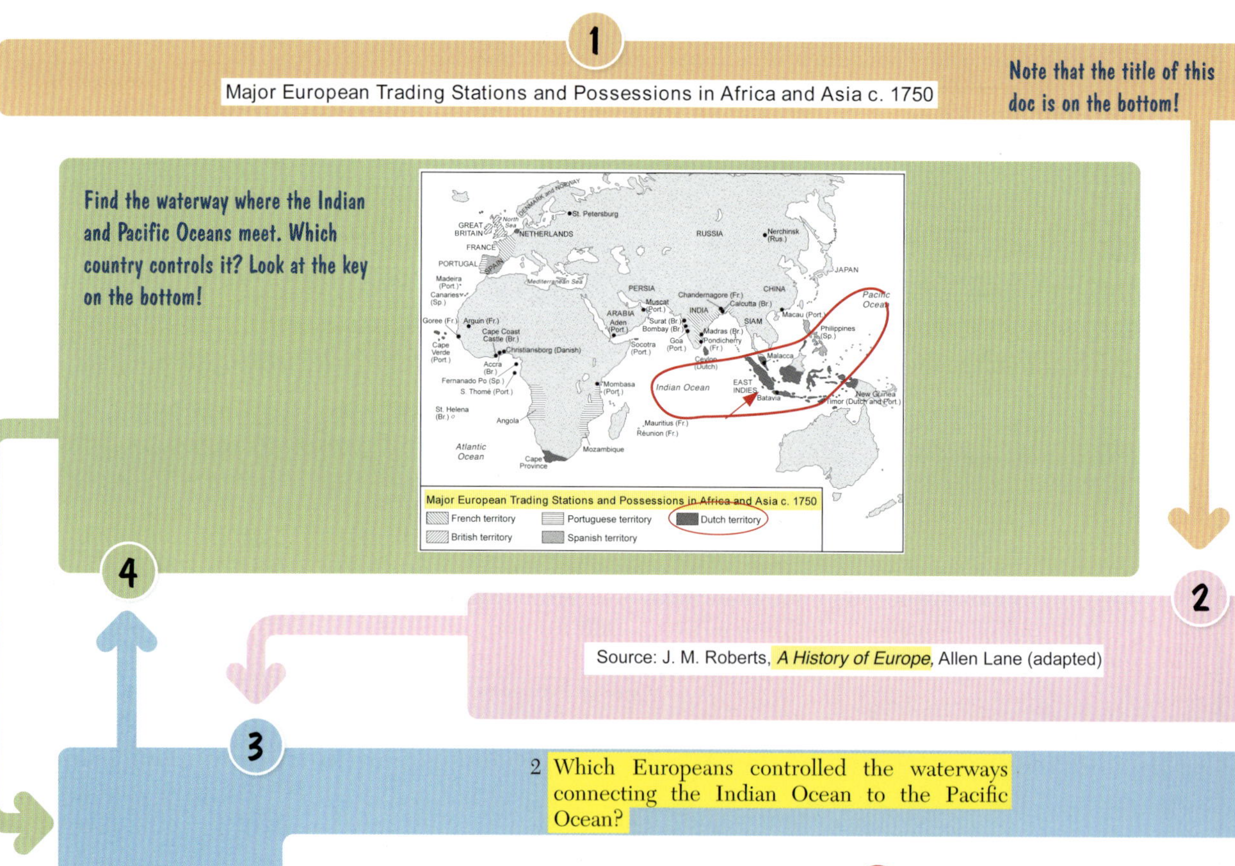

(1) Spanish
(2) Portuguese
(3) Dutch
(4) French

FYI: This question had nothing to do with your knowledge of history. Once you learn how to analyze maps, you'll be able to get lots of correct answers just by looking at the map!

UNIT 2

THE WORLD IN 1750

Trade in the 1750s

During this time, empires, states, and kingdoms around the world were gaining power.

Are you ready for a trip around the world, peeking in on cool empires? Think big!

Q: How did they gain power?

A: Empires expanded their empires through military conquest and trade.

- Global trade made empires wealthy and powerful. Countries competed over trade routes.
- Some trade routes were **sea-based** (MARITIME empires) and some routes were **land-based**.
- The more control a ruler had over trade, the more powerful and wealthy he became.
- Using trade, smaller states sometimes gained more power and wealth than larger states with trade!

World Map 1700

World Trade in the 1750s

TRADE = POWER AND WEALTH

- Some kingdoms traded mainly within their own territory; other countries traded with foreign countries.
- New global trade networks formed, disrupting regional (local) trade.
- Some kingdoms used land routes for trade; others used sea routes.

The expansions and increased trade introduced new challenges that had to be faced. Stay tuned!

World Trade in the 1700s

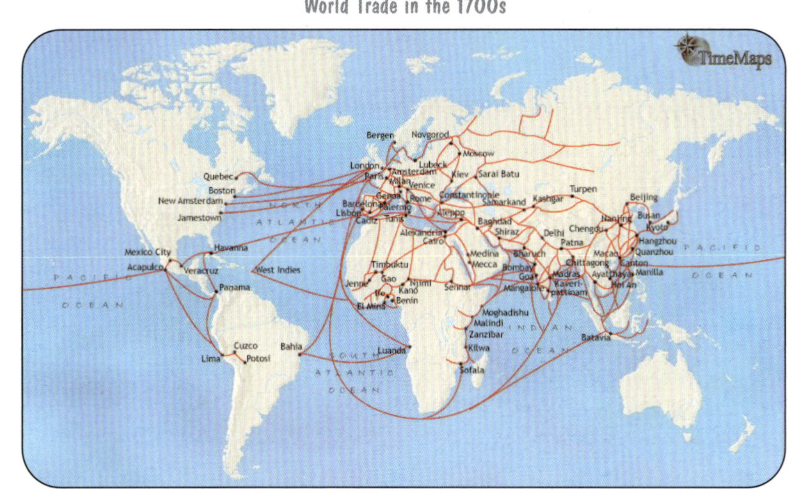

Interconnectedness: The empires were interconnected by trade.

Land Empires & Kingdoms in the 1750s

MAJOR LAND EMPIRES:

- Ottoman Empire
- Mughal Empire (India)
- Tokugawa Shogunate (Japan)
- Russian Empire
- Qing Dynasty (China)

Get ready for a trip around the world exploring each of these fascinating and diverse empires!

Eurasian Land Empires in the 1700s

The Ottoman Empire

- In 1453, the Ottoman Empire captured Constantinople, the capital of the Byzantine Empire, and established a Muslim empire. They renamed the capital ISTANBUL.
- Over time, they greatly expanded their territory to include parts of Europe, the Middle East, and North Africa, especially under Suleiman the Magnificent.

Suleiman the Magnificent

Ottoman Empire Expansion

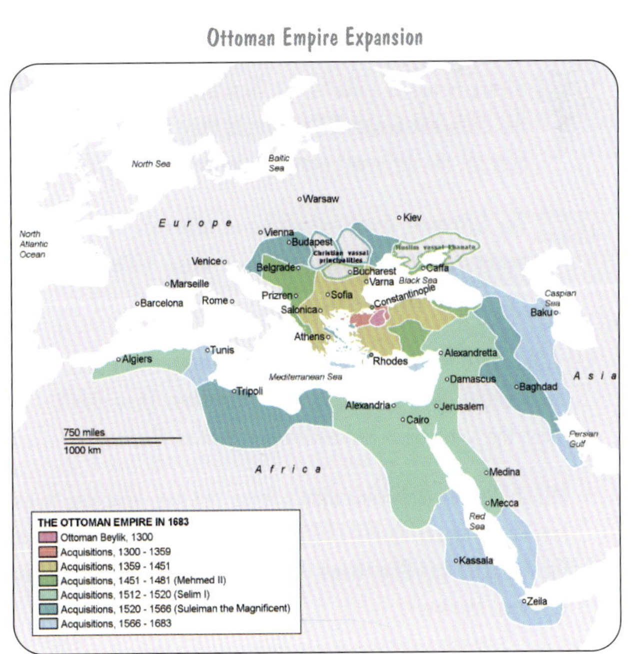

Ottoman Religious & Ethnic Tolerance

As the Ottoman Empire expanded, other religious and ethnic groups joined.

Q: Diversity posed a challenge. How would this massive empire keep peace among all the different groups? How would they maintain control over all the different parts of the empire?

HINT: Millet – Muslims let other religious groups practice their own religions.

A: The Ottomans practiced religious tolerance to maintain power over their diverse societies using millets and the devshirme system.

Read on to learn more.

Although Christians and Jews were tolerated and not persecuted, they still faced discrimination. They didn't have the same legal and political rights as Muslims.

- MILLETS: The Ottomans didn't force the non-Muslims to convert. Instead, they set up MILLETS – non-Muslim religious communities for the Jews and Christians. The groups were completely loyal to the Ottoman empire.

Millet

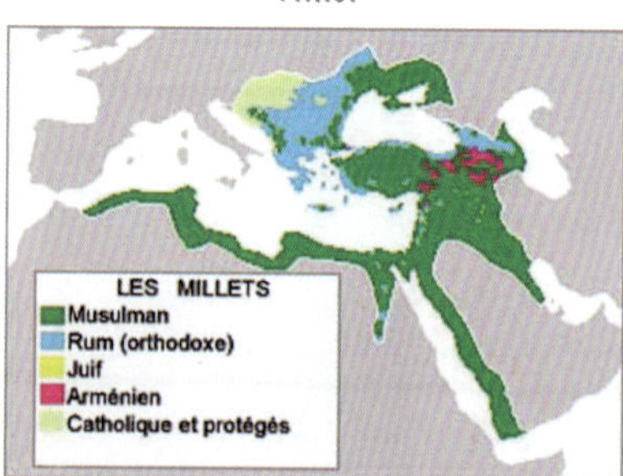

E: IDEAS AND BELIEFS: The Ottomans accepted and tolerated other religious groups.

Ottoman Political Organization

The Ottoman Empire was massive and included many different groups.

However, the Ottoman Empire successfully maintained control and order by setting up a BUREAUCRACY – appointed officials under one ruler.

The Ottoman Empire also set up systems to gain manpower for their government and army:

- DEVSHIRME SYSTEM: The Ottoman Empire required boys from the empire's Christian communities to join the Ottoman government, as a form of tax. The boys were forced to convert to Islam and then served in the bureaucracy or army.
- JANISSARIES: Most of the boys recruited from the devshirme system then joined the most elite part of the army, and were called JANISSARIES. They helped expand the Ottoman empire.

Devshirme

Ottoman Empire Commercial Activity

- The Ottoman government built up major commercial and industrial centers, where merchants and artisans traded goods.

Ottoman Trade

- The most important source of revenue was tax from trade.
- When the Ottoman Empire expanded, it took control of the important land and sea trade routes (including the Mediterranean Sea). Most trade took place within the massive empire.
- At its peak, the Ottoman Empire had a virtual monopoly on trade between Europe and Asia because it controlled most of the trade routes, including a large portion of the Silk Road.

The Fall of the Ottoman Empire

By the late 1600s, the Ottoman Empire began to lose power to its neighboring empires – the Russian Empire and the Austrian Hapsburg Empire.

Although the empire remained large until the 1900s, its influence was weakening.

Why?

- The government became corrupt.
- The Ottoman Empire controlled the existing trade routes, which interfered with Western Europe's trade with Asia, so eventually the Europeans found new trade routes. The Ottoman Empire then lost its monopoly on trade routes.
- European countries were gaining power – both militarily and economically. The Ottoman Empire couldn't keep up with the European technology, especially ships and navigation tools.

The Mughal Empire

- The Mughal Empire was a Muslim dynasty that ruled most of modern-day India and Pakistan from the 1500s to the mid-1700s.

- The Mughal Empire conquered areas that included two major religious groups: Hindus and Muslims.

Mughal Empire

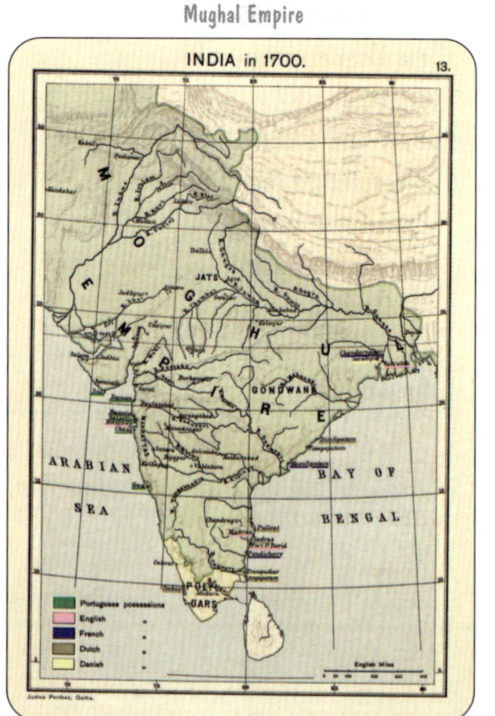

Akbar the Great & Political Organization / Commercial Activity

Akbar the Great

Akbar the Great (1556–1605) was the most powerful ruler of the Mughal Empire.

AKBAR THE GREAT:

- Strengthened the central government
- Expanded and strengthened the empire through trade
- Established a fair justice system
- Modernized the army
- Encouraged trade between the Ottoman and Mughal Empires

Power: Akbar the Great used his power to strengthen and expand the Mughal Empire.

Mughal Empire Religious Tolerance

Even though Akbar the Great was a Muslim, he encouraged religious tolerance by:

- Including Hindus in his government
- Ending the non-Muslim tax (called jizya)
- Allowing Hindus to control their own institutions and make their own laws

Ideas and beliefs: The Mughals tolerated other religions.
Human Rights: Akbar the Great protected the rights of different religions.

The Decline & Fall of the Mughal Empire

Several factors led to the end of the Mughal Empire:

- The Mughal leader Aurangzeb imposed Islamic law on the non-Muslims and ended religious tolerance.
- Religious groups rebelled and tried taking control of the government.
- The battles to fight these religious groups drained the empire's treasury.
- After Aurangzeb died, competition for leadership weakened the empire.

Now that the Mughal rulership was so weak, the British were able to take over the empire.

The British Take Over the Mughal Empire

- The Mughals welcomed and encouraged European trade.
- The Mughals allowed the Europeans to set up the East India Company inside their empire. The Mughals allowed them to build warehouses and forts.
- In the late 1700s, the British East India Company took control over the region and employed SEPOYS – Indian soldiers to maintain control.
- The Mughal Empire is over ☹. The Europeans kept control of India until 1947!

Mughal Interactions with the Outside World

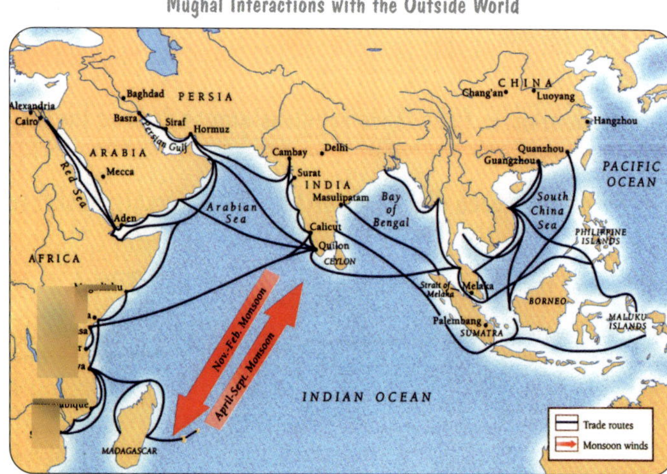

Ⓡ **Cause and effect:** The Mughals allowed Europeans to infiltrate their economy. This resulted in the fall of the Mughal Empire.

Regents Making Connections Time

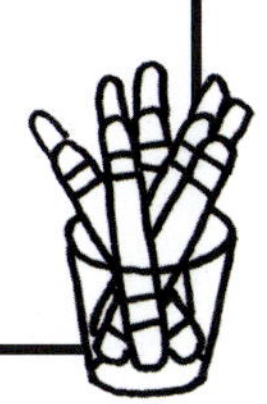

Compare and contrast the Ottoman Empire and the Mughal Empire in:

1. Religious and ethnic tolerance
2. Political organization
3. Commercial activity

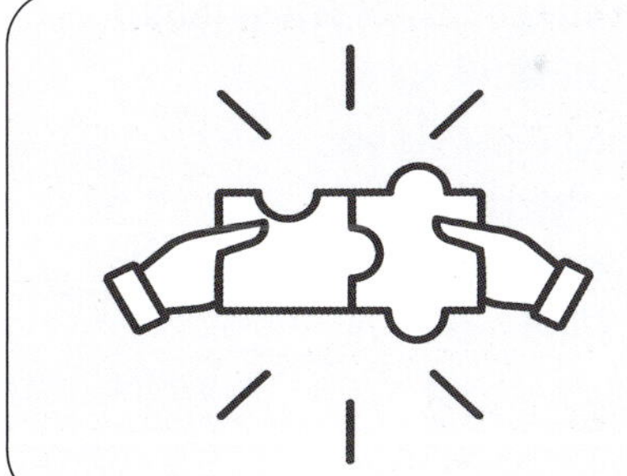

Skim through the last few pages and jot down the similarities and differences.

Japanese Political Organization

JAPANESE FEUDALISM (1185–1868):

- The EMPEROR had no political power. He was just a figurehead.
- The emperor appointed SHOGUNS – military dictators who set up dynasties called SHOGUNATES.
- The Shoguns gave land to the DAIMYO – landowners – in exchange for loyalty.
- The Daimyo gave land to the SAMURAI – warriors — who were loyal to them. They had to follow a strict code of conduct called BUSHIDO.
- PEASANTS, ARTISANS, and MERCHANTS provided services for the samurai in exchange for protection.

HINT: Shogun sounds like show gun- someone who has a gun shows he has power.

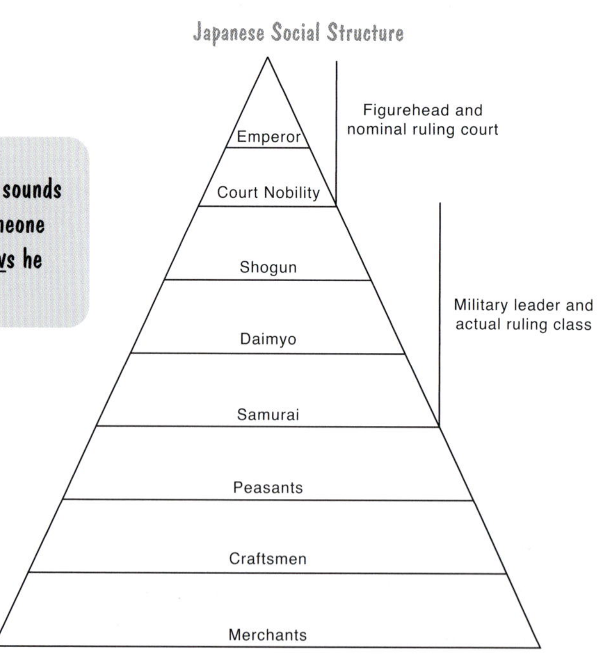

Tokugawa Shogunate in Japan

The Tokugawa Shogunate gained power in 1608 and ruled until 1868. Japan is made up of a series of large islands, which can be difficult to control. The Tokugawa Shogunate replaced the feudal system with a more centralized government.

A Tokugawa Shogun

How?

- The shoguns changed the city capital to EDO – present-day Tokyo – and established a new, powerful center.
- The shoguns upheld strict social hierarchies to maintain total control over the massive population.
- The shoguns kept strict control over the daimyo. The shoguns required the daimyo to live in Edo every other year and forced the daimyos' families to live in Edo as hostages.

Japanese Seclusion

- In the mid-1500s, Europeans began to trade with Japan, and they converted 300,000 Japanese to Christianity. In the late 1500s, Spain conquered the Philippines and then spread Christianity. Japanese rulers did not want this happening in Japan! Japan therefore limited missionary activity, by jailing and killing Christians.
- By the 1630s, the Tokugawa shoguns stopped nearly all contact with foreigners! Foreigners were banned from traveling to Japan and the Japanese weren't allowed to leave Japan.
- The seclusion lasted for 250 years! Japan was able to isolate because it is an ARCHIPELAGO – a group of islands, so it has greater control over entry to and exit from the country.
- During the seclusion, Japan was able to avoid Western domination and was able to protect its distinct culture.

Compare and contrast interactions with outsiders in the Mughal Empire and the Tokugawa Shogunate.

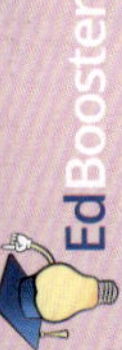

Tokugawa Shogunate Economy

- When the Tokugawa Shogunate unified, and isolated and stabilized the country, the economy skyrocketed!
- They established better farming methods, such as new tools and seeds.
- Trade increased within the country.
- They built travel routes, called the Tokaido System, to connect the provinces with the capital.
- During this period, the Japanese developed their culture, arts, literacy, and theater.

Power: The Tokugawa Shogunate maintained power by isolating themselves from the world.

Cause and effect: National isolation/stability led to a unified country and enhanced economy.

Tokugawa Shogunate Map

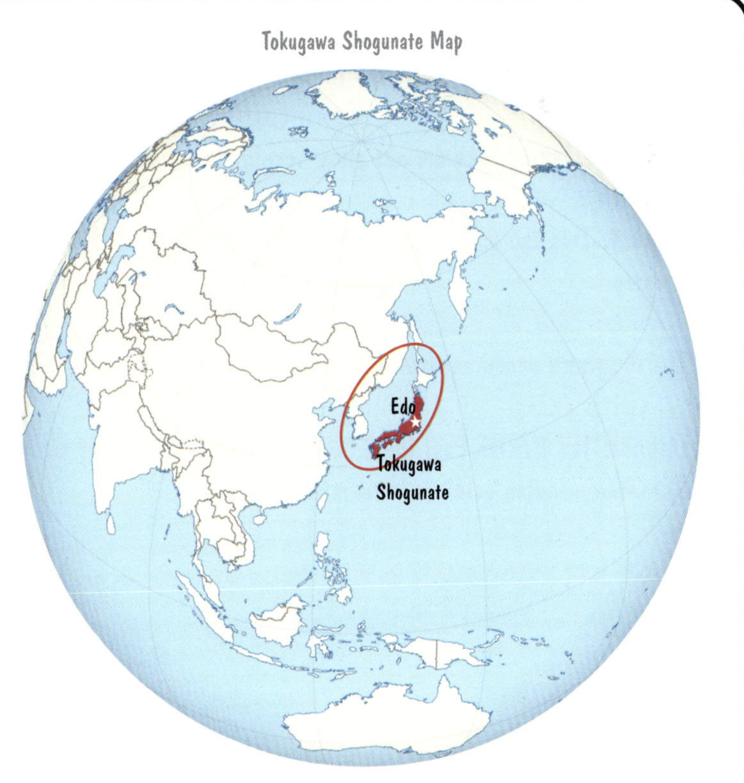

Regents Making Connections Time

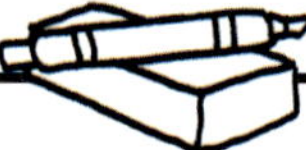

Q: Compare and contrast the Tokugawa and Mughal responses to outsiders.

A: The **Tokugawas** did not allow foreign interactions.

Impact: This increased internal trade and wealth and helped the rulers control the country.

The **Mughals** encouraged foreign trade.

Impact: The British East India Company took control over the region and employed SEPOYS – Indian soldiers to maintain control.

The Romanov Empire in Russia

- **PETER THE GREAT** (Russian czar from 1682 to 1725) expanded Russia's territory – extending it approximately 4,000 miles, from the Baltic Sea to the Pacific Ocean. Russia became the world's largest country!
- This major expansion helped Russia prosper from trade. But Russia needed warm water ports to use for trade all year round because most of Russia's ports freeze in the winter. Peter fought battles to gain a warm water port but failed.

Peter the Great

CATHERINE THE GREAT (1762–1796) was able to acquire warm water ports by defeating the Ottomans along the Black Sea. From there, the Russians were able to sail into the Mediterranean Sea and on to the oceans of the world.

- **Power:** Peter the Great used his power to expand the country and invite global trade.
- **Natural Resources:** Russia lacks warm water ports, which leads it to fight many wars.

Catherine the Great

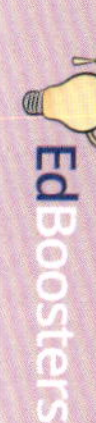

Qing Dynasty in China

- The Qing Dynasty (1644–1911) expanded China's borders through military conquest.
- They displayed ETHNOCENTRISM – they thought of themselves as the center of the universe.
- The Qing Dynasty did allow foreign trade, but with strict restrictions. Some countries accepted these restrictions, while others did not. The trade restrictions eventually led to Qing's decline.
- China traded its tea, porcelain, and silk in exchange for Europe's silver.

HINT: Ethnocentrism – Chinese thought of themselves as the center of the world.

Ideas and Beliefs: China displayed ethnocentrism; they thought they were the center of the world.

Maritime Empires & Kingdoms in the 1750s

- Maritime means sea-based.
- **EUROPEAN MARITIME EMPIRES:** France, Britain, the Netherlands (Dutch), Portugal, and Spain
- **WEST AFRICAN KINGDOMS**

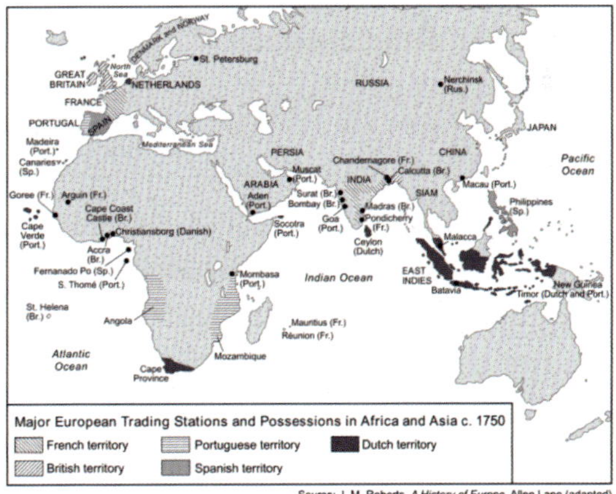

Source: J. M. Roberts, *A History of Europe*, Allen Lane (adapted)

Natural Resources: Countries that live near maritime trade routes are poised to become wealthy and powerful, even if they cover a small region.

The Dutch Netherlands controlled a large and wealthy empire (including profitable islands in Asia, the Caribbean, South America, and South Africa).

See you soon in Europe and West Africa. Bring along boating gear!

Bourbon France

In France, the power of the king increased over time, while the power of the nobles decreased.

LOUIS XIV (Louis the Fourteenth) was the king of France from 1652 to 1715. He was an ABSOLUTE MONARCH – he had complete control over his subjects. He called himself the SUN KING – the sun representing his power and control.

Louis XIV

- Louis XIV expanded the BUREAUCRACY, appointing officials to rule the provinces.
- He organized a strong, disciplined army. France became very powerful and wealthy.
- However, Louis XIV heavily taxed the peasants to fund his ostentatious palace and parties, which led to social unrest, poverty, and national debt.

Power: Louis XIV was an absolute monarch who called himself the "Sun King." He established a bureaucracy to maintain control of the people.

Louis XIV & the Palace of Versailles

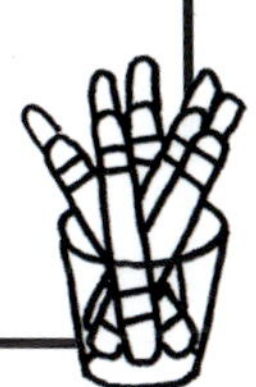

Louis XIV built the enormous and luxurious Palace of Versailles, whose magnificent décor included paintings, structures, statues of the king, and glorious gardens.

- The palace showcased Louis XIV's prestige and gave him power.
- The palace was able to hold 20,000 people. In it, Louis held court and entertained, requiring the attendance of the French aristocracy.
- The Palace of Versailles helped Louis subdue the nobles' power. A noble who wanted status or influence went to the palace, where Louis was able to control his power. This helped him maintain his absolute control over the bureaucracies.

Palace of Versailles

R This is a common Regents topic.

Regents Making Connections Time

Compare and contrast the **Tokugawa Shogunate** in Japan with the **Bourbon Dynasty** in France.

- What did Edo and Versailles have in common?
- How were both dynasties able to control their populations?

Ⓡ This is a common Regents question.

Skim through the previous few pages and jot down the similarities and differences.

The British Empire

Let's zoom in on the small island of Britain. Look how this small island created one of history's largest empires using their naval (ships) power.

The British Empire included India, 13 colonies of the USA, Canada, Ireland, Australia, the Caribbean Islands, and colonies in Africa and South America!

The British Empire (1763)

This is an example of how a small country can create a huge empire.

West African Kingdoms

WEST AFRICAN KINGDOMS:

- Ashanti Empire (1700–1902) – present-day Ghana
- Benin (1200–1897) – present-day southwest Nigeria
- Dahomey (1600–1894) – present-day Benin

West African Kingdoms in the 1700s

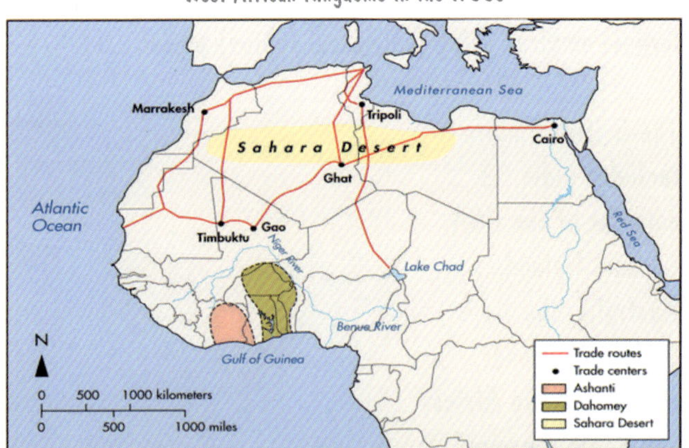

Africa was a major player in global trade, exporting wood, ivory, pepper, gold, and slaves.

Africa connects with other continents by sea:

- The **Mediterranean Sea** and the **Red Sea** connect Africa with the **Middle East** and **Europe**.
- The **Indian Ocean** connects Africa with **East Africa, India,** and **Asia.**

Q Look at the map. Do you see how small the Ashanti Empire is compared the rest of the region?

A The Ashanti Empire became powerful and wealthy due to its proximity to the sea. The Ashanti traded slaves and gold with the British and Dutch in return for guns, and used these weapons to fight and expand their territory.

Quick Review

Check off the boxes you know well. Whatever you don't know well (yet!), go back and review now!

- ☐ World trade in the 1750s
- ☐ The Ottoman Empire
  - Istanbul = capital
  - Religious/ethnic tolerance
  - Millets, devshirme, janissaries
  - Suleiman the Magnificent
- ☐ The Mughal Empire
  - Akbar the Great
  - Religious tolerance
- ☐ Tokugawa Shogunate in Japan
  - Feudal system: emperor, shoguns, daimyo, samurai
  - Edo = capital
  - National isolation
- ☐ Bourbon France
  - Louis XIV
  - Palace of Versailles
- ☐ Romanov Empire in Russia
  - Romanov Empire
  - Peter the Great
- ☐ Qing Dynasty – China
  - Ethnocentrism
- ☐ Land empires
- ☐ Maritime empires

Enduring Issues Essay Topics That Came Up in This Unit:

- **Power:**
  - Powerful monarchs strengthened and expanded their empires: Suleiman the Magnificent (Ottoman Empire), Akbar the Great (Mughal Empire), Louis XIV (France), Peter the Great (Russia)
  - Tokugawa Shogunate used feudalism to organize power.
  - Empires gained power through trade.
- **Scarcity:** Russia lacks warm water ports, which leads it to fight wars.
- **Environmental impact:** Countries that live near maritime trade routes can become wealthy and powerful, even if they cover only a small region.
- **Ideas and Beliefs:** Ethnocentrism, religious tolerance in the Ottoman and Mughal Empires
- **Interconnectedness:** Empires and kingdoms became more interconnected, which expanded global trade and reduced regional trade.

Regents Question Time!

Now it's time to test how well you know your stuff.

Have fun!

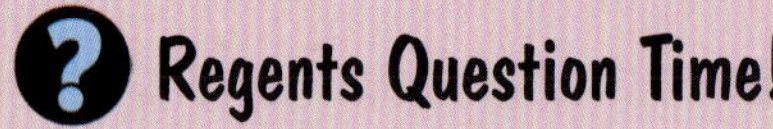

. . . In the Moghul [Mughal] empire the core contradiction had always been Hindus versus Muslims. Akbar the Great had worked out a sort of accommodation, but his great-grandson Aurangzeb reversed all his policies, enforcing orthodox Islam rigidly, restoring discrimination against Hindus, squashing smaller religious groups such as the Sikhs, and generally replacing tolerance with repression. And yet, say what you will about the man's narrow-minded zealotry [fanaticism], Aurangzeb was a titanic talent, so he not only held his empire together but extended it. The whole time, however, he was sowing the discord [division] and tension that would erupt to ruin the empire as soon as a less capable ruler took charge. . . .

. . . This glimpse into the Ottoman social clockwork does not begin to exhaust its fractal intricacy [complexity]: look closer and deeper into Ottoman society and you'll see the same order of complexity at every level. Everything was connected to everything else and connected in many ways, which was fine when all the connections balanced out and all of the parts were working. Centuries later, when the empire entered its decrepitude [decaying state], all the intertwining parts and intermeshing [connecting] institutions became a peculiarly Ottoman liability; their intricacy meant that trouble in one place or sphere translated mysteriously to trouble in a dozen other places or spheres—but that came later. In the sixteenth century, the Ottoman Empire was an awesomely well-functioning machine. . . .

Source: Tamim Ansary, *Destiny Disrupted: A History of the World Through Islamic Eyes*, Public Affairs

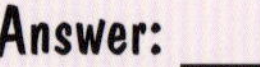

1

No title here. Move on.

Both the Mughal and Ottoman Empires experienced a period of success, then decline.

. . . In the Moghul [Mughal] empire the core contradiction had always been Hindus versus Muslims. Akbar the Great had worked out a sort of accommodation, but his great-grandson Aurangzeb reversed all his policies, enforcing orthodox Islam rigidly, restoring discrimination against Hindus, squashing smaller religious groups such as the Sikhs, and generally replacing tolerance with repression. And yet, say what you will about the man's narrow-minded zealotry [fanaticism], Aurangzeb was a titanic talent, so he not only held his empire together but extended it. The whole time, however, he was sowing the discord [division] and tension that would erupt to ruin the empire as soon as a less capable ruler took charge. . . .

. . . This glimpse into the Ottoman social clockwork does not begin to exhaust its fractal intricacy [complexity]: look closer and deeper into Ottoman society and you'll see the same order of complexity at every level. Everything was connected to everything else and connected in many ways, which was fine when all the connections balanced out and all of the parts were working. Centuries later, when the empire entered its decrepitude [decaying state], all the intertwining parts and intermeshing [connecting] institutions became a peculiarly Ottoman liability; their intricacy meant that trouble in one place or sphere translated mysteriously to trouble in a dozen other places or spheres—but that came later. In the sixteenth century, the Ottoman Empire was an awesomely well-functioning machine. . . .

Source: Tamim Ansary, *Destiny Disrupted: A History of the World Through Islamic Eyes*, Public Affairs

4

2

Source: Tamim Ansary, *Destiny Disrupted: A History of the World Through Islamic Eyes*, Public Affairs

3

4 Based on these passages, what is a primary similarity between the Mughal and Ottoman Empires?

(1) Social conflict did not exist in either empire.
(2) Each empire experienced a period of success.
(3) Each empire lasted less than a century.
(4) Hinduism had little influence in the development of either empire.

Regents Question Time!

. . . In the Moghul [Mughal] empire the core contradiction had always been Hindus versus Muslims. Akbar the Great had worked out a sort of accommodation, but his great-grandson Aurangzeb reversed all his policies, enforcing orthodox Islam rigidly, restoring discrimination against Hindus, squashing smaller religious groups such as the Sikhs, and generally replacing tolerance with repression. And yet, say what you will about the man's narrow-minded zealotry [fanaticism], Aurangzeb was a titanic talent, so he not only held his empire together but extended it. The whole time, however, he was sowing the discord [division] and tension that would erupt to ruin the empire as soon as a less capable ruler took charge. . . .

. . . This glimpse into the Ottoman social clockwork does not begin to exhaust its fractal intricacy [complexity]: look closer and deeper into Ottoman society and you'll see the same order of complexity at every level. Everything was connected to everything else and connected in many ways, which was fine when all the connections balanced out and all of the parts were working. Centuries later, when the empire entered its decrepitude [decaying state], all the intertwining parts and intermeshing [connecting] institutions became a peculiarly Ottoman liability; their intricacy meant that trouble in one place or sphere translated mysteriously to trouble in a dozen other places or spheres—but that came later. In the sixteenth century, the Ottoman Empire was an awesomely well-functioning machine. . . .

Source: Tamim Ansary, *Destiny Disrupted: A History of the World Through Islamic Eyes*, Public Affairs

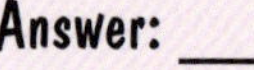

Answer: ___

1

No title here. Move on.

. . . In the Moghul [Mughal] empire the core contradiction had always been Hindus versus Muslims. Akbar the Great had worked out a sort of accommodation, but his great-grandson Aurangzeb reversed all his policies, enforcing orthodox Islam rigidly, restoring discrimination against Hindus, squashing smaller religious groups such as the Sikhs, and generally replacing tolerance with repression. And yet, say what you will about the man's narrow-minded zealotry [fanaticism], Aurangzeb was a titanic talent, so he not only held his empire together but extended it. The whole time, however, he was sowing the discord [division] and tension that would erupt to ruin the empire as soon as a less capable ruler took charge. . . .

. . . This glimpse into the Ottoman social clockwork does not begin to exhaust its fractal intricacy [complexity]: look closer and deeper into Ottoman society and you'll see the same order of complexity at every level. Everything was connected to everything else and connected in many ways, which was fine when all the connections balanced out and all of the parts were working. Centuries later, when the empire entered its decrepitude [decaying state], all the intertwining parts and intermeshing [connecting] institutions became a peculiarly Ottoman liability; their intricacy meant that trouble in one place or sphere translated mysteriously to trouble in a dozen other places or spheres—but that came later. In the sixteenth century, the Ottoman Empire was an awesomely well-functioning machine. . . .

Source: Tamim Ansary, *Destiny Disrupted: A History of the World Through Islamic Eyes*, Public Affairs

4

2

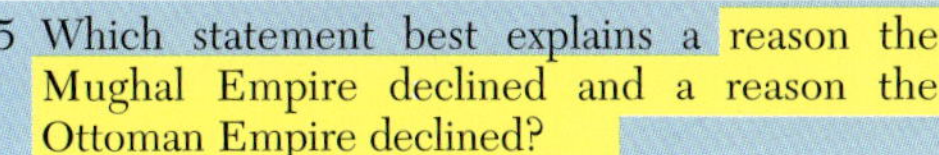
Source: Tamim Ansary, *Destiny Disrupted: A History of the World Through Islamic Eyes*, Public Affairs

3

5 Which statement best explains a reason the Mughal Empire declined and a reason the Ottoman Empire declined?

(1) Mughal leaders were ineffective; Ottoman society was too interconnected.
(2) Mughal society was too secular; policies of Ottoman sultans were inconsistent.
(3) Religious diversity in the Mughal Empire was lacking; the Ottoman Empire never worked efficiently.
(4) Mughal society paid little attention to the government; Ottoman social groups were too isolated.

Regents Question Time!

The sankin kōtai (lit., "alternate attendance") system was a device of the Tokugawa shogunate, the government of Japan from 1603 to 1868, designed to insure political control by the regime over the daimyo, or territorial lords, who exercised virtually autonomous authority over the more than 260 feudal states into which four-fifths of the country was divided. Under this system most of the daimyo were required to travel biennially [every two years] from their domains to the capital of the Tokugawa at Edo (present day Tokyo) and to spend alternate years in personal attendance at the shogunal court. Each daimyo was also required to maintain residences at the capital where his wife and children were permanently detained. . . .

Another important contribution of the operation of the sankin kōtai system to the modernization of Japan was to promote the intellectual and cultural unification of the country. The sankin kōtai served to bring a large part of the leadership elements from the whole country together in one place and to keep a constant stream of leaders and intellectuals moving back and forth between the capital and all parts of the country. This was important in giving Japan the tremendous intellectual unity with which it faced the West in the nineteenth century. It also enabled the people at large to have a stronger sense of national unity than would have been the case had the system not existed. By serving as the vehicle which spread the culture of Edo and Osaka to the countryside, the system influenced the diffusion of a truly national culture. . . .

Source: Toshio G. Tsukahira, *Feudal Control in Tokugawa Japan*, East Asian Research Center, Harvard University, 1966

Answer: ___

1

No title here. Move on.

The sankin kōtai (lit., "alternate attendance") system was a device of the Tokugawa shogunate, the government of Japan from 1603 to 1868, designed to insure political control by the regime over the daimyo, or territorial lords, who exercised virtually autonomous authority over the more than 260 feudal states into which four-fifths of the country was divided. Under this system most of the daimyo were required to travel biennially [every two years] from their domains to the capital of the Tokugawa at Edo (present day Tokyo) and to spend alternate years in personal attendance at the shogunal court. Each daimyo was also required to maintain residences at the capital where his wife and children were permanently detained. . . .

Another important contribution of the operation of the sankin kōtai system to the modernization of Japan was to promote the intellectual and cultural unification of the country. The sankin kōtai served to bring a large part of the leadership elements from the whole country together in one place and to keep a constant stream of leaders and intellectuals moving back and forth between the capital and all parts of the country. This was important in giving Japan the tremendous intellectual unity with which it faced the West in the nineteenth century. It also enabled the people at large to have a stronger sense of national unity than would have been the case had the system not existed. By serving as the vehicle which spread the culture of Edo and Osaka to the countryside, the system influenced the diffusion of a truly national culture. . . .

Source: Toshio G. Tsukahira, *Feudal Control in Tokugawa Japan*, East Asian Research Center, Harvard University, 1966

4

2

Source: Toshio G. Tsukahira, *Feudal Control in Tokugawa Japan*, East Asian Research Center, Harvard University, 1966

3

1 What was an important contribution of the sankin kōtai (alternate attendance) system to the modernization of Japan?

(1) Japan's people developed a stronger sense of national cultural unity.
(2) Japan's government established control over Western intellectuals forced to live in Osaka.
(3) Japan improved its railroad system by connecting the countryside to the cities.
(4) Japan increased the power of the daimyo during the Tokugawa shogunate.

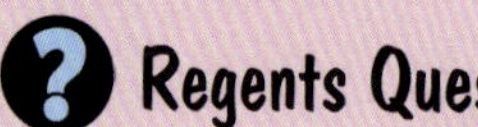

Regents Question Time!

The sankin kōtai (lit., "alternate attendance") system was a device of the Tokugawa shogunate, the government of Japan from 1603 to 1868, designed to insure political control by the regime over the daimyo, or territorial lords, who exercised virtually autonomous authority over the more than 260 feudal states into which four-fifths of the country was divided. Under this system most of the daimyo were required to travel biennially [every two years] from their domains to the capital of the Tokugawa at Edo (present day Tokyo) and to spend alternate years in personal attendance at the shogunal court. Each daimyo was also required to maintain residences at the capital where his wife and children were permanently detained. . . .

Another important contribution of the operation of the sankin kōtai system to the modernization of Japan was to promote the intellectual and cultural unification of the country. The sankin kōtai served to bring a large part of the leadership elements from the whole country together in one place and to keep a constant stream of leaders and intellectuals moving back and forth between the capital and all parts of the country. This was important in giving Japan the tremendous intellectual unity with which it faced the West in the nineteenth century. It also enabled the people at large to have a stronger sense of national unity than would have been the case had the system not existed. By serving as the vehicle which spread the culture of Edo and Osaka to the countryside, the system influenced the diffusion of a truly national culture. . . .

Source: Toshio G. Tsukahira, *Feudal Control in Tokugawa Japan*, East Asian Research Center, Harvard University, 1966

Answer: ____

1

No title here. Move on.

The sankin kōtai (lit., "alternate attendance") system was a device of the Tokugawa shogunate, the government of Japan from 1603 to 1868, designed to insure political control by the regime over the daimyo, or territorial lords, who exercised virtually autonomous authority over the more than 260 feudal states into which four-fifths of the country was divided. Under this system most of the daimyo were required to travel biennially [every two years] from their domains to the capital of the Tokugawa at Edo (present day Tokyo) and to spend alternate years in personal attendance at the shogunal court. Each daimyo was also required to maintain residences at the capital where his wife and children were permanently detained. . . .

Another important contribution of the operation of the sankin kōtai system to the modernization of Japan was to promote the intellectual and cultural unification of the country. The sankin kōtai served to bring a large part of the leadership elements from the whole country together in one place and to keep a constant stream of leaders and intellectuals moving back and forth between the capital and all parts of the country. This was important in giving Japan the tremendous intellectual unity with which it faced the West in the nineteenth century. It also enabled the people at large to have a stronger sense of national unity than would have been the case had the system not existed. By serving as the vehicle which spread the culture of Edo and Osaka to the countryside, the system influenced the diffusion of a truly national culture. . . .

Source: Toshio G. Tsukahira, *Feudal Control in Tokugawa Japan*, East Asian Research Center, Harvard University, 1966

4

2

Source: Toshio G. Tsukahira, *Feudal Control in Tokugawa Japan*, East Asian Research Center, Harvard University, 1966

3

2 The purpose of the Tokugawa's sankin kōtai (alternate attendance) system is similar to the purpose of

(1) British suffragettes who demanded Parliament grant women the right to vote
(2) King Louis XIV of France who required nobles to stay at Versailles
(3) Simón Bolívar who expected the indigenous people to rise up against the Spanish
(4) European countries that divided up the African continent

Louis XIV also maintained control over his empire by requiring the nobles to stay at his palace in Versailles.

UNIT 3

THE SCIENTIFIC METHOD & THE ENLIGHTENMENT

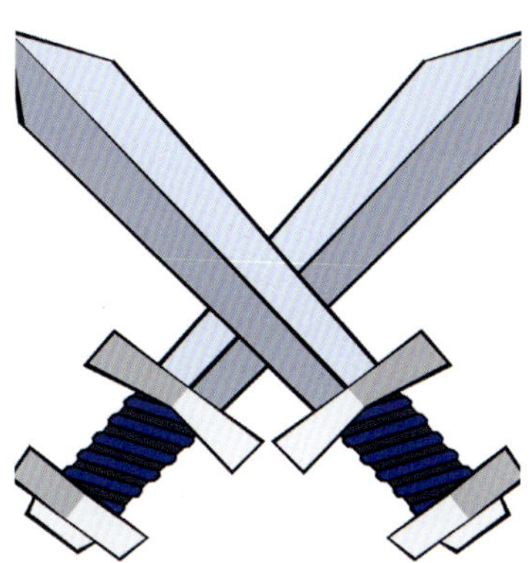

Revolutions

REVOLUTION: a major and quick change

There are different types of revolutions:

1. **INTELLECTUAL REVOLUTION:** a change in the way people view the world

   ex: Scientific Revolution, the Enlightenment

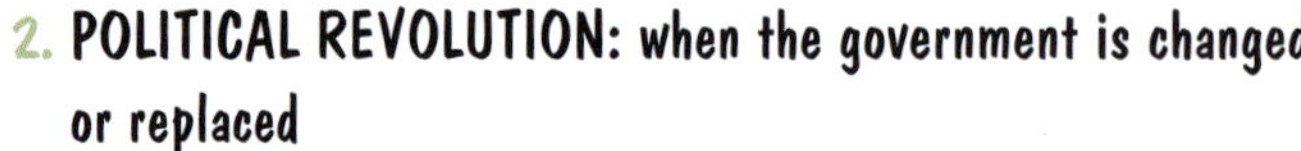

2. **POLITICAL REVOLUTION:** when the government is changed or replaced

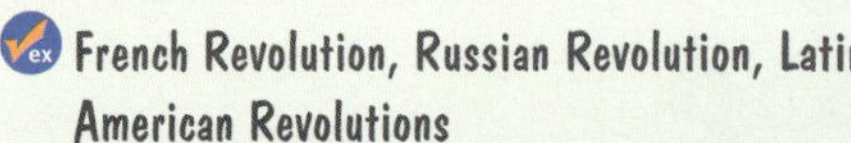

   ex: French Revolution, Russian Revolution, Latin American Revolutions

The Scientific Revolution (1500's & 1600's)

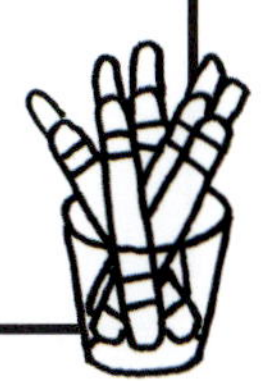

Until this point, most of European society accepted the beliefs of the Catholic Church.

Now, scientists started questioning old ideas and presenting new ones.
They challenged traditional beliefs and proved their new ideas through **observations** and **conclusions.**

Ⓡ Common Regents question

NEWTON introduced the idea that NATURAL LAWS govern the physical world.

Effects of the Scientific Revolution

1. People started challenging the traditional authority of the Church.

2. The ENLIGHTENMENT

3. Spread of new ideas throughout Europe

Ⓡ **Cause and effect:** People challenged the ideas of the Church (because of the Scientific Revolution) ➲ Enlightenment

Ⓡ **Turning Point:** The Scientific Revolution changed people's ideas and led to the Enlightenment.

The Enlightenment / Age of Reason

THE ENLIGHTENMENT/AGE OF REASON: Period when logic was used to try to improve society

<u>Scientific Revolution:</u>

Challenge Church

Scientists believed that **natural laws** governed the **physical world.**

→

<u>Enlightenment:</u>

New ideas

Political thinkers believed **natural laws** governed **human behavior.**

HINT: Enl<u>ight</u>enment: This era brought <u>light</u> to people, since it improved society and introduced new ideas about how a government should run.

The Enlightenment: Important People

Meet these guys and what they have to say:

1. JOHN LOCKE:
   - People have natural rights – life, liberty, and property.
   - The government must protect these rights.

   This was a totally new idea! In the past, the government was not expected to respect people's rights.

   Now, if the government doesn't protect the people's rights, the people have a right to overthrow the government.

HINT: Locke says that people's rights are protected – their rights are "locked in"!

The Enlightenment: More Important People

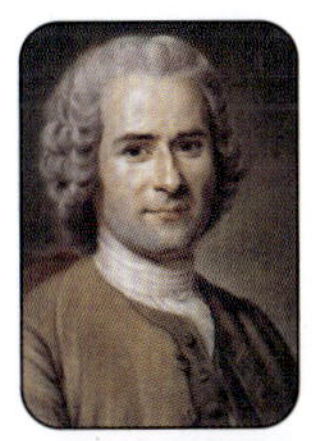

2. ROUSSEAU (pronounced ROO-SO): People choose to follow the authority of the government for their own good.

HINT: Rousseau (us) – Rousseau understood that we (us) choose to listen to authority for our (us) own good.

3. BARON de MONTESQUIEU: Separation of Powers – The government should be divided into 3 branches so that no single branch can become too powerful.

4. VOLTAIRE: Belief in freedom of speech and freedom of religion

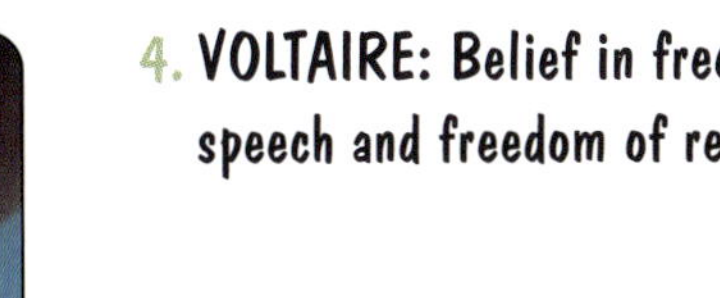

If only my students would follow my authority for their own good – so that they can learn! (Enlightenment!)

Effects of the Enlightenment

1. The ideas of the Enlightenment led to political revolutions.

Enlightenment	→	American Revolution French Revolution Latin American Revolutions

R **Cause and effect:** The Enlightenment led to the revolutions.

We'll learn about the American Revolution in the American History course. I hope you won't go crazy from curiosity in the interim!

The Enlightenment & Enlightened Despots

Enlightenment  Enlightened Despots

ENLIGHTENED DESPOTS: Monarchs (kings, queens, czars, etc.) who implemented the ideas of the Enlightenment

Catherine the Great

1. Peter the Great (Russia)
2. Maria Theresa (Habsburg)
   - Introduced a national educational system
3. Catherine the Great (Russia):
   - Prohibited religious persecution and torture
   - Made the legal system more just

The interesting part is that these rulers were **ABSOLUTIST** and dictator-like!

R **Turning point/cause and effect:** The Enlightenment brought new ideas about the government's role in protecting people's freedoms. This led to revolutions.

Individuals Influence Enlightenment Ideas

Enlightenment  Liberty for all people

Some important individuals influenced the Enlightenment ideas, including:

MARY WOLLSTONECRAFT wrote **A VINDICATION OF THE RIGHTS OF WOMAN**, which asserts that women are not naturally inferior to men and should be entitled to the rights of life, liberty, and the pursuit of happiness.

WILLIAM WILBERFORCE was a British leader who worked to abolish the slave trade.

His efforts led to a law that abolished slavery in most of the British Empire!

HINT: William Wilber<u>force</u> was the <u>force</u> behind slavery abolition in the British Empire.

Quick Review

Check off the boxes you know well. Whatever you don't know well (yet!), go back and review now!

- ☐ The Scientific Revolution
- ☐ The Scientific Method
- ☐ Copernicus (Heliocentric model)
- ☐ Galileo
- ☐ Newton
- ☐ Enlightenment
  - John Locke
  - Rousseau
  - Baron de Montesquieu
  - Voltaire
- ☐ Enlightenment leads to revolutions
- ☐ Enlightened despots

Enduring Issues Essay Topics That Came Up in This Unit:

- **Cooperation:** The Enlightenment philosophers developed philosophies on how to improve society. Feel free to list and discuss the philosophers we just met! (John Locke, Rousseau, Baron de Montesquieu, Voltaire)

- **Conflict:** The old theories of the Church versus the new theories

- **Ideas and beliefs:** Many new ideas were presented during the Scientific Revolution and the Enlightenment. Think about famous Enlightenment philosophers who presented ideas on how to improve society, and said that the government should respect people's freedoms.

Regents Question Time!

Now it's time to test how well you know your stuff.

Have fun!

Regents Question Time!

This excerpt is from a letter written by Galileo to Johannes Kepler on August 4, 1597.

> . . . "I have as yet read nothing beyond the preface of your book, from which, however, I catch a glimpse of your meaning, and feel great joy on meeting with so powerful an associate in the pursuit of truth, and, consequently, such a friend to truth itself; for it is deplorable that there should be so few who care about truth, and who do not persist in their perverse [improper] mode of philosophising.* But as this is not the fit time for lamenting [complaining about] the melancholy condition of our times, but for congratulating you on your elegant discoveries in confirmation of the truth, I shall only add a promise to peruse [study] your book dispassionately, and with the conviction that I shall find in it much to admire. . . .

Source: J. J. Fahie, Galileo: His Life and Work, John Murray

*Philosophising is the method used by some to understand the world in which they live.

1 Based on this 1597 letter excerpt, what goal are both Galileo and Kepler pursuing? [1]

____

Answer: ___

1

This excerpt is from a letter written by Galileo to Johannes Kepler on August 4, 1597.

Yes, the vocabulary here is complicated. No, you don't need to understand every word. You should understand some of it, which will give you the answer!

> . . . "I have as yet read nothing beyond the preface of your book, from which, however, I catch a glimpse of your meaning, and feel great joy on meeting with so powerful an associate in the pursuit of truth, and, consequently, such a friend to truth itself; for it is deplorable that there should be so few who care about truth, and who do not persist in their perverse [improper] mode of philosophising.* But as this is not the fit time for lamenting [complaining about] the melancholy condition of our times, but for congratulating you on your elegant discoveries in confirmation of the truth, I shall only add a promise to peruse [study] your book dispassionately, and with the conviction that I shall find in it much to admire. . . .

2

Source: J. J. Fahie, Galileo: His Life and Work, John Murray

3

1 Based on this 1597 letter excerpt, what goal are both Galileo and Kepler pursuing? [1]

4

Goal of Galileo and Kepler

Acceptable Answers:

- truth/pursuit of truth
- scientific truth
- discoveries that reveal the truth
- to make discoveries that confirm the truth/in confirmation of the truth
- to change how science is seen
- to understand the world in which they lived

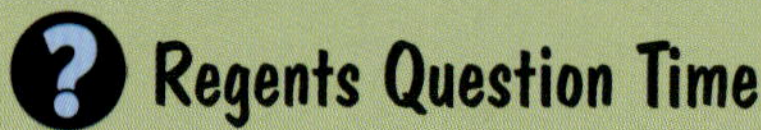

Regents Question Time!

Galileo explains his discoveries to the Pope.

Source: Chris Madden cartoons

2 Based on Chris Madden's cartoon, what risk did Galileo take in presenting his findings to the Church? [1]

Answer: ___

1

Galileo explains his discoveries to the Pope.

Galileo is explaining his findings to the pope. The pope is thinking about taking the telescope and hitting Galileo on the head with it! (Don't laugh!) Galileo is at risk of being punished by the Church.

2

Source: Chris Madden cartoons

No helpful info here. Too bad ☹.

3

2 Based on Chris Madden's cartoon, what risk did Galileo take in presenting his findings to the Church? [1]

Acceptable Answers:

- The pope would punish him/hit him; getting hit/punished by the Church
- he/Galileo would be in conflict with the Church
- being punished for explaining ideas that challenged Church teachings
- the anger of the Church/of Church officials
- fear of being rejected by the Church
- Galileo's/his findings would not be accepted or believed by the Church
- excommunication/being accused of heresy

Regents Question Time!

"... Finally, gather together all that we have said, so great and so august [important], about royal authority. You have seen a great nation united under one man: you have seen his sacred power, paternal and absolute: you have seen that secret reason which directs the body politic, enclosed in one head: you have seen the image of God in kings, and you will have the idea of majesty of kingship.

God is holiness itself, goodness itself, power itself, reason itself. In these things consists the divine majesty. In their reflection consists the majesty of the prince. ..."

— Jacques-Benigne Bossuet

15 Which individual most likely opposed the form of government described in this quotation?

(1) Ivan the Terrible
(2) Thomas Hobbes
(3) John Locke
(4) Louis XIV

Answer: ___

1

No title here. Move on.

Looks like it's praising absolutism (that the king/monarch has all the power)

"... Finally, gather together all that we have said, so great and so august [important], about royal authority. You have seen a great nation united under one man: you have seen his sacred power, paternal and absolute: you have seen that secret reason which directs the body politic, enclosed in one head: you have seen the image of God in kings, and you will have the idea of majesty of kingship.

God is holiness itself, goodness itself, power itself, reason itself. In these things consists the divine majesty. In their reflection consists the majesty of the prince. . . ."

2

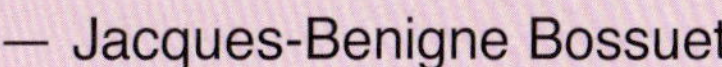

— Jacques-Benigne Bossuet

I don't see any help here.

3

15 Which individual most likely opposed the form of government described in this quotation?

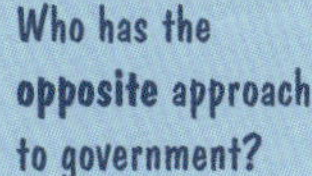

Who has the **opposite** approach to government?

(1) Ivan the Terrible
(2) Thomas Hobbes
(3) John Locke
(4) Louis XIV

4

Who has the opposite idea – that the government should NOT have all the power? That's right! John Locke

If there's no title, you'll obviously skip that step. I guess you don't have any other choice.

UNIT 4

AGE OF REVOLUTIONS

Quick Recap

Until this point (1780s), here's how government worked:

1. **ABSOLUTISM:** Monarchs had total control over their nations.
   Countries had a **CENTRALIZED GOVERNMENT**, where all the power was in one ruler's hands.

2. People believed in **DIVINE RIGHT:** the belief that kings received their power from God and should therefore have complete control over the people.

Now, things start changing...

Stay posted! Things are going to get exciting!

Political Revolutions

Until now, the people accepted the absolute reign of one ruler. True, the monarch often abused them. That was just life.

Then, the Enlightenment introduced new ideas, such as the idea that people should have freedoms and the government should protect those freedoms. The people heard these ideas and said –
"Hey! We're being treated unfairly. We are entitled to rights!"

How will they obtain those rights and get rid of the government? Here's where we enter a pretty bloody era of political revolutions.

- A POLITICAL REVOLUTION is when the people of a country overthrow an existing government and create a new government.

So hold up your shields and let's visit revolutions all over the world!

The French Revolution (1789-1799)

<u>Causes of the French Revolution:</u>

1. ABSOLUTE MONARCHY: People had no say in the government. Whatever the monarch decided is what happened. The French people believed that the kings abused their power and denied the people their rights.

2. SOCIAL INEQUALITY:
   - The FIRST and SECOND ESTATES (clergy and nobility) enjoyed special rights, had tons of money, and didn't pay taxes.
   - The THIRD ESTATE (middle and lower classes) had to pay most of the taxes and had no rights. No fair! They were very unhappy ☹!
     - The Third Estate included 2 groups:
       1. BOURGEOISIE: the wealthy middle class
       2. PEASANTS: the poor lower class

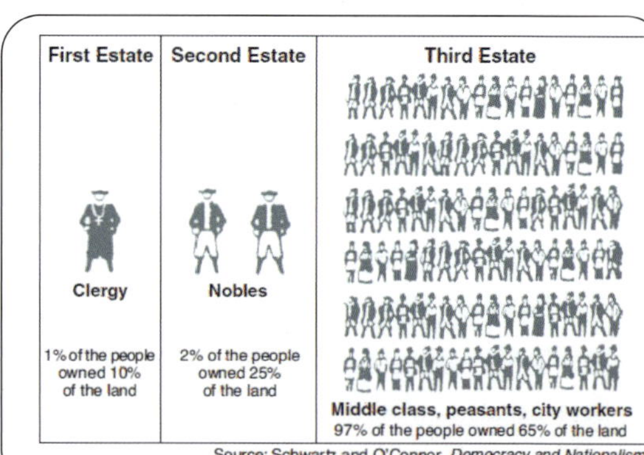

Source: Schwartz and O'Connor, *Democracy and Nationalism*, Globe Book Company (adapted)

The French Revolution (1789-1799)

<u>Causes of the French Revolution:</u> (continued)

3. **ECONOMIC PROBLEMS:**
   - The government spent tons of money on wars (including helping the Americans in the Revolutionary War).
   - There was a bad harvest.
   - Food became very expensive.

When people are hungry, they get angry. Sounds like the French were quite unhappy!

4. **THE ENLIGHTENMENT:** People challenged the traditional social inequality. The members of the Third Estate said, "Why should the nobles and clergy enjoy privileges at our expense?"

5. **AMERICAN REVOLUTION:** The French saw the Americans' success in the American Revolution. They said, "Let's do the same!"

HINT: Causes of the French Revolution: MEAT - <u>M</u>onarchy, <u>E</u>nlightenment, <u>A</u>merican Revolution, <u>T</u>hird Estate

Sounds like they have some good ideas to get them out of their misery!

The French Revolution Begins

The French people were really unhappy with the absolutist French monarchy.
So LOUIS XVI, the king of France called the Estates General (representatives of all 3 estates) into session. Many changes happened because of this gathering:

- The Third Estate felt ignored in the Estates General, so they withdrew. They formed the NATIONAL ASSEMBLY – the group that has the power to make laws. They met on a local tennis court and made an oath (called the TENNIS COURT OATH!) to keep meeting until the king recognized them as a legitimate government body.

- SEIZURE OF THE BASTILLE (1789): The Bastille Prison (the royal prison) symbolized the strength of the French monarchy. The Third Estate stormed the Bastille, starting the French Revolution!

This led to the fall of the French monarchy.

The National Assembly Rules

- The National Assembly signed a document called the DECLARATION OF THE RIGHTS OF MAN, which included:
  - Freedom of speech
  - Freedom of equality
  - Representation for all in government
  - Took away the privileges of the First and Second Estates

(This document was based on the Declaration of Independence and Enlightenment ideas.)

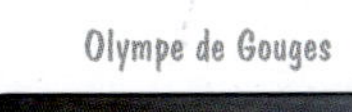
Olympe de Gouges

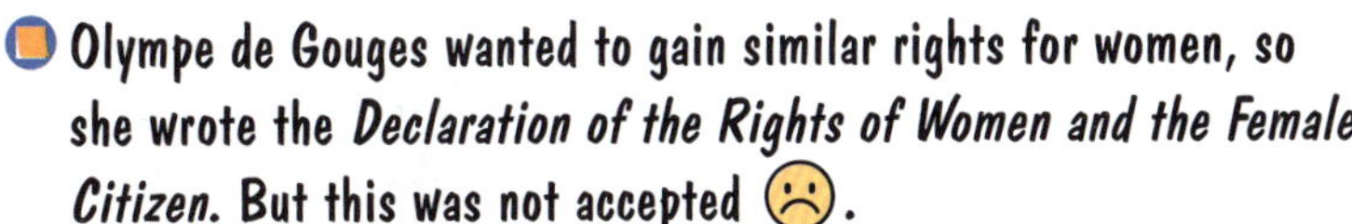

Olympe de Gouges wanted to gain similar rights for women, so she wrote the *Declaration of the Rights of Women and the Female Citizen*. But this was not accepted ☹.

- The National Assembly set up a limited monarchy and representative assembly, called the LEGISLATIVE ASSEMBLY.

First Stage of the French Revolution: The Reign of Terror

- Radicals, called JACOBINS, took control of the Assembly, killed the French king, and made France a REPUBLIC: a state in which the people and their elected representatives hold the power.

  This period, known as the REIGN OF TERROR, was a time of bloodshed, fighting, and instability.
  - Leader of the Jacobins: ROBESPIERRE
  - COMMITTEE OF PUBLIC SAFETY: The radicals created a group dedicated to wiping out the old regime. Anyone who was suspected of loyalty to the old leadership was killed on the GUILLOTINE (an instrument that cut off people's heads) or jailed!
  - The radicals' famous theme was "LIBERTY, EQUALITY, FRATERNITY (brotherhood)!"
- Then, Robespierre was killed, which ended the Reign of Terror.
- The FRENCH DIRECTORY government replaced the Jacobins. They were a weak and insufficient government.

Ⓡ **Cause and effect:** French Revolution ➲ Freedoms ➲ Napoleon (a dictator) comes to power

HINT: Robespierre (spear): When he ruled, thousands were killed.

That doesn't sound too "safe" to me!

I guess the "spear" hit Robespierre this time!

Second Stage of the French Revolution: Napoleon Bonaparte (1799-1815)

(1799) Napoleon overthrew the French Directory government in a COUP D'ÉTAT (rebellion by military leaders to overthrow the government).

Napoleon formed a new government and put himself in charge.
He called himself "EMPEROR OF THE FRENCH"– he had absolute power!

<u>Napoleon's Achievements:</u>

1. **Territory:** Napoleon conquered much of Europe and ruled over a huge empire.
2. **Economy/Education:** He made economic and educational improvements.
3. NAPOLEONIC CODE: He created a code of law called the NAPOLEONIC CODE, which gave legal equality and religious tolerance to all citizens.
4. **Stability:** He brought stability to France.

Napoleon sounds almost as good as my napoleon dessert!

HINT: TENS (Territory, Economic/educational improvements, Napoleonic code, Stability)

Third Stage of the French Revolution: The Fall of Napoleon

Napoleon invaded Russia in 1812, where he faced two problems:

1. It was during the bitter winter and the French were not equipped to deal with the brutal weather. Many Frenchmen froze to death!
   - R This is an example of how geography affects history.
   - E **Environmental impact:** The Russian weather affected the French Revolution.
2. SCORCHED EARTH POLICY: The Russians burned the earth as they retreated (moved back to escape from the French invaders).
   The French had no food, so they lost energy to fight.
   Many starved to death.

R **Making Connections:** Hitler made the same mistake as Napoleon. He also invaded Russia in the winter, which led to his downfall.

Napoleon lost the war and was sent to exile, where he died.

Effects of The French Revolution

1. The BOURGEOISIE (wealthy middle class that was part of the Third Estate) gained power.

2. NATIONALISM (pride in one's nation):
   - **In France:** France was proud of their revolution and of Napoleon's conquests.
   - **Globally:** The idea of nationalism spread to many areas as a result of Napoleon's conquests.

Ⓡ **Cause and effect:** French Revolution introduces the concept of nationalism ➲ Revolutions in Latin America and South America

Ⓡ **Cause and effect:** French Revolution ➲ Changes in the government (introduction of new freedoms and rights)

Congress of Vienna (1814)

The Napoleonic era was over. The world was a mess after so many revolutions and wars. Now what?

The European leaders met in the CONGRESS OF VIENNA to put Europe back in order.

Here's what they accomplished during this meeting:

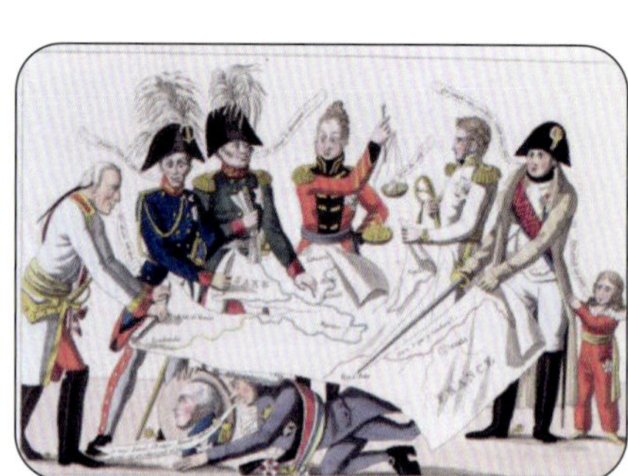

1. They "redrew" the map of Europe, assigning territories to different countries.
2. They established a "balance of power" so that no country could become too powerful.
3. They reinstated the French monarchy (the same type of government that existed before the French Revolution).

Ⓡ **Cause and effect:** French Revolution ➲ Congress of Vienna ➲ Reinstating monarchy and establishing a balance of power in Europe

Latin American Issues

After the French Revolution, the feeling of nationalism was in the air, and other countries decided to copy the French.

During this period, stronger countries controlled (imperialized) weaker countries.

European countries (such as Spain, Portugal, and France) controlled Latin America and South America.

The MOTHER COUNTRY was the stronger country that controlled the weaker country.
The COLONY was the weaker country being controlled.

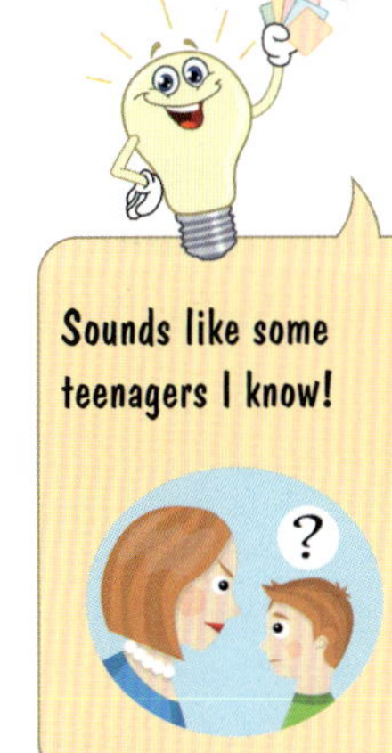

Latin American colonies were getting frustrated that the European countries were controlling them. They wanted more rights and independence!

Cause and effect: Imperialism ➲ Latin American Revolutions

Latin American Colonies

This is a map of Latin American countries in the late 1700s.
Notice how the Latin American colonies were controlled by stronger countries (mother countries): British, Danish, Dutch, French, Portuguese...

EdBoosters™

The Latin American Revolutions (1800-1830)

Latin American countries revolted (made revolutions) to gain independence from their mother countries.

Causes of the Latin American Revolutions:

1. SOCIAL INEQUALITY:
   The Peninsulares (Spanish-born people) had more rights and money than all the other classes (see diagram).
2. The ENLIGHTENMENT inspired the Latin American people to fight for their independence and rights.
3. The AMERICAN and FRENCH REVOLUTIONS: Revolutions were "in the air."

PENINSULARES: Spanish born
CREOLES: European origin, born in America
MESTIZOS: Mixed Europeans and Indian ancestry
MULATTOS: Mixed European and Negro ancestors
INDIANS, NEGROS

Latin American Social Classes

R **Cause and effect:** All these factors led to the Latin American revolutions.

R **Turning Point:** The Latin American revolutions changed the political face of Latin American countries.

South America Before and After the Revolutions

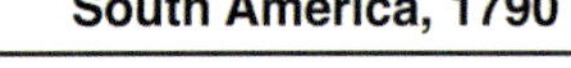

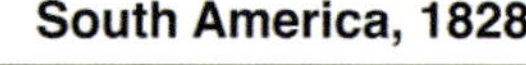

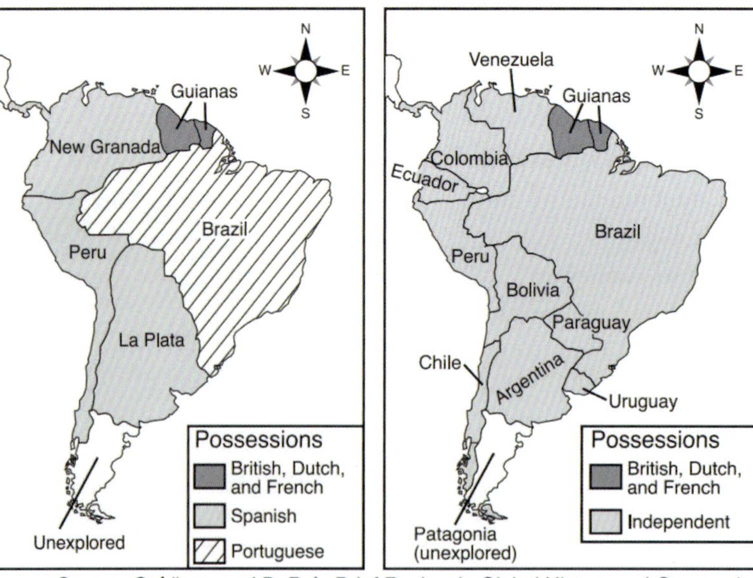

Source: Goldberg and DuPré, *Brief Review in Global History and Geography*, Prentice Hall (adapted)

South American Colonies

Latin American Revolutions: Haiti

France controlled Haiti. Haiti rebelled and became the first Latin American colony to revolt against European rule.

Causes of Haiti's Rebellion:

- Slaves made up 90% of the population, but had no rights!
- Slaves worked in terrible conditions.

Revolt:

TOUSSAINT LOUVERTURE was a nationalistic leader who took control of Haiti in 1798 and gained its freedom from the French.

HINT: Louverture - overturn. Louverture overturned the French rule of Haiti.

Latin American Revolutions: Nationalistic Leaders

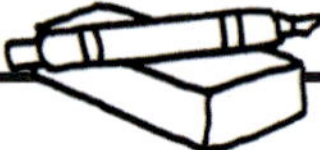

NATIONALISTIC LEADER: A leader who loves his nation and wants to free it of outside control

Famous Latin America Nationalistic Leaders:

SIMON BOLIVAR AKA: "The Liberator":

- AKA "The Liberator" – called GRAN COLOMBIA – to unite all of South America into one country.
- He led resistance movements against Spanish imperialism.
- He liberated Venezuela, Colombia, Ecuador, Peru, and Bolivia.

Gran Colombia sounds like one grand happy family!

Common Regents question: Bolivar was a nationalistic movement leader.

Ideas and Beliefs: Nationalistic leaders spread ideas of nationalism!

Conflict: Revolutions helped people gain independence.

Effects of the Independence Movements

- Spain's empire was divided into many separate states. Each state tried to create stability, social equality, and a good economy.
- They eliminated the problem of the Peninsulares being too powerful, but unequal social classes remained.
- Power remained in the hands of the wealthy landowners.

R **Cause and effect:** The independence movements led to these 3 developments.

R SOUTH AMERICA does not have political unity because of geographic factors, such as the Andes Mountains and the Amazon. Even though Bolivar tried to unite South America, he was unsuccessful because of these geographic features. This is an example of geography impacting history.

Quick Review

Check off the boxes you know well. Whatever you don't know well (yet!), go back and review now!

- ☐ Causes of Revolutions:
  - Enlightenment
  - Imperialism
  - Absolutism
- ☐ French Revolution
  - National Assembly
  - Seizure of the Bastille
  - Declaration of the Rights of Man
  - French Constitution
  - Reign of Terror – Robespierre
  - Napoleon – Nationalism
- ☐ Latin American Independence Movements: Louverture and Bolivar

Enduring Issues Essay Topics That Came Up in This Unit:

- **Conflict:** French Revolution, Latin American Revolution
- **Power:** During revolutions, power changes hands.
- **Inequality/Human Rights Violations:** People are upset about how they're treated and want change.
- **Ideas and Beliefs:** New ideas of freedom and nationalism spur revolutions. Nationalistic leaders promote these ideas.
- **Interconnectedness:** People connected in groups, which gave them the power to organize revolutions.

Now it's time to test how well you know your stuff.

Have fun!

Regents Question Time!

> . . . I shall tell you with what we must provide ourselves in order to expel the Spaniards and to found a free government. It is *union*, obviously; but such union will come about through sensible planning and well-directed actions rather than by divine magic. America stands together because it is abandoned by all other nations. It is isolated in the center of the world. It has no diplomatic relations, nor does it receive any military assistance; instead, America is attacked by Spain, which has more military supplies than any we can possibly acquire through furtive [stealthy] means.
>
> When success is not assured, when the state is weak, and when results are distantly seen, all men hesitate; opinion is divided, passions rage, and the enemy fans these passions in order to win an easy victory because of them. As soon as we are strong and under the guidance of a liberal nation which will lend us her protection, we will achieve accord [unity] in cultivating the virtues and talents that lead to glory. Then will we march majestically toward that great prosperity for which South America is destined. Then will those sciences and arts which, born in the East, have enlightened Europe, wing their way to a free Colombia, which will cordially bid them welcome. . . .

— Simón Bolívar, "Reply of a South American to a Gentleman of This Island [Jamaica]," September 6, 1815 (adapted)

3 In this letter, Simón Bolívar's goal is to

(1) become monarch of the strongest country in South America
(2) break off diplomatic relations with Europe
(3) form one nation that unifies all of South America
(4) convince Mexico to join in his fight against Spain

Answer: ____

1

No title here. Move on.

He's talking about unity for South America!

. . . I shall tell you with what we must provide ourselves in order to expel the Spaniards and to found a free government. It is *union,* obviously; but such union will come about through sensible planning and well-directed actions rather than by divine magic. America stands together because it is abandoned by all other nations. It is isolated in the center of the world. It has no diplomatic relations, nor does it receive any military assistance; instead, America is attacked by Spain, which has more military supplies than any we can possibly acquire through furtive [stealthy] means.

When success is not assured, when the state is weak, and when results are distantly seen, all men hesitate; opinion is divided, passions rage, and the enemy fans these passions in order to win an easy victory because of them. As soon as we are strong and under the guidance of a liberal nation which will lend us her protection, we will achieve accord [unity] in cultivating the virtues and talents that lead to glory. Then will we march majestically toward that great prosperity for which South America is destined. Then will those sciences and arts which, born in the East, have enlightened Europe, wing their way to a free Colombia, which will cordially bid them welcome. . . .

4

2

— Simón Bolívar, "Reply of a South American to a Gentleman of This Island [Jamaica]," September 6, 1815 (adapted)

3

What's Simon Bolivar's goal? PS: You may know the answer already!

3 In this letter, Simón Bolívar's goal is to

(1) become monarch of the strongest country in South America

(2) break off diplomatic relations with Europe

(3) form one nation that unifies all of South America

(4) convince Mexico to join in his fight against Spain

Regents Question Time!

. . . I shall tell you with what we must provide ourselves in order to expel the Spaniards and to found a free government. It is *union*, obviously; but such union will come about through sensible planning and well-directed actions rather than by divine magic. America stands together because it is abandoned by all other nations. It is isolated in the center of the world. It has no diplomatic relations, nor does it receive any military assistance; instead, America is attacked by Spain, which has more military supplies than any we can possibly acquire through furtive [stealthy] means.

When success is not assured, when the state is weak, and when results are distantly seen, all men hesitate; opinion is divided, passions rage, and the enemy fans these passions in order to win an easy victory because of them. As soon as we are strong and under the guidance of a liberal nation which will lend us her protection, we will achieve accord [unity] in cultivating the virtues and talents that lead to glory. Then will we march majestically toward that great prosperity for which South America is destined. Then will those sciences and arts which, born in the East, have enlightened Europe, wing their way to a free Colombia, which will cordially bid them welcome. . . .

— Simón Bolívar, "Reply of a South American to a Gentleman of This Island [Jamaica]," September 6, 1815 (adapted)

4 Simón Bolívar's actions were most likely influenced by the ideas of

(1) church officials
(2) Enlightenment thinkers
(3) laissez-faire economists
(4) Marxist followers

Answer: 

1

No title here. Move on.

The enlightened European ideas will travel to free Colombia...

. . . I shall tell you with what we must provide ourselves in order to expel the Spaniards and to found a free government. It is *union*, obviously; but such union will come about through sensible planning and well-directed actions rather than by divine magic. America stands together because it is abandoned by all other nations. It is isolated in the center of the world. It has no diplomatic relations, nor does it receive any military assistance; instead, America is attacked by Spain, which has more military supplies than any we can possibly acquire through furtive [stealthy] means.

When success is not assured, when the state is weak, and when results are distantly seen, all men hesitate; opinion is divided, passions rage, and the enemy fans these passions in order to win an easy victory because of them. As soon as we are strong and under the guidance of a liberal nation which will lend us her protection, we will achieve accord [unity] in cultivating the virtues and talents that lead to glory. Then will we march majestically toward that great prosperity for which South America is destined. Then will those sciences and arts which, born in the East, have enlightened Europe, wing their way to a free Colombia, which will cordially bid them welcome. . . .

2

— Simón Bolívar, "Reply of a South American to a Gentleman of This Island [Jamaica],"
September 6, 1815 (adapted)

3

Which ideas influenced Bolivar to seek freedom and unity for South America? PS: You many know the answer already 😊.

4 Simón Bolívar's actions were most likely influenced by the ideas of

(1) church officials
(2) Enlightenment thinkers
(3) laissez-faire economists
(4) Marxist followers

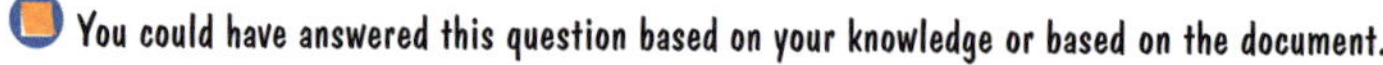

EdBoosters™

Regents Question Time!

Declaration of the Rights of Man and of the Citizen – 1789	Declaration of the Rights of Woman and Female Citizen – 1791
Articles: 1. Men are born and remain free and equal in rights. Social distinctions may be founded only upon the general good. 2. The aim of all political association is the preservation of the natural and imprescriptible [inalienable] rights of man. These rights are liberty, property, security, and resistance to oppression. . . . 4. Liberty consists in the freedom to do everything which injures no one else; hence the exercise of the natural rights of each man has no limits except those which assure to the other members of the society the enjoyment of the same rights. These limits can only be determined by law. . . . 6. Law is the expression of the general will. Every citizen has a right to participate personally, or through his representative, in its foundation. It must be the same for all, whether it protects or punishes. All citizens, being equal in the eyes of the law, are equally eligible to all dignities and to all public positions and occupations, according to their abilities, and without distinction except that of their virtues and talents. . . .	**FIRST ARTICLE** Woman is born free and remains equal to man in rights. Social distinctions can only be founded on common service. **II** The aim of all political associations is to preserve the natural and inalienable rights of Woman and Man: these are the rights to liberty, ownership, safety and, above all, resistance to oppression. . . . **IV** Liberty and justice lie in rendering everything which belongs to others as of right. Thus the exercise of woman's natural rights has no limit other than the perpetual tyranny of man's opposing them: these limits must be reformed by the laws of nature and reason. . . . **VI** The Law must be the expression of the general will; all citizens, female and male, should concur [agree] personally or through their representatives in its formation, and it must be the same for all. All citizens, being equal in its eyes, must be equally eligible to all honours, positions and public posts according to their abilities, and with no other distinction other than those of their virtues and talents. . . .
Source: The Avalon Project at Yale Law School	Source: Olympe de Gouges, 1791

3 Which political philosophy is best supported by both documents?

(1) Rule of law represents a social contract with the people.
(2) Tyranny encourages liberty and security.
(3) Separation of powers guarantees people fair treatment.
(4) Oppression promotes the general will.

Answer: ___

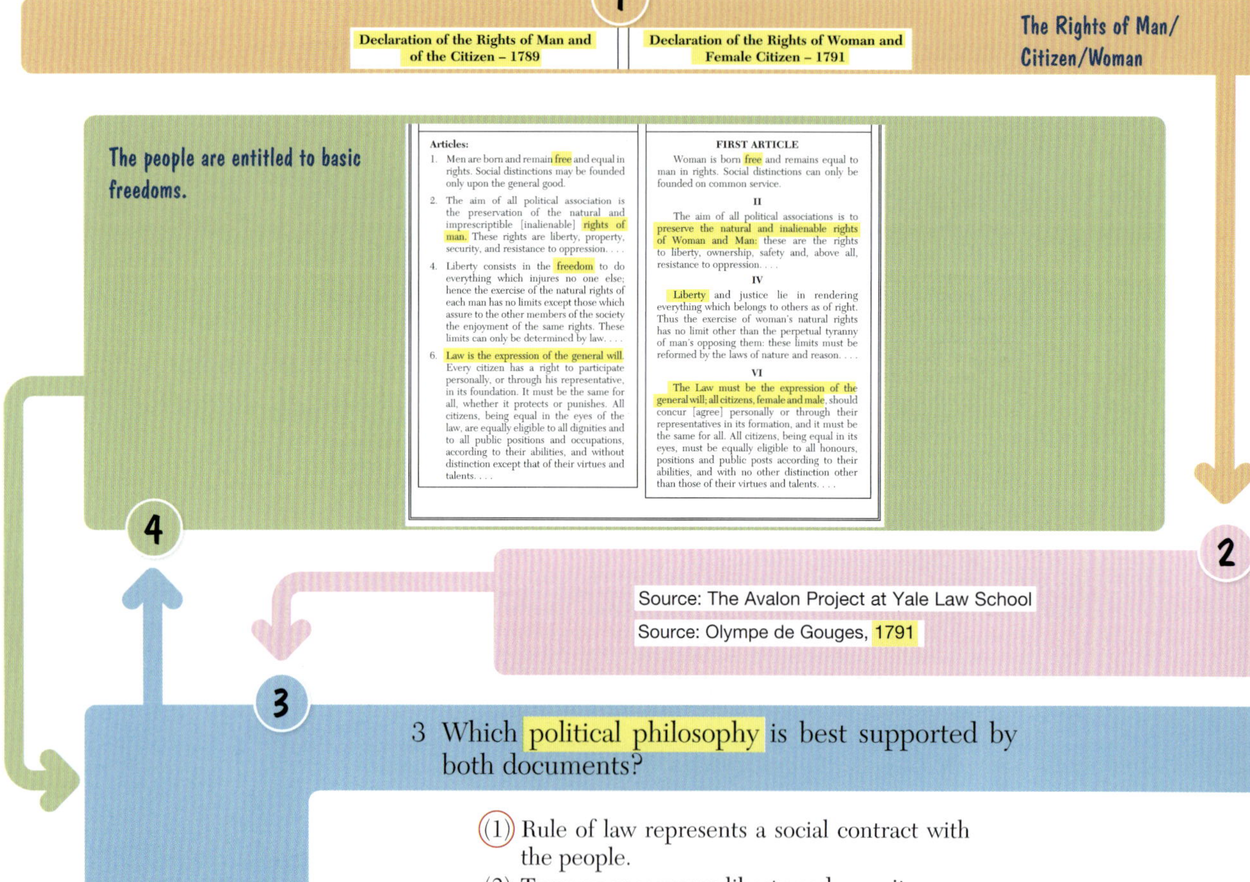

Articles:

1. Men are born and remain free and equal in rights. Social distinctions may be founded only upon the general good.
2. The aim of all political association is the preservation of the natural and imprescriptible [inalienable] rights of man. These rights are liberty, property, security, and resistance to oppression. . . .
4. Liberty consists in the freedom to do everything which injures no one else; hence the exercise of the natural rights of each man has no limits except those which assure to the other members of the society the enjoyment of the same rights. These limits can only be determined by law. . . .
6. Law is the expression of the general will. Every citizen has a right to participate personally, or through his representative, in its foundation. It must be the same for all, whether it protects or punishes. All citizens, being equal in the eyes of the law, are equally eligible to all dignities and to all public positions and occupations, according to their abilities, and without distinction except that of their virtues and talents. . . .

FIRST ARTICLE

Woman is born free and remains equal to man in rights. Social distinctions can only be founded on common service.

II

The aim of all political associations is to preserve the natural and inalienable rights of Woman and Man: these are the rights to liberty, ownership, safety and, above all, resistance to oppression. . . .

IV

Liberty and justice lie in rendering everything which belongs to others as of right. Thus the exercise of woman's natural rights has no limit other than the perpetual tyranny of man's opposing them: these limits must be reformed by the laws of nature and reason. . . .

VI

The Law must be the expression of the general will; all citizens, female and male, should concur [agree] personally or through their representatives in its formation, and it must be the same for all. All citizens, being equal in its eyes, must be equally eligible to all honours, positions and public posts according to their abilities, and with no other distinction other than those of their virtues and talents. . . .

3 Which political philosophy is best supported by both documents?

(1) Rule of law represents a social contract with the people.
(2) Tyranny encourages liberty and security.
(3) Separation of powers guarantees people fair treatment.
(4) Oppression promotes the general will.

A social contract is an agreement that people have rights that must be respected by the government. In return, the people agree to follow the law for the good of society.

Regents Question Time!

Declaration of the Rights of Man and of the Citizen – 1789	Declaration of the Rights of Woman and Female Citizen – 1791
Articles: 1. Men are born and remain free and equal in rights. Social distinctions may be founded only upon the general good. 2. The aim of all political association is the preservation of the natural and imprescriptible [inalienable] rights of man. These rights are liberty, property, security, and resistance to oppression. . . . 4. Liberty consists in the freedom to do everything which injures no one else; hence the exercise of the natural rights of each man has no limits except those which assure to the other members of the society the enjoyment of the same rights. These limits can only be determined by law. . . . 6. Law is the expression of the general will. Every citizen has a right to participate personally, or through his representative, in its foundation. It must be the same for all, whether it protects or punishes. All citizens, being equal in the eyes of the law, are equally eligible to all dignities and to all public positions and occupations, according to their abilities, and without distinction except that of their virtues and talents. . . .	**FIRST ARTICLE** Woman is born free and remains equal to man in rights. Social distinctions can only be founded on common service. **II** The aim of all political associations is to preserve the natural and inalienable rights of Woman and Man: these are the rights to liberty, ownership, safety and, above all, resistance to oppression. . . . **IV** Liberty and justice lie in rendering everything which belongs to others as of right. Thus the exercise of woman's natural rights has no limit other than the perpetual tyranny of man's opposing them: these limits must be reformed by the laws of nature and reason. . . . **VI** The Law must be the expression of the general will; all citizens, female and male, should concur [agree] personally or through their representatives in its formation, and it must be the same for all. All citizens, being equal in its eyes, must be equally eligible to all honours, positions and public posts according to their abilities, and with no other distinction other than those of their virtues and talents. . . .
Source: The Avalon Project at Yale Law School	Source: Olympe de Gouges, 1791

4 Which event most directly influenced the writing of both documents?

(1) Iranian Revolution
(2) Cuban Revolution
(3) French Revolution
(4) Russian Revolution

Answer: ___

1

Declaration of the Rights of Man and of the Citizen – 1789

Declaration of the Rights of Woman and Female Citizen – 1791

Declaration of Rights of Man... 1789
What was happening at this time?

We know that in 1789 and 1791, the French Revolution was happening.

Articles:

1. Men are born and remain free and equal in rights. Social distinctions may be founded only upon the general good.
2. The aim of all political association is the preservation of the natural and imprescriptible [inalienable] rights of man. These rights are liberty, property, security, and resistance to oppression. . . .
4. Liberty consists in the freedom to do everything which injures no one else; hence the exercise of the natural rights of each man has no limits except those which assure to the other members of the society the enjoyment of the same rights. These limits can only be determined by law. . . .
6. Law is the expression of the general will. Every citizen has a right to participate personally, or through his representative, in its foundation. It must be the same for all, whether it protects or punishes. All citizens, being equal in the eyes of the law, are equally eligible to all dignities and to all public positions and occupations, according to their abilities, and without distinction except that of their virtues and talents. . . .

FIRST ARTICLE

Woman is born free and remains equal to man in rights. Social distinctions can only be founded on common service.

II

The aim of all political associations is to preserve the natural and inalienable rights of Woman and Man: these are the rights to liberty, ownership, safety and, above all, resistance to oppression. . . .

IV

Liberty and justice lie in rendering everything which belongs to others as of right. Thus the exercise of woman's natural rights has no limit other than the perpetual tyranny of man's opposing them: these limits must be reformed by the laws of nature and reason. . . .

VI

The Law must be the expression of the general will; all citizens, female and male, should concur [agree] personally or through their representatives in its formation, and it must be the same for all. All citizens, being equal in its eyes, must be equally eligible to all honours, positions and public posts according to their abilities, and with no other distinction other than those of their virtues and talents. . . .

2

Source: The Avalon Project at Yale Law School

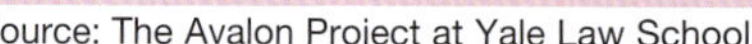
Source: Olympe de Gouges, 1791

3

4 Which event most directly influenced the writing of both documents?

(1) Iranian Revolution
(2) Cuban Revolution
(3) French Revolution
(4) Russian Revolution

4

UNIT 5

REVOLUTION & NATIONALISM

Nationalism

NATIONALISM: Strong devotion to one's country, and belief that each nation should have its own state

- Nationalism is often based on common background. For example: culture, history, religion, language, or territory.
- Nationalism had a **major** effect on many countries.
- Nationalism often leads to revolutions.

HINT: Nationalism: "ism" means belief. Nationalism means belief in one's nation (country).

NATIONALIST: A person who advocates for the unity of a country

R There are many Regents questions on nationalism and nationalist leaders.

Nationalism Can Unite or Break Up a Country

- **Sometimes, nationalism can unify a country.**

  ✓ex Germany and Italy

  R **Cause and effect:** Nationalism ⊃ Can unify a country

- **Sometimes, nationalism can break up a country.**

  ✓ex Austria and the Ottoman Empire

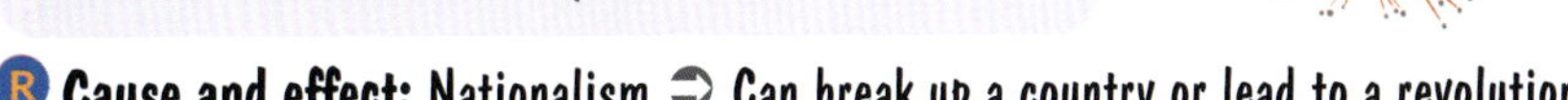

  R **Cause and effect:** Nationalism ⊃ Can break up a country or lead to a revolution

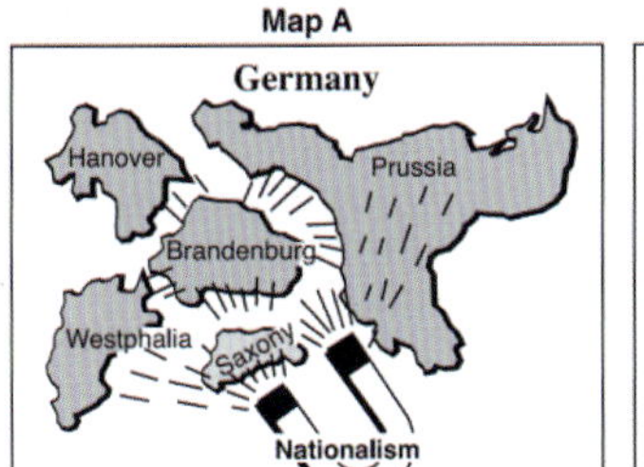

Source: Sol Holt and John R. O'Connor, *Exploring World History,* Globe Book Co. (adapted)

Nationalism can unite or break up a country.

The "Trend" of Nationalism Begins

In France, there was a strong sense of nationalism, which led to the French Revolution. France's nationalism and revolution inspired many other nations.

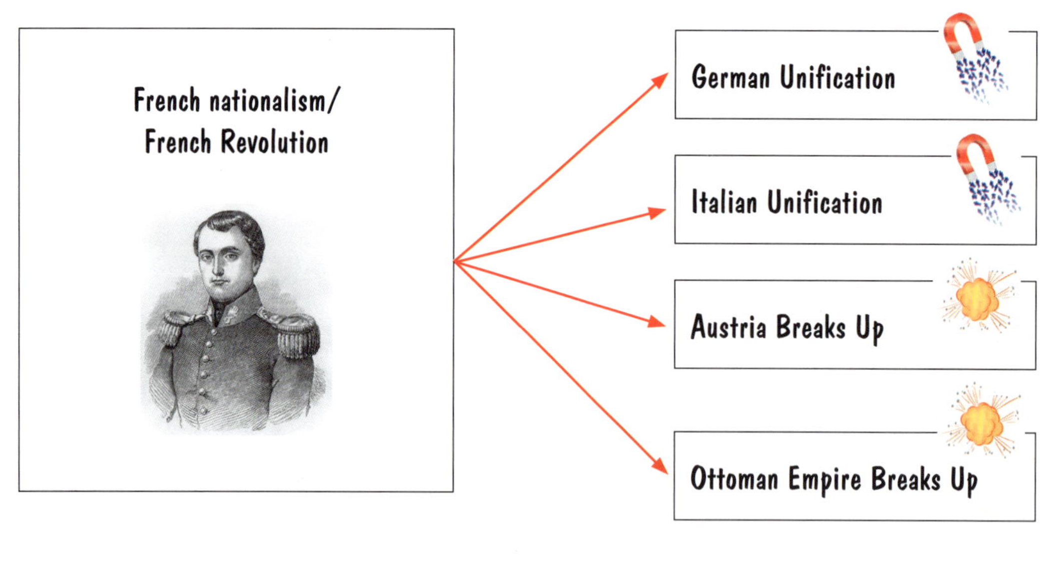

Ⓡ **Cause and effect:** French nationalism/French Revolution ➲ Nationalism around the world

Italian Unification

Italy was made up of many small states. Keep in mind that Italy wasn't even a country (as of 1870)!

Three nationalists helped unify Italy into one country.

Italy 1859

MAZZINI

GARIBALDI

CAVOUR

Italy 1861

German Unification

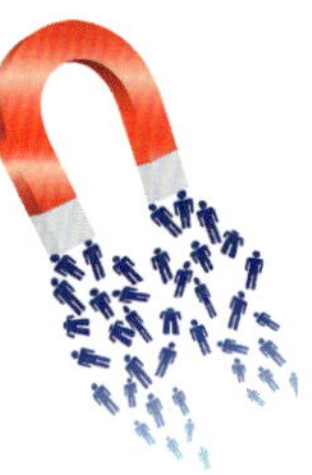

Germany was made up of small states since the 800s.
Nationalism inspired Germany to unite.

OTTO VON BISMARCK (a Prussian leader) united Germany with the policy of "blood and iron": military power and wars. He believed in practical, rather than idealistic policies to achieve his goals, which is known as REALPOLITIK.
Ⓡ Common Regents question

He led 3 wars:

1. Danish War
2. Austria-Prussian War
3. Franco-Prussian War

In 1871, Prussia united Germany.

Otto Von Bismarck

Ⓡ **Cause and effect:** The 3 wars ➲ United Germany

Ⓔ Conflict: The 3 wars
Ⓔ Power: Otto von Bismarck's policy of blood and iron

Nationalism in the Austro-Hungarian Empire

The royal Hapsburg family ruled this huge empire, which included Austria, Hungary, Bohemia, and other parts of Europe. They acquired these lands by wars, treaties, and royal marriages. There were now many different nationalities living in this empire.

However, these different groups were not happy to be ruled by the leaders of the Austro-Hungarian empire. They wanted independence and their say in government, due to feelings of nationalism.

In the 1800s, many different ethnic groups fought for self-government.

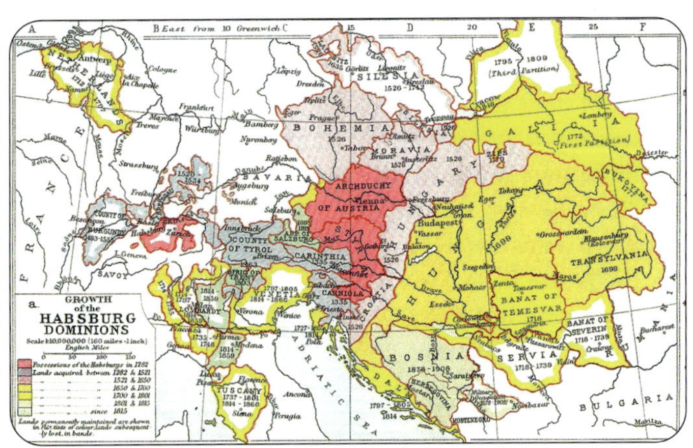

Austro-Hungarian Empire

Ottoman Nationalism

1400-1900: The Ottoman Empire controlled a massive area from Eastern Europe and the Balkans to North Africa and the Middle East, which included most of the world's strategic waterways.

The Ottoman Empire

Many groups lived in this area, including Serbs, Greeks, Romanians, and Bulgarians. The Ottoman Empire tolerated all these groups' cultures and religions.

But by the 1900s, it all went downhill ☹.

- All the ethnic groups living in the empire wanted self-rule AND
- The European powers (France, Britain, Germany, and Russia) wanted control over this area.
- The Ottoman Empire became known as the SICK MAN OF EUROPE. There were major political and economic issues in this area.

Sneak Preview: Eventually a nationalistic movement (Pan-Slavism) breaks up the Balkans and leads to World War I.

Ottoman Empire – The Armenian Massacre

The Muslim Turks abandoned the traditional Ottoman tolerance of different cultures and religions.

1914-1923: THE ARMENIAN MASSACRE: Muslim Turks persecuted and killed millions of Christian Armenians.

This is an example of GENOCIDE – a planned and systematic campaign to kill out an entire nation.

R This is a common Regents question.

E Human Rights Violation: In the Armenian Massacre, millions of people were killed because of their nationality.

More Nationalism

This feeling of nationalism was felt all over the world.

During this time period, nationalism was also found in:

1. The Middle East (Zionism)
2. India
3. The Balkans

We'll travel to these places a little later.

Check off the boxes you know well. Whatever you don't know well (yet!), go back and review now!

- ☐ Nationalism: strong devotion to one's country
- ☐ Nationalism often leads to revolutions.
- ☐ Sometimes nationalism unifies (Germany and Italy).
- ☐ Sometimes nationalism breaks up an empire (Austro-Hungary and Ottoman Empires).
- ☐ Italian Unification: Mazzini, Cavour, and Garibaldi unify Italy.
- ☐ German unification: Otto von Bismarck unifies Germany with "blood and iron" (wars).
- ☐ Ottoman Empire became the "sick man of Europe" when nationalities wanted their own independence
- ☐ The Armenian Massacre

Enduring Issues Essay Topics That Came Up in This Unit:

- **Conflict:** Revolutions that were caused by nationalism
- **Inequality:** Mother countries imperialized (controlled) colonies. The colonies did not want foreign control.
- **Power:** Nationalistic leaders exerted power, which led to revolutions and independence.
- **Human Rights Violation:** Armenian massacre (genocide)

Regents Question Time!

Now it's time to test how well you know your stuff.

Have fun!

Regents Question Time!

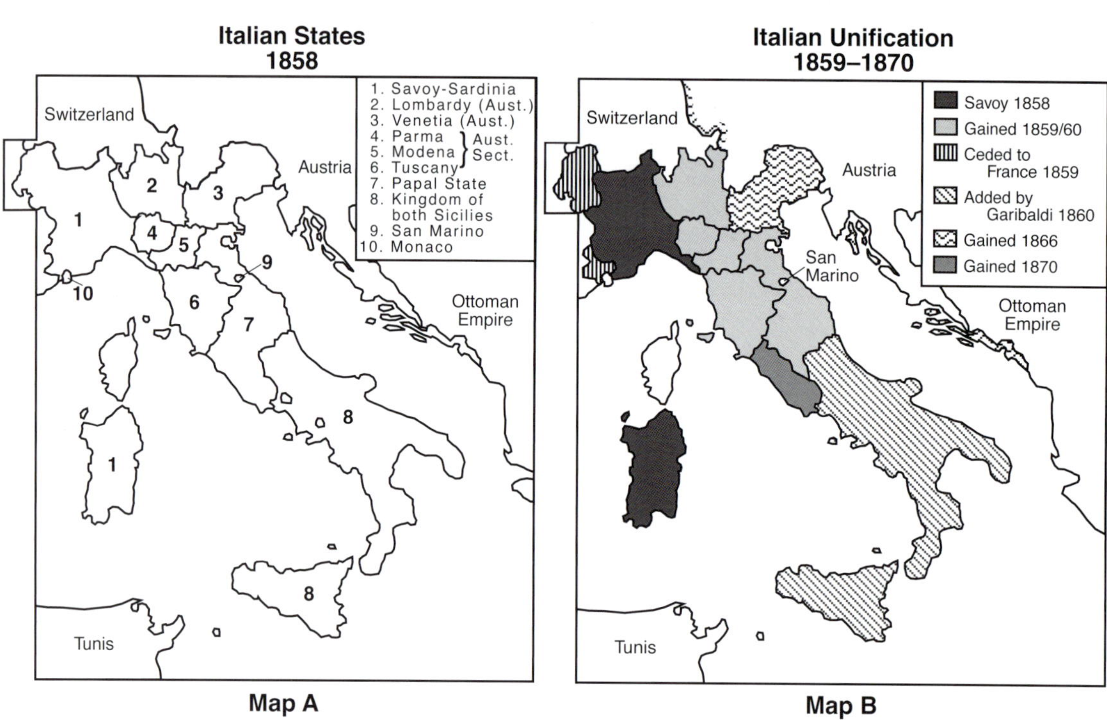

Map A

Map B

Source: Alexander Ganse, 2000 (adapted)

24 Which factor provided the motivation for the changes that took place between 1858 and 1870 as indicated on these maps?

(1) exploration
(2) appeasement
(3) religion
(4) nationalism

Answer: ____

1

Italian States
1858

Italian Unification
1859–1870

Italian States and Italian Unification

A bunch of separate states become unified.

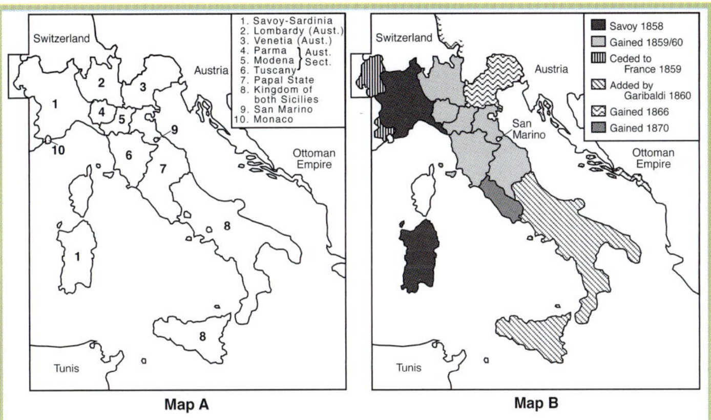

Switzerland
Austria
1. Savoy-Sardinia
2. Lombardy (Aust.)
3. Venetia (Aust.)
4. Parma } Aust.
5. Modena } Sect.
6. Tuscany
7. Papal State
8. Kingdom of both Sicilies
9. San Marino
10. Monaco
Ottoman Empire
Tunis

Map A

Switzerland
Austria
Savoy 1858
Gained 1859/60
Ceded to France 1859
Added by Garibaldi 1860
Gained 1866
Gained 1870
San Marino
Ottoman Empire
Tunis

Map B

2

Source: Alexander Ganse, 2000 (adapted)

Not helpful

3

24 Which factor provided the motivation for the changes that took place between 1858 and 1870 as indicated on these maps?

What's causing Italy's unification? PS: You know this already!

(1) exploration
(2) appeasement
(3) religion
(4) nationalism

4

Regents Question Time!

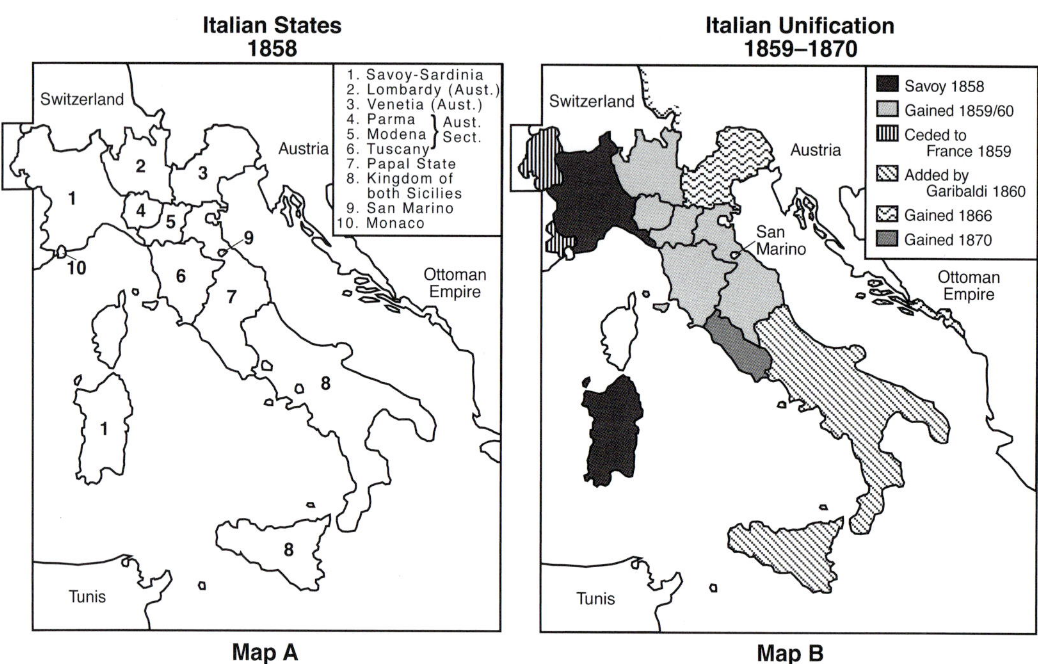

Source: Alexander Ganse, 2000 (adapted)

25 Which pair of individuals played a direct role in the changes that took place between Map A and Map B?

(1) Otto Von Bismarck and Wilhelm II
(2) Klemens von Metternich and Victor Emmanuel III
(3) Camillo di Cavour and Guiseppe Mazzini
(4) Alexander II and Frederick the Great

Answer: ____

1

Italian States and Italian Unification

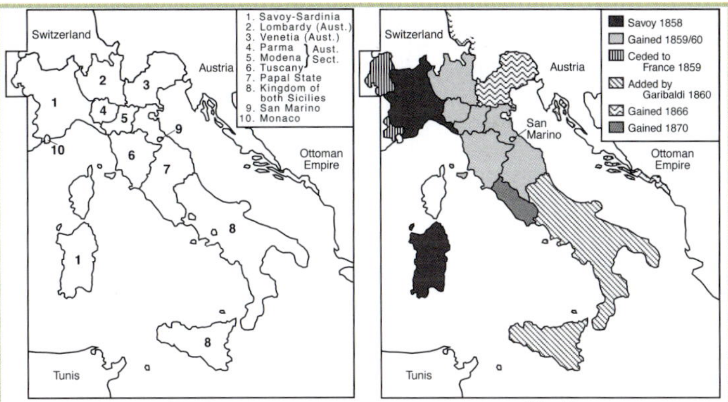

Italian States 1858 | Italian Unification 1859–1870

Map A: Switzerland, Austria, Ottoman Empire, Tunis
1. Savoy-Sardinia
2. Lombardy (Aust.)
3. Venetia (Aust.)
4. Parma } Aust. Sect.
5. Modena } Aust. Sect.
6. Tuscany } Aust. Sect.
7. Papal State
8. Kingdom of both Sicilies
9. San Marino
10. Monaco

Map B: Switzerland, Austria, San Marino, Ottoman Empire, Tunis
Savoy 1858
Gained 1859/60
Ceded to France 1859
Added by Garibaldi 1860
Gained 1866
Gained 1870

Map A | **Map B**

2

Source: Alexander Ganse, 2000 (adapted)

Not helpful

3

Who helped unify Italy?

25 Which pair of individuals played a direct role in the changes that took place between Map A and Map B?

(1) Otto Von Bismarck and Wilhelm II
(2) Klemens von Metternich and Victor Emmanuel III
(3) Camillo di Cavour and Guiseppe Mazzini
(4) Alexander II and Frederick the Great

4

Cavour and Mazzini unified Italy.

Regents Question Time!

Bismarck's German Empire

Zollverein Trade and Tariff Unions | **Danish War 1864** | **Austro-Prussian War 1866** | **North German Confederation 1867** | **Franco-Prussian War 1871**

Common Language, Customs, Race, and Historic Traditions

Source: Sue A. Kime et al., *World Studies: Global Issues & Assessments,* N & N Publishing Co. (adapted)

26 All the elements identified in the illustration contributed to German

(1) interdependence
(2) unification
(3) imperialism
(4) apathy

Answer: ___

1

Bismarck's German Empire

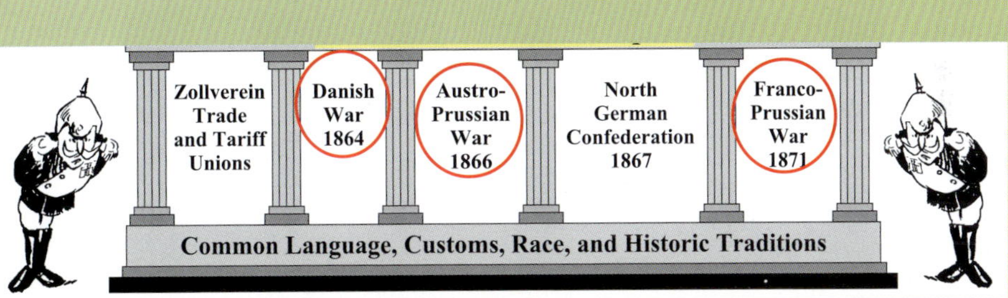

Bismarck fought wars to gain unification.

4

2

Source: Sue A. Kime et al., *World Studies: Global Issues & Assessments,* N & N Publishing Co. (adapted)

Not helpful, move on.

3

26 All the elements identified in the illustration contributed to German

(1) interdependence
(2) unification
(3) imperialism
(4) apathy

Bismarck unified Germany through "blood and iron" – lots of wars.

UNIT 6

INDUSTRIAL REVOLUTION

Economic & Social Revolutions

Overview:

- The Agrarian Revolution improved farming, which led to increased population.
- This led to the Industrial Revolution, when goods started to be produced in factories.
- This led to problematic working conditions and slums, which led to changes.

Agrarian Revolution → Industrial Revolution → Problems of Industrial Revolution lead to changes

Ⓡ **Cause and effect:** Agrarian Revolution ➲ Industrial Revolution

The Agrarian Revolution

Background: Until the mid-1700s, people lived in small villages and RURAL areas (countryside).

Rural area

HINT: The Agrarian Revolution improved agriculture (planting).

THE AGRARIAN REVOLUTION: In the mid-1700s, major changes in farming methods began.

Agrarian Revolution Changes:

- **Technology:** People discovered new methods to produce more food quickly.
  - Seed drills: They planted seeds in rows.
  - Crop rotation: They rotated the crops they planted on each piece of soil so that nutrients in the soil wouldn't get used up.
- ENCLOSURE MOVEMENT: They joined small strips of land together to make big fields. This made farming more efficient.

Seed drill

Instead of each "Farmer Brown" having his own little farm, they enclosed a bunch of small farms to make a big one.

Result of the Agrarian Revolution

There was much more food, so babies were born stronger and people lived longer. This caused a major increase in population: a population explosion.

R Cause and effect: Agrarian Revolution ➲ Population growth

E Innovation: New farming methods lead to enclosure and population growth.

The Industrial Revolution

Now that there are so many more people, more goods need to be produced at a faster rate.

In the past, people lived in an **AGRICULTURAL SOCIETY**, where goods were produced by "**HAND & HOME**" – without technology and at home.
In 1760, the **INDUSTRIAL REVOLUTION** began.
Goods started being produced with **MACHINERY** in **FACTORIES**.

Reminder: Revolution means a fundamental change. The economy changed from agricultural to industrial.

R Know this topic well. There are many Regents questions and good essay material on this topic!

R **Turning Point:** The Industrial Revolution changed many European economies from agricultural to industrial and changed where & how people lived and worked.

Where Did the Industrial Revolution Start?

The Industrial Revolution started in GREAT BRITAIN.
Then, it spread to Belgium, France, Germany, the United States, Japan and eventually to all over the world.

<u>Why Great Britain?</u>

POPULATION GROWTH:
More workers were available and less farmers were needed, so many people moved to cities to work in factories.

MONEY FOR INVESTMENT:
Great Britain gained a lot of wealth from its colonies, so it had money to invest into machinery and factories.

GEOGRAPHY:
1. Natural resources (coal, iron)
2. Transportation: natural harbors, rivers
3. Power sources: locations near water

GREAT BRITAIN
Starts the Industrial Revolution

ENERGY SOURCES:
They discovered STEAM POWER, and built steam powered machines.
Then, they discovered COAL POWER.

HINT: The Industrial Revolution started in Great Britain due to LLL – Land, Labor, Lots of money!

R This is an example of how geography affects history.

R **Cause and effect:** Note the causes that led to Great Britain starting the Industrial Revolution.
The Industrial Revolution then spread to Belgium, France, Germany, United States, Japan, and then to most of the world.

Factories

FACTORY: A building where goods are produced by machinery

Assembly line in cotton mill factory

Here's how the factory system works:

- **MASS PRODUCTION:** Factories produce goods in huge quantities.
- **ASSEMBLY LINES:** Each worker does one part of the production process.
  A bunch of people work together, but each person does only one part of the job. This makes the job get done faster and more efficiently.

Each worker puts in one type of screw to create a machine.

- Power sources:
  - **STEAM ENGINE:** an engine that uses steam to generate power
    The steam engine powered the factory machinery, boats, and trains.
  - Later, people got energy from **COAL.**

Steam Engine

Turning Point: The factory system changed the way goods were produced.

Industrial Revolution Inventions

New machinery was invented to help factories produce goods faster:

1. The FLYING SHUTTLE: A machine that wove thread into cloth quickly

2. The SPINNING JENNY: A machine that spun wool into thread

Flying Shuttle

Ⓡ Cause and effect: Industrialization ➲ Factory system ➲ New inventions and cheaper products

Ⓔ Innovation: These innovations made production of goods quicker and more efficient. Stay tuned for the negative impacts ☹.

Spinning Jenny

Factory Conditions

So, what was life like for factory workers?

- CHILD LABOR: People worked for 12-16 hours straight, even women and children!
- The factories had dangerous machinery that cut off limbs and caused many injuries. An injured worker was promptly fired!
- The machinery caused terrible air pollution, which caused lung damage.
- Factory workers were paid minimal wages, which often didn't cover basic food and living expenses.
- Because so many people were available for jobs, factory owners took advantage of the workers. They made them work very long hours and would fire workers for the slightest imperfections.

Innovation: The factory owners treated their workers poorly.

Child labor

Effects of the Industrial Revolution

1. **URBANIZATION:** People move from rural (countrylike) areas to cities. The cities became **SLUMS** – overcrowded areas where very poor people live. Living conditions were terrible.
   - There was no sewage, sanitation system, or running water. People drank water from rivers that were also used for dumping sewage! Many people became ill and died of cholera and typhoid, caused by germs in the rivers.

   - Cities were infested with rats and rodents (gross!).

   - Disease and crime were rampant.
   - As if that wasn't bad enough, machinery from the factories polluted the water and air, contaminating it with dangerous chemicals.

2. **IMPROVED TRANSPORTATION:** New roads, canals, railroads, steam engines, and powered ships were created, which helped people travel more efficiently.

More Effects of the Industrial Revolution

3. CULTURAL CHANGES: As people moved to cities, their traditional customs got lost:
- In the **middle class**, men now worked in factories, while women stayed home to care for the home and children. These children had a higher standard of living and better education.
- In the working class, women worked long hours in the factories and were paid less than men.

R Cause and effect: Industrialization, urbanization, improved transportation, and cultural changes

The Sadler Report

😊 The Industrial Revolution was great because it helped reform the economy and produce goods at a fast rate.

☹ But some terrible things were happening at the same time.
The factory conditions were simply unacceptable!

Michael Sadler, a British parliament member, decided to do something about it.
He wrote THE SADLER REPORT, which exposed the horrible working conditions in the factories.

Michael Sadler

HINT: The Sadler Report exposed the sad state of the factory's workers.

Many factory workers were interviewed in The Sadler Report. What they reported was shocking.

The Sadler Report documented that young children had to be at the factory from 5 AM to 9 PM! The machines were so dangerous; fingers were often cut off while people operated the machinery. Once workers were injured, the bosses promptly fired them. Children didn't go to school and learn; instead, they labored day and night, not receiving adequate nutrition or sleep.

A young child working in a factory

Once these dark facts were exposed, many reforms were enacted.

Reforms to Solve Industrial Revolution Problems in Great Britain

1. FACTORIES REGULATION ACT OF 1833:
   - Barred children under 9 from working in textile (fabric and clothing) factories
   - Limited the hours that children under 18 could work
2. MINES ACT: Banned children under 10 years old from working in coal mines, which were very dangerous
3. LABOR UNIONS: Workers join together to form unions (organization of workers) to protect themselves.
4. Labor unions demanded and received better wages and working conditions. When their demands were not met, they went on strike.

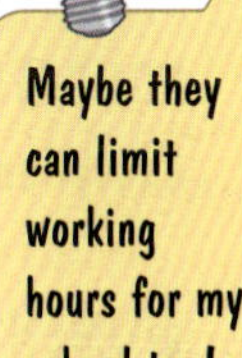

Maybe they can limit working hours for my school too!

Great news! Many problems caused by the Industrial Revolution were now solved!

R **Cause and effect:** Industrialization ➲ Factories ➲ Factory workers mistreated ➲ Sadler Report ➲ Government reforms

More Reforms to Solve Industrial Revolution Problems in Great Britain

5. Better housing: The government paved the streets and created sewer systems, and houses were built from sturdy steel.

6. EDUCATION ACT OF 1870 funded elementary education for the public.

7. WOMEN'S SUFFRAGE MOVEMENT led by Emmeline Pankhurst fought for women's rights, with protests and violence.

Great news! Many problems caused by the Industrial Revolution were now solved!

Emmeline Pankhurst

Population Explosion

Improved living conditions (sewer systems, workplace reforms) and technology, people lived safer lives

Fewer children died and people lived longer

Huge rise in population

New Economic Policies

The Industrial Revolution brought many changes to the economy.
New issues and ideas cropped up as a result.

People came up with new economic policies to solve the issues.

Innovation: New economic policies – some were good, others were bad.

Adam Smith

ADAM SMITH was an Enlightenment thinker who wanted to follow the "natural laws" of the economy.

Adam Smith

He advocated the idea of a laissez-faire **CAPITALIST ECONOMY** – let the economy flow without government intervention.

- All business decisions are made by private owners, not the government.

HINT: Laissez-faire – pronounced "lazay fair" – sounds like lazy. The government becomes "lazy" at controlling businesses. (They're not really lazy; they purposely back off to let private citizens run the economy.)

Adam Smith wrote a book called **THE WEALTH OF NATIONS**, which introduced the concept of **CAPITALISM**.

- This book significantly impacted the world economy.

What's capitalism? Turn the page to find out!

Capitalism

CAPITALISM: An economic system where a country's trade is controlled by private owners for profit

Also known as:

- MARKET ECONOMY
- FREE ENTERPRISE

HINT: A market is a place where people buy goods. In a market economy, the people are determining the economy.

HINT: Free Enterprise: Free – freedom in enterprise (business)

The economy changed from being government-controlled to being controlled by private business owners.

Main ideas of Capitalism

1. Businesses and factories are owned and profited by individuals (not the government).

2. Laissez-Faire Economy: The government has little or no control over businesses.

3. Businesses sell SHARES and STOCKS (parts) of their businesses to individuals.
   - Each STOCKHOLDER and shareholder owns a part of the big company.
   - Results: There's an increase in big businesses, and the middle class grows.

4. Competition: Businesses compete for customers.

5. Prices are determined by SUPPLY and DEMAND. (See next page.)

R There are many Regents questions on this topic.

E **Innovation:** Capitalism was a new economic policy.

R **Cause and effect:** Industrialization ➲ New economic policies (including capitalism/laissez-faire)

Supply and Demand (Capitalism)

When there's high supply and low demand, prices drop.
When there's low supply and high demand, prices rise.

High supply of apples + low demand = prices drop

Low supply of apples + high demand = prices rise

Social Darwinism

During the Industrial Revolution, some people became factory owners, were successful, and became very rich.

Others worked long and hard hours and made pennies.
Some people argued that this wasn't fair!
The idea of Social Darwinism emerged, saying, tough luck!
Some people are more talented and will be more successful and some people are less talented and won't be successful.
They used this belief to justify unfair business practices.

SOCIAL DARWINISM: The belief that some people are more successful in business because they are more "fit" to succeed

- This concept led to RACISM and IMPERIALISM.
- Socialists believed that the government should serve the needs of everyone and give access to better pricing.

This economic policy was adapted from Darwin's theory of evolution.

R There are many Regents questions on this topic.

R Cause and effect: Industrialization ➲ New economic policies – Social Darwinism (negative) ➲ Causes racism and imperialism

Marxism

During the Industrial Revolution, within the capitalist economy, rich business owners took advantage of the factory workers.

KARL MARX and FRIEDRICH ENGELS did not like this at all!

Marx (left)
Engels (right)

They thought capitalism was bad because:

- It's unfair that some people are rich (factory owners) while others are poor (workers).
- The greedy factory owners took advantage of the poor factory workers and didn't treat them properly.

Marxism is named after Marx!

The Communist Manifesto

KARL MARX and **FRIEDRICH ENGELS** wrote a book called **THE COMMUNIST MANIFESTO** to spread their ideas.

Ideas of Marxism:

1. There is a conflict between the wealthy factory owners (**BOURGEOISIE**) and the poor factory workers (**PROLETARIAT**).
2. The rich prosper and take advantage of the workers' hard labor, while the workers live in poverty.
3. Marx and Engels predicted that workers will unite and eventually overthrow the bourgeoisie with a bloody revolution. Since there are so many workers, they will have a lot of power. They will then create their own society where wealth and power will be shared, and they won't need a government.
4. They wanted to get rid of laissez-faire capitalism.

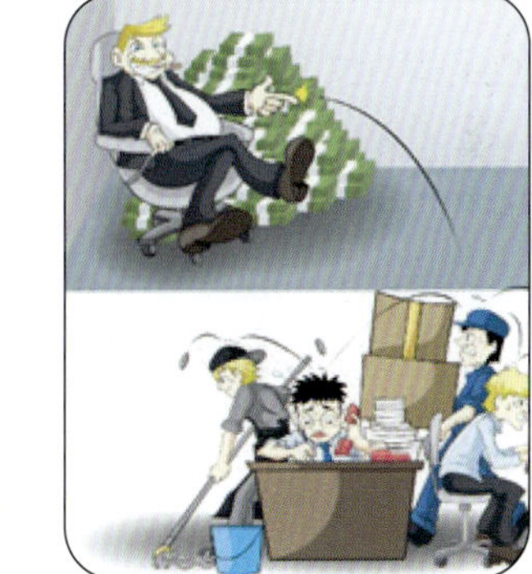

R **Cause and effect:** Marxism ➲ Communism. Russia was the first country to adopt a communist system.

R There are many Regents questions on this topic.

E **Innovation:** Marxism and Social Darwinism had many negative effects.

E **Ideas and Beliefs:** Books can be a powerful source of new ideas.

Capitalism vs. Marxism

CAPITALISM

1. The people control the economy.
2. Businesses are privately owned.
3. Classes are determined by wealth.

MARXISM

1. The government controls the economy.
2. There are no privately owned businesses.
3. All citizens are equal.

Ideas and beliefs: Adam Smith and Karl Marx had opposing ideas, both of which spread extensively.

Irish Potato Famine

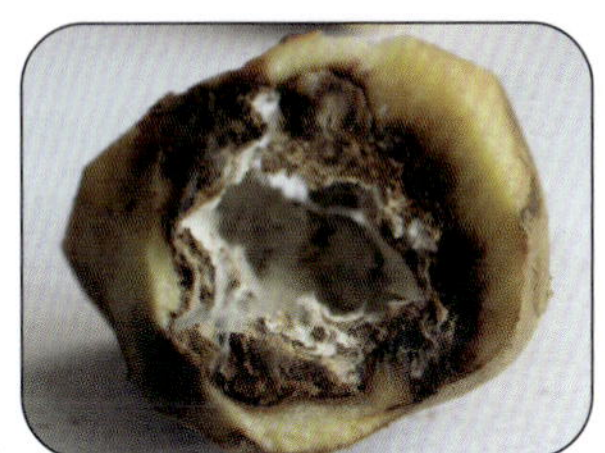
Potato Blight

Background: Britain thrived in the Agricultural and Industrial Revolutions, but their colony, Ireland did not.
The British landlords forced the Irish to grow and export most of their crops, leaving them with only potatoes.
In the mid-1800s, a disease called blight destroyed the potato crops, causing a famine that killed a million people and drove millions more to emigrate to America to escape the famine.
The British government did little to help, fueling Irish resistance and intensifying the fight for independence.
Ireland fought to break free from Great Britain—Southern Ireland succeeded, Northern Ireland stayed, and religious tensions flared.

- The Irish Potato Famine shows what can happen with laissez-faire capitalism: the British government did not intervene, causing a massive disaster.
- R Environmental Impact/Scarcity: A disease of the potato crop caused a million Irish people to die from starvation. The lack of food caused death and vast emigration to the United States.
- R Cause and effect: Famine caused Irish Nationalism and mass emigration to the USA.

Check off the boxes you know well. Whatever you don't know well (yet!), go back and review now!

- ☐ Agrarian Revolution: new agricultural practices
- ☐ Industrial Revolution
  - Starts in Great Britain
  - Factories, urbanization, mass production, assembly line, slums, poor working conditions, Sadler Report and reforms
- ☐ Capitalism – Adam Smith
  - The Wealth of Nations, trade controlled by private owners, laissez-faire, supply and demand
- ☐ Social Darwinism
- ☐ Marxism: Marx and Engels
  - The Communist Manifesto, businesses are government-owned, all citizens are equal, basis for Communism

Enduring Issues Essay Topics That Came Up in This Unit:

- **Scarcity:** There wasn't enough room for people to live because of urbanization.
- **Environmental Impact:** Great Britain's geography contributed to the Industrial Revolution. Great Britain had natural resources (coal and iron), and water for transportation and power. Also, major population growth occurred, which caused major pollution in the environment.
- **Innovation:** (some good, some bad)
  - Goods were now produced in factories using machinery and steam/coal power. This caused more goods to be produced, but also resulted in unsafe and unfair working conditions and pollution.
  - New economic systems: capitalism/laissez-faire/Adam Smith
Marxism/Marx and Engel/Social Darwinism
- **Interconnectedness:** Labor unions are groups of workers in similar industries who come together to demand more rights and better wages.

Now it's time to test how well you know your stuff.

Have fun!

Regents Question Time!

DEATH'S DISPENSARY.

OPEN TO THE POOR, GRATIS [free of charge], BY PERMISSION OF THE PARISH.

Source: George Pinwell, "Death's Dispensary," Fun Magazine, August 18, 1866 (adapted)

In cities and towns, drinking water was drawn from the same rivers into which raw sewage flowed. This sewage contaminated the water with the bacteria that cause cholera and typhoid fever. However, a direct link between germs and diseases had yet to be made. In England, London's Thames river was so polluted that in the summer of 1858, the "Great Stink" drove Members of Parliament out of the House of Commons, situated close to the river.

— Richard Walker, *Epidemics & Plagues*, Kingfisher, 2006

5 This illustration and excerpt depict events from which time and place in history?

(1) Revolutionary France
(2) Victorian England
(3) Meiji Japan
(4) Soviet Russia

Answer: ___

FUN.—August 18, 1866.

1866 – The factories with all their machinery were causing major pollution at this time.

The excerpt tells us straight out that this happened in England!

Source: George Pinwell, "Death's Dispensary," Fun Magazine, August 18, 1866 (adapted)

In cities and towns, drinking water was drawn from the same rivers into which raw sewage flowed. This sewage contaminated the water with the bacteria that cause cholera and typhoid fever. However, a direct link between germs and diseases had yet to be made. In England, London's Thames river was so polluted that in the summer of 1858, the "Great Stink" drove Members of Parliament out of the House of Commons, situated close to the river.

— Richard Walker, *Epidemics & Plagues,* Kingfisher, 2006

— Richard Walker, *Epidemics & Plagues,* Kingfisher, 2006

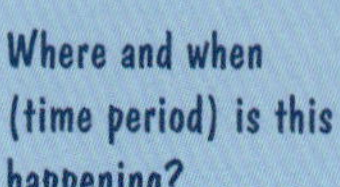

5 This illustration and excerpt depict events from which time and place in history?

Where and when (time period) is this happening?

(1) Revolutionary France
(2) Victorian England
(3) Meiji Japan
(4) Soviet Russia

Regents Question Time!

Source: George Pinwell, "Death's Dispensary," Fun Magazine, August 18, 1866 (adapted)

In cities and towns, drinking water was drawn from the same rivers into which raw sewage flowed. This sewage contaminated the water with the bacteria that cause cholera and typhoid fever. However, a direct link between germs and diseases had yet to be made. In England, London's Thames river was so polluted that in the summer of 1858, the "Great Stink" drove Members of Parliament out of the House of Commons, situated close to the river.

— Richard Walker, *Epidemics & Plagues*, Kingfisher, 2006

6 Which characteristic of the Industrial Revolution most directly contributed to the health concern highlighted in this illustration and excerpt?

(1) urban population growth
(2) improved communication
(3) new power sources
(4) trade union movement

Answer: ___

FUN.—August 18, 1866.

1866 – The factories with all its machinery were causing major pollution at this time.

Excerpt: The drinking water contained tons of germs, which caused many people to get sick and die.

Cartoon: The cartoon shows "Death" distributing water. This shows the water source being a serious cause of death.

Now think: what led to this major water pollution issue?

Since so many people were moving to cities, there was a tremendous increase in pollution.

Note: When they give you 2 documents, one document may help you understand the next.

FUN.—August 18, 1866.

DEATH'S DISPENSARY.

OPEN TO THE POOR, GRATIS [free of charge].
BY PERMISSION OF THE PARISH.

Source: George Pinwell, "Death's Dispensary," Fun Magazine, August 18, 1866 (adapted)

In cities and towns, drinking water was drawn from the same rivers into which raw sewage flowed. This sewage contaminated the water with the bacteria that cause cholera and typhoid fever. However, a direct link between germs and diseases had yet to be made. In England, London's Thames river was so polluted that in the summer of 1858, the "Great Stink" drove Members of Parliament out of the House of Commons, situated close to the river.

— Richard Walker, *Epidemics & Plagues*, Kingfisher, 2006

4

2

— Richard Walker, *Epidemics & Plagues*, Kingfisher, 2006

3

What led to this health issue?

6 Which characteristic of the Industrial Revolution most directly contributed to the health concern highlighted in this illustration and excerpt?

(1) urban population growth
(2) improved communication
(3) new power sources
(4) trade union movement

EdBoosters™

Regents Question Time!

DEATH'S DISPENSARY.
OPEN TO THE POOR, GRATIS [free of charge], BY PERMISSION OF THE PARISH.

Source: George Pinwell, "Death's Dispensary," Fun Magazine, August 18, 1866 (adapted)

> In cities and towns, drinking water was drawn from the same rivers into which raw sewage flowed. This sewage contaminated the water with the bacteria that cause cholera and typhoid fever. However, a direct link between germs and diseases had yet to be made. In England, London's Thames river was so polluted that in the summer of 1858, the "Great Stink" drove Members of Parliament out of the House of Commons, situated close to the river.

— Richard Walker, *Epidemics & Plagues*, Kingfisher, 2006

7 Which action effectively addressed the specific public health concern raised in this illustration and excerpt?

(1) installation of electric lighting in poor neighborhoods
(2) burning herbs to purify the air
(3) improvements in water treatment
(4) relocation of government offices

Answer: ____

FUN.—August 18, 1866.

1866 – The factories with all its machinery were causing major pollution at this time.

The issue is water pollution.

DEATH'S DISPENSARY.
OPEN TO THE POOR, GRATIS [free of charge].
BY PERMISSION OF THE PARISH.

Source: George Pinwell, "Death's Dispensary," Fun Magazine, August 18, 1866 (adapted)

In cities and towns, drinking water was drawn from the same rivers into which raw sewage flowed. This sewage contaminated the water with the bacteria that cause cholera and typhoid fever. However, a direct link between germs and diseases had yet to be made. In England, London's Thames river was so polluted that in the summer of 1858, the "Great Stink" drove Members of Parliament out of the House of Commons, situated close to the river.

— Richard Walker, *Epidemics & Plagues*, Kingfisher, 2006

2

— Richard Walker, *Epidemics & Plagues*, Kingfisher, 2006

4

3

What action helped fix this issue?

7 Which action effectively addressed the specific public health concern raised in this illustration and excerpt?

(1) installation of electric lighting in poor neighborhoods
(2) burning herbs to purify the air
(3) improvements in water treatment
(4) relocation of government offices

Choice #3 is the only choice that gives a solution to the water pollution issue.

Regents Question Time!

. . . "I started from Cork, by the mail [coach] (says our informant), for Skibbereen and saw little until we came to Clonakilty, where the coach stopped for breakfast; and here, for the first time, the horrors of the poverty became visible, in the vast number of famished poor, who flocked around the coach to beg alms: amongst them was a woman carrying in her arms the corpse of a fine child, and making the most distressing appeal to the passengers for aid to enable her to purchase a coffin and bury her dear little baby. This horrible spectacle induced me to make some inquiry about her, when I learned from the people of the hotel that each day brings dozens of such applicants into the town. . . ."

Source: James Mahony, "Sketches in the West of Ireland," *The Illustrated London News*, February 13, 1847 (adapted)

5 What is the most likely purpose of this document?

(1) to highlight the benefits of free market
(2) to record the negative effects of child labor
(3) to minimize the impacts of agricultural innovations
(4) to inspire social and political reform

Answer: ___

1

No title here. Move on.

The poverty in Ireland was terrible and a woman was holding a dead child and didn't have enough money to bury him. Sounds sensational. Think why someone would write this...

. . . "I started from Cork, by the mail [coach] (says our informant), for Skibbereen and saw little until we came to Clonakilty, where the coach stopped for breakfast; and here, for the first time, the horrors of the poverty became visible, in the vast number of famished poor, who flocked around the coach to beg alms: amongst them was a woman carrying in her arms the corpse of a fine child, and making the most distressing appeal to the passengers for aid to enable her to purchase a coffin and bury her dear little baby. This horrible spectacle induced me to make some inquiry about her, when I learned from the people of the hotel that each day brings dozens of such applicants into the town. . . ."

4

2

Source: James Mahony, "Sketches in the West of Ireland," *The Illustrated London News*, February 13, 1847 (adapted)

What was happening in Ireland in the 1800s? The Irish Potato Famine

3

5 What is the most likely purpose of this document?

Think: Why would someone write this?

(1) to highlight the benefits of free market
(2) to record the negative effects of child labor
(3) to minimize the impacts of agricultural innovations
(4) to inspire social and political reform

Regents Question Time!

. . . "I started from Cork, by the mail [coach] (says our informant), for Skibbereen and saw little until we came to Clonakilty, where the coach stopped for breakfast; and here, for the first time, the horrors of the poverty became visible, in the vast number of famished poor, who flocked around the coach to beg alms: amongst them was a woman carrying in her arms the corpse of a fine child, and making the most distressing appeal to the passengers for aid to enable her to purchase a coffin and bury her dear little baby. This horrible spectacle induced me to make some inquiry about her, when I learned from the people of the hotel that each day brings dozens of such applicants into the town. . . ."

Source: James Mahony, "Sketches in the West of Ireland," *The Illustrated London News*, February 13, 1847 (adapted)

6 The conditions described in this passage directly resulted in

(1) Ireland invading Britain
(2) millions of Irish emigrating to the United States
(3) most landlords forgiving the rent the Irish owed
(4) Britain agreeing to withdraw from Ireland

Answer: ___

1

No title here. Move on.

. . . "I started from Cork, by the mail [coach] (says our informant), for Skibbereen and saw little until we came to Clonakilty, where the coach stopped for breakfast; and here, for the first time, the horrors of the poverty became visible, in the vast number of famished poor, who flocked around the coach to beg alms: amongst them was a woman carrying in her arms the corpse of a fine child, and making the most distressing appeal to the passengers for aid to enable her to purchase a coffin and bury her dear little baby. This horrible spectacle induced me to make some inquiry about her, when I learned from the people of the hotel that each day brings dozens of such applicants into the town. . . ."

4

2

Source: James Mahony, "Sketches in the West of Ireland," *The Illustrated London News*, February 13, 1847 (adapted)

What was happening in Ireland in the 1800s? The Irish Potato Famine

3

What was the result of the Irish Potato Famine?

6 The conditions described in this passage directly resulted in

(1) Ireland invading Britain
(2) millions of Irish emigrating to the United States
(3) most landlords forgiving the rent the Irish owed
(4) Britain agreeing to withdraw from Ireland

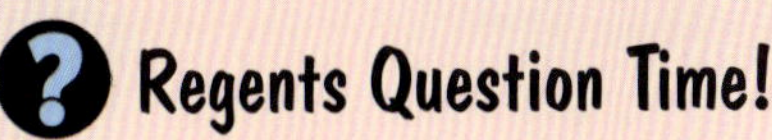

Regents Question Time!

EFFECTS OF A STRIKE
UPON THE CAPITALIST and UPON THE WORKING MAN

Source: *Punch*, 1852

21 Which statement reflects the overall effect of labor strikes as shown in this cartoon?

(1) Workers get to take a well-earned vacation.
(2) Workers are deprived of their income and suffer hardships.
(3) Employers can manage their businesses from home.
(4) Employers generally meet workers' demands quickly.

Answer: ___

EFFECTS OF A STRIKE
UPON THE CAPITALIST and UPON THE WORKING MAN

The capitalist is drinking wine and relaxing in wealth. The worker sits and suffers in poverty.

4

2

Source: *Punch*, 1852

1852 – this is the time period when Industrial Revolution workers were being mistreated.

3

21 Which statement reflects the overall effect of labor strikes as shown in this cartoon?

(1) Workers get to take a well-earned vacation.
(2) Workers are deprived of their income and suffer hardships.
(3) Employers can manage their businesses from home.
(4) Employers generally meet workers' demands quickly.

Regents Question Time!

EFFECTS OF A STRIKE
UPON THE CAPITALIST and UPON THE WORKING MAN

Source: *Punch,* 1852

22 Based on this cartoon, which government policy is most likely influencing the situation experienced by the working man?

(1) laissez-faire
(2) universal suffrage
(3) limiting immigration
(4) public sanitation laws

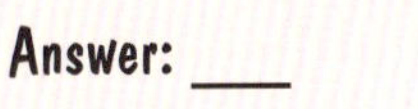

Answer: ____

1

EFFECTS OF A STRIKE
UPON THE CAPITALIST and UPON THE WORKING MAN

The capitalist is drinking wine and relaxing in luxury. The worker sits and suffers in poverty.

4

2

Source: *Punch,* 1852

1852 – a time when capitalism reigned and wealthy factory owners controlled the economy

3

22 Based on this cartoon, which government policy is most likely influencing the situation experienced by the working man?

(1) laissez-faire
(2) universal suffrage
(3) limiting immigration
(4) public sanitation laws

The economy was controlled by the capitalists, who abused their power. The government remained uninvolved.

Regents Question Time!

LOGINS FOR THRAVELERS
GOOD BEDS.
LOGINS FOR THRAVELERS

A COURT FOR KING CHOLERA.

Source: *Punch*, September 25, 1852 (adapted)

24 This 1852 drawing most likely would have been used to argue for improvements in

(1) workhouse rules
(2) sanitation regulations
(3) factory conditions
(4) suffrage laws

Answer: ____

A COURT FOR KING CHOLERA.

Notice that the title was on the bottom.

People lived in slums with terrible sanitation conditions, which caused terrible illnesses, including cholera.

A COURT FOR KING CHOLERA.

4

2

Source: *Punch*, September 25, 1852 (adapted)

1852 – a time of urbanization, pollution, and illness, which were effects of the Industrial Revolution

3

What would be an improvement for this problem?

24 This 1852 drawing most likely would have been used to argue for improvements in

(1) workhouse rules
(2) sanitation regulations
(3) factory conditions
(4) suffrage laws

UNIT 7

JAPANESE MODERNIZATION & IMPERIALISM

Japan & Isolation

Background: During the TOKUGAWA SHOGUNATE, Japan was isolated from the world for 200 years (1600s-1800s)!

The Japanese people weren't allowed to have any outside contact with the world. Therefore, Japan experienced much internal trade and development.

(During this time period, FEUDALISM was the economic system – people worked and fought for nobles who gave them land and protection in return.)

Japan Comes Out of Isolation

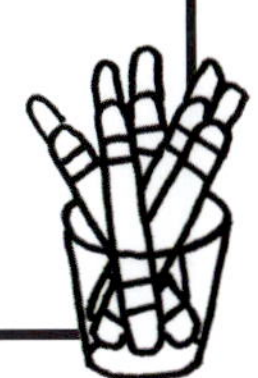

In the 1800s, an American Navy captain, MATTHEW PERRY, sailed to Japan and forced Japan to sign a treaty permitting trade with American ships.

The Tokugawa Shogunate signed this treaty agreeing to trade with United States.

Eventually, this led to the downfall of the Tokugawa Shogunate and the rise of Emperor Meiji.

Matthew Perry

Meiji

HINT: Perry – pier. A pier is a place where boats dock. Perry "opened up" the pier of Japan.

The Meiji Restoration (1868-1912)

Time period in Japanese history when Emperor Meiji modernized and Westernized Japan

- **Modernization:** Japan industrialized, building factories, machines, roads, and communication.
- **Westernization:** Japan adopted Western customs, government, education, and military systems.

HINT: Meiji effected major changes and modernization in Japan.

M&M: Meiji = Modernization

- (R) There are many Regents questions on this topic.
- (R) **Turning Point:** Japan's economy changes from feudalism to a modern and successful economy.
- (R) **Cause and effect:** Meiji Restoration (modernization and Westernization) ➲ Japan becomes a powerful country
- (E) **Ideas and beliefs:** During the Meiji Restoration, Japan implements Western ideas.
- (E) **Power:** Meiji Restoration turns Japan into a powerful nation.

Quick Review

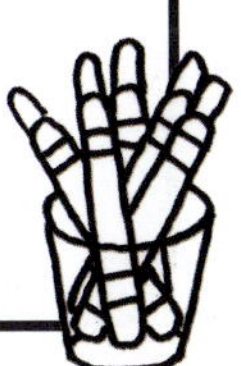

Check off the boxes you know well. Whatever you don't know well (yet!), go back and review now!

- ☐ Tokugawa isolation
- ☐ Matthew Perry opens Japan's doors
- ☐ Meiji Restoration – modernization, Westernization

Enduring Issues Essay Topics That Came Up in This Unit:

- **Power:**
  The Meiji Restoration turned Japan into a powerful nation.
  Japan fought and won wars and land, which increased its power.

- **Conflict:** Japan fought wars to gain land and natural resources.

- **Scarcity:** Japan lacked natural resources, so it fought wars to gain control over colonies that would provide it with natural resources.

- **Ideas and beliefs:** Meiji Restorations implements ideas of modernization in Japan.

Regents Question Time!

Now it's time to test how well you know your stuff.

Have fun!

Regents Question Time!

Ladies with western musical instruments

Source: Published by Ōmori Kakutarō, wood block print (detail), c. 1890, Museum of Fine Arts, Boston

31 This late 19th-century Japanese print illustrates

(1) isolationism
(2) ethnocentrism
(3) cultural diffusion
(4) democracy

Answer: ___

1

Ladies with western musical instruments

Western musical instruments

2

Source: Published by Ōmori Kakutarō, wood block print (detail), c. 1890, Museum of Fine Arts, Boston

1890

3

31 This late 19th-century Japanese print illustrates

(1) isolationism
(2) ethnocentrism
(3) cultural diffusion
(4) democracy

4

The Japanese women in this image are playing Western musical instruments. This is an example of the spread of cultures.

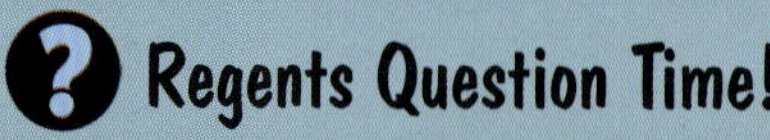

Regents Question Time!

Ladies with western musical instruments

Source: Published by Ōmori Kakutarō, wood block print (detail), c. 1890, Museum of Fine Arts, Boston

32 During which period of Japanese history was this print most likely created?

(1) Tokugawa shogunate
(2) Meiji Restoration
(3) Russo-Japanese War
(4) post–World War II occupation

Answer: ___

1

Ladies with western musical instruments

Western musical instruments

2

Source: Published by Ōmori Kakutarō, wood block print (detail), c. 1890, Museum of Fine Arts, Boston

1890

3

32 During which period of Japanese history was this print most likely created?

During what time period did Japan Westernize?

(1) Tokugawa shogunate
(2) Meiji Restoration
(3) Russo-Japanese War
(4) post–World War II occupation

4

Regents Question Time!

In the very heart of Tokyo sits the imperial palace, site of the former Edo Castle. Inside a colossal moat with ramparts that dwarf anything seen in Europe, vast open spaces enclose the last fragments of one of the world's most imposing seventeenth-century monuments. Across the globe in France, Louis XIV's palace and gardens of Versailles form a similar impression of artificial mastery of nature and society. Miles of formal gardens punctuated [decorated] with fountains and statuary surround a palace known for its cold magnificence, with the entire ensemble of town, palace, and park orienting itself around a single, central focal point: the Sun King's bedroom. Each complex symbolizes a system of power. Edo evokes [brings to mind] the Tokugawa rule by status, which decreed that the daimyo lords, who were themselves forced to spend alternate years in Edo away from their regional domains, lived administratively and spatially segregated from the various other categories of subjects, all ranged in a pattern of residential sectors spiraling around the castle. Versailles, in similar fashion, bespeaks [indicates] the domestication of the French aristocracy in a "gilded cage," where they scrambled for favors while the Sun King undermined their authority and deprived them of their independence. . . .

— William Beik, "Louis XIV and the Cities," *Edo and Paris: Urban Life and the State in the Early Modern Era*, Cornell University Press, 1994

1 Based on this passage, one way the castle at Edo and the palace at Versailles are similar is that both

(1) became symbols of power and wealth
(2) developed into monastic centers of learning
(3) were meant to provide protection and prevent attacks
(4) served as monuments to the military

Answer: ___

1

No title here. Move on.

In the very heart of Tokyo sits the imperial palace, site of the former Edo Castle. Inside a colossal moat with ramparts that dwarf anything seen in Europe, vast open spaces enclose the last fragments of one of the world's most imposing seventeenth-century monuments. Across the globe in France, Louis XIV's palace and gardens of Versailles form a similar impression of artificial mastery of nature and society. Miles of formal gardens punctuated [decorated] with fountains and statuary surround a palace known for its cold magnificence, with the entire ensemble of town, palace, and park orienting itself around a single, central focal point: the Sun King's bedroom. Each complex symbolizes a system of power. Edo evokes [brings to mind] the Tokugawa rule by status, which decreed that the daimyo lords, who were themselves forced to spend alternate years in Edo away from their regional domains, lived administratively and spatially segregated from the various other categories of subjects, all ranged in a pattern of residential sectors spiraling around the castle. Versailles, in similar fashion, bespeaks [indicates] the domestication of the French aristocracy in a "gilded cage," where they scrambled for favors while the Sun King undermined their authority and deprived them of their independence. . . .

4

2

— William Beik, "Louis XIV and the Cities," *Edo and Paris: Urban Life and the State in the Early Modern Era*, Cornell University Press, 1994

3

What's the similarity between the castle at Edo and the palace at Versailles?

1 Based on this passage, one way the castle at Edo and the palace at Versailles are similar is that both

(1) became symbols of power and wealth
(2) developed into monastic centers of learning
(3) were meant to provide protection and prevent attacks
(4) served as monuments to the military

This question was purely a reading comprehension question.

Regents Question Time!

In the very heart of Tokyo sits the imperial palace, site of the former Edo Castle. Inside a colossal moat with ramparts that dwarf anything seen in Europe, vast open spaces enclose the last fragments of one of the world's most imposing seventeenth-century monuments. Across the globe in France, Louis XIV's palace and gardens of Versailles form a similar impression of artificial mastery of nature and society. Miles of formal gardens punctuated [decorated] with fountains and statuary surround a palace known for its cold magnificence, with the entire ensemble of town, palace, and park orienting itself around a single, central focal point: the Sun King's bedroom. Each complex symbolizes a system of power. Edo evokes [brings to mind] the Tokugawa rule by status, which decreed that the daimyo lords, who were themselves forced to spend alternate years in Edo away from their regional domains, lived administratively and spatially segregated from the various other categories of subjects, all ranged in a pattern of residential sectors spiraling around the castle. Versailles, in similar fashion, bespeaks [indicates] the domestication of the French aristocracy in a "gilded cage," where they scrambled for favors while the Sun King undermined their authority and deprived them of their independence. . . .

— William Beik, "Louis XIV and the Cities," *Edo and Paris: Urban Life and the State in the Early Modern Era*, Cornell University Press, 1994

2 Which claim can best be supported by this passage?

(1) The more independent the nobles were the higher their status.
(2) Nobles maintained their authority by remaining isolated.
(3) Rulers controlled their nobles by influencing where they lived.
(4) Spending time in segregated sectors guaranteed nobles the support of their ruler.

Answer: ___

1

No title here. Move on.

The Tokugawa rulers forced the lords to live separate from other people. The French rulers forced the aristocrats to live in a "cage."

In the very heart of Tokyo sits the imperial palace, site of the former Edo Castle. Inside a colossal moat with ramparts that dwarf anything seen in Europe, vast open spaces enclose the last fragments of one of the world's most imposing seventeenth-century monuments. Across the globe in France, Louis XIV's palace and gardens of Versailles form a similar impression of artificial mastery of nature and society. Miles of formal gardens punctuated [decorated] with fountains and statuary surround a palace known for its cold magnificence, with the entire ensemble of town, palace, and park orienting itself around a single, central focal point: the Sun King's bedroom. Each complex symbolizes a system of power. Edo evokes [brings to mind] the Tokugawa rule by status, which decreed that the daimyo lords, who were themselves forced to spend alternate years in Edo away from their regional domains, lived administratively and spatially segregated from the various other categories of subjects, all ranged in a pattern of residential sectors spiraling around the castle. Versailles, in similar fashion, bespeaks [indicates] the domestication of the French aristocracy in a "gilded cage," where they scrambled for favors while the Sun King undermined their authority and deprived them of their independence. . . .

4

2

— William Beik, "Louis XIV and the Cities," *Edo and Paris: Urban Life and the State in the Early Modern Era*, Cornell University Press, 1994

3

2 Which claim can best be supported by this passage?

(1) The more independent the nobles were the higher their status.
(2) Nobles maintained their authority by remaining isolated.
(3) Rulers controlled their nobles by influencing where they lived.
(4) Spending time in segregated sectors guaranteed nobles the support of their ruler.

This question was purely a reading comprehension question.

Regents Question Time!

Japanese Imperialism, 1875–1910

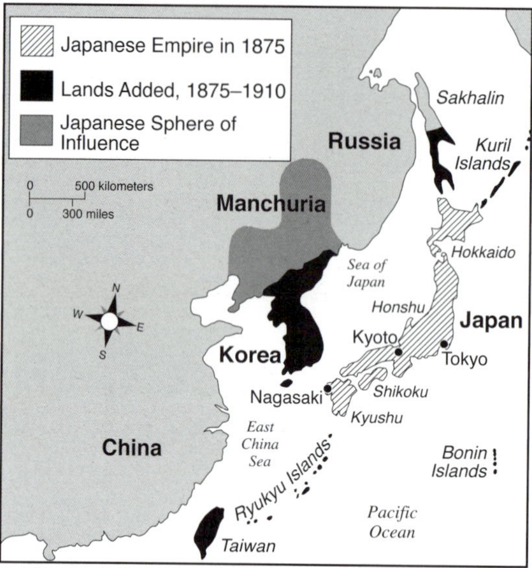

Source: Henry Brun et al., *Reviewing Global History and Geography*, AMSCO (adapted)

28 What was a basic cause of the political changes shown on this map?

(1) Russia and Japan formed an alliance.
(2) Korea defeated Japan in the Sino-Japanese War.
(3) The Japanese people wanted to spread the beliefs of Shinto.
(4) Japan needed raw materials for industrialization.

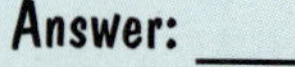

1

Japanese Imperialism, 1875–1910

Japan expanded significantly

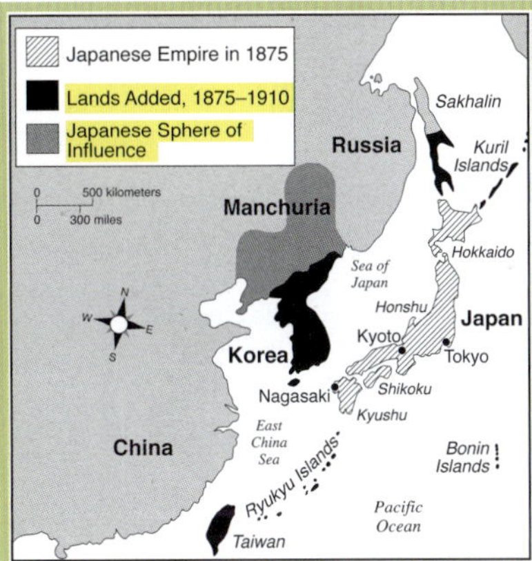

4

2

Source: Henry Brun et al., *Reviewing Global History and Geography*, AMSCO (adapted)

No help here

3

What caused Japan to imperialize? You know this!

28 What was a basic cause of the political changes shown on this map?

(1) Russia and Japan formed an alliance.
(2) Korea defeated Japan in the Sino-Japanese War.
(3) The Japanese people wanted to spread the beliefs of Shinto.
(4) Japan needed raw materials for industrialization.

Regents Question Time!

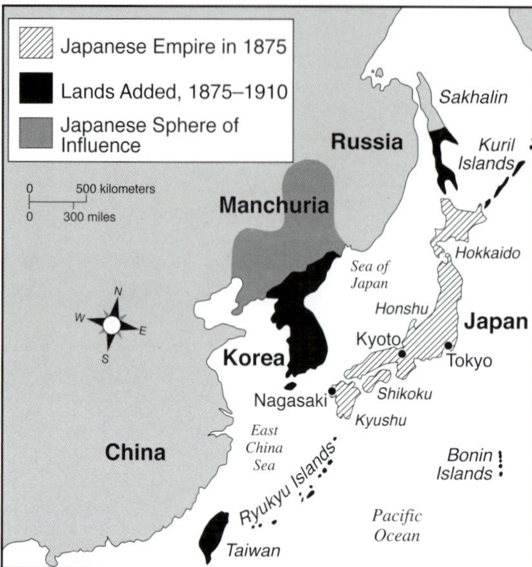

Source: Henry Brun et al., *Reviewing Global History and Geography*, AMSCO (adapted)

29 Which event is associated with the changes shown on this map?

(1) Opium War
(2) Meiji Restoration
(3) Chinese Nationalist Revolution
(4) rise of the Soviet Union

Answer: ___

1

Japanese Imperialism, 1875–1910

Japan expanded significantly.
When did Japan expand so much?

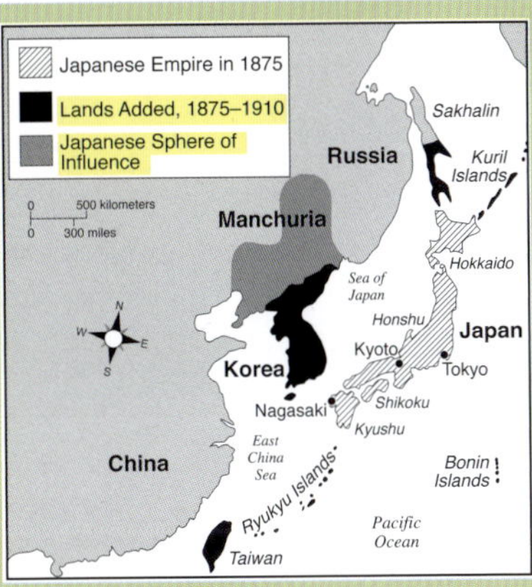

2

Source: Henry Brun et al., *Reviewing Global History and Geography*, AMSCO (adapted)

No help here

3

29 Which event is associated with the changes shown on this map?

(1) Opium War
(2) Meiji Restoration
(3) Chinese Nationalist Revolution
(4) rise of the Soviet Union

4

EdBoosters™

UNIT 8

IMPERIALISM

EdBoosters™

Imperialism

IMPERIALISM/COLONIALISM: when a strong country has economic/political control over a weaker country
COLONY: the country being controlled
MOTHER COUNTRY: the controlling country

Britain (strong country) imperialized India (weaker country).

Britain was the mother country. India was the colony.

- **Power:** European countries had power over its colonies and denied them of their freedoms.
- **Inequality:** The colonies were exploited (taken advantage of) and their freedoms were denied.
- **Conflict:** Colonies were not so happy that foreign countries were controlling them.

Let's explore global imperialism – imperialism around the world!

HINT: A mother country is similar to a mother and a colony is similar to a child. The mother country bosses around the colonies, just as mothers boss their kids around.

Causes of Imperialism

Over time, the concept of stronger countries taking over weaker countries became accepted for these reasons:

1. **NATIONALISM, SOCIAL DARWINISM:**
   The stronger countries thought that they were so large or so great and believed they had the right to dominate (control) weaker countries.
   They believed in "survival of the fittest" – some countries are stronger and better and will therefore succeed, prosper, and take advantage of the "less fit" countries.

2. **ECONOMIC MOTIVES:**
   Imperialists needed raw materials, customers for their manufactured products, and places to invest their profits. Taking over colonies seemed liked a perfect solution.
3. **WHITE MAN'S BURDEN:**
   KIPLING wrote THE WHITE MAN'S BURDEN (1899), a racist poem that justified imperialism.
   He wrote that white imperialists have a duty to educate the underdeveloped nations.
   Missionaries saw it as their duty to spread Christian and Western ideas to Africa and Asia.

R **Cause and effect:** Note the causes that led to imperialism.

R **Cause and effect:** The Industrial Revolution led to Imperialism.

HINT: Nationalism, Economic motives, White Man's Burden – acronym for NEW. This NEW idea of imperialism spread for these reasons.

White Man's Burden

This cartoon depicts Kipling's famous poem, *The White Man's Burden.*

Forms of Imperialism

- **DIRECT RULE:** The imperialist country rules the colony directly.
- **INDIRECT RULE:** The imperialist country lets the local leaders rule, but rules indirectly.
- **PROTECTORATE:** Local rulers rule, but are under the control of the imperialistic country.
- **SPHERE OF INFLUENCE:** An outside power claims exclusive rights to investment and trading in the colony.

Imperialists used a "divide and conquer" strategy to gain and maintain power.

- They combined Muslims and Hindus, allowing them to fight with each other.
- They split up African tribes and combined rivaling tribes.
- The colonies were busy fighting with each other, so they didn't resist the imperialist country as much.

You don't need to memorize; just be familiar with the different styles of imperialism.

Britain: The Leading Imperialistic Power

During the Victorian era (1837-1901), Britain was the leading imperialistic nation. It controlled territory all over the world, including the Americas, Asia, and Australia.

- Because Britain controlled territory in so many time zones, a famous saying emerged: "The sun never sets on the British Empire."
- Because the British industrialized first, they became the most powerful imperialists.
- Germany and France competed fiercely with Britain for control over colonies. They especially fought over Africa and China.

The Europeans successfully imperialized Africa and Asia because they had a stronger military and economy. They also "divided and conquered" – they separated Muslims and Hindus in India and the rival tribes in Africa.

Power: Europe's power and military led to imperialism.

Human Rights Violation/Inequality: The stronger European countries took advantage of the weaker countries' resources and denied them basic rights.

The British in India

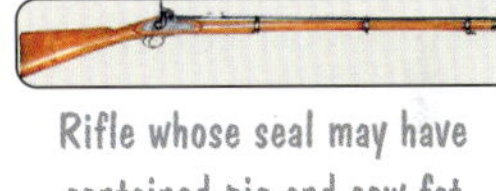

Rifle whose seal may have contained pig and cow fat

Background: The BRITISH EAST INDIA COMPANY (a British company) controlled three-fifths of India. They employed Indian soldiers, called SEPOYS.

The British East India Company demanded that the Sepoys (Indian soldiers) follow orders that were against their religious beliefs (Islam and Hinduism).

FYI: A rumor spread that the bullet casings of the soldiers' rifles contained traces of pig or cow fat. The soldiers needed to bite off the casing to fill the bullet with gun powder. The problem was that Hindus do not eat cows and Muslims do not eat pigs.

HINT: Mutiny means rebellion. The Sepoy Mutiny means the Sepoys rebelled.

THE SEPOY MUTINY (1857): Angered by the British East India Company's rules, the Indian soldiers revolted.

- This is an example of resistance against imperialism.

The British government crushed the rebellion and took direct control of India.

- Until now, the British East India Company controlled India.
- Now, the British government controlled India. Britain now had even more control over India!

Power: The Sepoy Rebellion increased British control of India.

Human Rights Violation/Inequality: British imperialism in India infringed on the Indians' rights.

The British Empire in India (Continued)

The British government imperialized India.

- **Mother country:** Great Britain
- **Colony:** India

When Britain became the mother country of India, it modernized and Westernized India.

ex Great Britain built roads, railroads, bridges, a sanitation system, and school systems in India.

India became known as the "crown jewel" of the British Empire. Why?

- India provided the British with raw materials, such as jute (a plant that produces fiber to make sacks and mats) and cotton.
- India was also a great market for Britain's manufactured goods.

Effects of the British Empire on India

Positive Effects:

1. New roads and railroads that linked all parts of India
2. Telegraphy and mail systems
3. Irrigation systems
4. British schools that offered education to Indians

Negative Effects:

1. Most Indian resources went to Britain.
2. British-made goods replaced locally made goods.
3. The Indian people were treated as inferior.
4. Britain attempted to Westernize India, which destroyed Indian culture.

R **Cause and effect:** British imperialism of India ➲ All the effects listed above

E **Inequality:** Britain controlled the Indians.

E **Power:** Britain used its power to help India, and to exploit (take advantage of) its people.

E **Conflict:** The British fought to gain power over India.

The Berlin Conference

BERLIN CONFERENCE (1884): European leaders met in Berlin, Germany, took a map of Africa, and divided it among themselves.
By 1914, European countries controlled over 90% of Africa.

Now, you have to understand that Africa was made up of a bunch of different tribes and ethnic groups, with diverse cultures. These tribes did not get along with each other. When the European leaders divided Africa, they did not pay any attention to tribal boundaries. They broke up tribes and put opposing tribes together. This created serious tension and fights among the different tribes, which lasts until today. Not a good situation!

Cartoon of Otto von Bismarck and other European leaders at the Berlin Conference sharing Africa as if it's a cake

- R Cause and effect: Berlin Conference ➲ Scramble for Africa ➲ European countries control 90% of Africa.
- E Power: Europe exerts power over Africa.
- E Conflict: The Europeans divided Africa without being sensitive to tribal boundaries. Therefore, there is serious conflict between the African tribes until today.

The Scramble for Africa: (1880-1914)

European powers, including France, Great Britain, Germany, Italy, Spain, and Portugal wanted control of Africa.

Why did these countries want control of Africa?

1. **Natural resources:** gold, copper, rubber, and ivory
   The European countries wanted to get their hands on Africa's valuable gold and ivory by imperializing the continent.
2. **Nationalism and racism:**
   The imperialistic countries felt that they were great and better than others and wanted to expand.
3. European countries also wanted to **missionize** (educate and encourage Catholic religion) Africa.
4. **White Man's Burden:** This poem encouraged countries to educate and help weaker countries.

Rubber tree

Ivory

Gold

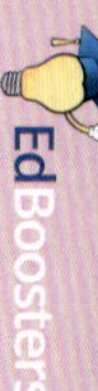

Abuse in the Congo

King Leopold II of Belgium took control of the Congo Free State in Africa and exploited (took advantage of for his own benefit) its natural resources, such as rubber and ivory.

He also forced the Africans to work really hard for him under brutal conditions and terror.

congo

This cartoon depicts King Leopold II abusing the Africans to gain natural resources from them, such as rubber.

Africa Before and After the Scramble of Africa

Document 1

Africa in 1879

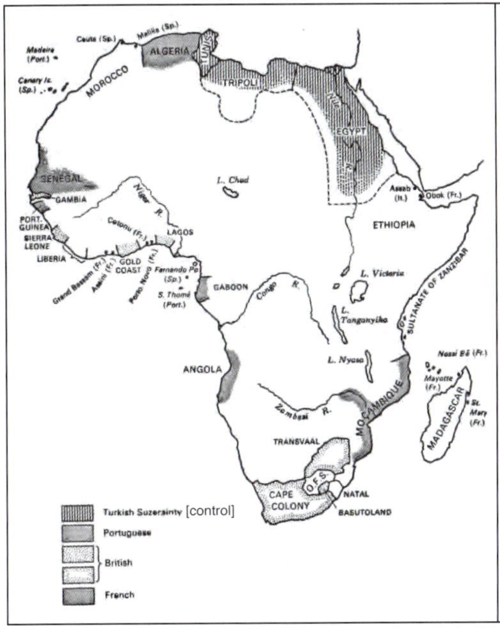

Turkish Suzerainty [control]
Portuguese
British
French

Africa in 1914

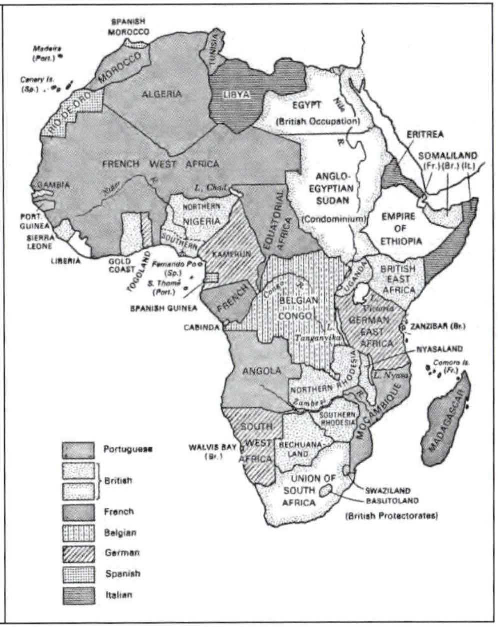

Portuguese
British
French
Belgian
German
Spanish
Italian

Source: Raymond F. Betts, ed., *The Scramble for Africa: Causes and Dimensions of Empire*, D.C. Heath and Company, 1972 (adapted)

Imperialism in South Africa – The Boer War

In the mid-1600s, Dutch farmers moved to South Africa.
They became known as BOERS and AFRIKANERS.
The Boers settled in Cape Town.

Then, the British imperialized Cape Town and took control over the area. The Boers were not interested in being under British rule. So they moved North, away from the British, and established the Boer Republics.

THE BOER WAR (1899-1902):
The British decided to imperialize the Boer Republics. A very bloody war followed, with many losses.
At the end, the British won control of South Africa. But bad feelings and hatred persisted between the Boers and the British.

FYI: Boers means "farmers" in the Dutch language.

More Resistance to Imperialism

As you can imagine, many countries did not take well to this imperialism! Some countries tried to resist. Most failed, but Ethiopia succeeded!

Ethiopia resistance against imperialism:

EMPEROR MENELIK II built up a large army and weapon supply. When Italy tried attacking to imperialize Ethiopia, the country fought back with its powerful army... and won!

This was the first time in history that an African army defeated an European army!

Emperor Menelik II

Imperialism in Africa – Segregation

Britain now had control over South Africa.
It created SEGREGATION rules – separation between black and white people.
This would be called APARTHEID, but more on that later.

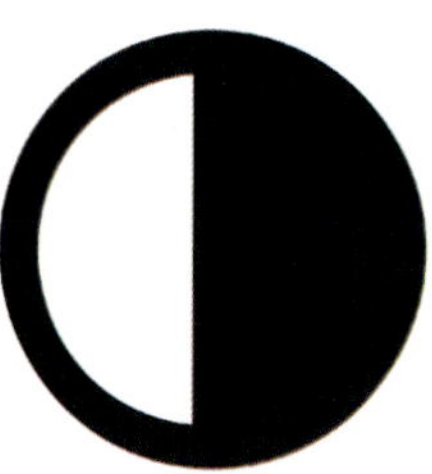

R **Cause and effect:** Imperialism in South Africa ➲ Boer War ➲ British control over South Africa ➲ Segregation (apartheid)

E **Inequality:** Apartheid – white people have far more rights than the black people.
E **Power:** Great Britain exerts power over South Africa.
E **Conflict:** The Europeans fought to control South Africa.

Imperialism in China

(1644-1912) The Qing dynasty was ETHNOCENTRIC – they felt they were the center of the world.
They had a very successful economy and were very proud of themselves.
They didn't want to adopt Western ways and were totally isolated from the world.

HINT: The Qing dynasty thought of themselves as "king" – center of the world.

Europe wanted to imperialize China because it possessed a wealth of raw materials and had a huge population to trade with.

THE OPIUM WAR (1839):
The British sneaked into China and sold OPIUM, an addictive drug, to the Chinese people. Millions of Chinese became addicted to the opium, and this weakened them. The Chinese government tried stopping the British from selling the opium. War broke out! Great Britain won the war because it had better weapons.

- R There are many Regents questions on this topic.
- R Cause and effect: Opium War ➲ British win and imperialize China
- E Conflict: Opium War was fought so that Britain would gain control of China.
- E Power: Britain exerts power over China.

FYI: Opium is obtained from the juice of poppy seeds.

Treaty of Nanjing (Imperialism in China)

After the Opium War, Great Britain forced China to sign the TREATY OF NANJING.

TREATY OF NANJING:

1. Britain can sell opium in China.
2. China must open ports for British trade.
3. British gained control of Hong Kong.
4. The British did not have to follow Chinese law when they were in China.
   - This concept is called EXTRATERRITORIALITY: people visiting from another country may follow their own country's laws and do not have to follow the local laws of the place they are visiting.
   - Usually, when you visit a country, you must follow their laws! The British got away with this.
5. The British carved SPHERES OF INFLUENCE in China – they divided China among the Imperialist nations as if they were cutting a pizza pie!
   The Imperialist countries had a lot of influence in China, but not total control.

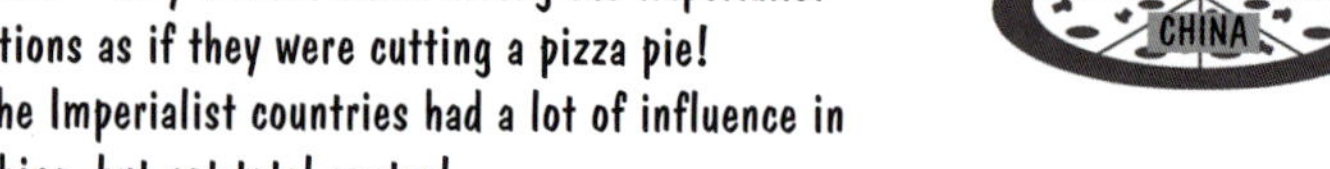

Sometimes the Treaty of Nanjing is called the Treaty of Nanking.

R There are many Regents questions on this topic.

HINT: Extraterritoriality: Extra-territory – people don't need to follow the "extra" laws of the "territory" they are visiting.

HINT: Treaty of Nanking: Just as a "king" gives orders to his people, Britain gave orders to China.

Spheres of Influence

- **A SPHERE OF INFLUENCE** is when an outside country claims investment and trading privileges from a weaker country.
- The weaker country is called a **COLONY**.

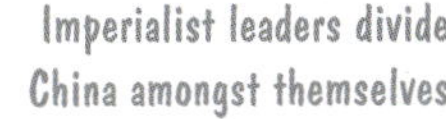

Imperialist leaders divide China amongst themselves.

HINT: Sphere of influence: One country has influence over another sphere (area).

R Cause and effect: Treaty of Nanjing ➲ China is "carved" into "spheres of influence"

R Turning Point: The Treaty of Nanjing resulted in increased foreign control over China.

E Conflict: Powerful countries had significant influence on China and China wanted its independence.

E Power: Powerful countries exert power over China.

E Inequality: Powerful countries have power over the Chinese.

Chinese Rebellions – Taiping Rebellion

If you were a Chinese person living during this time, would you be happy that the Western world is opening doors for you, or would you resent those people for intruding?
Circle the face that shows how you would feel.
Let's see how the Chinese people felt.

Some Chinese rulers and people held on to the old beliefs of ethnocentrism and resisted change. For example, EMPRESS CiXi of the Qing Dynasty held on to tradition and stopped reforms.

Chinese people fight the Qing Dynasty

TAIPING REBELLION (1850-1864):
But many Chinese people wanted to modernize and adopt Western cultures to improve their economic situation. These people revolted against the Qing dynasty. Millions of Chinese were killed in this internal battle ☹.

- Ⓡ Cause and effect: European Imperialism ➲ Rebellions
- Ⓔ Power and Conflict: European powers have a power struggle with the Chinese dynasty.
- Ⓔ Interconnectedness: Because of the European presence in China, some Chinese people wanted Westernization.

HINT: Taiping Rebellion: The Qing Dynasty was "taped" down to its old ways and many Chinese people wanted reforms.

Chinese Rebellion – The Boxer Rebellion

Britain entered China, turned its people into opioid addicts, fought a war with them, and then foisted its influence on China.
How do you think the Chinese reacted?

How would you feel if your sister enters your room, wrecks it, fights with you, and then forces you to listen to her?!

THE BOXER REBELLION (1900):
Many Chinese resented and feared the outside influence of foreign imperialism.
A Chinese group, called BOXERS, rebelled against British control.

The imperialists crushed the rebellion and forced China to accept Western reforms.

The Chinese Boxers fight against the British

- R There are many Regents questions on this topic.
- R Cause and effect: European imperialism ➲ Boxer rebellion ➲ Europeans crushed the rebellion and the Chinese were forced to accept Western reforms.
- E Power and Conflict: A major power struggle between foreign imperialists and the Chinese government led to rebellions.

HINT: Boxing is a fighting sport. The Boxers fought against the British. (But I wouldn't exactly call it a sport, if you know what I mean.)

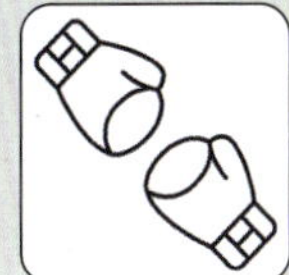

Sun Yat-Sen & The Chinese Revolution: (1911)

Chinese nationalism increased, and the Chinese wanted a different kind of government. Workers and peasants fought to end the Chinese monarchy. SUN YAT-SEN replaced the Qing dynasty and became the president.

Sun Yat-Sen

<u>Sun Yat-Sen instituted reforms:</u>

1. No foreign country may control China.
2. He created a representative government.
3. He improved the economic situation.

Ⓡ Cause and effect: Chinese nationalism ➲ Sun Yat-Sen becomes president

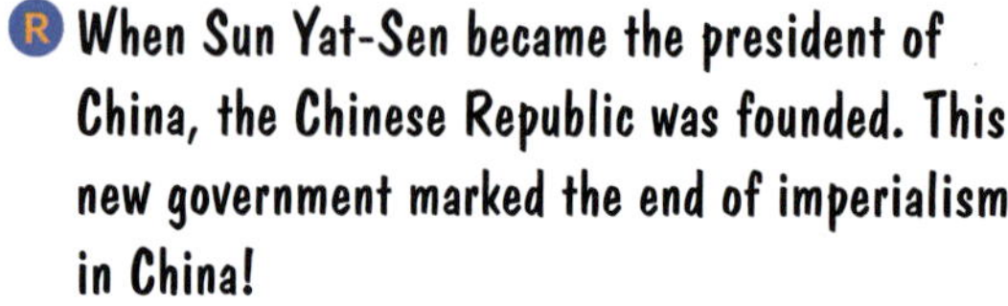

Ⓡ When Sun Yat-Sen became the president of China, the Chinese Republic was founded. This new government marked the end of imperialism in China!

HINT: A <u>sun</u> brings light to earth. <u>Sun</u> Yat-Sen brought light to China.

Japan Becomes a World Power

Once Japan built factories, they needed NATURAL RESOURCES and RAW MATERIALS to manufacture products.

- NATURAL RESOURCES: substances that occur in nature

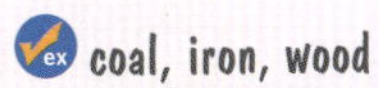 coal, iron, wood

- RAW MATERIALS: materials needed to produce useful products

Problem: Japan had very limited natural resources and raw materials ☹.
Solution: They would have to get the raw materials from other countries 😊.

In order to obtain raw materials, Japan took control over weaker countries. This is called IMPERIALISM: when a stronger country takes control over a weaker country. The weaker country that's being controlled is called a COLONY.

Japan gained colonies by fighting wars:

1. SINO-JAPANESE WAR: Japan took Formosa (Taiwan) from China, gaining access to China's ports.
2. RUSSO-JAPANESE WAR: Japan took Korea and Manchuria from Russia.
   PS: This was a major embarrassment to Russia, which was considered a powerful country!

R Cause and effect: Japan lacked natural resources ➲ Japan fought wars to gain natural resources.

E Scarcity: Japan imperialized because it didn't have enough natural resources.

Positive Effects of Imperialism

1. Colonies get Westernized.
2. CULTURAL DIFFUSION: spread of beliefs and cultures
3. Economies are more interconnected.
4. Improvements in transportation, education, medicine
5. The West discovers new goods, such as tea and tomatoes.

- R Cause and effect: Imperialism of China ➲ The five effects above
- E Interconnectedness: The influence of the West (specifically Europe) spreads.
- E Ideas and beliefs: Western technologies, culture, and ideas spread.
- Generally, cultural diffusion occurs when there is war, trade, or immigration.

HINT: Cultural diffusion: The culture of one country diffuses (spreads) to other countries.

Western culture and ideas spread all over the world.

Negative Effects of Imperialism

1. Colonies lost control and self-rule.
2. Colonies were forced to give their natural resources to their mother country.
3. Competition for colonies leads to wars.

- Imperialism was generally good for the mother country, but bad for the colonies.
- R Cause and effect: Imperialism of China ➲ The three effects above
- E Power: The mother countries exerted power over the colonies.

Quick Review

Check off the boxes you know well. Whatever you don't know well (yet!), go back and review now!

- ☐ Imperialism: a stronger country gains control of a weaker country
  - Causes of imperialism: NEW (nationalism, economic reasons, White Man's Burden)
  - Mother country
  - Colony
- ☐ British imperialism:
  - British East India Company
  - Sepoy Mutiny
- ☐ Scramble for Africa
  - Berlin conference
  - Boer War
- ☐ Imperialism in China
  - Opium War
  - Treaty of Nanjing
  - Taiping Rebellion, Boxing Rebellion
  - Sun Yat-Sen
- ☐ Effects of imperialism

Enduring Issues Essay Topics That Came Up in This Unit:

- Power: Stronger countries imperialize weaker countries and exert control over them.
- Conflict: Many wars were fought to help mother countries gain land. Often, the imperialized colony resisted foreign control.
- Ideas and beliefs: Mother countries spread Western ideas to the colonies.
- Interconnectedness: Some citizens of the mother countries settled in the colonies, and they became connected to the colonies and spread their ideas.
- Human Rights Violation/Inequality: Mother countries exerted power and control over the colonies.

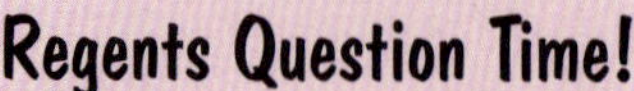

Now it's time to test how well you know your stuff.

Have fun!

Regents Question Time!

Document 1

Source: Mrs. Ernest Ames, *An ABC for Baby Patriots,* Dean & Sons, 1898 (adapted)

29 Explain the historical circumstances that led to British attitudes about their empire as shown in this excerpt from *An ABC for Baby Patriots.* [1]

____

____

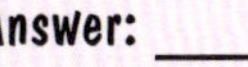

Answer: ___

1

No title here. Move on.

Document 1

This cartoon is showing that Britain thought it was the greatest!

2

Source: Mrs. Ernest Ames, *An ABC for Baby Patriots*, Dean & Sons, 1898 (adapted)

1898 – Imperialization time period

3

29 Explain the historical circumstances that led to British attitudes about their empire as shown in this excerpt from *An ABC for Baby Patriots*. [1]

4

What historical circumstance led to Britain feeling so great about itself? What was going on at this time that led to British imperialism?

Any of these answers is correct:

- Britain wanted a large empire so that it could acquire new markets/military bases.
- The British wanted to expand their markets to sell the goods being manufactured as a result of the Industrial Revolution.
- They believed in/supported British nationalism.
- Military conquest led to prestige/new colonies/power.
- Belief in Social Darwinism supported their actions.
- They wanted to spread their culture.

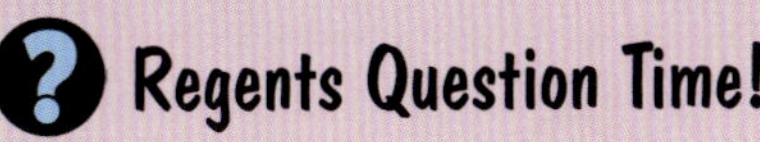

Document 2

The Discovery of India was written by Jawaharlal Nehru during his imprisonment at Ahmadnagar Fort in British India from April to September 1944. Nehru was a leader in the Indian National Congress.

> The Chief business of the East India Company in its early period, the very object for which it was started, was to carry Indian manufactured goods—textiles, etc., as well as spices and the like—from the East to Europe, where there was a great demand for these articles. With the developments in industrial techniques in England a new class of industrial capitalists rose there demanding a change in this policy. The British market was to be closed to Indian products and the Indian market opened to British manufactures. The British parliament, influenced by this new class, began to take a greater interest in India and the working of the East India Company. To begin with, Indian goods were excluded from Britain by legislation, and as the company held a monopoly in the Indian export business, this exclusion influenced other foreign markets also. This was followed by vigorous attempts to restrict and crush Indian manufactures by various measures and internal duties which prevented the flow of Indian goods within the country itself. British goods meanwhile had free entry. The Indian textile industry collapsed, affecting vast numbers of weavers and artisans. The process was rapid in Bengal and Bihar; elsewhere it spread gradually with the expansion of British rule and the building of railways. It continued throughout the nineteenth century, breaking up other old industries also, shipbuilding, metalwork, glass, paper, and many crafts.
>
> To some extent this was inevitable as the older manufacturing came into conflict with the new industrial technique. But it was hastened by political and economic pressure, and no attempt was made to apply the new techniques to India. Indeed every attempt was made to prevent this happening, and thus the economic development of India was arrested [stopped] and the growth of the new industry prevented. Machinery could not be imported into India. A vacuum was created in India which could only be filled by British goods, and which also led to rapidly increasing unemployment and poverty. The classic type of modern colonial economy was built up, India becoming an agricultural colony of industrial England, supplying raw materials and providing markets for England's industrial goods. . . .

Source: Jawaharlal Nehru, *The Discovery of India*, The John Day Company, 1946

30 Identify Jawaharlal Nehru's point of view concerning British colonialism in India based on this excerpt. [1]

____

____

Answer: ____

1

No title here. Move on.

Document 2

The Discovery of India was written by Jawaharlal Nehru during his imprisonment at Ahmadnagar Fort in British India from April to September 1944. Nehru was a leader in the Indian National Congress.

> The Chief business of the East India Company in its early period, the very object for which it was started, was to carry Indian manufactured goods—textiles, etc., as well as spices and the like—from the East to Europe, where there was a great demand for these articles. With the developments in industrial techniques in England a new class of industrial capitalists rose there demanding a change in this policy. The British market was to be closed to Indian products and the Indian market opened to British manufactures. The British parliament, influenced by this new class, began to take a greater interest in India and the working of the East India Company. To begin with, Indian goods were excluded from Britain by legislation, and as the company held a monopoly in the Indian export business, this exclusion influenced other foreign markets also. This was followed by vigorous attempts to restrict and crush Indian manufactures by various measures and internal duties which prevented the flow of Indian goods within the country itself. British goods meanwhile had free entry. The Indian textile industry collapsed, affecting vast numbers of weavers and artisans. The process was rapid in Bengal and Bihar; elsewhere it spread gradually with the expansion of British rule and the building of railways. It continued throughout the nineteenth century, breaking up other old industries also, shipbuilding, metalwork, glass, paper, and many crafts.
>
> To some extent this was inevitable as the older manufacturing came into conflict with the new industrial technique. But it was hastened by political and economic pressure, and no attempt was made to apply the new techniques to India. Indeed every attempt was made to prevent this happening, and thus the economic development of India was arrested [stopped] and the growth of the new industry prevented. Machinery could not be imported into India. A vacuum was created in India which could only be filled by British goods, and which also led to rapidly increasing unemployment and poverty. The classic type of modern colonial economy was built up, India becoming an agricultural colony of industrial England, supplying raw materials and providing markets for England's industrial goods. . . .

4

2

Source: Jawaharlal Nehru, *The Discovery of India*, The John Day Company, 1946

3

30 Identify Jawaharlal Nehru's point of view concerning British colonialism in India based on this excerpt. [1]

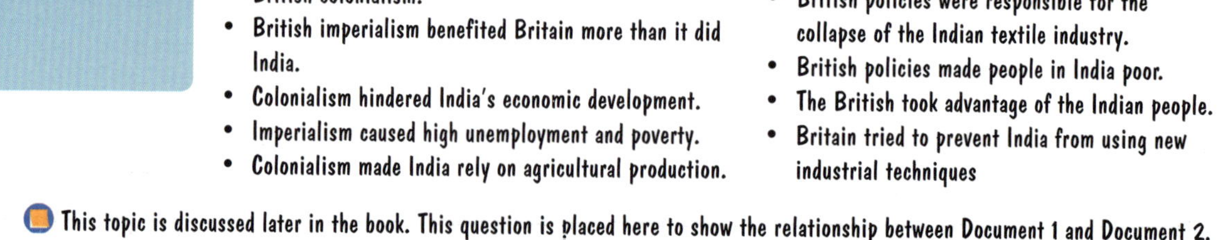

Any of these answers is correct:

- India's traditional industries were damaged/hurt by British colonialism.
- British imperialism benefited Britain more than it did India.
- Colonialism hindered India's economic development.
- Imperialism caused high unemployment and poverty.
- Colonialism made India rely on agricultural production.
- Britain monopolized trade with India.
- British policies were responsible for the collapse of the Indian textile industry.
- British policies made people in India poor.
- The British took advantage of the Indian people.
- Britain tried to prevent India from using new industrial techniques

This topic is discussed later in the book. This question is placed here to show the relationship between Document 1 and Document 2.

Regents Question Time!

Base your answer to question 31 on ***both*** Documents 1 and 2 and on your knowledge of social studies.

Cause—refers to something that contributes to the occurrence of an event, the rise of an idea, or the bringing about of a development.

Effect—refers to what happens as a consequence (result, impact, outcome) of an event, an idea, or a development.

31 Identify ***and*** explain a cause-and-effect relationship associated with the historical developments in documents 1 and 2. Be sure to use evidence from ***both*** documents 1 and 2 in your response. [1]

____

____

____

____

Answer: ____

CRQ Answer

This is a typical CRQ Regents question. Here's how to answer:

We'll discuss CRQ Regents questions at the end of the book.

1. Find the general concept of each document.
   Document 1: British imperialism
   Document 2: Problems with imperialism in India
2. Which concept led to the other?
   British imperialism led to problems with imperialism in India.
3. Write out your answer!
   Any of these answers is correct:
   - Because Great Britain wanted a large empire, it colonized India and exploited the Indian economy/resources.
   - British imperialism/capitalism led to the collapse of India's native industries/domestic system.
   - British imperialism led to the loss of India's economic self-sufficiency. British imperialism led to the eventual rise of Indian nationalism and resistance.
   - Britain's desire for raw materials led to the exploitation of Indian agricultural products.
   - Britain defeated India and colonized it.

Regents Question Time!

The Partition of Africa

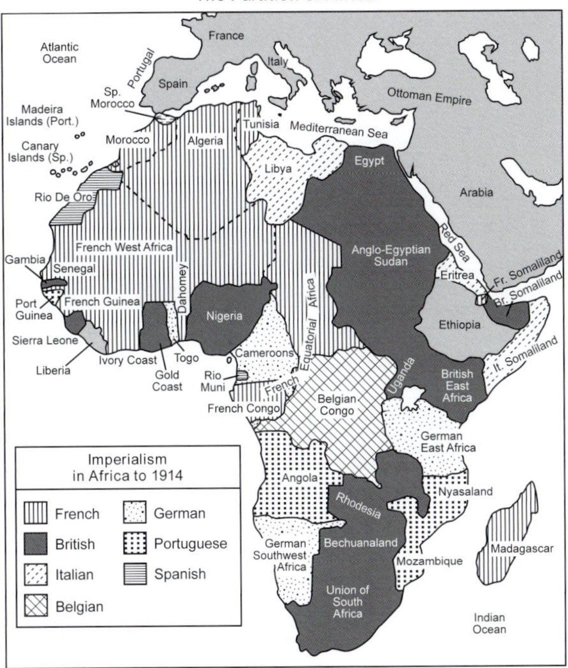

Source: Costello et al., World History: Book 3, 1815–1919, The Center for Learning, 1992 (adapted)

8 What was a result of the political situation shown on this map?

(1) Most local rulers had power equal to that of European leaders.

(2) The economic prosperity of the African nationalist leaders increased their power.

(3) African leaders willingly adopted European forms of governance including constitutions.

(4) The boundaries that were established led to the division of traditional cultures and commerce.

Answer: ____

The Partition of Africa

European countries imperialized African countries.

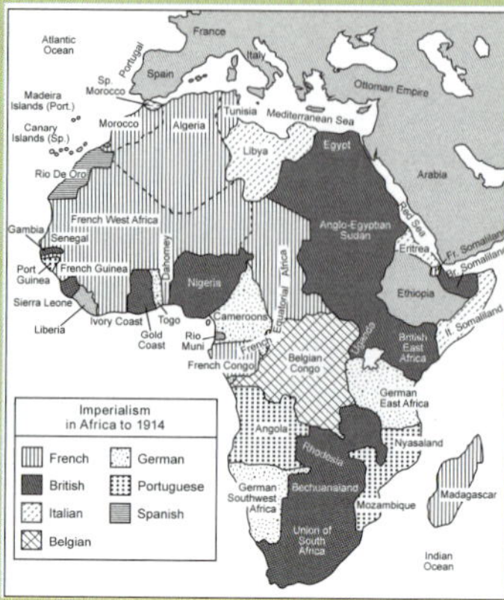

Source: Costello et al., World History: Book 3, 1815–1919, The Center for Learning, 1992 (adapted)

8 What was a result of the political situation shown on this map?

(1) Most local rulers had power equal to that of European leaders.
(2) The economic prosperity of the African nationalist leaders increased their power.
(3) African leaders willingly adopted European forms of governance including constitutions.
(4) The boundaries that were established led to the division of traditional cultures and commerce.

What was a result of the European countries dividing up Africa without taking tribal boundaries into account? This divided the cultures and trade unique to each African tribe.

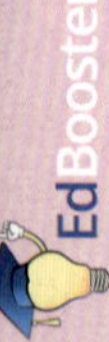

UNIT 9

WORLD WAR I (1914-1918)

Causes of World War I

World War I was a terribly bloody war. Over 35 million people were killed! What caused this war?

1. **Nationalism:**
   - Germany was unified and proud to show off its strength.
   - France wanted to regain the power it lost in the Franco-Prussian War.
   - The ethnic groups in the Ottoman and Austro-Hungarian empires wanted self-rule.

2. **Militarism:**
   Each country competed to have the best army, navy, and weapons. So they built up their military and had it available for use.
3. **Imperialism & economic rivalry:**
   Germany, France, and Britain competed for colonies, to gain economic power.

4. **Alliances:**
   Countries made alliances with each other — a deal that if anyone starts up with me, you'll come and protect me and vice versa.

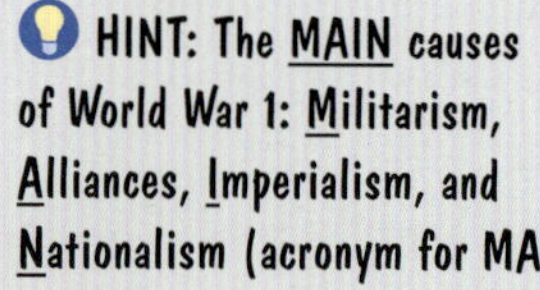

HINT: The MAIN causes of World War 1: Militarism, Alliances, Imperialism, and Nationalism (acronym for MAIN)

Cause and effect: The four causes listed above ➲ World War I

Alliances (Teams)

Countries made deals with each other. If another country decides to fight us, you'll come help us fight.

These were the teams in World War I:

Central Powers:

1. Germany
2. Austria-Hungary
3. Ottoman Turks

Allies:

1. Britain
2. France
3. Russia
4. *Italy joined later
5. *USA joined at the end of the war

These alliance systems were created to keep peace in Europe. Instead they did the opposite!
Stay posted to see why.

Interconnectedness: Alliances create powerful connections, which eventually leads to war.

HINT: AGO: Austria-Hungary, Germany, Ottoman Turks

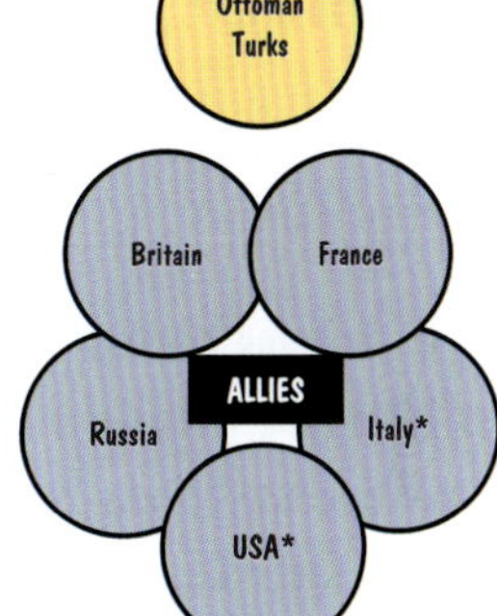

HINT: Notice that the first letters of these countries correspond to this phrase: Best Friends (Allies) Unite In Rivalry (Britain, France, USA, Italy, Russia).

The Balkans

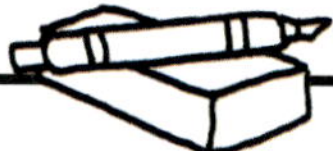

The Balkans is an area in Europe that contained Austria-Hungary, Bosnia, Serbia, and other countries (in the early 1900s).

Notice how many different ethnic groups lived in this area. (See map key on bottom left.)

This area experienced much ethnic tension, which was fueled by nationalism.

The Balkans became known as THE POWDER KEG OF EUROPE.
Powder keg is gunpowder. If a tiny spark hits gunpowder, it can cause a massive explosion.
Since the Balkans were experiencing so much tension, a tiny spark there would cause a massive world war!

The Balkans

- Ⓡ Common Regents question
- Ⓡ **Cause and effect:** Tension in the Balkans ➲ War
- Ⓔ **Interconnectedness:** The Balkans is located in the heart of Europe and sets off tensions among its neighbors.

HINT: <u>Bal</u>-<u>kan</u>: <u>ball</u> <u>cans</u> – or more like <u>cannon</u><u>balls</u>! The Balkans was like a cannonball ready to explode!

The Slavs

Now that we discussed official alliances, let's talk about an ethnic group that caused countries to be very connected and intertwined with each other.

The SLAVS were an ethnic group that share a similar culture and language.
The Slavic nations looked out for each other and would help each other in times of need.

Some Slavic Countries:

1. Bosnia
2. Serbia
3. Russia

PS: Eventually these countries would become allies.

Interconnectedness: The Slavic nations are very intertwined and join as allies in war.

The Spark that Sets Off World War I

Here's what happened:
(Follow along with the numbers in the images.)

1. The Austro-Hungarian empire controlled Bosnia.

2. Serbia was home to members of the same Slavic ethnic group as Bosnia.

3. The Serbians felt bad for Bosnia, which was controlled by the Austro-Hungarian empire.

The Slavs

The Spark that Sets Off World War I

A Serbian man was mad that the Austro-Hungarian empire was controlling Bosnia (a fellow Slav country).

So, while Austro-Hungarian duke FRANZ FERDINAND was visiting Bosnia, this Serbian fellow assassinated the duke and his expectant wife!

Serbian man kills Austro-Hungarian duke

Domino Effect – The World Joins In

1. Austria-Hungary blamed Serbia for the assassination. So Austria-Hungary declared war on Serbia.

2. Russia was part of the SLAVIC ethnic group and had an agreement to help Serbia. So Russia declared war on Austria-Hungary.

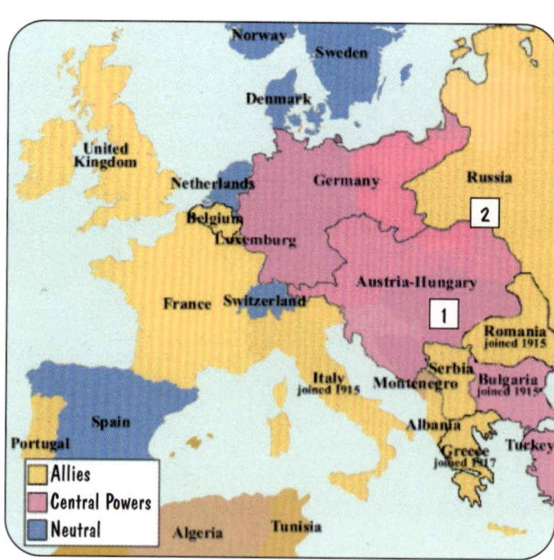

The Allies Join the War

Russia and Austria-Hungary each had their own allies.
Each of their allies came to help them fight.

Germany came to help Austria-Hungary.

CENTRAL POWERS

Germany

Austria-Hungary

Ottoman Turks

Britain and France came to help Russia.

Britain

France

ALLIES

Russia

Because of the Slavs' interconnection and the alliances, these six major countries became involved in the war.

- R **Cause and effect:** Events above ➲ The allies got involved and the war began.
- E **Interconnectedness:** Countries and ethnic groups were interconnected, so a major world war broke out.
- E **Cooperation:** Allies joined forces.
- E **Power:** Major world powers joined together and used their powers to fight this major war.
- E **Conflict:** The war...

Warfare in World War I

New and improved weapons were used:

- Machine guns
- Poison gas
- Submarines
  - By the way, the U.S. eventually joined the war because of unrestricted submarine warfare.
- Airplanes
- Tanks

This war was fought using TRENCH WARFARE:
Armies dug deep trenches along the fronts and fought from there. This caused a stalemate, in which neither team was able to progress for many months on the Western front.

Trench Warfare

Advanced warfare caused much more killing and destruction.
Over 35 million civilians and soldiers died in this war!

R **Cause and effect:** New technologies used in war ➲ Millions of people died.

E **Innovation:** New technologies used in war had a major world impact. Look how much damage it caused!

Total War

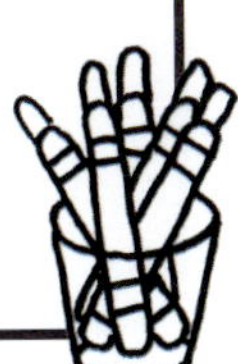

World War I was a TOTAL WAR – military and civilian resources were completely affected by the war.

The government took complete control over civilian resources, (including factories, homes, and farms), money, and media to try to win the war.

- Millions died because of warfare, starvation, and diseases.
- Factories, homes, and farms were destroyed.
- Governments raised taxes and borrowed money for the war, which affected the economy.
- Women joined the workforce to help as nurses or provide other army services.
- The government used propaganda to influence public opinion and keep the morale high.

R **Cause and effect:** Total war ➲ Destruction, loss of life, and economic disaster

E **Conflict:** The war caused large-scale death and destruction.

USA Joins the War

Lusitania Ship

At the beginning of World War I, the USA was neutral – it was not involved in the war.
Then, two things happened to make the USA join the war (1917):

1. Germany's submarine ships attacked the LUSITANIA – a British ship carrying US passengers. 128 American passengers were killed.
2. The ZIMMERMAN NOTE: Germany wanted Mexico to help it fight in the war. So Germany promised Mexico that when it would win the war, it would give Mexico some US land as a reward.

When the USA heard about this, it declared war on Germany.
Now, the USA became part of the Allies' team.

- **Interconnectedness:** Since the United States was so interconnected with other countries, they were compelled to join the war.
- **Cooperation:** The United States joined the Allies' team.
- **Turning Point:** The USA provided fresh soldiers and boosted the morale when they joined the Allies' team. This helped the Allies win the war.

The Zimmerman note sparked the USA's decision to join the war.

World War I Ends

(1917) Russia underwent a revolution and its new leader signed the Treaty of Brest-Litovsk, allowing it to leave the war. Russia withdrew from the war.

(1918) When the USA joined the war, Germany surrendered.

Turning Point: Russia withdrew from the war and the United States entered the war. These two factors caused the Allies to win the war.

Post-World War I

1. The 14 Points
2. Treaty of Versailles
3. League of Nations
4. Effects of World War I

Let's learn about each of these.

The 14 Points

After the war ended, Woodrow Wilson, president of the USA, gave a speech called THE 14 POINTS.

- The speech outlined a plan for peace and the end of World War I.
- He encouraged the world not to punish Germany and the Central Powers harshly because he felt it would backfire in the future.
- He stressed "self-determination" – that people should be able to choose their own government.

President Woodrow Wilson

Sounds like a nice speech? Maybe, but not everyone thought so. Wilson's plan was not widely accepted. Read on...

Ideas and beliefs: Wilson had some great ideas on how to promote world peace.

Treaty of Versailles

The Allied rulers of USA, Britain, France, and Italy, nicknamed the "BIG 4", met at the Palace of Versailles (outside Paris) to discuss a plan for peace.

They signed the TREATY OF VERSAILLES, which officially ended World War I. Germany was defeated and was forced to sign the treaty.

HINT: LAMB – Land, Army, Money, Blame

Treaty of Versailles – Main Points:

Germany had to:

1. Accept responsibility for World War I.
2. Pay WAR REPARATIONS – compensation payments to the other side.
   FYI: They had to pay 30 billion dollars to other countries!
3. Decrease the size of its military.
4. Give back land.

Germany felt that these conditions were unfair and that they had been punished too harshly. These feelings of anger led to World War II.

Most European countries preferred this peace plan over Wilson's.

HINT: Treaty of Versailles – it's pronounced Treaty of Ver-sigh. Germany "sighed" (very loudly!!) as a result of this treaty.

R **Cause and effect:** World War I (Treaty of Versailles) ➲ World War II

League of Nations

40 nations joined together to maintain world peace and avoid another world war.
FYI: US President Wilson wanted to join, but the US Congress didn't let him.

First League of Nations Meeting (1920)

In the end, the League of Nations was a failure because they had no way to enforce world peace.

R Common Regents questions

E **Cooperation:** The US Congress did not consent to join the League of Nations, which contributed to its failure.

Effects of World War I

1. Germany's economy was in bad shape due to war debt and reparations.
2. Germany was angered by the terms in the Treaty of Versailles. This led to World War II.

3. Major empires collapsed as a result of World War I:

- The Austro-Hungarian empire collapsed and was divided into smaller states (e.g., Czechoslovakia and Yugoslavia).
- The Ottoman Empire collapsed and many of its colonies became French and British MANDATES, which means that France and Britain now had legal control of those areas.

Ⓡ **Cause and effect:** Economic fall of Germany + Anger due to the Treaty of Versailles ➲ World War II and the rise of a totalitarian government in Germany

Map Time

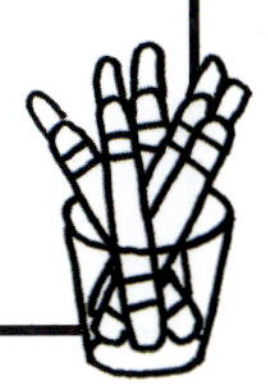

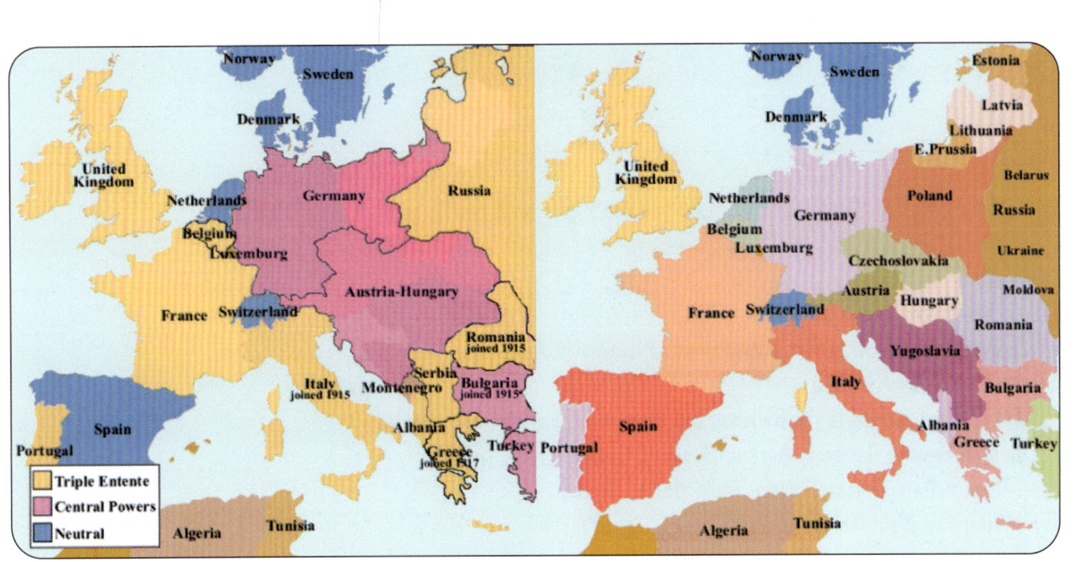

Before and after World War I

Notice how large empires were divided into smaller states.

Check off the boxes you know well. Whatever you don't know well (yet!), go back and review now!

- ☐ Causes of World War I
  - Nationalism, militarism, imperialism, alliances (MAIN)
- ☐ World War I: 1914-1918
- ☐ World War I started in the Balkans, and then many countries got involved
- ☐ Central Powers: Germany, Austria-Hungary, Ottoman Turks (AGO)
- ☐ Allies: Britain, France, Russia, Italy, United States
- ☐ Military struggle (trench warfare)
- ☐ USA enters the war and Russia withdraws. This leads to the war's end.
- ☐ Treaty of Versailles: Makes Germany take responsibility for war, pay war reparations, and return land.
- ☐ League of Nations
- ☐ Effects of World War I: Angry feelings (due to the Treaty of Versailles) leads to World War II; debt; collapse of empires.

Enduring Issues Essay Topics That Came Up in This Unit:

- **Power:** Germany built up its military, which made it more powerful and led to World War I.
- **Conflict:** World War I...
- **Interconnectedness/Cooperation:** The various allies were interconnected and cooperated with each other to fight in World War I.
- **Environmental impact/Scarcity:** World War I led to destruction and shortages in Germany.
- **Interconnectedness:** The Treaty of Versailles led to the next world war.

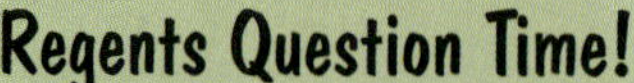

Now it's time to test how well you know your stuff.

Have fun!

Regents Question Time!

Attack

At dawn the ridge emerges massed and dun [brownish dark grey]
In the wild purple of the glowering [glaring] sun,
Smouldering through spouts of drifting smoke that shroud
The menacing scarred slope; and, one by one,
Tanks creep and topple forward to the wire.
The barrage roars and lifts. Then, clumsily bowed
With bombs and guns and shovels and battle-gear,
Men jostle and climb to meet the bristling fire.
Lines of grey, muttering faces, masked with fear,
They leave their trenches, going over the top,
While time ticks blank and busy on their wrists,
And hope, with furtive eyes and grappling fists,
Flounders in mud. O Jesu, make it stop!

— Siegfried Sassoon, 1918

10 This poem describes events related to which international conflict?

(1) World War I
(2) World War II
(3) Korean War
(4) Vietnam War

Answer: ___

1

No title here. Move on.

Tanks, guns, trenches... were used in

Attack

At dawn the ridge emerges massed and dun [brownish dark grey]
In the wild purple of the glowering [glaring] sun,
Smouldering through spouts of drifting smoke that shroud
The menacing scarred slope; and, one by one,
Tanks creep and topple forward to the wire.
The barrage roars and lifts. Then, clumsily bowed
With bombs and guns and shovels and battle-gear,
Men jostle and climb to meet the bristling fire.
Lines of grey, muttering faces, masked with fear,
They leave their trenches, going over the top,
While time ticks blank and busy on their wrists,
And hope, with furtive eyes and grappling fists,
Flounders in mud. O Jesu, make it stop!

4

2

— Siegfried Sassoon, 1918

Which attack happened in 1918?

3

10 This poem describes events related to which international conflict?

(1) World War I
(2) World War II
(3) Korean War
(4) Vietnam War

Regents Question Time!

Attack

At dawn the ridge emerges massed and dun [brownish dark grey]
In the wild purple of the glowering [glaring] sun,
Smouldering through spouts of drifting smoke that shroud
The menacing scarred slope; and, one by one,
Tanks creep and topple forward to the wire.
The barrage roars and lifts. Then, clumsily bowed
With bombs and guns and shovels and battle-gear,
Men jostle and climb to meet the bristling fire.
Lines of grey, muttering faces, masked with fear,
They leave their trenches, going over the top,
While time ticks blank and busy on their wrists,
And hope, with furtive eyes and grappling fists,
Flounders in mud. O Jesu, make it stop!

— Siegfried Sassoon, 1918

11 Which claim about modern warfare is best supported by this poem?

(1) Soldiers were not as brave as in the past.
(2) Technology made combat more deadly.
(3) Religion became more central to long-standing conflicts.
(4) Scientific research did not supply battle-ready innovations.

Answer: ___

1

No title here. Move on.

Advanced weapons and warfare were used, which made this war so deadly.

Attack

At dawn the ridge emerges massed and dun [brownish dark grey]
In the wild purple of the glowering [glaring] sun,
Smouldering through spouts of drifting smoke that shroud
The menacing scarred slope; and, one by one,
Tanks creep and topple forward to the wire.
The barrage roars and lifts. Then, clumsily bowed
With bombs and guns and shovels and battle-gear,
Men jostle and climb to meet the bristling fire.
Lines of grey, muttering faces, masked with fear,
They leave their trenches, going over the top,
While time ticks blank and busy on their wrists,
And hope, with furtive eyes and grappling fists,
Flounders in mud. O Jesu, make it stop!

4

2

— Siegfried Sassoon, 1918

3

11 Which claim about modern warfare is best supported by this poem?

(1) Soldiers were not as brave as in the past.
(2) Technology made combat more deadly.
(3) Religion became more central to long-standing conflicts.
(4) Scientific research did not supply battle-ready innovations.

Regents Question Time!

> . . . At times, gas has been known to travel, with dire results, fifteen miles behind the lines.
>
> A gas, or smoke helmet, as it is called, at the best is a vile-smelling thing, and it is not long before one gets a violent headache from wearing it.
>
> Our eighteen-pounders were bursting in No Man's Land, in an effort, by the artillery, to disperse the gas clouds.
>
> The fire step was lined with crouching men, bayonets fixed, and bombs near at hand to repel the expected attack.
>
> Our artillery had put a barrage of curtain fire on the German lines, to try and break up their attack and keep back re-inforcements.
>
> I trained my machine gun on their trench and its bullets were raking the parapet [spraying the wall].
>
> Then over they came, bayonets glistening. In their respirators, which have a large snout in front, they looked like some horrible nightmare. . . .

— Arthur Empey, "Over the Top," G. P. Putnam's Sons, 1917

7 A historian could best use this passage to study which topic of World War I?

(1) events that started the war
(2) impact of combat on civilians
(3) equipment utilized by soldiers
(4) propaganda that supported the war effort

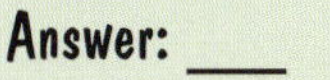

1

No title here. Move on.

Notice all the equipment used by the soldiers.

. . . At times, gas has been known to travel, with dire results, fifteen miles behind the lines.

A gas, or smoke helmet, as it is called, at the best is a vile-smelling thing, and it is not long before one gets a violent headache from wearing it.

Our eighteen-pounders were bursting in No Man's Land, in an effort, by the artillery, to disperse the gas clouds.

The fire step was lined with crouching men, bayonets fixed, and bombs near at hand to repel the expected attack.

Our artillery had put a barrage of curtain fire on the German lines, to try and break up their attack and keep back re-inforcements.

I trained my machine gun on their trench and its bullets were raking the parapet [spraying the wall].

Then over they came, bayonets glistening. In their respirators, which have a large snout in front, they looked like some horrible nightmare. . . .

4

2

— Arthur Empey, "Over the Top," G. P. Putnam's Sons, 1917

3

7 A historian could best use this passage to study which topic of World War I?

(1) events that started the war
(2) impact of combat on civilians
(3) equipment utilized by soldiers
(4) propaganda that supported the war effort

Regents Question Time!

> . . . At times, gas has been known to travel, with dire results, fifteen miles behind the lines.
>
> A gas, or smoke helmet, as it is called, at the best is a vile-smelling thing, and it is not long before one gets a violent headache from wearing it.
>
> Our eighteen-pounders were bursting in No Man's Land, in an effort, by the artillery, to disperse the gas clouds.
>
> The fire step was lined with crouching men, bayonets fixed, and bombs near at hand to repel the expected attack.
>
> Our artillery had put a barrage of curtain fire on the German lines, to try and break up their attack and keep back re-inforcements.
>
> I trained my machine gun on their trench and its bullets were raking the parapet [spraying the wall].
>
> Then over they came, bayonets glistening. In their respirators, which have a large snout in front, they looked like some horrible nightmare. . . .

— Arthur Empey, "Over the Top," G. P. Putnam's Sons, 1917

8 Which claim can best be supported by this passage?

(1) New technology made warfare more destructive.
(2) Warfare had a limited impact on the environment.
(3) Countries engaged in war were punished for their actions.
(4) Illness and disease took many lives.

Answer: ___

1

No title here. Move on.

Advanced warfare caused major damage and death.

. . . At times, gas has been known to travel, with dire results, fifteen miles behind the lines.

A gas, or smoke helmet, as it is called, at the best is a vile-smelling thing, and it is not long before one gets a violent headache from wearing it.

Our eighteen-pounders were bursting in No Man's Land, in an effort, by the artillery, to disperse the gas clouds.

The fire step was lined with crouching men, bayonets fixed, and bombs near at hand to repel the expected attack.

Our artillery had put a barrage of curtain fire on the German lines, to try and break up their attack and keep back re-inforcements.

I trained my machine gun on their trench and its bullets were raking the parapet [spraying the wall].

Then over they came, bayonets glistening. In their respirators, which have a large snout in front, they looked like some horrible nightmare. . . .

2

— Arthur Empey, "Over the Top," G. P. Putnam's Sons, 1917

3

8 Which claim can best be supported by this passage?

(1) New technology made warfare more destructive.
(2) Warfare had a limited impact on the environment.
(3) Countries engaged in war were punished for their actions.
(4) Illness and disease took many lives.

4

UNIT 10

RUSSIAN REVOLUTION & TOTALITARIANISM (1905-1950s)

Russia Under Czarist Rule

Around the world, countries were modernizing and Westernizing. But not Russia. Why?

From the 1500s to the end of the 1900s, the CZARS (Russian kings) ruled Russia and had a lot of power. They abused their power, denied people's rights, and persecuted their subjects. The czars were afraid they'd lose their power if they would modernize.

So the Russian people lived very primitively. The landowning nobles were rich, while the peasants (the poorest social group in Russia) and workers were very poor.

The peasants were unhappy. And they did not stand by quietly...

- **Inequality:** The lower class was very poor and not happy about it.
- **Power:** The Russian czars had absolute power and didn't allow Westernization.

Causes of the Russian Revolution

1. The czar's rule was harsh. He was a total dictator.
2. Peasants were unhappy about the big gap between the rich and the poor.
3. People were poor and food was scarce.
4. The czars enforced a policy of RUSSIFICATION – Russians need to think, act, and believe as Russians. Several ethnic groups living in Russia felt stifled by this idea.
5. BLOODY SUNDAY (1905):
   - The Russians tried to hold a peaceful march to get the czar, CZAR NICHOLAS II, to reform.
   - Czar Nicholas II got scared and ordered his soldiers to kill the protesters.
   - The Russians were furious with him! They made a peaceful protest to encourage reforms and the czar murdered them!
6. The Russian people suffered massive losses in World War I and wanted to leave the war. They had enough problems of their own and weren't interested in fighting a world war. But the czar stayed in the war.

R **Cause and effect:** Czar's harsh rule and Russification ➲ Bloody Sunday ➲ Russian Revolution

E **Scarcity:** Poverty and lack of food led to the Russian Revolution.

E **Ideas and beliefs:** The czars enforced Russification – the Russians had to think, act, and believe as Russians.

The Russian Revolution (1905-1917)

The Russian people revolted.
Czar Nicholas II of the Romanov dynasty was forced to give up power.
He was the last czar to rule in Russia.

A temporary government was set up, but it soon collapsed. This temporary government decided to keep fighting in World War I and didn't implement enough reforms.

- **Cause and effect:** The czar's harsh rule prevents Russia's modernization ➲ Russian Revolution
- **Conflict:** A conflict between the czar's rule and the Russian people's desire to modernize led to the Russian Revolution.

Czar Nicholas II

The Bolshevik Revolution (1917)

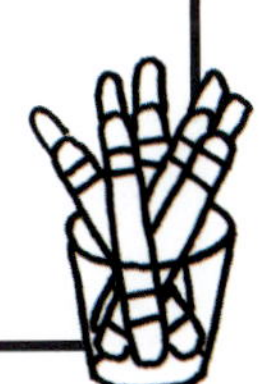

Vladimir Lenin

Leon Trotsky

VLADIMIR LENIN and **LEON TROTSKY** started a revolutionary group called **THE BOLSHEVIKS**, also known as **THE REDS**.

The Bolsheviks promised: "**PEACE, BREAD, AND LAND**"

- Peace: We'll pull Russia out of World War I.
- Bread: We'll end poverty.
- Land: We'll make sure the peasants get land.

- They called their political party **COMMUNIST**.
  They used Karl Marx's ideas as the basis of their movement, but adapted these ideas.

R There are many Regents questions on this topic.

E **Ideas and beliefs:** Lenin and Trotsky spread and implemented communist beliefs.

Lenin & Communism

Lenin and his communist party overthrew the temporary government and took over.

<u>Lenin modified Karl Marx's theory</u>:

1. He believed that a small group of party members could lead a country to communist equality.
2. He felt Russia needed a "temporary dictatorship."

Lenin, the dictator

<u>Lenin's Rule</u>:

1. The USSR withdrew from World War I. It signed the Treaty of Brest-Litovsk, which gave some of its land to Germany, but allowed it to leave the war.
2. Lenin gave land to the peasants.
3. Industries were NATIONALIZED – taken over by the government.
4. Lenin established strict military rule with secret police.

Lenin established a TOTALITARIAN/AUTOCRATIC government – where one ruler completely controls the people. Many Russian leaders followed in this path.

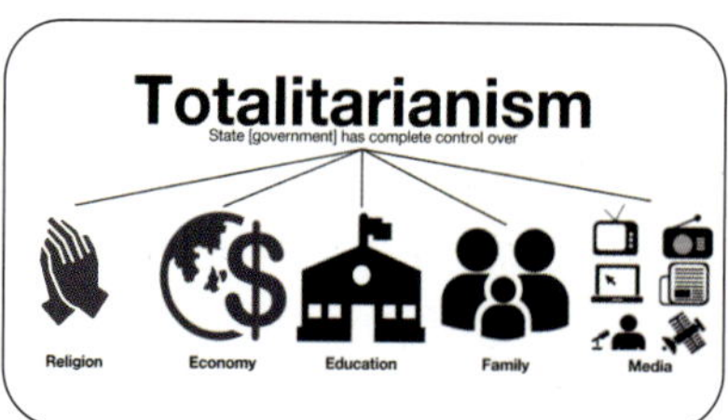

HINT: <u>Total</u>itarian – <u>total</u>. The leader has <u>total</u> control over the people.

Civil War in Russia (1918-1921)

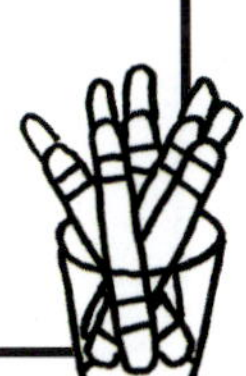

Some people agreed with Lenin and liked his ideas. Others wanted czarist rule to continue.

A civil war broke out.

- The REDS: Lenin's supporters
- The WHITES: Lenin's opponents, who were still loyal to the czar

The communists had murdered Czar Nicholas II and his family to end czarist rule. Both sides used brutal war tactics, causing many casualties.

FYI: Western countries joined to help the Whites, but this just increased Russian nationalism.

In the end, the REDS, Lenin's supporters, won.

- They changed Russia's name to USSR (Union of Soviet Socialist Republics), also known as the SOVIET UNION.

Lenin seized power from the czar and got rid of anyone who didn't agree with him.

USSR symbol

The New Economic Policy (N.E.P.)

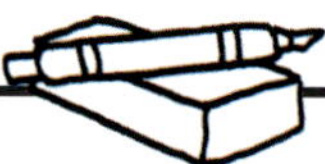

Lenin and his communist party took control of all factories, trade, and banks.

But the economy was suffering. Peasants weren't producing enough food because they were scared that the communist government would take control of it.

So Lenin instituted the **NEW ECONOMIC POLICY:** there can be some privately owned small factories and agricultural companies.

This new policy helped the Russian economy recover.

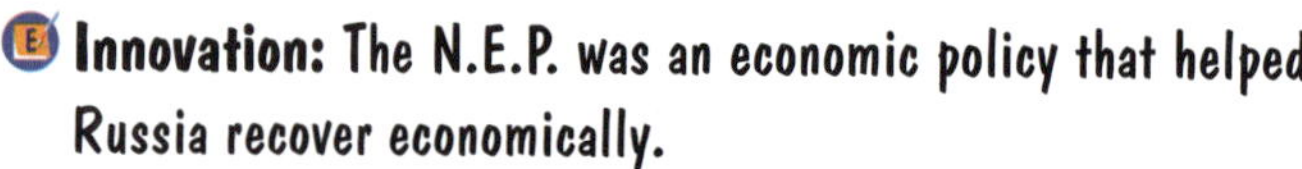

Innovation: The N.E.P. was an economic policy that helped Russia recover economically.

Stalin and Communist Russia

Lenin died in 1924.
JOSEPH STALIN seized power and continued COMMUNIST rule.

Stalin

Stalin's leadership:

- Stalin ran a totalitarian government, where the government controlled every detail of life with secret police and strict censorship of speech, media, music, and art. The purpose of all media was to praise communism.
- Communist leaders killed, exiled, or jailed anyone they suspected of not being fully loyal to communism. Stalin ruled with terror and cruelty. People lived in total fear of the police. If Russian citizens would disobey the government, they would be killed or sent to SIBERIA – a frigid slave camp where millions of people died.
  - The GREAT PURGE (1936–1938): Stalin accused thousands of people of not being loyal to communism and punished them harshly.
- Stalin glorified himself in Russia. He named streets and cities after himself, placed statues and pictures of himself all over the country, and made schoolchildren learn about his greatness.

R There are many Regents questions on this topic.

E **Power:** Stalin abused his power and was a cruel ruler who terrorized and killed millions of Russian citizens.

E **Human Rights Violations:** In the Great Purge, Stalin punished thousands of people for not being loyal to communism.

Command Economy

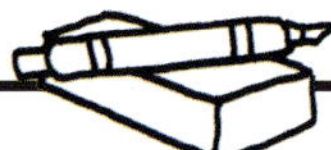

Stalin instituted a COMMAND ECONOMY, where the government controlled all aspects of the economy.

HINT: In a command economy, the government commands how all aspects of the economy should run.

Command Economy:

- The government owns all businesses.
- The government makes economic decisions.
- The government plans the economy.
- The economy is focused on industrial growth.

The Soviet Union (Russia) was the first to institute a command economy. Later, other communist countries adopted command economies as well.

HINT: Communist countries use a command economy. COMMUNIST economy = COMMAND economy

Ideas and beliefs: A command economy was a new economic idea.

Stalin's Policies

FIVE-YEAR PLAN:

Stalin instituted a five-year plan to help the Russian economy. He set up a five-year quota to help Russia industrialize quickly.

- He transformed Russia's economy from AGRICULTURAL to INDUSTRIAL.
- He created huge factories, but these did not produce consumer goods (goods needed for consumers).
  - They produced massive amounts of oil, steel, coal, military goods.
  - They built power stations and railroads.
- The five-year plan did succeed in making the Soviet Union a major world industrial power.
- Despite the economic efforts, the Russians remained poor.

R Stalin's Five-Year Plan is often compared to Chinese modernizations.

Collective farm

COLLECTIVIZATION:

Stalin took privately owned land and combined it into huge government land plots.
He forced the peasants to give up their land and move to the COLLECTIVES – government-owned plots.

- Whoever disobeyed didn't get food. Many peasants resisted the collectives, and died of starvation. Millions of people died.
- In Soviet Ukraine, the people resisted Stalin's plan. 5 million people died from hunger! This became known as the HOLODOMOR (death by hunger)genocide.
- Feeding so many people in the collectives was a huge problem.

E **Scarcity:** The Five-Year Plan and collectivization led to a major food shortage in Russia.

E **Human Rights Violation:** Stalin starved or murdered people who disobeyed him.

HINT: Collectivization: collect. The government collected all the small plots of land into a huge piece of government-owned land.

Quick Review

Check off the boxes you know well. Whatever you don't know well (yet!), go back and review now!

- ☐ Russians unhappy with czarist rule
- ☐ Bloody Sunday
- ☐ Russian Revolution of 1905 – Czar Nicholas II gives up power
- ☐ Russia pulls out of World War I
- ☐ Bolshevik Revolution (1917)
- ☐ Lenin, Trotsky – Communism
- ☐ Russian Civil War – Reds and Whites
- ☐ New Economic Policy (Lenin)
- ☐ Stalin
  - Communism/totalitarianism
  - The Great Purge
  - Collectivization
  - Five-Year Plan
  - Command economy

Enduring Issues Essay Topics That Came Up in This Unit:

- **Power:**
  - The czars abused their power and didn't allow Russia to modernize.
  - The communists abused their power by terrorizing their subjects through strict military rule and secret police.
  - Stalin abused his power and ruled with cruelty, killing anyone who didn't accept his beliefs.
- **Inequality:**
  - Russian peasants and workers were very poor and had very little power during czarist rule.
- **Conflict:**
  - Blood Sunday, Russian Revolution of 1905, Bolshevik Revolution, civil war in Russia
- **Scarcity:**
  - Poverty and food shortages led to the Russian Revolution of 1905 and the Bolshevik Revolution.
  - Scarcity of food led Lenin to create the New Economic Policy.
  - The Five-Year Plan and collectivization led to food shortages.
- **Ideas and Beliefs:**
  - Russification – Russians need to think, act, and believe as Russians
  - Communism and command economy
  - New Economic Policy
- **Human Rights Violation:** The Great Purge and Stalin's rule

Regents Question Time!

Now it's time to test how well you know your stuff.

Have fun!

Regents Question Time!

Source: Philip Dorf, *Visualized World History*, Oxford Book Company

*Tsar – Czar

9 Which point of view is expressed in this illustration?

(1) The Russian Orthodox Church caused the fall of the Romanov dynasty.

(2) The Russian government encouraged a diversity of opinions.

(3) The Romanovs suppressed Enlightenment ideas within their empire.

(4) The Russian Revolution made conditions worse for most minorities.

Answer: ___

1

THE ROMANOVS MAINTAIN THE OLD RÉGIME IN RUSSIA

The title here is "The Romanovs Maintain the Old Regime in Russia." Note: Sometimes the title is found at the bottom of the document.

This Russian regime blocks out liberalism and democratic ideas and promotes its own agenda (orthodoxy, autocracy – absolute power of one leader, Pan-Slavism – the movement to unite all the Slavic people).

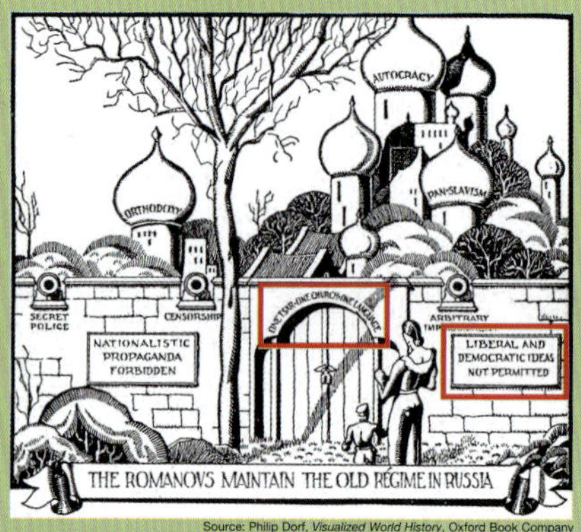

*Tsar – Czar

Source: Philip Dorf, *Visualized World History*, Oxford Book Company

4

2

Source: Philip Dorf, *Visualized World History*, Oxford Book Company

3

9 Which point of view is expressed in this illustration?

(1) The Russian Orthodox Church caused the fall of the Romanov dynasty.

(2) The Russian government encouraged a diversity of opinions.

(3) The Romanovs suppressed Enlightenment ideas within their empire.

(4) The Russian Revolution made conditions worse for most minorities.

EdBoosters™

Regents Question Time!

Source: Philip Dorf, *Visualized World History*, Oxford Book Company

*Tsar – Czar

10 Which long-term historical circumstance about Russia is shown in this illustration?

(1) appeal of Marxism to the Russian nobles
(2) autocratic rule of Russian royalty
(3) rejection of the Pan-Slavism movement
(4) support of the Russian Orthodox Church for democratic ideals

Answer: ___

1

THE ROMANOVS MAINTAIN THE OLD RÉGIME IN RUSSIA

The title here is "The Romanovs Maintain the Old Regime in Russia." Note: Sometimes the title is found at the bottom of the document.

This Russian regime blocks out liberalism and democratic ideas and promotes its own agenda (orthodoxy, autocracy – absolute power of one leader, Pan-Slavism – the movement to unite all the Slavic people).

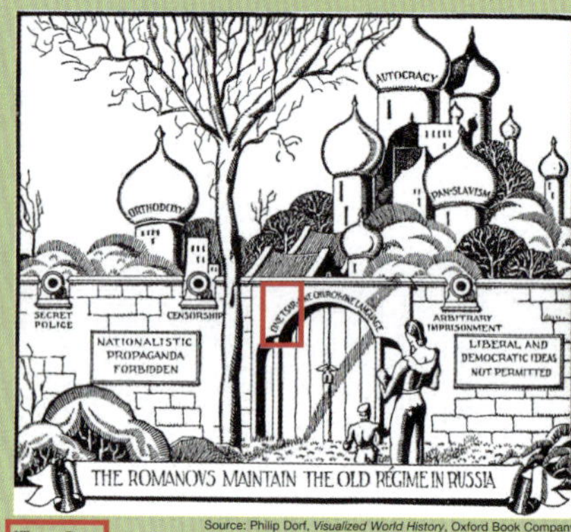

Source: Philip Dorf, *Visualized World History*, Oxford Book Company

*Tsar – Czar

4

2

Source: Philip Dorf, *Visualized World History*, Oxford Book Company

3

10 Which long-term historical circumstance about Russia is shown in this illustration?

(1) appeal of Marxism to the Russian nobles
(2) autocratic rule of Russian royalty
(3) rejection of the Pan-Slavism movement
(4) support of the Russian Orthodox Church for democratic ideals

Autocracy means a system of government by one person with absolute power.

EdBoosters

UNIT 11

BETWEEN THE WORLD WARS (1918-1939)

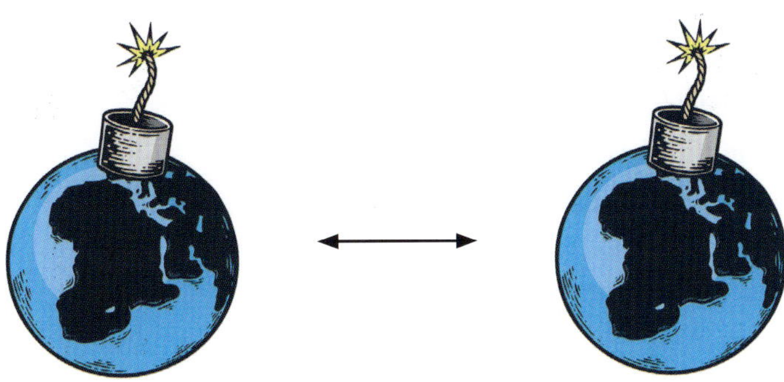

National Movements Between the World Wars

A few years after World War I, World War II broke out.
What was happening during the years in between the wars?

Lots of nationalism!
Nationalistic feelings spread contagiously from one country to the next.

- Countries in the Middle East, Africa, and Asia fought for self-determination (self-government).
- These countries were influenced by the West but wanted to get rid of Western rule.

Turkish Nationalism

KEMEL ATATURK was the general and hero in Turkey who led the nationalistic movement and made Turkey a republic.

Ataturk modernized and Westernized Turkey:

1. New law system based on European models (instead of Islamic law)
2. Western dress, calendar, and education
3. Women can vote and don't need to wear veils.
4. Industrialization: roads, railroads, factories

- Ataturk was a dictator who arrested critics, censored media, and persecuted minorities, such as the Armenians.

R There are many Regents questions about Ataturk's modernizations.

R The Regents often compares Ataturk to Emperor Meiji from Japan, and Raza Pahlavi from Iran.

Innovation: Ataturk modernized and Westernized Turkey. This led to many positive impacts (see above). On the flip side, many Muslims resented Ataturk's rule because he secularized Turkey (made Turkey less religious). Note the conflict between modernization and traditionalism.

HINT: Ataturk led Turkey's nationalistic movement.

Arab Nationalism

After World War I, Britain and France divided the Ottoman empire into MANDATES – territories controlled by the Europeans.

In the 1920s and 1930s, Arab nationalists wanted self-government.

They started PAN ARABISM: a movement to create unity between all Arabs.

Heads up: This will create much future conflict and lead to Arab-Israeli wars.

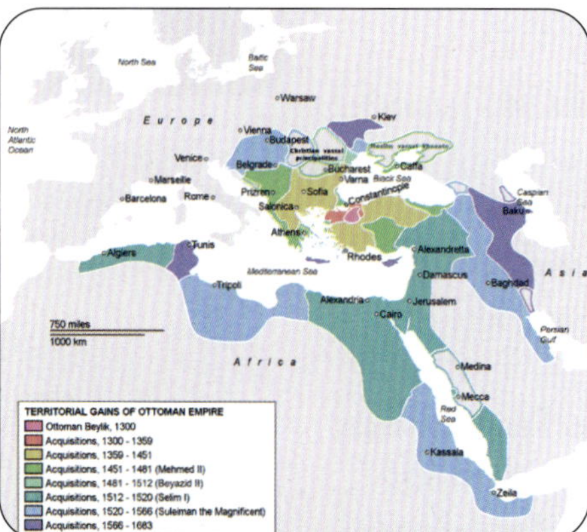

Ottoman Empire Mandates

Unity among Arabs

Indian Nationalism

The Indians were feeling nationalistic and wanted independence from Great Britain.

AMRITSAR MASSACRE (1919):

- The British made a rule that Indians cannot gather in public.
- But the Indians gathered in Amritsar anyway. The British fired on the crowd and killed many Indians.
- The Indians were furious and wanted their independence from Great Britain.

R **Cause and effect:** Amritsar Massacre ➲ Fuels independence movements in India

E **Power, Conflict, Inequality:** The British imperialized India and exerted power over them. The Indians resisted the British influence, which led to the Amritsar Massacre.

Mohandas Gandhi & Indian Nationalism

MOHANDAS GANDHI headed the Indian nationalistic movement and dedicated himself to helping India gain independence from Britain. Mohandas Gandhi encouraged **CIVIL DISOBEDIENCE** – nonviolent/passive refusal to obey unjust rules.

HINT: Civil disobedience: They disobeyed in a civil way.

Nonviolent Campaign Protests Against Britain:

1. **HOMESPUN CLOTHING MOVEMENT:**
   Gandhi encouraged people to spin clothing at home.
   Gandhi told them to **BOYCOTT** (stop buying) British goods. He wanted them to become less dependent on Britain and more independent.
2. **SALT MARCH:**
   Gandhi led a march for hundreds of miles to produce salt from seawater to avoid Britain's tax on salt.
   FYI: The march lasted 25 days.
   Britain arrested Gandhi and many other Indians.
3. Gandhi went on many hunger strikes as a means of nonviolent protest.
   FYI: He fasted 17 times, and his longest fast was 21 days.

One year later, in 1947, India received its independence. Five months later, Gandhi was assassinated.

Mohandas Gandhi

Regents Alert!

The Regents is obsessed with asking about Gandhi and his civil disobedience practices. There are plenty of questions on this topic in every section of the Regents.

- **Ideas and Beliefs:** Gandhi's civil disobedience philosophy
- **Conflict:** British imperialism vs. India's anti-imperialism campaign
- **Human Rights Violations:** Gandhi led a major campaign to end the human rights violations the Indian people were experiencing.

Women's Suffrage (1920s)

During World War I, women showed that they were able to contribute to society by taking over men's jobs. As modernization progressed, women demanded SUFFRAGE rights – rights to vote. Many countries began to allow women to vote:

ex New Zealand, Britain, United States, Canada, Finland, Germany, Sweden

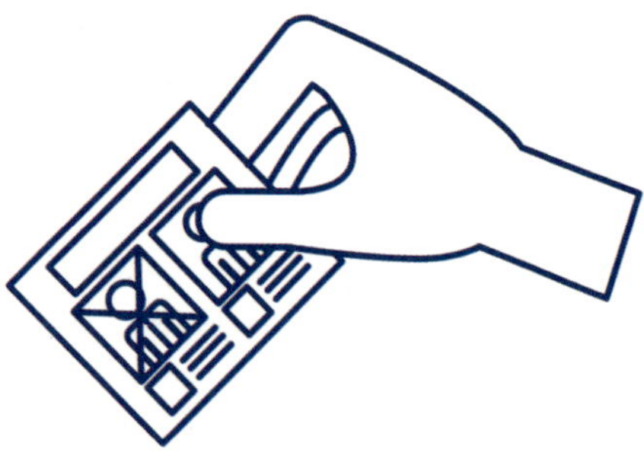

- **Inequality:** Women felt they were being treated unequally because they weren't allowed to vote. Suffrage rights corrected that inequality.
- **Interconnectedness:** The concept of women's suffrage caught on in many places around the world.

Japanese Nationalism & Militarism (1920s-1930s)

Japan became militaristic and aggressive and imperialized other countries.
Japan invaded China to take over Manchuria for natural resources. The League of Nations tried stopping Japan, but Japan ignored them and withdrew from the League.
Then, Japan teamed up with Germany. (Bad news!)

R Japan imperializes ➲ Japan invades China ➲ Japan teams up with Germany ➲ This leads to World War II!

E **Power and Conflict:** Japan uses its power to imperialize, which leads to conflict.

The Great Depression (1929-1930s)

The US stock market crashed, which caused the US economy to crash.

- A domino effect ensued, and the whole world economy took a plunge. For the next decade, millions of people were out of jobs!
- America was loaning money to Germany to pay war reparations. Now that America was experiencing the Great Depression, it asked for the money back.
- Germany couldn't repay its loans. So the German economy plummeted (fell).
- Angry and fearful Germans began to seek answers from Fascist leaders who gave them scapegoats and aggressive solutions.

Cause and effect: The Great Depression ➲ Germany's economy plummets ➲ World War II

Scarcity: The Great Depression led to scarcity (shortages) all over the world. Germany was hit hard, and this eventually led to World War II.

Interconnectedness: Economies all over the world are interconnected. The Great Depression in the United States affected countries all over the world.

The Rise of Fascism

FASCISM: a form of totalitarianism in which a nationalistic dictator rules the people

Fascism is characterized by:

- Blind loyalty to the leader
- Extreme militarism, strict discipline
- Belief in absolutism (the acceptance of the leader's absolute principles) and imperialism
- Strong nationalism
- Government **CENSORSHIP** (prohibition of media that opposes the beliefs of the government)
- Aggression that squashes people's feelings and beliefs and basic civil rights are denied
- **PROPAGANDA:** information (often biased) used to promote or publicize a point of view and influence people's thoughts and behaviors.

Fascism started in Germany and Italy.

Ⓡ There are many Regents questions on this topic.

Ⓡ **Turning Point:** Fascism leads to brutal rulership.

Ⓔ **Power:** Fascism promotes absolute power.

Ⓔ **Ideas and Beliefs:** Fascism

Ⓔ **Interconnectedness:** Fascism spreads.

Fascism in Italy – Mussolini

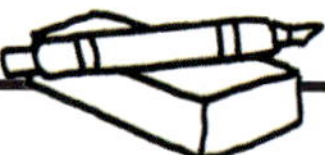

Italy was a mess after World War I. It lost land in treaties and was experiencing high unemployment.

BENITO MUSSOLINI took advantage of the situation, gained power, and became a fascist leader.

- He used violence and terror to gain control.
- He abolished freedom of speech, freedom of the press, and democratic elections.

Italy became a TOTALITARIAN state (dictatorship).

Benito Mussolini

R **Cause and effect:** Italy's weakness after World War I ➲ Mussolini and a totalitarian state

E **Power:** Fascism/totalitarianism

HINT: Mussolini – muscle: Mussolini used "muscle"/violence in his fascist rulership.

Fascism in Germany — Hitler

After World War I, the WEIMAR REPUBLIC (a very weak government) ruled. Germany was in ruins:

- Economically — because of INFLATION (money loses value, so prices rise) and because of the effects of the Great Depression
- Emotionally — because of the unfair terms in the Treaty of Versailles

ADOLF HITLER took advantage of Germany's poor economy and weak government and rose to power.

Adolf Hitler

Hitler promised to rebuild German pride. He called Germany the SUPERIOR RACE and created a nationalistic party called the NAZI PARTY.

Power: Fascism/totalitarianism

Hitler Writes Mein Kampf (1925)

Germany put Hitler in jail.
There, he wrote the book MEIN KAMPF, which means "my struggle."

Main Ideas of *Mein Kampf*:

- The "Third Reich" (Nazi regime) should rule for 1,000 years.
- The ARYAN RACE (Indo-European people) is superior and everyone else is inferior.
- Anyone who is inferior should be killed.
- The book was packed with hate, ANTI-SEMITISM (hostility toward Jews), and encouragement to annihilate non-Aryans, specifically the Jews.

Hitler's ideas spread quickly because of this book.

R This is an example of how a written work influenced world history.
R **Cause and effect:** *Mein Kampf* ➲ Nazi Regime ➲ World War II
E **Ideas and Beliefs:** Hitler spreads his anti-Semitic ideas with *Mein Kampf*.

Hitler Becomes the German Fuhrer (1933)

After Hitler's release from jail, he was appointed the chancellor of Germany.

- Hitler made himself the DICTATOR (ruler with total power) of Germany.
- He called himself FUHRER ("leader" in German).
- He replaced all German political parties with the Nazi party.
- He was a very powerful speaker and his speeches caused thousands to support his ideas.
- He used propaganda very well to brainwash Germans into thinking that he's a god and that all problems were caused by other races, mainly the Jews.
- Germany became a totalitarian country called the THIRD REICH.

Nazi Regime (1930s)

Hitler's political party was called the **NAZI REGIME.**

<u>The Nazi regime</u>:

- Ended civil rights
- Put businesses under government control
- Rebuilt the military
- Committed human rights violations
- Established anti-Semitic policies:
  - Boycotting Jewish businesses
  - Confiscating Jewish property
  - Enacting the **NUREMBERG LAWS OF 1935** which stripped the Jews of political rights
  - Creating the **HITLER YOUTH** group, which brainwashed children and teens to hate and discriminate against any non-Aryan

Anti-Semitism

Ⓡ **Human Rights Violations:** Nazi regime's anti-Semitic policies

Quick Review

Check off the boxes you know well. Whatever you don't know well (yet!), go back and review now!

- ☐ Turkish nationalism – Kemel Ataturk
- ☐ Arab nationalism – Pan Arabism
- ☐ Indian nationalism
    - Amritsar Massacre
    - Mohandas Gandhi
        - Civil disobedience, passive aggression
        - Salt March, hunger strikes
- ☐ Fascism
    - Mussolini in Italy
    - Hitler in Germany
        - Mein Kampf
        - Nazi Regime

Enduring Issues Essay Topics That Came Up in This Unit:

- **Power:**
  - British imperialism in India
  - Nazi regime abuses its power and mistreats minorities.
- **Conflict:** Amritsar Massacre
- **Scarcity/Interconnectedness:** The Great Depression leads to economic problems worldwide, specifically in Germany.
- **Ideas and Beliefs:** Gandhi spreads the idea of civil disobedience.
  - Fascism, totalitarianism
  - Anti-Semitism/Hitler/Mein Kampf
- **Human Rights Violations:** Nazi regime and anti-Semitism

Regents Question Time!

Now it's time to test how well you know your stuff.

Have fun!

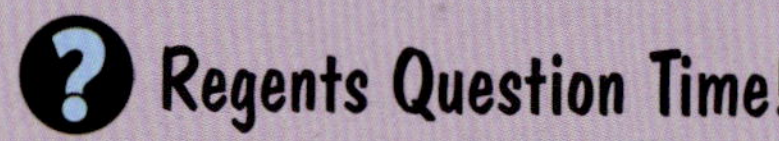

Regents Question Time!

BOMBAY, SUNDAY

The great test has come for "Mahatma" Gandhi, the Indian Nationalist leader, in his efforts to obtain the complete independence of India from British rule. Wading into the sea this morning at Dandi, the lonely village on the Arabian Sea shore, Gandhi and his followers broke the salt monopoly laws and so inaugurated the campaign of mass civil disobedience. There was no interference by the authorities, although a detachment of 150 police officers had been drafted into Dandi and a further force of 400 police was at Jalalpur.

The actual breaking of the salt monopoly law was witnessed by a large crowd who gathered at the seashore. Surrounded by about 100 volunteers—including those who had made the 200-mile march from Ahmedabad,—Gandhi waded into the sea and bathed. Pots were then filled with seawater and boiled or left in the sunshine and the salt residue sprinkled on the ground. Gandhi was hailed by Mrs. Sarojini Naidu, the Indian poetess, as "the lawbreaker." . . .

— *The Manchester Guardian,* April 7, 1930

12 The actions taken by Gandhi and his followers, as described in this excerpt, are examples of

(1) political espionage
(2) economic terrorism
(3) collective bargaining
(4) nonviolent resistance

Answer: ____

1

BOMBAY, SUNDAY

Gandhi arranged the Salt March, which was a way to get what he wanted (to stop paying taxes on salt) without breaking the law.

BOMBAY, SUNDAY

The great test has come for "Mahatma" Gandhi, the Indian Nationalist leader, in his efforts to obtain the complete independence of India from British rule. Wading into the sea this morning at Dandi, the lonely village on the Arabian Sea shore, Gandhi and his followers broke the salt monopoly laws and so inaugurated the campaign of mass civil disobedience. There was no interference by the authorities, although a detachment of 150 police officers had been drafted into Dandi and a further force of 400 police was at Jalalpur.

The actual breaking of the salt monopoly law was witnessed by a large crowd who gathered at the seashore. Surrounded by about 100 volunteers—including those who had made the 200-mile march from Ahmedabad,—Gandhi waded into the sea and bathed. Pots were then filled with seawater and boiled or left in the sunshine and the salt residue sprinkled on the ground. Gandhi was hailed by Mrs. Sarojini Naidu, the Indian poetess, as "the lawbreaker." . . .

4

2

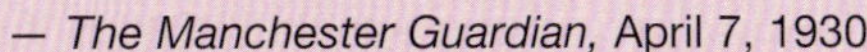

— *The Manchester Guardian,* April 7, 1930

3

12 The actions taken by Gandhi and his followers, as described in this excerpt, are examples of

This is a very straightforward question. You probably know the answer even before you read the document!

(1) political espionage
(2) economic terrorism
(3) collective bargaining
(4) nonviolent resistance

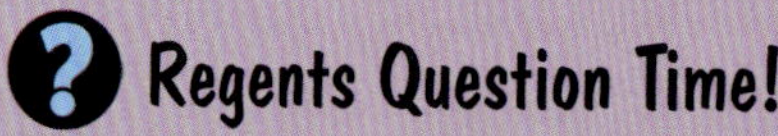

BOMBAY, SUNDAY

The great test has come for "Mahatma" Gandhi, the Indian Nationalist leader, in his efforts to obtain the complete independence of India from British rule. Wading into the sea this morning at Dandi, the lonely village on the Arabian Sea shore, Gandhi and his followers broke the salt monopoly laws and so inaugurated the campaign of mass civil disobedience. There was no interference by the authorities, although a detachment of 150 police officers had been drafted into Dandi and a further force of 400 police was at Jalalpur.

The actual breaking of the salt monopoly law was witnessed by a large crowd who gathered at the seashore. Surrounded by about 100 volunteers—including those who had made the 200-mile march from Ahmedabad,—Gandhi waded into the sea and bathed. Pots were then filled with seawater and boiled or left in the sunshine and the salt residue sprinkled on the ground. Gandhi was hailed by Mrs. Sarojini Naidu, the Indian poetess, as "the lawbreaker." . . .

— *The Manchester Guardian,* April 7, 1930

13 Which statement best summarizes the effects actions like those expressed in this excerpt had on India?

(1) International support for British colonial rule in India grew.
(2) The call for Indian self-government was abandoned.
(3) Separatist movements in India ended the fear of oppression.
(4) British control of India gradually weakened and ended.

Answer: ____

1

BOMBAY, SUNDAY

The Salt March succeeded in helping the Indians resist British control.

BOMBAY, SUNDAY

The great test has come for "Mahatma" Gandhi, the Indian Nationalist leader, in his efforts to obtain the complete independence of India from British rule. Wading into the sea this morning at Dandi, the lonely village on the Arabian Sea shore, Gandhi and his followers broke the salt monopoly laws and so inaugurated the campaign of mass civil disobedience. There was no interference by the authorities, although a detachment of 150 police officers had been drafted into Dandi and a further force of 400 police was at Jalalpur.

The actual breaking of the salt monopoly law was witnessed by a large crowd who gathered at the seashore. Surrounded by about 100 volunteers—including those who had made the 200-mile march from Ahmedabad,—Gandhi waded into the sea and bathed. Pots were then filled with seawater and boiled or left in the sunshine and the salt residue sprinkled on the ground. Gandhi was hailed by Mrs. Sarojini Naidu, the Indian poetess, as "the lawbreaker." . . .

4

2

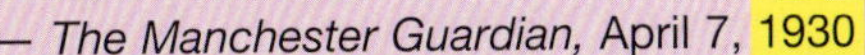

— *The Manchester Guardian,* April 7, 1930

3

13 Which statement best summarizes the effects actions like those expressed in this excerpt had on India?

The question is asking about the EFFECTS of civil disobedience.

(1) International support for British colonial rule in India grew.
(2) The call for Indian self-government was abandoned.
(3) Separatist movements in India ended the fear of oppression.
(4) British control of India gradually weakened and ended.

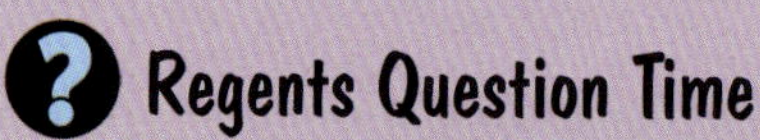

Atatürk's Fashion Police

Turkey's restrictions on wearing overtly religious-oriented attire are rooted in the founding of the modern, secular Turkish state, when the republic's founding father, Mustafa Kemal Atatürk, introduced a series of clothing regulations designed to keep religious symbolism out of the civil service. The regulations were part of a sweeping series of reforms that altered virtually every aspect of Turkish life—from the civil code to the alphabet to education to social integration of the sexes.

The Western dress code at that time, though, was aimed at men. The fez—the short, conical, red-felt cap that had been in vogue [fashion] in Turkey since the Ottoman Sultan Mahmud II made it part of the official national attire in 1826—was banished. Atatürk himself famously adopted a Panama hat to accent his Western-style gray linen suit, shirt, and tie when he toured the country in the summer of 1925 to sell his new ideas to a deeply conservative population. That autumn, the Hat Law of 1925 was passed, making European-style men's headwear de rigueur [fashionable] and punishing fez-wearers with lengthy sentences of imprisonment at hard labor, and even a few hangings. . . .

— Roff Smith, "Why Turkey Lifted Its Ban on the Islamic Headscarf,"
National Geographic, October 12, 2013

21 According to this article by Roff Smith, the goal of Atatürk's reforms was to

(1) prevent the elimination of the civil service system

(2) implement a legal system based on religious teachings

(3) revive Turkey's interest in Ottoman-era customs

(4) modernize Turkey in the image of European nations

Answer: ___

Atatürk's Fashion Police

Ataturk did not allow the Turkish people to wear religious clothing because he was trying to establish a modern state.

Turkey's restrictions on wearing overtly religious-oriented attire are rooted in the founding of the modern, secular Turkish state, when the republic's founding father, Mustafa Kemal Atatürk, introduced a series of clothing regulations designed to keep religious symbolism out of the civil service. The regulations were part of a sweeping series of reforms that altered virtually every aspect of Turkish life—from the civil code to the alphabet to education to social integration of the sexes.

The Western dress code at that time, though, was aimed at men. The fez—the short, conical, red-felt cap that had been in vogue [fashion] in Turkey since the Ottoman Sultan Mahmud II made it part of the official national attire in 1826—was banished. Atatürk himself famously adopted a Panama hat to accent his Western-style gray linen suit, shirt, and tie when he toured the country in the summer of 1925 to sell his new ideas to a deeply conservative population. That autumn, the Hat Law of 1925 was passed, making European-style men's headwear de rigueur [fashionable] and punishing fez-wearers with lengthy sentences of imprisonment at hard labor, and even a few hangings. . . .

— Roff Smith, "Why Turkey Lifted Its Ban on the Islamic Headscarf," *National Geographic*, October 12, 2013

You can probably answer this question already!

21 According to this article by Roff Smith, the goal of Atatürk's reforms was to

(1) prevent the elimination of the civil service system
(2) implement a legal system based on religious teachings
(3) revive Turkey's interest in Ottoman-era customs
(4) modernize Turkey in the image of European nations

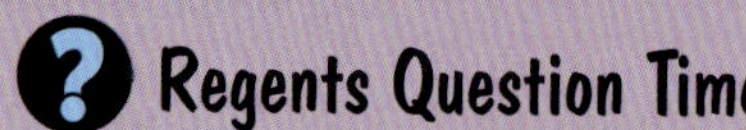

Atatürk's Fashion Police

> Turkey's restrictions on wearing overtly religious-oriented attire are rooted in the founding of the modern, secular Turkish state, when the republic's founding father, Mustafa Kemal Atatürk, introduced a series of clothing regulations designed to keep religious symbolism out of the civil service. The regulations were part of a sweeping series of reforms that altered virtually every aspect of Turkish life—from the civil code to the alphabet to education to social integration of the sexes.
>
> The Western dress code at that time, though, was aimed at men. The fez—the short, conical, red-felt cap that had been in vogue [fashion] in Turkey since the Ottoman Sultan Mahmud II made it part of the official national attire in 1826—was banished. Atatürk himself famously adopted a Panama hat to accent his Western-style gray linen suit, shirt, and tie when he toured the country in the summer of 1925 to sell his new ideas to a deeply conservative population. That autumn, the Hat Law of 1925 was passed, making European-style men's headwear de rigueur [fashionable] and punishing fez-wearers with lengthy sentences of imprisonment at hard labor, and even a few hangings. . . .

— Roff Smith, "Why Turkey Lifted Its Ban on the Islamic Headscarf," *National Geographic,* October 12, 2013

22 The phrases "deeply conservative population," "lengthy sentences of imprisonment," and "a few hangings" suggest that

(1) Atatürk's reforms were eagerly embraced throughout Turkey
(2) tensions existed between reformers and traditionalists in Turkey
(3) the policy of westernization was abandoned by the Turkish government
(4) most Turks preferred punishment to rapid change

Answer: ____

1

Atatürk's Fashion Police

Fashion Police – this title suggests that there was a conflict about clothing and therefore police were needed.

Turkey's restrictions on wearing overtly religious-oriented attire are rooted in the founding of the modern, secular Turkish state, when the republic's founding father, Mustafa Kemal Atatürk, introduced a series of clothing regulations designed to keep religious symbolism out of the civil service. The regulations were part of a sweeping series of reforms that altered virtually every aspect of Turkish life—from the civil code to the alphabet to education to social integration of the sexes.

The Western dress code at that time, though, was aimed at men. The fez—the short, conical, red-felt cap that had been in vogue [fashion] in Turkey since the Ottoman Sultan Mahmud II made it part of the official national attire in 1826—was banished. Atatürk himself famously adopted a Panama hat to accent his Western-style gray linen suit, shirt, and tie when he toured the country in the summer of 1925 to sell his new ideas to a deeply conservative population. That autumn, the Hat Law of 1925 was passed, making European-style men's headwear de rigueur [fashionable] and punishing fez-wearers with lengthy sentences of imprisonment at hard labor, and even a few hangings. . . .

2

— Roff Smith, "Why Turkey Lifted Its Ban on the Islamic Headscarf," *National Geographic*, October 12, 2013

3

22 The phrases "deeply conservative population," "lengthy sentences of imprisonment," and "a few hangings" suggest that

(1) Atatürk's reforms were eagerly embraced throughout Turkey
(2) tensions existed between reformers and traditionalists in Turkey
(3) the policy of westernization was abandoned by the Turkish government
(4) most Turks preferred punishment to rapid change

4

These phrases show that some people resisted the changes and were punished harshly.

Regents Question Time!

For a fortnight Gandhi's march is intended to be only a demonstration. Then, when he expects to be at the sea, he will begin to produce salt from brine [salt water], and so infringe [violate] the Government salt monopoly, defying the Government to arrest and punish him. At the same time his supporters everywhere have been incited by him to refuse to pay local taxes.

— Gandhi's March to the Sea, *The Guardian*, 1930

14 The actions taken by Gandhi reflect his commitment to which policy?

(1) collectivization
(2) religious intolerance
(3) civil disobedience
(4) censorship

Answer: ___

1

No title here. Move on.

Gandhi led a demonstration in which he produced salt from the sea to avoid paying the salt tax to the government.

> For a fortnight Gandhi's march is intended to be only a demonstration. Then, when he expects to be at the sea, he will begin to produce salt from brine [salt water], and so infringe [violate] the Government salt monopoly, defying the Government to arrest and punish him. At the same time his supporters everywhere have been incited by him to refuse to pay local taxes.
>
> – Gandhi's March to the Sea, *The Guardian*, 1930

4

2

The Salt March

3

Which policy did the Salt March reflect?

14 The actions taken by Gandhi reflect his commitment to which policy?

(1) collectivization
(2) religious intolerance
(3) civil disobedience
(4) censorship

Regents Question Time!

For a fortnight Gandhi's march is intended to be only a demonstration. Then, when he expects to be at the sea, he will begin to produce salt from brine [salt water], and so infringe [violate] the Government salt monopoly, defying the Government to arrest and punish him. At the same time his supporters everywhere have been incited by him to refuse to pay local taxes.

— Gandhi's March to the Sea, *The Guardian*, 1930

15 The actions of Gandhi and his supporters, as described in this passage, helped lead to the

(1) banning of Western books and music
(2) removal of British control from the subcontinent
(3) development of an economic alliance for South Asian nations
(4) peaceful partitioning of British India into India and Pakistan

Answer: ___

1

No title here. Move on.

Gandhi and his supporters resisted the British government's taxes in a peaceful way.

> For a fortnight Gandhi's march is intended to be only a demonstration. Then, when he expects to be at the sea, he will begin to produce salt from brine [salt water], and so infringe [violate] the Government salt monopoly, defying the Government to arrest and punish him. At the same time his supporters everywhere have been incited by him to refuse to pay local taxes.

2

The Salt March

— Gandhi's March to the Sea, *The Guardian*, 1930

3

What did the Salt March lead to?

15 The actions of Gandhi and his supporters, as described in this passage, helped lead to the

(1) banning of Western books and music
(2) removal of British control from the subcontinent
(3) development of an economic alliance for South Asian nations
(4) peaceful partitioning of British India into India and Pakistan

4

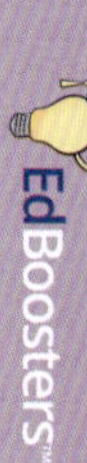

UNIT 12

WORLD WAR II (1939-1945)

Long-Term Causes of World War II

1. Resentment after World War I (Treaty of Versailles)
2. Germany, Italy, and Japan wanted to imperialize and build world empires at the expense of others.
3. Effects of the Great Depression
4. Rise of Fascism (see Unit 9)

R **Cause and effect:** 4 causes listed above ➲ World War II

Short-Term Causes of World War II

1. Hitler violated the Treaty of Versailles:
   - He stopped paying reparations.
   - He built up the German military.
   - He created a union with Austria.

2. Germany invaded the Sudetenland and Czechoslovakia, and annexed Austria.
3. The Japanese army invaded China in a brutal invasion known as the "Rape of Nanjing" (1937). They fought wars and took Chinese territory. No one was able to stop them.
4. Britain and France adopted the POLICY OF APPEASEMENT – they gave in to Japanese and German aggression in order to keep the peace and avoid war.

During the Munich Conference of 1938, Western democracies gave Sudetenland to Hitler.

- The League of Nations was ineffective in stopping German aggression.

HINT: This concept of appeasement is similar to a pacifier. When you give a crying baby a pacifier, you are not solving the problem; you are just stopping the crying.

Countries Form Alliances

Axis Powers:

1. Germany
2. Italy
3. Japan

Allied Powers/Allies:

1. France
2. Britain
3. Soviet Union*
4. China*
5. USA*

*Joined later

HINT: Axes jig (move quickly).

Axes (Axis powers) JIG: acronym for Japan, Italy, Germany

World War II Begins

Great Britain and France promised to protect Poland if Germany would attack.

(1939) Germany invaded Poland in a BLITZKREIG – lightning warfare. They used planes, tanks, and troop carriers to quickly enter the enemy's territory.

Britain declared war on Germany.

HINT: Blitzkrieg: "blitz" means lightning and "krieg" means war. Blitzkrieg means lightning warfare.

World War II (1939-1945)

The Axis Powers used advanced technology in the war – machine guns, atom bombs, improved planes, submarines, and walkie-talkies. This led to massive destruction.

World War II was a TOTAL WAR – it affected everyone and everything.

- An astronomical number of people were killed. Sit down when you read this number: close to 75 million. Wow!
- Civilians were targeted. Cities were bombed.
- Millions of men were drafted into the military.
- Women worked in the factories to produce planes, ships, and ammunition during the war. Women also served as nurses, truck drivers, and message decoders.
- Economies in Europe and Asia plummeted.

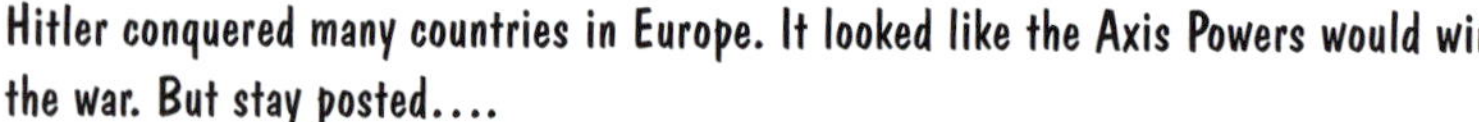

Hitler conquered many countries in Europe. It looked like the Axis Powers would win the war. But stay posted....

Conflict: The war!

Power: Hitler used his power to destroy and exterminate.

Innovation: Tanks, bombs, blitzkrieg, and new ammunition are used to fight the war, leading to massive destruction.

Environmental impact: Cities were destroyed in World War II.

The Holocaust

Hitler considered the Aryan race superior to all the other nations and wanted to destroy anyone "inferior." He targeted Jews, Slavs, Gypsies, and disabled people.

- He passed the **NUREMBERG LAWS** (1935) which stripped all Jews of citizenship, forced them to wear a yellow star badge at all times, and banned them from many jobs.

- **KRISTALLNACHT** (1938): The Nazis organized a massive pogrom (violent riot) against the Jews, destroying hundreds of Jewish synagogues, businesses, hospitals, and homes.

Yellow star the Jews were forced to wear

Kristallnacht

Hitler introduced **THE FINAL SOLUTION**, a plan to murder every Jew on earth.

GENOCIDE is an attempt to destroy an entire ethnic group or religion. The **HOLOCAUST** was Nazi German's genocide of Jews during World War II.

- Hitler forced the Jews to live in **GHETTOS** (poor, crowded sections of cities) and imposed curfews on them.

- He set up concentration camps and other brutal killing methods to exterminate the Jews.

HINT: "Kristallnacht" means "night of glass," referring to the glass windows broken during the pogrom.

Swastika – Nazi Symbol

The Holocaust – Concentration Camps

Concentration camp

CONCENTRATION CAMPS: The Nazis built labor and death camps in which millions of Jews were tortured and killed in the cruelest ways.

- Millions of Jews were killed in the **GAS CHAMBERS**, enclosed chambers filled with deadly gas.
- **CREMATORIA:** The Nazis burned the bodies of their Jewish victims in massive ovens that had to burn all day and night to accommodate the victims.
- The Nazis performed inhumane medical experiments on Jews, such as testing lethal drugs on them, freezing people, injecting chemicals into children's eyes to change eye color, amputations, cold water immersion experiments, and removing organs for dissections.
- **MASS SHOOTINGS:** The Nazis commanded hundreds of Jews to line up and give up all their valuables. They told them to dig their own mass graves and then shot them all.
- **DEATH MARCHES:** The Nazis forced starving and sickly Jews to march for days at a time, often in the freezing snow, without food, shelter, or proper shoes and clothing. Anyone caught lagging was shot and killed. Many died along the way from starvation and exhaustion.

A few individuals helped some Jews escape the persecution.
But most of the world turned a blind eye.

E **Human Rights Violations:** The Nazis persecuted and killed the Jews and other minorities in the cruelest ways.

FYI: Auschwitz and Bergen-Belsen were famous concentration camps.

Turning Point – The United States Enters the War (1941)

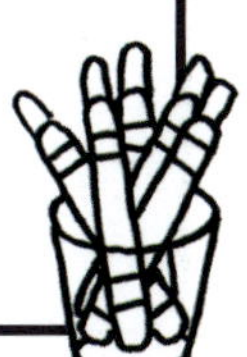

In the beginning, the United States was neutral in World War II.
Then, in 1941, Japan attacked the American military base at PEARL HARBOR.

Many Americans died in the attack. The United States could no longer stay neutral and entered the war (on the Allies' side).

Pearl Harbor

- **Interconnectedness:** Japan attacks an American military base, which causes the United States to enter World War II.
- **Cooperation:** The United States joins the Allies.
- **Power:** The United States uses its powerful army, navy, and air force to end the war.

More Turning Points in the War

1. BATTLE OF STALINGRAD: Hitler tried to capture Stalingrad, a city in the Soviet Union. But the Nazi soldiers were not able to withstand the frigid Russian weather. So the Allies won this major battle.

   Ⓡ Napoleon made the same mistake as the Nazis – trying to fight in the Russian winter.

2. INVASION OF NORMANDY – D-DAY (1944): The Allies landed on the coast of Normandy, France, and invaded Nazi-controlled territory.

   Now, Germany had to fight a war on two fronts – the British and US armies in the west, and the Russian army in the east.

   Though there were thousands of casualties on both sides, the Allies won this battle!

D-Day

Ⓡ **Cause and Effect:** United States enters the war ➲ Battle of Stalingrad and invasion of Normandy ➲ Allies begin to win the war

World War II Ends

1945: Germany surrenders!

The YALTA CONFERENCE:
When the Allies saw they were winning the war, three major leaders got together to divide Germany temporarily between the Allied Powers.

The Yalta Conference: Churchill, Roosevelt, Stalin

The three leaders were:

1. Roosevelt (USA)
2. Churchill (Great Britain)
3. Stalin (Russia)

Cooperation: Major world leaders gather to divide Germany.
Power: Major military forces join to use their power to divide Germany.

The Atom Bomb: Hiroshima & Nagasaki

While the war ended in Europe, it continued in Japan. The Japanese were not ready to surrender. They wanted to fight until the end.
(Great Britain and the United States weren't willing to risk millions of soldiers in a drawn-out conflict.)

United States dropped an atomic bomb on HIROSHIMA and then on NAGASAKI (Japanese cities).
These bombs killed over 100,000 people!
Many children born after the bombing were severely disfigured and missing organs.

Japan finally surrendered.

1945: World War II ends.

- R **Cause and effect:** Japan doesn't surrender ➲ United States drops two atom bombs ➲ Japan surrenders
- E **Innovations:** The atom bomb was a major technological innovation. Look how much damage it caused!
- E **Environmental impact:** The atom bombs caused long-lasting environmental damage to Hiroshima and Nagasaki.
- E **Power:** The United States used its power to take the drastic step of dropping the atom bombs. This action led to the end of the war.

Effects of World War II

1. Economies in Europe and Asia declined dramatically.
2. War crime trials: Violent leaders were punished for their atrocities.
   - NUREMBERG TRIALS: 22 Nazi leaders were tried and punished for crimes against humanity.
   - TOKYO TRIALS: Japanese officials were punished for war crimes.
   - This showed that government and military officials could be held accountable for their actions during wartime.
   - R Common Regents question

Nuremberg Trial

3. Europe was divided and Allied Powers occupied smaller countries.
4. The UNITED NATIONS was created to keep world peace.

R **Cause and effect:** World War II ➲ 5 effects listed above

E **Human Rights Violations:** The people responsible for World War II atrocities were punished in the Nuremberg Trials.

The United Nations (UN)

In 1945, the Allies created an international peacekeeping organization called the United Nations (UN). (This organization replaced the unsuccessful League of Nations.)

Main bodies of the United Nations:

1. **GENERAL ASSEMBLY:** Each country has a representative who can vote on resolutions.
2. **SECURITY COUNCIL:** representatives of a select group of countries dedicated to maintaining world peace

The United Nations drafted the **DECLARATION OF HUMAN RIGHTS**, which states that all people should have basic rights such as freedom of speech and the right to live.

Unfortunately, the United Nations was not effective in preventing future human rights violations, such as those in Rwanda, Africa.

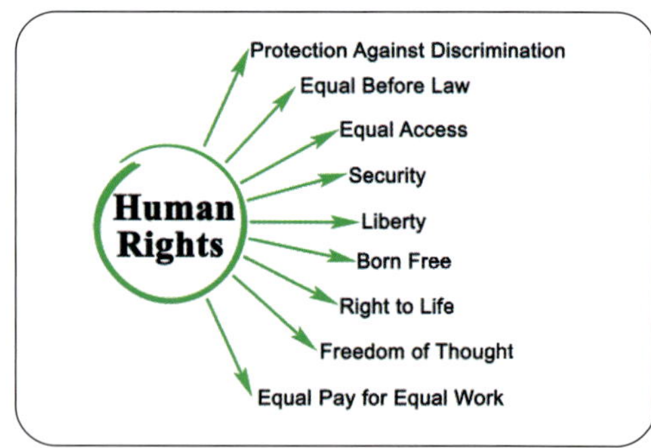

Declaration of Human Rights

Ideas and Beliefs/Innovation: The United Nations was created to maintain world peace.

Cooperation/Interconnectedness: Countries joined together to create an organization to preserve world peace.

Quick Review

Check off the boxes you know well. Whatever you don't know well (yet!), go back and review now!

- ☐ 1939-1945: World War II
- ☐ Causes of World War II: imperialism, resentment after World War I, Great Depression, Fascism
- ☐ Immediate causes of World War II: Treaty of Versailles is violated, Germany invades countries, Policy of Appeasement
- ☐ Axis: Germany, Italy, Japan (Axes JIG)
- ☐ Allies: France, Britain, later – Soviet Union, China, United States
- ☐ Blitzkrieg
- ☐ Genocide – Holocaust, Final Solution
- ☐ Pearl Harbor
- ☐ Battle of Stalingrad, Invasion of Normandy
- ☐ Yalta conference – Roosevelt, Churchill, Stalin
- ☐ Atomic bombs on Hiroshima and Nagasaki
- ☐ Nuremberg Trials
- ☐ United Nations

Enduring Issues Essay Topics That Came Up in This Unit:

- Human Rights Violations:
  - Holocaust, genocide, Final Solution, concentration camps
  - Nuremberg Trials and Tokyo Trials show that wartime atrocities can be punished.
- Scarcity: Economic problems in Germany (caused by the Great Depression and reparations) led to World War II.
- Conflict: World War II
- Innovation:
  - Tanks, bombs, blitzkrieg, and new ammunition were used to fight the war, leading to massive destruction.
  - United Nations
- Environmental impact:
  - Cities were destroyed in World War II.
  - Hiroshima and Nagasaki: Radiation from the atomic bombs caused long-term environmental damage and health issues.

Regents Question Time!

Now it's time to test how well you know your stuff.

Have fun!

 **Regents Question Time!**

"THEY SAY THEY WON'T WAIT ANY LONGER"

Source: Vaughn Shoemaker, *1939 A.D.*, *Chicago Daily News* (adapted)

26 What is the main idea of this cartoon?

(1) Natural forces can disrupt human planning.
(2) Seasonal differences can be safely ignored.
(3) Warm-water ports are necessary for survival.
(4) Faulty maps can have negative consequences.

Answer: ___

1

"THEY SAY THEY WON'T WAIT ANY LONGER"

The Nazis were not able to withstand the frigid Russian weather (in the Battle of Stalingrad). So the Allies won this major battle.

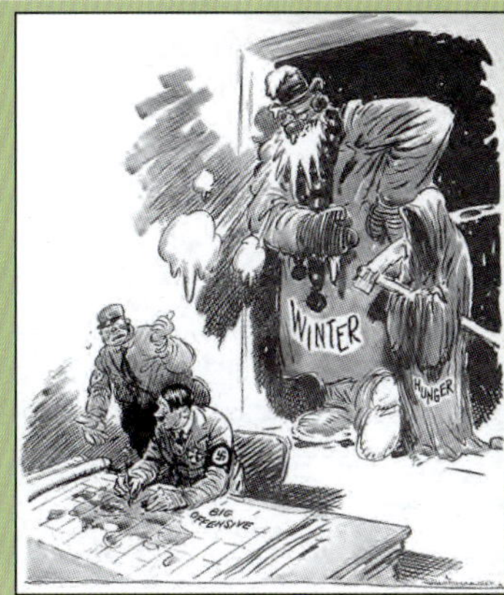

4

2

Source: Vaughn Shoemaker, 1939 A.D., *Chicago Daily News* (adapted)

3

26 What is the main idea of this cartoon?

(1) Natural forces can disrupt human planning.
(2) Seasonal differences can be safely ignored.
(3) Warm-water ports are necessary for survival.
(4) Faulty maps can have negative consequences.

Regents Question Time!

Source: Dr. Seuss, PM Magazine in *Dr. Seuss Goes to War,* August 13, 1941

16 This 1941 cartoon expresses the opinion that the policy of appeasement

(1) poses no threat to peace
(2) will not be tolerated
(3) is costly but necessary
(4) is shortsighted and unwise

Answer: ____

1

'Remember . . . One More Lollypop, and Then You All Go Home!'

The cartoon shows animals with Nazi swastika symbols who look ready to pounce. In the center, the "appeaser" is giving out lollypops to calm them. It's quite obvious that the lollypops may calm them down for a few minutes, but not for too long. This cartoon represents Britain and France's policy of giving in to Japanese and German aggression to keep peace and avoid war.

4

2

Source: Dr. Seuss, PM Magazine in *Dr. Seuss Goes to War,* August 13, 1941

1941 – World War II

3

16 This 1941 cartoon expresses the opinion that the policy of appeasement

(1) poses no threat to peace
(2) will not be tolerated
(3) is costly but necessary
(4) is shortsighted and unwise

UNIT 13

THE COLD WAR (1946-1991)

The Cold War

The Cold War was a conflict between the United States and the Soviet Union (Russia).

The Cold War was not a typical war with battles and guns. Instead, there was massive tension and competition between these two countries.

How did it all start?

The United States, Britain, and the Soviet Union worked together to win World War II but had major disagreements that eventually led to the Cold War.

Let's eavesdrop in on two major conferences that led to the "chilling" trouble ahead.

After World War II (1946), two SUPERPOWERS (powerful, influential nations) emerged: the United States and the Soviet Union.

The Yalta Conference

Churchill, Roosevelt, and Stalin at the Yalta Conference

YALTA CONFERENCE (1945):
Towards the end of World War II, Allied leaders met to try to create peace in Europe.

First, let's discuss the good parts 😊:

- The United States (Roosevelt), the United Kingdom (Churchill), and the Soviet Union (Stalin) agreed to demilitarize and split Germany into four spheres/ zones of occupation.
  - The US, Great Britain, and France would control **West** Germany.
  - The Soviet Union would control **East** Germany.
- They agreed to start an international organization called the UNITED NATIONS (UN).

Now let's explore the bad parts ☹️:

- The Soviet Union warned that it wanted to expand throughout the world and spread communism.
- The Soviet Union agreed that there would be free elections in East Germany. But they did not keep to this agreement!

The Potsdam Conference

POTSDAM CONFERENCE (1945):

Now that World War II ended, the "Big 3" — the leaders of the United States, Britain, and the Soviet Union — met in Potsdam, Germany.

The United States dropped the atomic bomb the day before, which made Stalin anxious about his power in the Soviet Union.

An atom bomb would make me kinda anxious too!

- They all agreed that Germany must demilitarize, pay war reparations, and give up their territories in the east.
- They disagreed on how to manage their zones.
  - The USA and Britain wanted to install **capitalism** and **democracy** in their zones.
  - The Soviet Union wanted to install **communism** and **totalitarianism** in their zones. They did not want to end there. They wanted to expand their zone and communist influence even further.

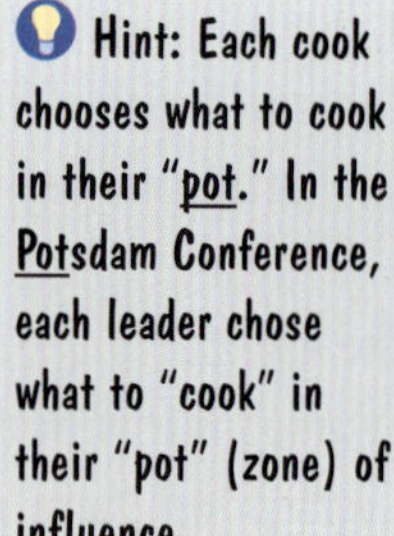

Hint: Each cook chooses what to cook in their "pot." In the Potsdam Conference, each leader chose what to "cook" in their "pot" (zone) of influence.

The Cold War

The United States and the Soviet Union had two major disagreements:

1. Economic disagreement:
   - The United States believed in CAPITALISM – where private owners control the economy.
   - The Soviet Union believed in having a COMMAND ECONOMY – where the government controls the economy.

2. Political disagreement:
   - The United States believed in DEMOCRACY – a government based on the participation and interests of the people.
   - The Soviet Union believed in COMMUNISM – a system in which all possessions are owned by a classless society.

The Soviet Union, under Stalin, imposed communism on many countries (including Poland, Czechoslovakia, and others). The United States was scared that Communism would spread all over the world. The United States spent the next 40 years trying to "contain" communism so that it wouldn't spread.

USSR flag

Ideas and Beliefs: Communism vs. capitalism and communism vs. democracy

Power: Different governments promote different political ideas.

The World Divided

After World War II, Europe was divided according to political views:

- DEMOCRACY: United States and Western Europe (The Western Bloc)
- COMMUNISM: Soviet Union (east)
  The Soviet Union had SATELLITE COUNTRIES – countries that it controlled politically and economically. Some of its satellite countries were Czechoslovakia, Hungary, and Poland.
- NONALIGNMENT: Some nations chose not to take sides in the Cold War. They felt it was a version of imperialism and did not want to get involved in other countries' affairs. They stayed out of the conflict and made economic progress.

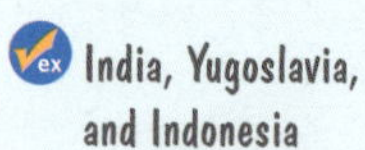

ex India, Yugoslavia, and Indonesia

HINT: A satellite revolves around a planet. A satellite country "revolves around" (depends on) the country that controls it.

The Iron Curtain

- There was an imaginary division between the east and west that was named the IRON CURTAIN.
- This represented the divide between the democratic and communist camps.
- The cartoon below depicts Prime Minister Winston Churchill of Britain (representing democracy) on one side of the curtain, with "Joe" – Joseph Stalin of the USSR (representing communism) – on the other side of the wall.

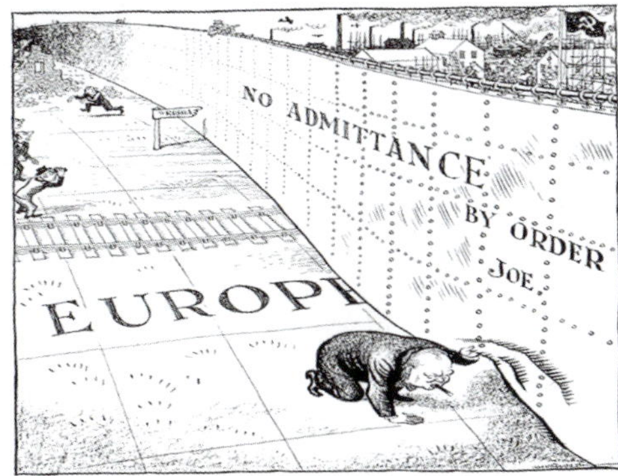

Cartoon depicting an "iron curtain" dividing the communists and the democrats

Interconnectedness: Satellite countries spread communism. Western countries remained democratic.

Power: Communists wanted to use their power to spread communism all over the world.

The Truman Doctrine & Containment (1947)

The United States feared the spread of communism. So President Truman created an economic and military program to help countries resist Soviet aggression.

- Truman sent military and economic aid to countries to help them resist communism.

ex USA sent aid to Greece and Turkey.

- This was based on the theory of CONTAINMENT, whose goal was to limit communism and stop it from spreading.

R Common Regents question

R **Turning Point:** The Truman Doctrine began a history of foreign aid to stop the spread of communism.

R **Cause and effect:** Spread of communism ➲ containment and foreign aid

President Truman

The Truman Doctrine tried to stop the "communism virus" by providing aid to non-Communist countries.

HINT: President Truman was a "true man." He noticed a big issue and worked to fix the problem.

HINT: In the theory of containment, communism is contained.

Marshall Plan (1947)

After World War II, many countries' economies were in ruins.

FOR EUROPEAN RECOVERY

SUPPLIED BY THE

UNITED STATES OF AMERICA

THE MARSHALL PLAN:

The United States took advantage of the terrible economy and offered billions of dollars to countries that would resist communism. This money helped the countries strengthen their democratic governments and build up their economies.

Many Western European countries took advantage of this offer, which helped democracy spread and stopped the spread of communism.

- R Common Regents question
- R **Cause and effect:** Truman Doctrine and Marshall Plan ➲ Communism is contained in many countries.
- E **Interconnectedness/Cooperation:** The United States works together with other countries to contain communism.

HINT: A marshal is a military commander. With the Marshall Plan, the United States was sort of like a commander, influencing countries to strengthen democracy.

Division in Germany

After World War II, the Allies (United States, Great Britain, France, the Soviet Union) divided Germany among themselves.

- Great Britain, United States, and France were democratic.
- The Soviet Union was communist.

Germany divided

BERLIN (the capital of Germany) was divided: West Berlin was democratic and East Berlin was communist. But Berlin was located in communist territory (East Germany) and therefore West Berlin was isolated.

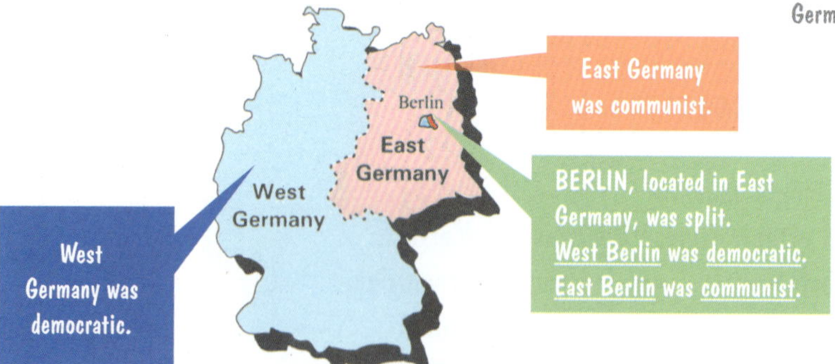

West Germany was democratic (blue), while East Germany was communist (red).
Berlin, the capital, was divided: West Berlin was democratic (blue), and East Berlin was communist (red).

The Berlin Blockade (1948)

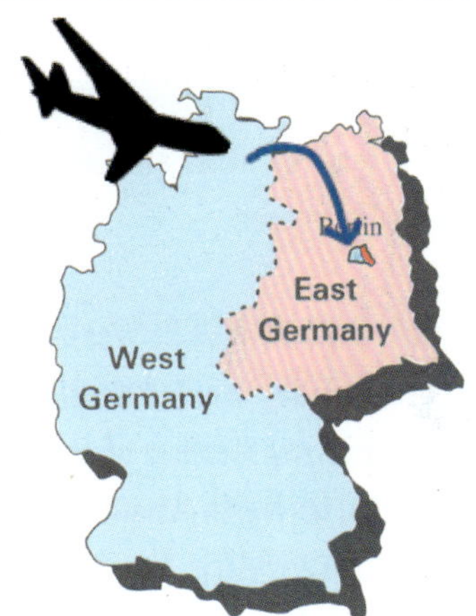

The Soviet Union was very unhappy that the Allied powers controlled West Germany. They were even more upset to have democratic West Berlin sitting in middle of their communist area! They wanted these democratic powers out of West Berlin.

The Soviet Union blocked all land routes through which food and supplies were brought to West Berlin (which was democratic, but surrounded by communist East Germany). They were trying to get rid of the democratic Allied powers in Berlin.

That's not what happened, though!
THE BERLIN AIRLIFT: Western powers flew food and supplies into West Berlin for close to a year. Eventually, the Soviets ended the blockade.

Cooperation: The Berlin Airlift was a success due to cooperation between the Western powers.

Military Alliances

Each side – west (democracy) and east (communism) – was afraid that the other side would attack. Therefore, they created alliances.

- NATO ALLIANCES: Western countries (including the US and Canada) created a military alliance to support each other if any member of the alliance was attacked.
  - NATO: North Atlantic Treaty Organization
- WARSAW PACT: The Soviet Union and its satellites (Poland, Czechoslovakia, Hungary, Romania, Bulgaria, and East Germany) in Eastern Europe made an alliance to support each other if any member of the alliance was attacked.

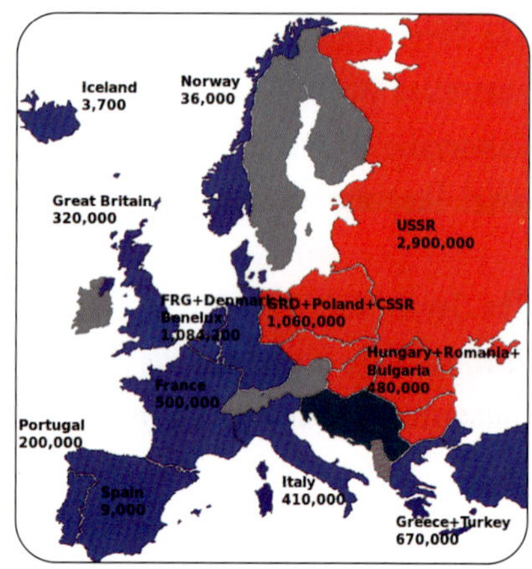

NATO Alliances – Blue
Warsaw Pact – Red

Cause and effect: Cold War tensions ➲ NATO and the Warsaw Pact

Cooperation: NATO alliances and the Warsaw Pact

The Hungarian Revolution (1956)

The Soviet Union controlled its satellites with an iron fist. However, some satellite countries wanted independence.

THE HUNGARIAN REVOLUTION:
A Hungarian nationalist led a revolt against the Soviet Union and gained Hungary's independence.
But the Soviets fought back and killed thousands of Hungarians to reclaim full power.
Hungary remained communist. ☹

- Other countries also tried to revolt, but the Soviet Union always managed to maintain control.

- **Conflict:** Communist control vs. independence

The Arms Race

The United States and the Soviet Union built up stocks of weapons in case one of them would attack the other.

ARMS RACE: a race to see who can build up the biggest nuclear arsenal (collection of nuclear weapons)

- First, the United States built an atom bomb. (Yikes!)
- Then, the Soviets built an atom bomb. (Double yikes!)
- For 40 years, each country spent loads of money improving their weapons.

Here's what was happening in history terminology:

- NUCLEAR PROLIFERATION: the spread of nuclear weapons
- MILITARY-INDUSTRIAL COMPLEX: network to produce weapons and military technologies

Many people worldwide were afraid that the United States or the Soviet Union would attack each other with their nuclear weapons and destroy the world.

- **Innovation:** Both countries made technological advancements (building atom bombs and nuclear weapons) that had the power to cause major damage.
- **Conflict:** Arms race
- **Power:** The United States and the Soviet Union gained power by building their military strength.

The Space Race

To prove how powerful they were, the United States and the Soviet Union competed over space exploration.

The Sputnik

- The Soviets built the SPUTNIK – a satellite to orbit Earth.
- The US established NASA (National Aeronautics and Space Administration) to improve America's space technology.
- The US created its first satellite.
- The Soviets sent the first man to space (1957).
- The US sent the first man to the moon (1969).
- Both superpowers built spy satellites.

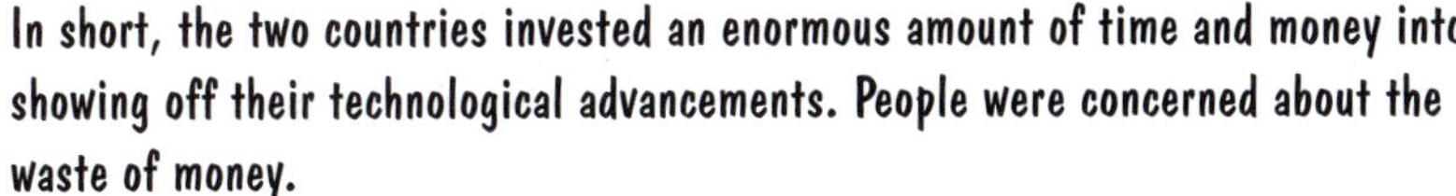

In short, the two countries invested an enormous amount of time and money into showing off their technological advancements. People were concerned about the waste of money.

Ⓡ Just know that the United States and the Soviet Union competed in space exploration – the "Space Race." You don't need to memorize the details.

Ⓔ **Conflict:** The Space Race

Ⓔ **Innovations:** The US and USSR spent much time and money on advancing science and technology.

The Cold War Around the World

America and the Soviet Union didn't actually go to war with each other. But they did support their satellite states (the countries that were on their side) in their wars for democracy or communism.

- The United States supported the democratic countries.
- The Soviet Union supported the communist countries.

Regions involved in wars (conflicts of democracy versus communism): East Asia, Middle East, Africa, and Latin America

Let's travel to each of these regions to see what happened at each place. Get out your bulletproof vest!

The Cold War in East Asia – The Korean War (1950-1953)

After World War II, Korea was divided into two:

- **North Korea:** under communist control (supported by the Soviet Union)
- **South Korea:** under democratic control (supported by the United States)

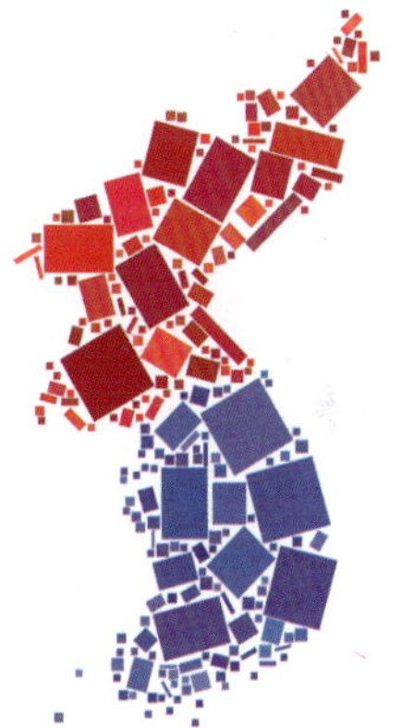

North Korea wanted to unify Korea and make the whole country communist. So North Korea invaded South Korea.

The United Nations stopped North Korea. The United States sent soldiers to North Korea to "contain" communism there.

At this point, the United States started sending troops to foreign countries to contain communism. One of these countries was Vietnam.

An ARMISTICE (end of conflict) was signed.

The end result was that Korea remained divided, as before.

Cooperation: The United States sent troops to North Korea to contain communism.

Conflict: Korean War/communism vs. democracy

The Cold War in East Asia – The Vietnam War (1955-1975)

HO CHI MINH, the communist leader of North Vietnam, freed Vietnam from France. He helped Vietnam gain independence by setting up ambushes, raids and surprise attacks on the French.

Ho Chi Minh

Then, in 1954, Vietnam was divided into two:

- North Vietnam: under communist control (supported by the Soviet Union)
- South Vietnam: under democratic control (supported by the United States)

North Vietnam wanted to unite Vietnam and make the whole country communist.

Sounds super familiar!
(Hint – Korea!)

American troops were not able to stop the unification.

In 1975, North Vietnam reunited with the South and made it communist.

R **Connections:** Ho Chi Minh and Gandhi were both nationalist leaders against an imperial power. However, Ho Chi Minh called for violence, while Gandhi did not.

The Cold War in the Middle East –

Arab States vs. Israel

NASSER (the nationalistic Arab leader in Egypt) tried to end Western control of Egypt:

- He nationalized the Suez Canal (1956).
- He used Soviet funding to make the Aswan High Dam.
- He fought two wars against Israel. The United States supported Israel.

Suez Canal

Iran & Iraq

- Conflict over oil resources in the Middle East caused major tensions during the Cold War.
- The USA and the Soviet Union wanted to gain control of Iran and Iraq because of their vast oil fields.

The Cold War in Cuba – The Cuban Missile Crisis (1962)

CUBAN REVOLUTION (1959):
FIDEL CASTRO seized power and made Cuba communist.

The United States was involved in the BAY OF PIGS INVASION. The goal of this invasion was to overthrow Castro and gain democracy in Cuba. The invasion failed.

After this incident, Castro asked the Soviet Union to protect Cuba from the United States.
So Soviet leader KHRUSHCHEV began building up missiles in Cuba, claiming that he was doing so to defend Cuba from the United States.

Fidel Castro

HINT: Castro made Cuba communist.

Cuba is in missile range of the United States. So there was a major danger of a nuclear war between the Soviet Union and the US!
The United States demanded that the missiles be removed.

The happy ending: Diplomacy succeeded and there was no need for war 😊.

Cooperation: Cooperation between the United States and Cuba averted a crisis.

HINT: Khrushchev rushed to create weapons.

Détente

- After the Cuban Missile Crisis, the Soviet Union and the United States recognized how close they had come to a nuclear war, which was quite scary! They wanted to make sure this didn't happen again.

- Also, both sides wanted to stop wasting so much money on the arms and space race.

  DÉTENTE (1967-1979) is the period of time that the Cold War tension started to ease.

- Both sides signed the SALT agreements to reduce weapons.

The Soviet-Afghanistan War

The communists are losing!
The United States was slowly succeeding in influencing Middle Eastern countries to adopt capitalism. The Soviet Union saw that it was losing power and was in trouble. It broke the Détente promises!

Afghanistan (a country in the Middle East) was still under communist rule, but rebel groups called the MUJAHIDEEN were fighting to topple it.

The Soviet Afghan War (1979-1989)

- In 1979, the Soviet army invaded Afghanistan to try to prop up the communist government against the rebels. They badly wanted to hold onto their communist proxy (representation) in the Middle East!
- The Soviet Union invested huge amounts of money, used advanced weapons, and sent over 600,000 soldiers to try to maintain the communist regime.
- The United States funded the Mujahideen to fight against the Soviet army.

Despite the Soviets' major investment, they lost the war!

FYI: Here's the biggest irony. After the war, the Mujahideen split into extremist groups including Al-Qaeda, with leader Osama bin Laden. This group eventually attacked the United States on 9/11!

West and East Germany Unite

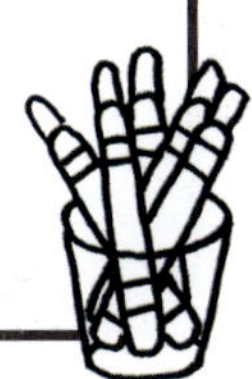

In 1961, East Germany (which was communist) built the **BERLIN WALL**, which separated it from democratic West Germany.

The Berlin Wall became a symbol of the Cold War.
"Tear down the wall" became a slogan towards the end of the Cold War.

FALL OF THE BERLIN WALL (1989):
East Germany wanted to join West Germany's freedom and success. So the Germans tore down the Berlin wall!

Sounds great? Not quite!
The results: West Germany had to pay higher taxes to rebuild the east; East Germany suffered from unemployment and social unrest as they transitioned to a market economy. ☹

Source: Clyde Wells, The Augusta Chronicle, 1989

Ⓡ Common Regents question
Ideas and Beliefs: Democracy wins over communism.

The Soviet Union Breaks Up (1980-1990)

Mikhail Gorbachev

When Mikhail GORBACHEV became the leader of the Soviet Union, he loosened the political restrictions further and tried to fix the economic issues.

Gorbachev instituted these policies:

1. PERESTROIKA: a policy to revitalize the Soviet economy and make it more like a free market economy
2. GLASNOST: a policy that called for more openness with the west and encouraged people to talk about the problems in the Soviet Union

Results:

- Nationalism among ethnic groups increased.
- The Soviet Union's satellite countries received their independence.
- The Berlin Wall fell (1989).
- The Soviet Union collapsed (1991)!

R Common Regents questions

R **Cause and effect:** Détente ➲ Perestroika and glasnost ➲ Fall of the Berlin Wall ➲ Soviet Union collapses

E **Ideas and Beliefs:** Gorbachev instituted policies that weakened the power of communism.

E **Interconnectedness:** Once communism loosened up in the Soviet Union, satellite countries got their independence.

HINT: Perestroika – rest. The Soviets decided to "rest" their control over the economy a bit.

HINT: Glasnost-glass. You can see through glass. Glasnost was a policy that encouraged people to expose the problems in the USSR.

Effects of the Fall of the Soviet Union

Now that the Soviet Union was dismantled, many "pieces of the puzzle" around the world shifted.

1. The United States became the sole superpower.
2. Countries that were Soviet Republics became independent.

 Ukraine

3. Corruption in Russia increased.
4. Nationalism among ethnic groups increased.

In Poland, LECH WALESA led the Solidarity party, which was the first non-communist government in the Soviet satellite!

Lech Walesa

Quick Review

Check off the boxes you know well. Whatever you don't know well (yet!), go back and review now!

- ☐ Superpowers: The United States and the Soviet Union
- ☐ Capitalism vs. command economy
- ☐ Democracy vs. communism
- ☐ Satellite countries
- ☐ The Truman Doctrine/Containment
- ☐ The Marshall Plan
- ☐ Berlin blockade/Berlin airlift
- ☐ NATO alliances, Warsaw Pact
- ☐ The Hungarian Revolution
- ☐ The Space Race
- ☐ The Arms Race
- ☐ Korean War
- ☐ Vietnam War
- ☐ Cuban Missile Crisis
- ☐ Gorbachev
- ☐ Fall of the Iron Curtain

Enduring Issues Essay Topics That Came Up in This Unit:

- **Conflict:**
  - Major conflict during the Cold War over communism vs. democracy and capitalism vs. command economy
  - Berlin Blockade
  - Hungarian Revolution
  - Arms Race
  - Space Race
  - Cuban Missile Crisis
- **Innovation:** Arms Race and Space Race
- **Interconnectedness:** Communism spread from the Soviet Union to satellite countries. Democracy spread among Western countries.
- **Cooperation:**
  - The Berlin airlift helps democratic West Berlin during the Berlin Blockade.
  - Fall of the Berlin Wall
  - NATO alliances and the Warsaw Pact
- **Power:**
  - The United States and the Soviet Union showcased their power in the Space Race and the Arms Race.
  - The United States used its power to contain communism (Truman Doctrine and Marshall Plan).

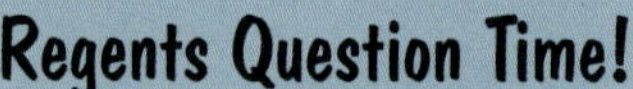

Now it's time to test how well you know your stuff.

Have fun!

Regents Question Time!

Peep Under the Iron Curtain

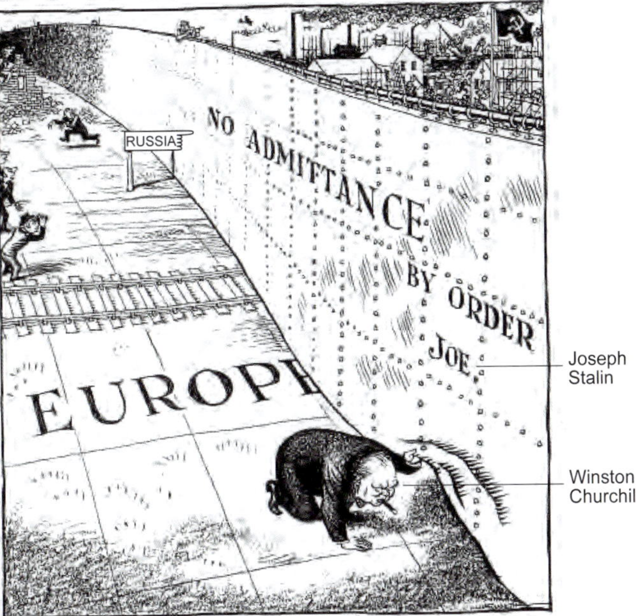

Source: Leslie Gilbert Illingworth, Daily Mail, March 6, 1946 (adapted)

Geographic Context—refers to where this historical development/event is taking place and why it is taking place there.

32 Explain the geographic context for the historical development/event shown in this 1946 cartoon. [1]

____

____

Answer: ___

Peep Under the Iron Curtain

Cold War

Europe is divided: Prime Minister Winston Churchill of Britain (democracy) is on one side of the wall. Joseph Stalin of USSR (communism) is on the other side of the wall.

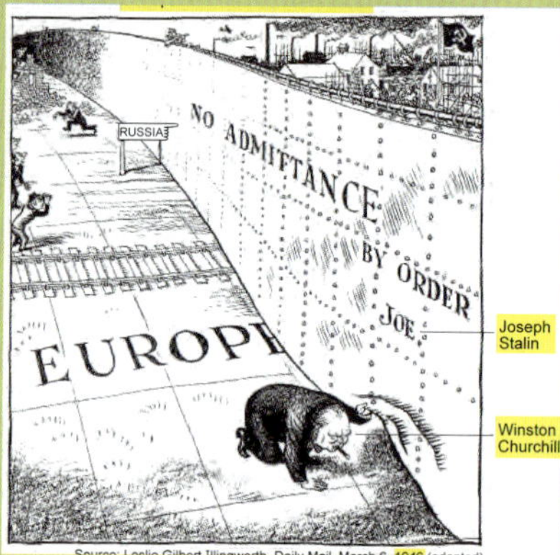

4

2

Source: Leslie Gilbert Illingworth, Daily Mail, March 6, 1946 (adapted)

Geographic Context—refers to where this historical development/event is taking place and why it is taking place there.

1946 = Cold War

3

Geographic context – where is this taking place and why is it taking place there?

32 Explain the geographic context for the historical development/event shown in this 1946 cartoon. [1]

Any of these answers is correct:

- Europe was divided after World War II into communist countries and non-communist countries.
- Europe was divided after World War II as a result of decisions made at the Yalta Conference.
- The Iron Curtain divided Europe during the Cold War.

Make sure your answer includes *where* it happened and *why* it happened there.

Regents Question Time!

Interactions Between the United States of America and the Soviet Union		
1948–49	**1962**	**1979**
In June 1948, the Soviet Union blockades democratic West Berlin. The U.S. and its allies fly in supplies daily to keep the city from starving. The Soviets lift the blockade in May 1949.	U.S. spy planes discover Soviet-built nuclear sites in Cuba. After a tense 13-day standoff with President John F. Kennedy, the Soviets remove the missiles.	Soviet troops invade Afghanistan. Aided by the U.S., Islamic fighters wage a 10-year guerrilla war against the Soviets, who withdraw in 1989.

— Carl Stoffers, "Are We Heading Toward a New Cold War?" *New York Times Upfront*, October 10, 2016 (adapted)

11 Which foreign policy action best explains the United States response to Cold War situations?

(1) repeated reliance on appeasement
(2) consistent attempts to bring about détente
(3) a continuing pursuit of nonalignment
(4) a long-term commitment to containment

Answer: ___

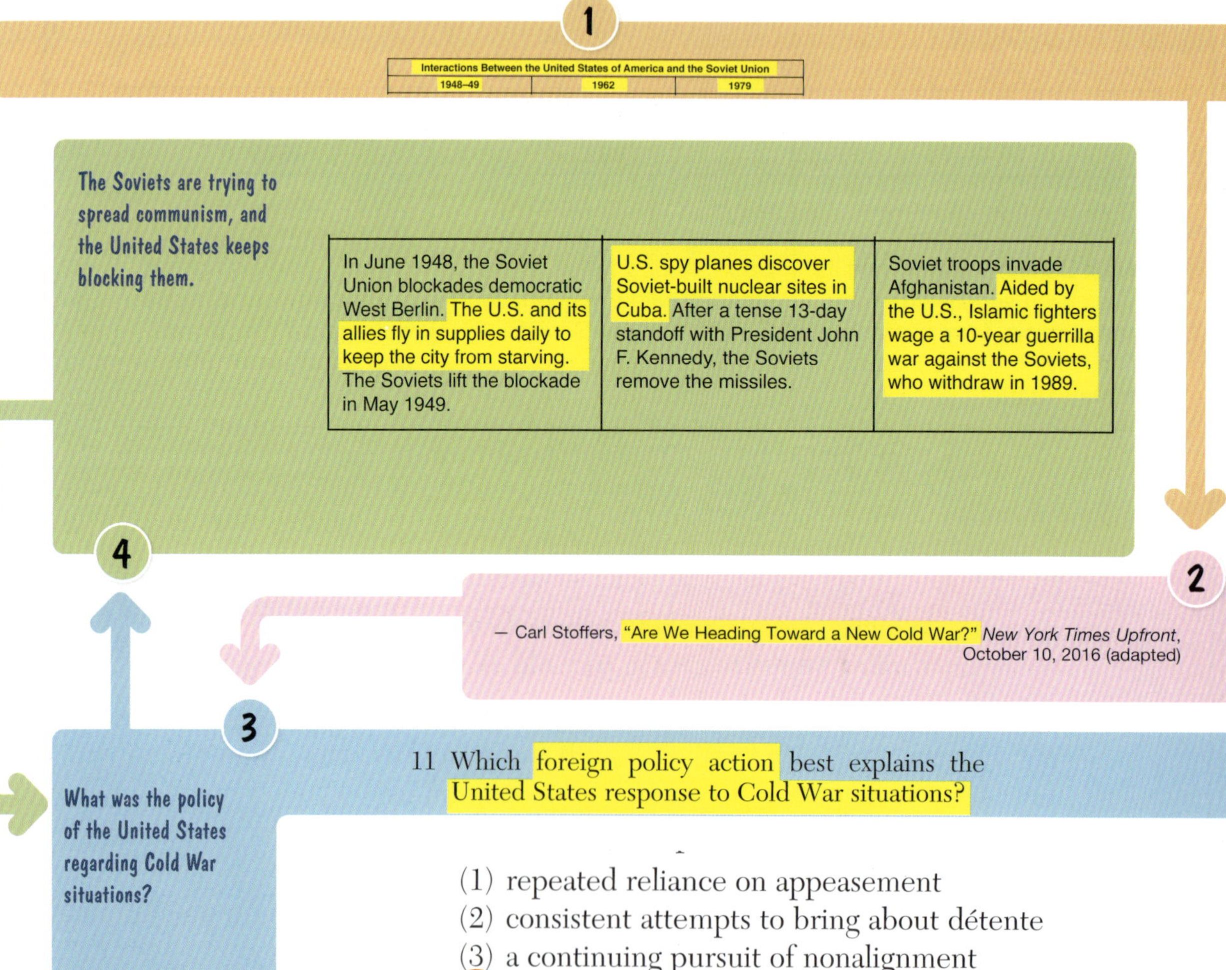

Interactions Between the United States of America and the Soviet Union		
1948–49	1962	1979
In June 1948, the Soviet Union blockades democratic West Berlin. The U.S. and its allies fly in supplies daily to keep the city from starving. The Soviets lift the blockade in May 1949.	U.S. spy planes discover Soviet-built nuclear sites in Cuba. After a tense 13-day standoff with President John F. Kennedy, the Soviets remove the missiles.	Soviet troops invade Afghanistan. Aided by the U.S., Islamic fighters wage a 10-year guerrilla war against the Soviets, who withdraw in 1989.

— Carl Stoffers, "Are We Heading Toward a New Cold War?" *New York Times Upfront*, October 10, 2016 (adapted)

11 Which foreign policy action best explains the United States response to Cold War situations?

(1) repeated reliance on appeasement
(2) consistent attempts to bring about détente
(3) a continuing pursuit of nonalignment
(4) a long-term commitment to containment

Containment was the USA's policy to stop the spread of communism in the world.

 Regents Question Time!

Source: Edmund S. Valtman, 1991

38 Which set of problems most directly contributed to the situation shown in this 1991 cartoon featuring Mikhail Gorbachev?

(1) refusal to adopt and accept aid from the Marshall Plan
(2) a forced famine in Ukraine and rebellions in the gulags
(3) invasions by foreign troops and Soviet cities under military siege
(4) a deteriorating Soviet economy and secessionist republics desiring independence

Answer: ___

1

No title here. Move on.

Gorbachev is looking at a broken-up symbol of the USSR.

2

Source: Edmund S. Valtman, 1991

3

38 Which set of problems most directly contributed to the situation shown in this 1991 cartoon featuring Mikhail Gorbachev?

(1) refusal to adopt and accept aid from the Marshall Plan
(2) a forced famine in Ukraine and rebellions in the gulags
(3) invasions by foreign troops and Soviet cities under military siege
(4) a deteriorating Soviet economy and secessionist republics desiring independence

4

UNIT 14

MODERN DAY ASIA & THE PACIFIC

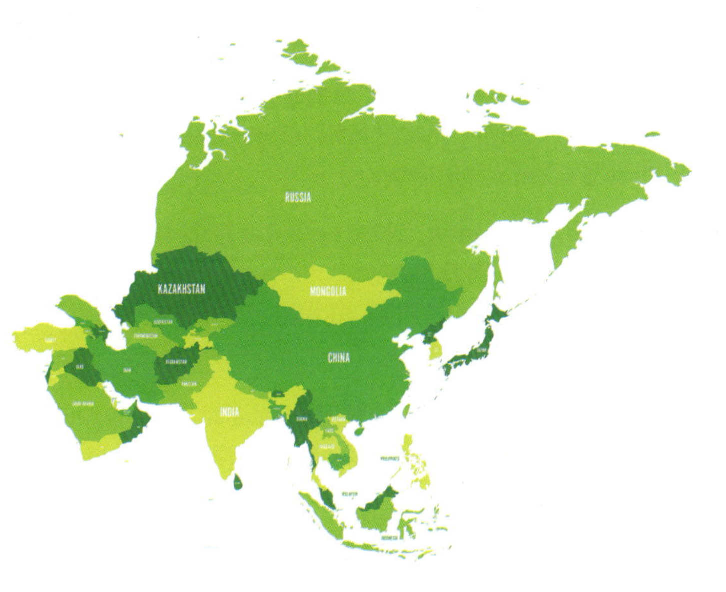

EdBoosters

India

Prime Minister Nehru

RECAP: India was imperialized by Great Britain. Nationalist leaders created the **INDIAN NATIONAL CONGRESS** to promote democracy and human rights. The **MUSLIM LEAGUE** safeguarded the rights of Indian Muslims. Mohandas Gandhi led an independence movement based on passive resistance. India gained independence from Britain in 1947.

PROBLEM: The Hindus and Muslims had ongoing serious religious conflict for a while. Therefore, when the British granted India independence, they divided India into a Hindu area and a Muslim area.

This was called the **PARTITION OF INDIA**, which separated India into two countries: India and Pakistan (1947).

- India's leader: Prime Minister **JAWAHARLAL NEHRU**
- Pakistan's leader: **MUHAMMED ALI JINNA**

SIKHS are people who have combined Hindu and Muslim beliefs. Since they have different beliefs than the Hindus and Muslims, they are considered a religious minority. They face discrimination from the Muslims and Hindus until today.

Conflict: Hindus vs. Muslims in India

Hindus & Muslims in India—Religious Conflict

- Notice the way India was split: Pakistan is divided into two parts with India in between them. Check out the map below. India is shaded orange and the Pakistans are shaded green. Notice how Hindu India is at the center and Muslim Pakistans are on opposite sides of India.

- The Muslims had to get to one of the Pakistans and the Hindus had to get to India. During these mass migrations, millions of people were killed at the borders. The Hindus killed the Muslims and the Muslims killed the Hindus. Gandhi tried to make peace, but a Hindu fanatic assassinated him. Now the Indian peace guy is out of the picture.

- The Muslims and Hindus had such hard feelings towards each other following the mass migrations. So despite the partition, the Hindus and Muslims continued to fight. Tension and violence between the Hindus and Muslims persist until today ☹.

Ⓡ This is an example of religious conflict and discrimination.

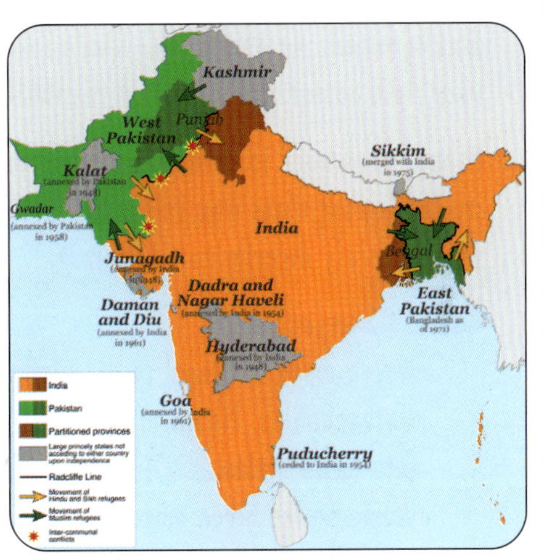

THE PARTITION OF INDIA

Hindu India is in the center. One part of Pakistan is east of India and one part of Pakistan is west of India.

Social Changes in India

Background: As part of the Hindu religion, the Indians had very rigid social classes called the CASTE SYSTEM.

People were born into their class and could not move out of it. The lowest class was called the UNTOUCHABLES and they were severely discriminated against.

Brahmin
priests
Kshatriya
warriors, kings
Vaishya
merchants, landowners
Sudra
commoners, peasants, servants
Untouchable, outcast, out of cast
street sweepers, latrine cleaners

Caste System in India

Social Changes:

1. Nehru made it illegal to discriminate against the Untouchables. He gave them jobs and allowed them entry into universities.
2. Women were given more rights.
3. MOTHER TERESA founded a charity to provide food and medical care to those in need.

Sounds great, no? Bad news: Despite the reforms, discrimination against the Untouchables continues until today, especially in rural areas.

R Mother Teresa is an example of an individual who improved human rights.

E **Innovation:** Social changes

E **Inequality:** The Untouchables were considered inferior and were mistreated.

India Today

- India today has a democratic government.
- India was so fed up with being bossed around by Britain. So when Nehru led India to independence, they adopted a policy of NONALIGNMENT, which means that they refuse to form alliances with other nations, especially communist or non-communist blocs during the Cold War.
- MIXED ECONOMY: The economy is partially government owned and partially privately owned (capitalism).
- Many companies worldwide outsource their work to India, where labor is cheap. This is an example of GLOBALIZATION: a process through which the world's businesses have become interconnected and interdependent.

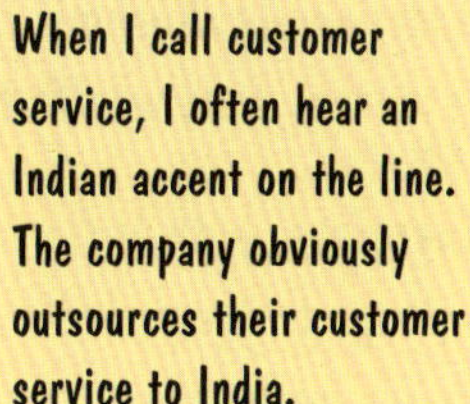

When I call customer service, I often hear an Indian accent on the line. The company obviously outsources their customer service to India.

- The Indian government launched the GREEN REVOLUTION, which introduced major changes in the agricultural system (1965) in an effort to solve the food shortage issue for the growing population. They began using advanced agricultural technology, such as pesticides, fertilizers, and tractors, which boosted their crop production. This revolution made a massive impact on India's agricultural success.
- Overpopulation: People moved to urban areas to get jobs. Too many people now live in the cities.

Environmental Impact: Green Revolution and overpopulation

Ideas and Beliefs: Nonalignment

Interconnectedness: Outsourcing jobs to India

Ethnic Tension in Kashmir, India

Kashmir is an area that was split between India and Pakistan in 1947. Kashmir is a very important area, as it provides fresh water and electricity to neighboring areas. Additionally, Kashmir is gifted with a wealth of natural resources (and wealth to the country that controls it!).

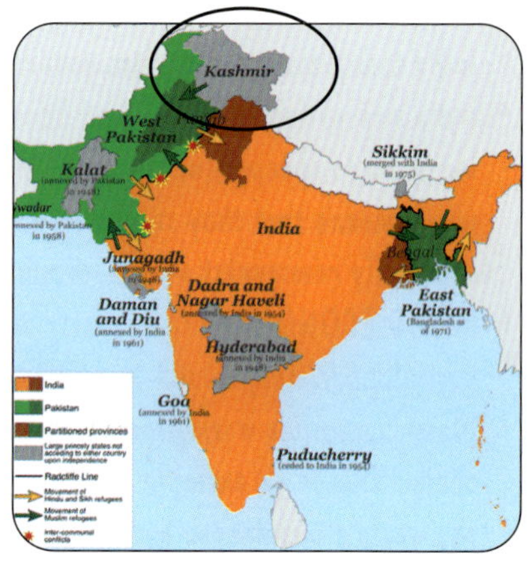

Therefore, both India and Pakistan claim that Kashmir belongs to them. India and Pakistan fight bitterly over this region until today.

It's kind of scary because both sides have nuclear weapons, and we're afraid of a nuclear attack.

FYI: Kashmir is unique in that it has a secular Indian government, but is made up mostly of Muslim people.

R This is an example of ethnic tension/religious conflict in a region.

E **Conflict:** India and Pakistan are fighting over control of Kashmir.

E **Innovation:** Availability of nuclear weapons makes this conflict frightening!

Tension in East Pakistan

As we discussed, West and East Pakistan were separated, with India in the middle.

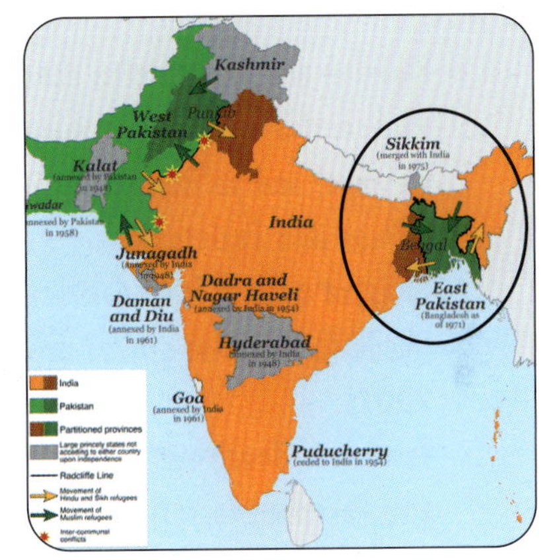

East Pakistan wanted independence from West Pakistan. After all, they're really far from West Pakistan!

They fought and won their independence, and renamed their country BANGLADESH.

FYI: Bangladesh is an extremely poor and overpopulated country that suffers from monsoons and bad storms. Was their independence worth it after all?

Conflict: East Pakistan and West Pakistan

HINT: They fought with a "bang" to create Bangladesh.

Problems in Pakistan

1. Pakistan and Afghanistan share a mountainous border. Afghanistan has many problems, including terrorism, violence, and political issues. These problems often diffuse into Pakistan.
2. Pakistan suffers from political instability because Al Qaeda (a terrorist group) overthrew the government (in 2007).
3. Terrorism flourishes because Afghani terrorist groups give Pakistani terrorist groups aid. Since 9/11, over 60,000 Pakistanis were killed in terrorist attacks!
4. Ethnic tensions exist between Muslims and Hindus, especially in Kashmir.

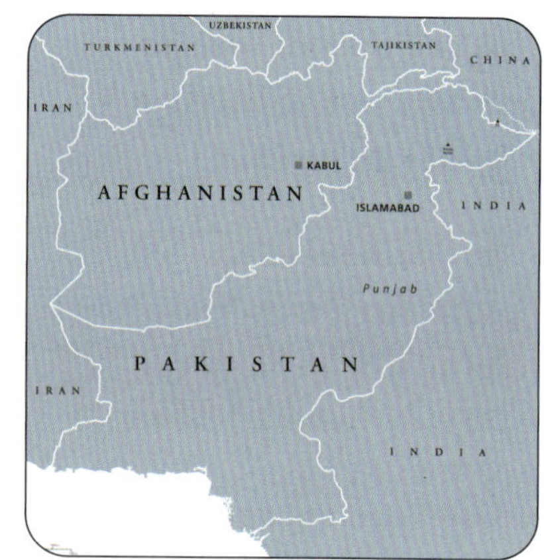

Interconnectedness: Pakistan and Afghanistan share a border, and their problems therefore diffuse into each other's regions.

Conflict: Pakistan is politically unstable and fraught with terrorism.

Human Rights Violation: Terrorism in Pakistan and Afghanistan

Korea

Recap: During the Korean War (1950-1953), Korea was divided into two.

- North Korea became a communist country.
- South Korea became a democratic country.

Let's take a tour of North and South Korea and see what became of them.

South Korea Today:

- South Korea remains non-communist.
- South Korea experienced tremendous economic growth and is one of the Four Asian Tigers (highly developed economies which include Hong Kong, Singapore, South Korea and Taiwan).
- South Korea is famous for exporting textiles and other well-priced items.

South Korea is a famous for its international trade. Notice the South Korean flag shown with import and export signs.

North Korea is a whole different story!

North Korea Today:

Cartoon of President Trump and Kim Jong-Un

KIM JONG-UN is the leader of North Korea. He is a communist dictator.

- He invests huge amounts of money and resources into advancing his military, without focusing on the growth of the country.
- Under his rule, North Korea developed nuclear weapons and often conducts nuclear testing. He frequently threatens the United States and South Korea that he will attack them.
- He kills anyone whom he sees as a threat to his regime. North Korea has no freedom of speech or freedom of the press. Human rights are not protected. (In other words, stay far away!)
- The USA is trying to initiate peace and denuclearize North Korea to remove the nuclear threat.

Human Rights Violation: North Korea's brutality against anyone opposed to Kim Jong-Un's regime; nuclear proliferation

Burma

This country was governed by military rule, and human rights were consistently violated.

AUNG SAN SUU KYI battled the human rights violations.

- She founded the National League for Democracy (NLF) and won the election in the 1990s.
- The military refused to hand over power to her, and placed her under house arrest for 15 years!
- While under house arrest, she won the Nobel Peace Prize for her non-violent struggle for democracy and human rights.
- When she finally rose to power, she was accused of allowing genocide to take place under her rule!

Aung San Suu Kyi

Human rights violations: Aung San Suu Kyi fought against human rights violations, but then violated them herself.

Vietnam

Background info: Vietnam was separated into two parts: The north became communist and the south became democratic (1954). North Vietnam was not satisfied with their lot. They wanted to unite with South Vietnam and make the entire area communist.

Communist Vietnam

THE VIETNAM WAR (1955-1975)

- North Vietnam tried uniting with South Vietnam.
- United States sent troops to South Vietnam to make sure it wouldn't fall to communism.
  The United States was afraid that if South Vietnam became communist, this would have a domino effect and cause surrounding countries to become communist, too. Although they invested much resources, they were unsuccessful.
- North Vietnam won the war and united with South Vietnam under communist rule.

R In the Vietnam War, the United States intervened to contain communism, but South Vietnam fell to communism. In the Korean War, the U.S.was able to contain communism, and South Korea remained non-communist. (Notice the contrast.)

E **Conflict:** The Vietnam War

E **Cooperation:** United States aids South Vietnam to help contain communism.

Cambodia

Background: The Cambodian Civil War was fought from 1967-1975 between the Cambodian government and the KHMER ROUGE (the communist party). The Khmer Rouge won the war and created a communist government.

During the Vietnam War, Cambodia served as a supply route for the communists. America bombed and invaded Cambodia during the Vietnam War to destroy this route in an effort to contain communism.

Pol Pot

Cambodia

After the American troops left, the KHMER ROUGE seized power, using guerrilla warfare (1975-1979).

- POL POT was the ruthless leader of the Khmer Rouge. He led the Khmer Rouge to act with extreme cruelty.
- The Khmer Rouge murdered over a million people in their effort to remove all Western influence from the country. Horrific!
- The places where the murders took place became known as KILLING FIELDS (for obvious reasons).
- The civil war officially ended. However, fighting continues until today.

R Common Regents question

R This is an example of human rights violations/genocide. Other examples of genocide in recent history include the Armenian Genocide, the Holocaust, and killing in Rwanda.

E **Human Rights Violations:** The Khmer Rouge murdered over a million people in order to eliminate Western influence. The world stood there like bystanders, failing to step in and stop this genocide!

E **Conflict/Power:** The Khmer Rouge abused its power and started a civil war.

Japan

Japan was devastated after World War II. Millions of people died, and entire cities (Hiroshima and Nagasaki) were devastated by the atomic bombs.

In the Tokyo Trials, the United States tried and convicted some Japanese people for wartime atrocities. The US also guided Japan to set up a democratic government and end militarism. This helped Japan become the successful country it is today.

Japan Today:

- Japan became economically successful. Today it is considered an economic superpower.
- Japan is experiencing strain between the forces of modernization and traditionalism.
  - Tradition was always very important in Japanese culture, which emphasizes a code of behavior, in which families are dominated by males, and people have a responsibility to a family or group.
  - During imperialism, when Japan modernized, they became more Westernized, which weakened traditions.

Japan is trying to preserve tradition while embracing modernization.

FYI: Japan modernized and Westernized during the Meiji Restoration (1866-1868). Japan modernized again after World War II.

Conflict: Traditionalism vs. modernization

Cooperation/Interconnectedness: The United States helped Japan establish a democratic government, which led to Japan's success.

China

Background info:

China was imperialized by Great Britain. Then, Sun Yat-Sen became the president. He tried to eliminate foreign control and improve China's economic and political situation (early 1900s).

Mao Zedong
Chinese communist leader

Chiang Kai-Shek became the next leader and led the **Nationalist Party.**

Meanwhile, **communism** became more popular and powerful during World War II.

Kai-Shek wanted to stop this, so he began a civil war between his **Nationalist Party** and the **Communist Party** (1927-1949).

- Kai-Shek led the LONG MARCH, hunting down and killing 80,000 communists along the way!
- MAO ZEDONG survived the Long March and became the leader of the Communist Party.
- The Communist Party won the civil war and established the **communist**-run People's Republic of China (PRC).

Kai-Shek fled to Taiwan and set up a **nationalist**-run country there.

R **Cause and effect:** Karl Marx and the *Communist Manifesto* ➲communism in China, Korea, and Vietnam

E **Ideas and Beliefs:** Mao Zedong spread the ideas of communism.

Mao Zedong – The Great Leap Forward (1958)

THE GREAT LEAP FORWARD:

Mao Zedong introduced this new program to increase agricultural and industrial growth.

- He created COMMUNES – groups of people who lived and worked together and had to produce quotas of goods.
- This program was a massive failure.
- It caused the worst man-made famine in history! Millions of Chinese people died.
- But if anyone protested, they were imprisoned in "reeducation camps" or killed.

Ⓡ Common Regents question

Ⓡ The Regents often compares Mao Zedong's Great Leap Forward to Stalin's Five-Year Plan and collectivization in Russia. Both of these communist leaders imposed a command economy and tried instituting economic reforms. Both weren't very successful.

Ⓔ **Innovation/Environmental Impact:** The Great Leap Forward

Mao Zedong – The Cultural Revolution (1966)

Mao Zedong renewed communism and strengthened Chinese culture.

- Mao Zedong closed all schools and universities, and invited 11 million students called RED GUARDS to attack all professionals (writers, scientists, doctors, etc.) who opposed communism.
- The Red Guards were extremely violent and caused major destruction.

HINT: The Cultural Revolution was a revolution of the culture of China.

E **Power/Inequality/Conflict:** Mao Zedong used force to strengthen communism.

R **Connections:** Mao Zedong's Cultural Revolution was similar to Stalin's Purges.

The Next Chinese communist Leader – Deng Xiaoping (1976)

After Mao Zedong died, DENG XIAOPING rose to power.
He managed to improve the economy, but not the political situation.

THE FOUR MODERNIZATIONS – Xiaoping's economic reforms:

1. Modernized farming
2. Upgraded industry
3. Growth in technology
4. Improved defense

Economic Improvements under Xiaoping:

- He changed the economy from a COMMAND ECONOMY to a SOCIALIST MARKET ECONOMY – a market economy with public ownership and state-owned businesses
- Xiaoping got rid of the communes.
- He allowed partial private ownership.
- He allowed foreign business.

The political situation was another story...

Deng Xiaoping and Tiananmen Square Massacre

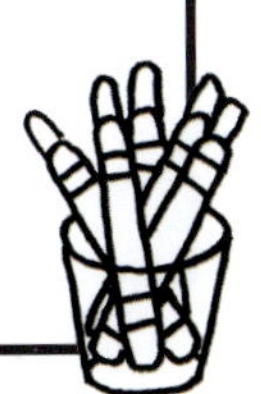

TIANANMEN SQUARE MASSACRE(1989):

Isn't it ironic how a protest for human rights resulted in such severe human rights violations?!

The Chinese people were fed up with the government's inflation, corruption, lack of freedom of press, and freedom of speech. They organized a demonstration to protest for more rights and freedoms.

Tiananmen Square

Instead of the government listening to their complaints, they sent tanks and troops to fight them! The government quashed the protests, killing and wounding thousands of people in the process.

- (R) Common Regents question
- (E) **Innovation:** The Four Modernizations and improved economy under Xiaoping
- (E) **Conflict/Power:** Political unrest – Tiananmen Square
- (R) This is an example of human rights violations.

HINT: Tiananmen (tie men): Chinese men and women felt tied down and wanted more freedoms.

Return of Hong Kong to China

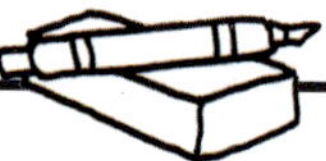

(1842) Britain took control of Hong Kong (an island off the coast of China). Britain helped Hong Kong modernize and become wealthy.

(1997) Britain returned Hong Kong to China. Hong Kong then became known as the SPECIAL ADMINISTRATIVE REGION – it enjoys some self-rule and has a separate political and economic system from that of mainland China.

To this day, the people of Hong Kong continue to protest and struggle for more independence. How will this conflict be resolved? Only time will tell....

Power/Conflict: China partially controls Hong Kong, and Hong Kong wants more independence.

China Today

China is the biggest exporter of goods in the world today.
It is an economic superpower because of the massive amount of international trading it does.

President XI JINPING is working to advance the economy, while maintaining a strict form of communism.

President Xi Jinping

Current Issues in China:

1. China controls the Buddhist region of TIBET. The people of Tibet want their independence.
2. The Chinese people suffer from human rights violations, and do not have freedom of speech or press or the right to vote. They also suffer from poor working conditions and minimal pay.
3. OVERPOPULATION: The Chinese government was concerned that the cities were becoming so overcrowded that the natural resources would run out and there'd be too much pollution.
    - Therefore, the government enacted a ONE-CHILD POLICY, which meant that each Chinese family was only allowed to have one child. This law caused serious problems, including killing of female babies and the aging of China's population. Many outsiders disagree with this approach as the world was ultimately created for people.
    - Since 2013, the government has eased up on this policy, and now allows families to have two children.

Power: China has become an economic superpower globally.

Interconnectedness: Countries around the world are dependent on China's exports.

Inequality/Human Rights Violation: People are deprived of freedom of speech and the press, and the right to vote.

Scarcity/Environmental Impact: Overpopulation – the Chinese government is concerned that the natural resources will get used up and therefore limits the population.

The Asian Tigers

THE ASIAN TIGERS:

1. Taiwan
2. Singapore
3. Hong Kong
4. South Korea

These four countries, located on the Pacific Rim, were nicknamed "Asian Tigers" because of their rapid economic growth. They are known for their massive financial and manufacturing centers, which make them prosperous.

Quick Review

Check off the boxes you know well. Whatever you don't know well (yet!), go back and review now!

- ☐ India
  - Religious tension between Hindus and Muslims
  - Partition of India
  - Sikhs
  - Caste system stopped
  - Mixed economy
  - Green Revolution
  - Religious tension in Kashmir
  - East Pakistan becomes Bangladesh
- ☐ Korea – South Korea experiences economic growth, North Korea (Kim Jong-Un) is communist and abuses military power.
- ☐ Vietnam – Ho Chi Minh and guerrilla warfare
- ☐ Cambodia – Khmer Rouge, Pol Pot, and human rights violations
- ☐ Japan – modernization vs. traditionalism
- ☐ China
  - Mao Zedong – the Great Leap Forward, communes, the Cultural Revolution
  - Deng Xiaoping – the Four Modernizations, economic improvement
  - Tiananmen Square Massacre
  - Hong Kong is returned to China – Special Administrative Region
  - Xi Jinping and economic success
- ☐ Asian Tigers: Taiwan, Singapore, Hong Kong, South Korea

Enduring Issues Essay Topics That Came Up in This Unit:

- **Conflict:**
  - Hindus vs. Muslims in India
  - India and Pakistan fight over control of Kashmir.
  - Pakistan and Afghanistan are politically instable and fraught with terrorism.
  - Korean War and Vietnam War
  - Traditionalism vs. modernization in Japan
  - Tiananmen Square Massacre
- **Human Rights Violations:**
  - Terrorism in Pakistan and Afghanistan
  - North Korea's brutality against those opposed to Kim Jong-Un's regime, nuclear proliferation
  - Khmer Rouge (Pol Pot) murdered over a million people in Cambodia to remove Western influence.
- **Inequality:** The Untouchables in India are considered inferior and are mistreated.
- **Interconnectedness:** India, China, and the Asian Tigers manufacture goods for countries around the world. Also, countries around the world outsource jobs to India, China, and the Asian Tigers.
- **Cooperation:**
  - The United States aids South Vietnam to help contain communism.
  - The United States helps Japan establish a democratic government, which leads to Japan's success.

More Enduring Issues Essay Topics That Came Up in This Unit:

- **Power:** China and the Asian Tigers became economic world powers.
- **Ideas and Beliefs:** communism vs. containment
- **Innovation:**
  - Social changes in India (Nehru and Mother Teresa)
  - The Great Leap Forward/communes during Mao Zedong's rule in China
  - The Four Modernizations and improved economy under Xiaoping

- **Scarcity:** Overpopulation – the Chinese government is concerned that the natural resources will get used up and therefore limits the population.
- **Environmental Impact:**
  - Green Revolution and overpopulation
  - The Great Leap Forward/communes during Mao Zedong's rule in China
  - Overpopulation in China – the Chinese government is concerned that the natural resources will get used up and therefore limits the population.

Regents Question Time!

Now it's time to test how well you know your stuff.

Have fun!

Regents Question Time!

Excerpt of a Speech Given by Nehru at the Bandung Conference in 1955

> . . . If all the world were to be divided up between these two big blocs what would be the result? The inevitable result would be war. Therefore every step that takes place in reducing that area in the world which may be called the unaligned area is a dangerous step and leads to war. It reduces that objective, that balance, that outlook which other countries without military might can perhaps exercise. . . .

— George Kahin, ed., *The Asian-African Conference,* Bandung, Indonesia, April 1955
Cornell University Press, 1956

16 Which historical development led Nehru to promote the policy of unaligned areas?

(1) expansion of Cold War blocs
(2) political pressure from his Parliament to pursue isolationism
(3) partitioning of India and Pakistan at independence
(4) internal friction between various Indian ethnic groups

Answer: ____

Excerpt of a Speech Given by Nehru at the Bandung Conference in 1955

Nehru is explaining why he never took sides between the "two big blocs" – communism and democracy.

. . . If all the world were to be divided up between these two big blocs what would be the result? The inevitable result would be war. Therefore every step that takes place in reducing that area in the world which may be called the unaligned area is a dangerous step and leads to war. It reduces that objective, that balance, that outlook which other countries without military might can perhaps exercise. . . .

— George Kahin, ed., *The Asian-African Conference,* Bandung, Indonesia, April 1955
Cornell University Press, 1956

What was going on in the world that led to Nehru's nonalignment policy?

16 Which historical development led Nehru to promote the policy of unaligned areas?

(1) expansion of Cold War blocs
(2) political pressure from his Parliament to pursue isolationism
(3) partitioning of India and Pakistan at independence
(4) internal friction between various Indian ethnic groups

Regents Question Time!

Excerpt of a Speech Given by Nehru at the Bandung Conference in 1955

> . . . If all the world were to be divided up between these two big blocs what would be the result? The inevitable result would be war. Therefore every step that takes place in reducing that area in the world which may be called the unaligned area is a dangerous step and leads to war. It reduces that objective, that balance, that outlook which other countries without military might can perhaps exercise. . . .

— George Kahin, ed., *The Asian-African Conference,* Bandung, Indonesia, April 1955
Cornell University Press, 1956

17 Which countries would be most likely to agree to adopt the policy Nehru is discussing?

(1) democracies in Western Europe
(2) communist nations in Asia
(3) newly independent Asian and African nations
(4) satellite countries in Central and Eastern Europe

Answer: ____

1

Excerpt of a Speech Given by Nehru at the Bandung Conference in 1955

Nehru explains his views on nonalignment.

> . . . If all the world were to be divided up between these two big blocs what would be the result? The inevitable result would be war. Therefore every step that takes place in reducing that area in the world which may be called the unaligned area is a dangerous step and leads to war. It reduces that objective, that balance, that outlook which other countries without military might can perhaps exercise. . . .

2

— George Kahin, ed., *The Asian-African Conference,* Bandung, Indonesia, April 1955
Cornell University Press, 1956

3

Which countries would agree with the nonalignment policy?

4

17 Which countries would be most likely to agree to adopt the policy Nehru is discussing?

(1) democracies in Western Europe
(2) communist nations in Asia
(3) newly independent Asian and African nations
(4) satellite countries in Central and Eastern Europe

You can find the answer to this question using the process of elimination. The democratic, communist, and satellite countries each took sides in the Cold War and did not follow the nonalignment policy. Cross out those choices. The only one left is "newly independent Asian and African nations."

Regents Question Time!

Mao's cult of personality also went beyond the badges and the Little Red Book. There were propaganda posters inside homes, classrooms, meeting halls, office buildings, and factories. The line beneath Mao's image says: Wishing Chairman Mao a long life.

Source: International Institute of Social History

18 Which political leader other than Mao Zedong utilized this type of poster?

(1) Otto Von Bismarck
(2) Emperor Meiji
(3) Joseph Stalin
(4) Nelson Mandela

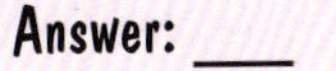
Answer: ____

1

No title here. Move on.

Mao Zedong is portrayed in this document and image as a dictator who uses propaganda to promote himself.
Joseph Stalin was also a dictator who used propaganda to promote himself.

Mao's cult of personality also went beyond the badges and the Little Red Book. There were propaganda posters inside homes, classrooms, meeting halls, office buildings, and factories. The line beneath Mao's image says: Wishing Chairman Mao a long life.

2

Source: International Institute of Social History

3

18 Which political leader other than Mao Zedong utilized this type of poster?

(1) Otto Von Bismarck
(2) Emperor Meiji
(3) Joseph Stalin
(4) Nelson Mandela

4

Regents Question Time!

Mao's cult of personality also went beyond the badges and the Little Red Book. There were propaganda posters inside homes, classrooms, meeting halls, office buildings, and factories. The line beneath Mao's image says: Wishing Chairman Mao a long life.

Source: International Institute of Social History

19 The design and use of this poster suggests its purpose was to

(1) advertise advancements in Chinese healthcare
(2) build support for China's leader among the people
(3) warn the Chinese people about the dangers of capitalism
(4) improve the literacy rates of children and adults throughout China

Answer: ___

1

No title here. Move on.

It's a propaganda poster to promote Mao Zedong.

Mao's cult of personality also went beyond the badges and the Little Red Book. There were propaganda posters inside homes, classrooms, meeting halls, office buildings, and factories. The line beneath Mao's image says: Wishing Chairman Mao a long life.

4

2

Source: International Institute of Social History

3

What was the purpose of this poster?

19 The design and use of this poster suggests its purpose was to

(1) advertise advancements in Chinese healthcare
(2) build support for China's leader among the people
(3) warn the Chinese people about the dangers of capitalism
(4) improve the literacy rates of children and adults throughout China

Regents Question Time!

Mao's cult of personality also went beyond the badges and the Little Red Book. There were propaganda posters inside homes, classrooms, meeting halls, office buildings, and factories. The line beneath Mao's image says: Wishing Chairman Mao a long life.

Source: International Institute of Social History

20 Which historical development is most closely associated with this poster?

(1) establishment of special economic zones
(2) efforts to confront the opium crisis
(3) nationalist rebellions against Qing rule
(4) the Cultural Revolution

Answer: ___

1

No title here. Move on.

Mao's cult of personality also went beyond the badges and the Little Red Book. There were propaganda posters inside homes, classrooms, meeting halls, office buildings, and factories. The line beneath Mao's image says: Wishing Chairman Mao a long life.

2

Source: International Institute of Social History

3

What was going on during this period that was connected to Mao Zedong's dictatorship?

20 Which historical development is most closely associated with this poster?

(1) establishment of special economic zones
(2) efforts to confront the opium crisis
(3) nationalist rebellions against Qing rule
(4) the Cultural Revolution

4

Mao Zedong started the Cultural Revolution to reignite Chinese culture. He used his position as a dictator to snuff out non-Chinese culture.

Regents Question Time!

. . . China is such a powerhouse of low-cost manufacturing that even though the NAFTA accord has given Mexico a leg up with the United States, and even though Mexico is right next door to us, China in 2003 replaced Mexico as the number two exporter to the United States. (Canada remains number one.) Though Mexico still has a strong position in big-ticket exports that are costly to ship, such as cars, auto parts, and refrigerators, China is coming on strong and has already displaced Mexico in areas such as computer parts, electrical components, toys, textiles, sporting goods, and tennis shoes. But what's even worse for Mexico is that China is displacing some Mexican companies in Mexico, where Chinese-made clothing and toys are now showing up on store shelves everywhere. No wonder a Mexican journalist told me about the day he interviewed a Chinese central bank official, who told him something about China's relationship with America that really rattled him: "First we were afraid of the wolf, then we wanted to dance with the wolf, and now we want to be the wolf.". . .

— Thomas L. Friedman, *The World Is Flat: A Brief History of the Twenty-first Century,* Farrar, Straus and Giroux, 2005

25 According to Thomas Friedman, why is it surprising that Mexico is being replaced by China as the number two exporter to the United States?

(1) Mexico is geographically close to the United States.
(2) China's relationship with the United States has been damaged.
(3) Mexico has the world's strongest economy.
(4) China's industry lacks low-cost manufacturing ability.

Answer: ____

1

No title here. Move on.

Mexico shares a border with the USA ("right next door to us"), which makes it strange that they're not exporting as much to the USA as China is.

. . . China is such a powerhouse of low-cost manufacturing that even though the NAFTA accord has given Mexico a leg up with the United States, and even though Mexico is right next door to us, China in 2003 replaced Mexico as the number two exporter to the United States. (Canada remains number one.) Though Mexico still has a strong position in big-ticket exports that are costly to ship, such as cars, auto parts, and refrigerators, China is coming on strong and has already displaced Mexico in areas such as computer parts, electrical components, toys, textiles, sporting goods, and tennis shoes. But what's even worse for Mexico is that China is displacing some Mexican companies in Mexico, where Chinese-made clothing and toys are now showing up on store shelves everywhere. No wonder a Mexican journalist told me about the day he interviewed a Chinese central bank official, who told him something about China's relationship with America that really rattled him: "First we were afraid of the wolf, then we wanted to dance with the wolf, and now we want to be the wolf.". . .

4

2

— Thomas L. Friedman, *The World Is Flat: A Brief History of the Twenty-first Century*, Farrar, Straus and Giroux, 2005

3

Why is it surprising that Mexico isn't exporting as much goods to the USA as China is?

25 According to Thomas Friedman, why is it surprising that Mexico is being replaced by China as the number two exporter to the United States?

(1) Mexico is geographically close to the United States.
(2) China's relationship with the United States has been damaged.
(3) Mexico has the world's strongest economy.
(4) China's industry lacks low-cost manufacturing ability.

See what the question is asking. Read the wording carefully to make sure you are answering the question being asked.

Regents Question Time!

. . . China is such a powerhouse of low-cost manufacturing that even though the NAFTA accord has given Mexico a leg up with the United States, and even though Mexico is right next door to us, China in 2003 replaced Mexico as the number two exporter to the United States. (Canada remains number one.) Though Mexico still has a strong position in big-ticket exports that are costly to ship, such as cars, auto parts, and refrigerators, China is coming on strong and has already displaced Mexico in areas such as computer parts, electrical components, toys, textiles, sporting goods, and tennis shoes. But what's even worse for Mexico is that China is displacing some Mexican companies in Mexico, where Chinese-made clothing and toys are now showing up on store shelves everywhere. No wonder a Mexican journalist told me about the day he interviewed a Chinese central bank official, who told him something about China's relationship with America that really rattled him: "First we were afraid of the wolf, then we wanted to dance with the wolf, and now we want to be the wolf.". . .

— Thomas L. Friedman, *The World Is Flat: A Brief History of the Twenty-first Century,* Farrar, Straus and Giroux, 2005

26 In the quotation "First we were afraid of the wolf, then we wanted to dance with the wolf, and now we want to be the wolf," what does the "wolf" symbolize?

(1) an economic powerhouse
(2) an exporting country
(3) a valuable trade item
(4) a low-cost manufacturer

Answer: ____

1

No title here. Move on.

First, China was afraid of USA, which was considered the world's economic leader, then it tried competing with the USA, and now it is becoming the world's economic leader.

. . . China is such a powerhouse of low-cost manufacturing that even though the NAFTA accord has given Mexico a leg up with the United States, and even though Mexico is right next door to us, China in 2003 replaced Mexico as the number two exporter to the United States. (Canada remains number one.) Though Mexico still has a strong position in big-ticket exports that are costly to ship, such as cars, auto parts, and refrigerators, China is coming on strong and has already displaced Mexico in areas such as computer parts, electrical components, toys, textiles, sporting goods, and tennis shoes. But what's even worse for Mexico is that China is displacing some Mexican companies in Mexico, where Chinese-made clothing and toys are now showing up on store shelves everywhere. No wonder a Mexican journalist told me about the day he interviewed a Chinese central bank official, who told him something about China's relationship with America that really rattled him: "First we were afraid of the wolf, then we wanted to dance with the wolf, and now we want to be the wolf." . . .

4

2

— Thomas L. Friedman, *The World Is Flat: A Brief History of the Twenty-first Century*, Farrar, Straus and Giroux, 2005

3

26 In the quotation "First we were afraid of the wolf, then we wanted to dance with the wolf, and now we want to be the wolf," what does the "wolf" symbolize?

(1) an economic powerhouse
(2) an exporting country
(3) a valuable trade item
(4) a low-cost manufacturer

Regents Question Time!

. . . Yet in recent months something has changed. Kim Jong Il, whose regime was responsible for the first test and who died in 2011, had only a rudimentary [basic] nuclear device, useful mainly for blackmail. Under his son, Kim Jong Un, the programme has rapidly gathered pace, with two nuclear tests this year alone. The North has also conducted 21 missile tests this year, including one from a submarine—a first. The ability to miniaturise a tactical nuclear weapon on a working missile could be just two or three years away, with an intercontinental ballistic missile capable of hitting California possible in five years' time. Chun Yung-woo, a South Korean former national security adviser, talks of "growing outrage. . .after five tests, a change of mood, a sense of urgency."

Once, it was possible to hope that the North's isolated regime would implode [fail] under its own contradictions before it gained a proper nuclear capability. But the spread of informal markets and, for some North Koreans, a measure of prosperity may have strengthened the regime's chances of survival. A consensus in Seoul is forming that Mr Kim now aims to dictate events on the peninsula—including the ability to demand that the Americans leave. One senior foreign diplomat in Seoul says that for the first time he hears people wondering openly whether there will be a major conflict on the peninsula in their lifetime. . . .

— "A Shrimp Among Whales," *The Economist*, October 27, 2016

20 The tensions between North Korea and South Korea described in this passage began over

(1) boundaries drawn during the Cold War
(2) ethnic conflict on the Korean peninsula
(3) trade disputes centered on fishing rights in the Yellow Sea
(4) China's purchase of submarine technology from North Korea

Answer: ___

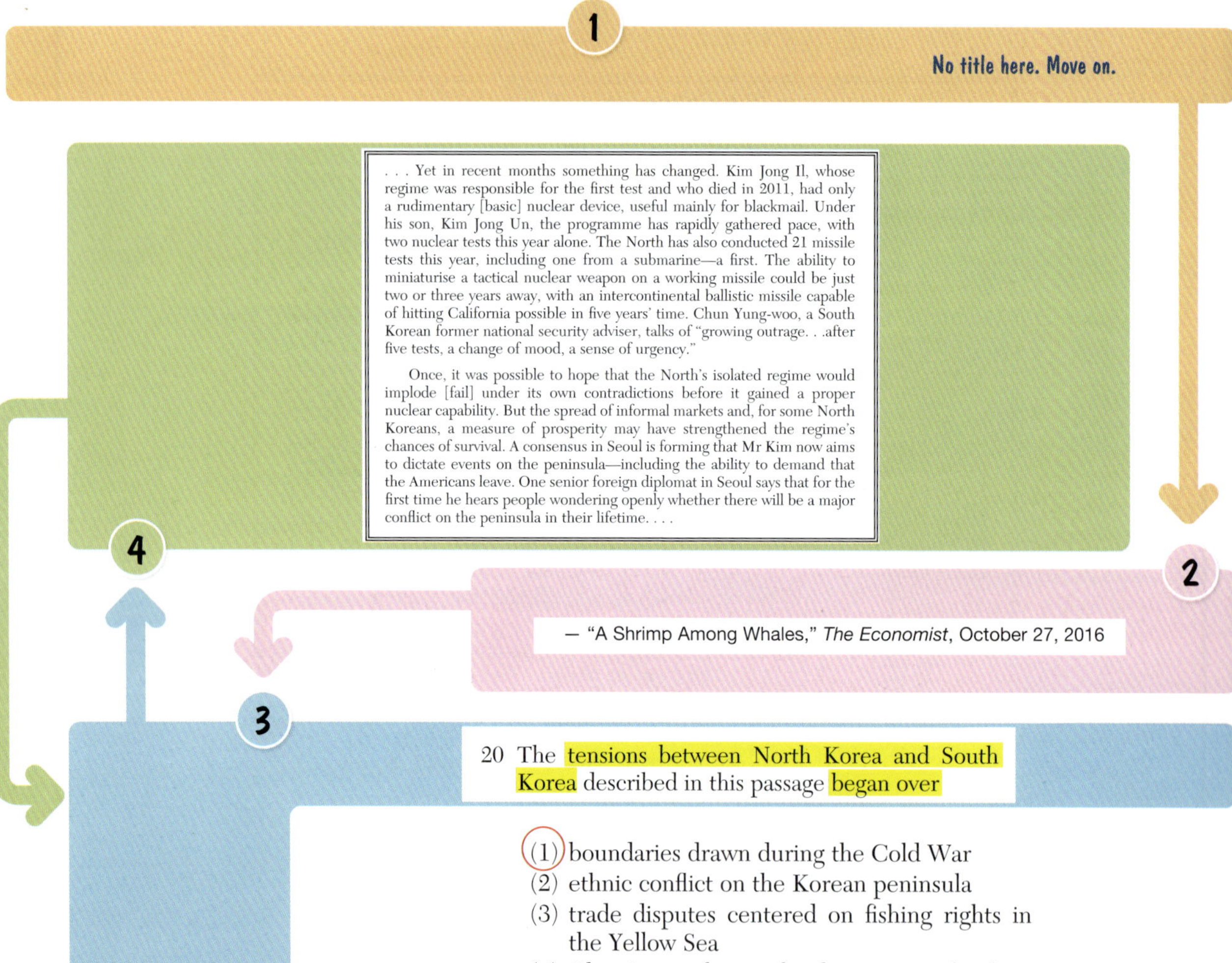

. . . Yet in recent months something has changed. Kim Jong Il, whose regime was responsible for the first test and who died in 2011, had only a rudimentary [basic] nuclear device, useful mainly for blackmail. Under his son, Kim Jong Un, the programme has rapidly gathered pace, with two nuclear tests this year alone. The North has also conducted 21 missile tests this year, including one from a submarine—a first. The ability to miniaturise a tactical nuclear weapon on a working missile could be just two or three years away, with an intercontinental ballistic missile capable of hitting California possible in five years' time. Chun Yung-woo, a South Korean former national security adviser, talks of "growing outrage. . .after five tests, a change of mood, a sense of urgency."

Once, it was possible to hope that the North's isolated regime would implode [fail] under its own contradictions before it gained a proper nuclear capability. But the spread of informal markets and, for some North Koreans, a measure of prosperity may have strengthened the regime's chances of survival. A consensus in Seoul is forming that Mr Kim now aims to dictate events on the peninsula—including the ability to demand that the Americans leave. One senior foreign diplomat in Seoul says that for the first time he hears people wondering openly whether there will be a major conflict on the peninsula in their lifetime. . . .

— "A Shrimp Among Whales," *The Economist*, October 27, 2016

20 The tensions between North Korea and South Korea described in this passage began over

(1) boundaries drawn during the Cold War
(2) ethnic conflict on the Korean peninsula
(3) trade disputes centered on fishing rights in the Yellow Sea
(4) China's purchase of submarine technology from North Korea

The document didn't answer the question. Sometimes you just have to pull things out from your brain. Sorry!

Regents Question Time!

. . . Yet in recent months something has changed. Kim Jong Il, whose regime was responsible for the first test and who died in 2011, had only a rudimentary [basic] nuclear device, useful mainly for blackmail. Under his son, Kim Jong Un, the programme has rapidly gathered pace, with two nuclear tests this year alone. The North has also conducted 21 missile tests this year, including one from a submarine—a first. The ability to miniaturise a tactical nuclear weapon on a working missile could be just two or three years away, with an intercontinental ballistic missile capable of hitting California possible in five years' time. Chun Yung-woo, a South Korean former national security adviser, talks of "growing outrage. . .after five tests, a change of mood, a sense of urgency."

Once, it was possible to hope that the North's isolated regime would implode [fail] under its own contradictions before it gained a proper nuclear capability. But the spread of informal markets and, for some North Koreans, a measure of prosperity may have strengthened the regime's chances of survival. A consensus in Seoul is forming that Mr Kim now aims to dictate events on the peninsula—including the ability to demand that the Americans leave. One senior foreign diplomat in Seoul says that for the first time he hears people wondering openly whether there will be a major conflict on the peninsula in their lifetime. . . .

— "A Shrimp Among Whales," *The Economist*, October 27, 2016

21 Based on this passage, in which way is the situation in the Korean peninsula comparable to the history of South Asia since World War II?

(1) Peaceful protests led colonial powers to surrender their control of the region.
(2) Increased prosperity has accompanied a shift from totalitarian to democratic rule.
(3) Regional conflicts have contributed to the proliferation of nuclear weapons.
(4) Technological progress reduced tension and led to improved trade relationships.

Answer: ___

1 No title here. Move on.

2 Kim Jong-Un is advancing his nuclear program in the Korean peninsula.

. . . Yet in recent months something has changed. Kim Jong Il, whose regime was responsible for the first test and who died in 2011, had only a rudimentary [basic] nuclear device, useful mainly for blackmail. Under his son, Kim Jong Un, the programme has rapidly gathered pace, with two nuclear tests this year alone. The North has also conducted 21 missile tests this year, including one from a submarine—a fi miniaturise a tactical nuclear weapon on a working missile could be just two or three years away, with an intercontinental ballistic missile capable of hitting California possible in five years' time. Chun Yung-woo, a South Korean former national security adviser, talks of "growing outrage. . .after five tests, a change of mood, a sense of urgency."

Once, it was possible to hope that the North's isolated regime would implode [fail] under its own contradictions before it gained a proper nuclear capability. But the spread of informal markets and, for some North Koreans, a measure of prosperity may have strengthened the regime's chances of survival. A consensus in Seoul is forming that Mr Kim now aims to dictate events on the peninsula—including the ability to demand that the Americans leave. One senior foreign diplomat in Seoul says that for the rst time he hears people wondering openly whether there will be a major conflict on the peninsula in their lifetime. . . .

— "A Shrimp Among Whales," *The Economist*, October 27, 2016

3 **4**

21 Based on this passage, in which way is the situation in the Korean peninsula comparable to the history of South Asia since World War II?

(1) Peaceful protests led colonial powers to surrender their control of the region.
(2) Increased prosperity has accompanied a shift from totalitarian to democratic rule.
(3) Regional conflicts have contributed to the proliferation of nuclear weapons.
(4) Technological progress reduced tension and led to improved trade relationships.

It was possible to answer this question even if you didn't know a thing about South Asia. Using process of elimination, you'd see there's only one choice that matches this document.

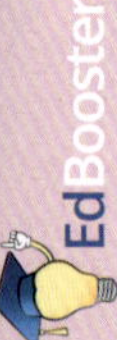

Regents Question Time!

. . . Yet in recent months something has changed. Kim Jong Il, whose regime was responsible for the first test and who died in 2011, had only a rudimentary [basic] nuclear device, useful mainly for blackmail. Under his son, Kim Jong Un, the programme has rapidly gathered pace, with two nuclear tests this year alone. The North has also conducted 21 missile tests this year, including one from a submarine—a first. The ability to miniaturise a tactical nuclear weapon on a working missile could be just two or three years away, with an intercontinental ballistic missile capable of hitting California possible in five years' time. Chun Yung-woo, a South Korean former national security adviser, talks of "growing outrage. . .after five tests, a change of mood, a sense of urgency."

Once, it was possible to hope that the North's isolated regime would implode [fail] under its own contradictions before it gained a proper nuclear capability. But the spread of informal markets and, for some North Koreans, a measure of prosperity may have strengthened the regime's chances of survival. A consensus in Seoul is forming that Mr Kim now aims to dictate events on the peninsula—including the ability to demand that the Americans leave. One senior foreign diplomat in Seoul says that for the first time he hears people wondering openly whether there will be a major conflict on the peninsula in their lifetime. . . .

— "A Shrimp Among Whales," *The Economist*, October 27, 2016

22 Which claim is best supported in this passage?

(1) An arms race will help defuse tensions on the Korean peninsula.
(2) Economic cooperation between the two Koreas would spread democracy to the North.
(3) An invasion by the United States could remove Kim Jong Un from power with few casualties.
(4) North Korea's successful military tests have increased the likelihood of war.

Answer: ____

1

No title here. Move on.

Kim Jong-Un is advancing his nuclear program. People are very concerned about future nuclear conflict.

. . . Yet in recent months something has changed. Kim Jong Il, whose regime was responsible for the first test and who died in 2011, had only a rudimentary [basic] nuclear device, useful mainly for blackmail. Under his son, Kim Jong Un, the programme has rapidly gathered pace, with two nuclear tests this year alone. The North has also conducted 21 missile tests this year, including one from a submarine—a fi miniaturise a tactical nuclear weapon on a working missile could be just two or three years away, with an intercontinental ballistic missile capable of hitting California possible in five years' time. Chun Yung-woo, a South Korean former national security adviser, talks of "growing outrage. . .after five tests, a change of mood, a sense of urgency."

Once, it was possible to hope that the North's isolated regime would implode [fail] under its own contradictions before it gained a proper nuclear capability. But the spread of informal markets and, for some North Koreans, a measure of prosperity may have strengthened the regime's chances of survival. A consensus in Seoul is forming that Mr Kim now aims to dictate events on the peninsula—including the ability to demand that the Americans leave. One senior foreign diplomat in Seoul says that for the first time he hears people wondering openly whether there will be a major conflict on the peninsula in their lifetime. . . .

2

— "A Shrimp Among Whales," *The Economist*, October 27, 2016

3

22 Which claim is best supported in this passage?

(1) An arms race will help defuse tensions on the Korean peninsula.

(2) Economic cooperation between the two Koreas would spread democracy to the North.

(3) An invasion by the United States could remove Kim Jong Un from power with few casualties.

(4) North Korea's successful military tests have increased the likelihood of war.

4

UNIT 15

MODERN DAY MIDDLE EAST

The Middle East Today

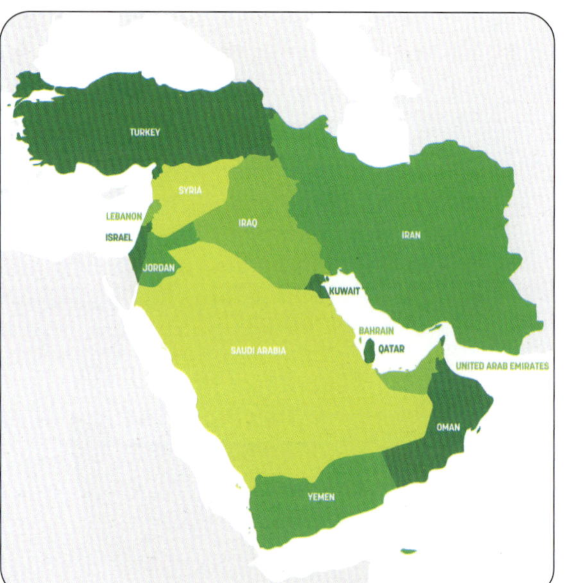

Map of the Middle East

In this unit, we'll explore the conflicts and challenges of the Middle East.

The Middle East is a crossroads for people from Africa, Asia, and Europe, and the area contains major cultural and religious diversity. This often leads to conflict...

Oil in the Middle East

As you may know from the news, the Middle East plays a huge role in world politics. Why? The Middle East has oil fields that the whole world is dependent on. Oil is the most important energy source.

As long as we're driving cars fueled by gas and using gas and oil to power appliances and heating systems, we are dependent on the Middle East for the gas.

The type of oil we're talking about is NOT cooking oil! It's oil/gas that's an energy source for cars, machinery, appliances, and heat.

How Middle Eastern oil impacts politics:

- Middle Eastern countries go to war to control oil-rich lands.
- Countries all over the world take interest in these countries because they need their oil.

Oil and OPEC

Several countries established an organization called OPEC (Organization of Petroleum Exporting Countries) to control the oil industry by setting prices and production levels.

- This organization was founded by Iraq, Iran, Kuwait, Saudi Arabia, and Venezuela.
- OPEC has a lot of power because it controls most of the world's oil.
- OPEC sometimes refuses to sell oil to specific countries for political reasons.

R This is an example of how geography impacts history.

E **Environmental Impact:** Oil in the Middle East has a significant effect on world politics.

Iraq

SADDAM HUSSEIN was the nationalistic Arab leader of Iraq. He was involved in several Middle Eastern conflicts:

Saddam Hussein

Now let's travel around the Middle East and visit Iraq, Iran, Afghanistan, Israel, Egypt and some other cool places.

1. IRAN-IRAQ WAR (1980-1988):
   War between Iran and Iraq over borders
2. PERSIAN GULF WAR (1990-1991):
   Saddam Hussein (Iraqi leader) invaded Kuwait for its oil. America went to war against Iraq to defend Kuwait and forced Iraqi troops to leave Kuwait.

3. US-IRAQ WAR (2003):
   The United States thought that Iraq was hiding weapons of mass destruction (WMDs), so the US invaded Iraq and overthrew Saddam Hussein. He was tried and then executed (killed).
   FYI: No evidence of weapons of mass destruction were ever found.

There was no strong leadership after the last war with Iraq, and ISIS (a terror organization) has taken control.

Conflict: Many wars have been fought in Iraq.

Cooperation: The United States invaded Iraq to stop the spread of nuclear weapons.

Environmental Impact: Iraq invaded Kuwait for its oil.

Iran and Reza Pahlavi

REZA PAHLAVI overthrew the SHAH (leader) and made himself the new Shah, in 1941.
He used terror to modernize and Westernize Iran.

Pahlavi Westernized and modernized Iran by:

1. Building factories and railroads
2. Strengthening the army
3. Adopting Western dress and law
4. Establishing secular schools
5. Integrating women into public life

Shah Reza Pahlavi
(Notice his Western dress.)

- R The Regents often compares Reza Pahlavi to Ataturk from Turkey and Meiji from Japan. They all modernized their countries.
- R Pahlavi and Ataturk both faced Islamic opposition.
- E **Conflict:** There is often a clash between forces of modernization and traditionalism/religion.

Iran and Ayatollah Khomeini

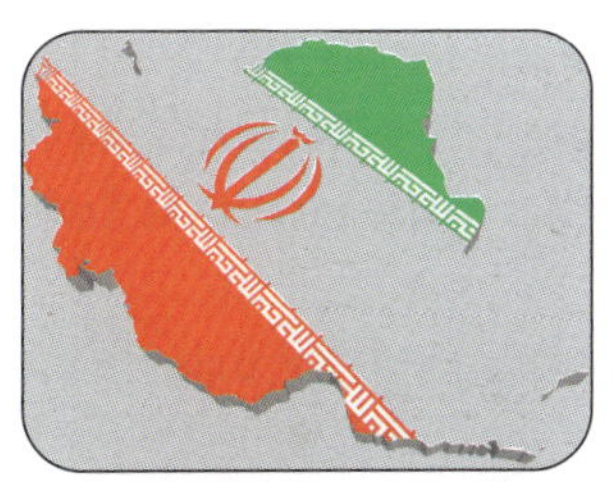

AYATOLLA KHOMEINI and others opposed Westernization.

The IRANIAN REVOLUTION (1979): Khomeini and other Iranians overthrew the Shah. Khomeini took power.

- Khomeini, a strict Muslim, established a strict Muslim traditional government that rules according to sharia law (Islamic religious law).
- He believed in ISLAMIC FUNDAMENTALISM – adherence to strict Muslim religious tradition and opposition to Westernization.

AHMADINEJAD took over and created a huge nuclear program (2005). He refused to end it despite intense world pressure.

In 2015, the Iran Nuclear Deal was signed with the goal of Iran dismantling its nuclear program in exchange for billions of dollars. President Trump withdrew from the deal in 2018 because Iran was not complying with the deal.

Ayatolla Khomeini

R Common Regents questions

R **Connections:** Both Iran and Turkey (think Ataturk) struggle with modernization vs. traditionalism.

Afghanistan

Background: The Soviet Union invaded Afghanistan in 1979. The United States provided financial and military aid to defend Afghanistan against the Soviet Union.

When the Soviet Union left Afghanistan, there was no leadership. A terrorist group called the TALIBAN/AL QAEDA took over (1988). The leader was OSAMA BIN LADEN.

- On September 11, 2001 (9/11), al Qaeda attacked the Twin Towers in New York City and the Pentagon in Washington, D.C.
- The United States invaded Afghanistan to fight al Qaeda terrorists. Nine years later, US forces killed Osama bin Laden.
- The United States left Afghanistan in 2021. The Taliban, who are known to abuse human rights, took over the government and remain in power.

Ⓡ **Conflict:** The al Qaeda terrorist group attacked the United States.
Ⓡ **Ideas and Beliefs:** Terrorism

The Israeli-Palestinian Conflict

You see that tiny country called Israel? Jewish Israelis and Palestinian Arabs are in a serious conflict over whose homeland this country is.

- The Jewish Israelis claim that the land was promised to them by God in the Bible and that it's their homeland. They were kicked out of the land by the Romans thousands of years ago and they want it back.
- The Palestinian Arabs claim that the land is their homeland and belongs to them. They were living there for hundreds of years and they want to maintain control over the land. Neighboring Arab countries support them.

Notice how Israel is surrounded by Arab states – including Egypt, Lebanon, Syria, Jordan, Iraq, and Saudi Arabia.

Map of the Middle East

The History Behind the Israeli-Palestinian Conflict

Herzl: Founder of Zionism

1. The Jews were living in Israel until the Romans destroyed their settlement and banned them from living there (70CE). The country was called PALESTINE. Later, Arabs settled the land and then over the years, groups of Jews returned to live there, too.

2. In Europe, the Jews were facing persecution and pogroms. So THEODOR HERZL led a movement called ZIONISM (1800s). This was a nationalistic movement to create a Jewish state.

   In 1917, the British (who were trying to gain control of Palestine from the Ottomans) signed the BALFOUR DECLARATION, which promised the Jews a national homeland in Palestine. Many Jews moved to Palestine and bought and farmed land there.

3. Then, during World War II, the Holocaust happened: six million European Jews were murdered by the Nazis. Many surviving Jews needed a safe place to settle and wanted to return to their homeland. There was an international effort to create a Jewish state in Palestine.

R The Regents often asks about conflict in the Middle East. There is an ongoing conflict between the Jews and the Arabs over whose HOMELAND Israel is.

R **Turning Point:** The Holocaust leads to the creation of the State of Israel, which leads to ongoing regional conflict.

E **Conflict:** Jews and Arabs over Israel

E **Ideas and Beliefs:** Zionism

The State of Israel

(1948) Britain withdrew from Palestine. The United Nations made a plan to split Palestine (present-day Israel) between the Jews and the Arabs. The Jews agreed to the plan, but the Arabs did not.

So the Jews declared an independent State of Israel.

The Arabs (in Israel and the surrounding countries) attacked the Jews and fought a series of wars over borders. Israel won territory in these wars.

Israeli/Arab Wars:

1. War of Independence(1948)
2. Six Day War(1967)
3. Yom Kippur War(1973)

Arab Terrorism in Israel

The Palestinian Arabs are upset that they lost so much land in the wars. They also have many internal issues including poverty, refugees, and infighting. Radicals among Palestinian Arabs use terrorism to gain land back.

Arab TERRORISM:

- The PLO (Palestine Liberation Organization) was started by YASIR ARAFAT, an Arab leader who promoted terrorism to regain Palestinian land.
- INTIFADA (1987): Arab radicals made an uprising against the Jews, boycotting Israel and throwing stones and bombs at Israelis. Their goal was to gain more territory from Israel.
- SUICIDE BOMBINGS: Young Arab radicals attach bombs to themselves and blow themselves up in highly populated Israeli areas, such as buses and cafés, to kill Israelis.
- Hamas is a Palestinian terrorist organization that controls the West Bank. They engage in terrorism with the goal of wiping Israel off the map.

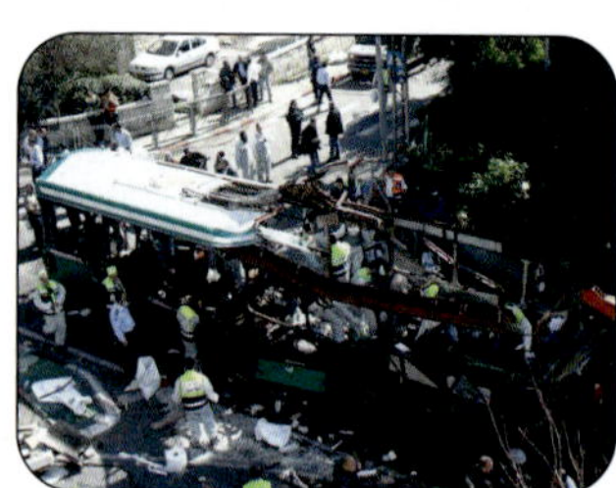

Bus bombing terrorism

Human Rights Violation: Arab terrorism against Israeli Jews

Peace Attempts in Israel

There have been many attempts to resolve the Israeli-Palestinian conflict, often called "a roadmap to peace."

1. CAMP DAVID ACCORDS(1978):
   President JIMMY CARTER of the US brokered a peace treaty between MENACHEM BEGIN (Israel) and ANWAR SADAT (Egypt).

   Results:
   - Israel returned the Sinai Desert to Egypt.
   - Egypt was the first Arab country to recognize Israel as an independent state.

2. OSLO ACCORDS(1993): "Land for Peace"
   President BILL CLINTON of the US attempted to make peace in the Middle East. The agreement was that if Israel gives back land, the Palestinians will stop the terrorism.

   YITZCHAK RABIN, the Israeli Prime Minister, signed a treaty to give Palestinians part of the Gaza Strip. YASIR ARAFAT, the Arab leader, signed as well.

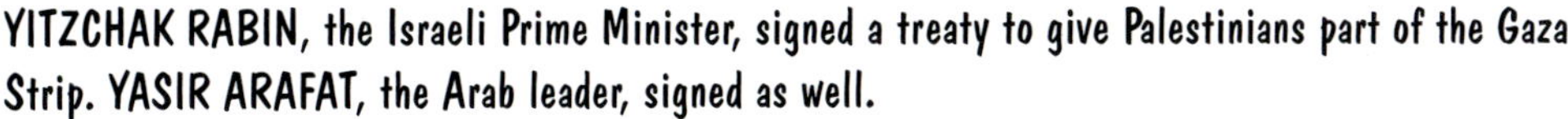

   Results: The Palestinians violated the agreement and continued attacking Israel. Unfortunately, Arab terrorism continues....

More Peace Attempts in Israel

3. Another idea has been proposed – a Two-State Solution. This involves two separate states, Israel and Palestine, living side by side with secure and recognized borders.

4. ABRAHAM ACCORDS (2020):

President **DONALD TRUMP** coordinated a peace agreement between Israel and Arab states to normalize relations. While some Arab countries signed and are cooperating, others haven't, and tensions remain.

And so, the conflict continues. The Arabs still want more territory and self-rule in Israel. Terrorism continues until today.

Conflict: Conflict between Jews and Arabs over Israeli territory.

Arab Spring

ARAB SPRING:
A series of anti-government protests, uprisings, and rebellions that spread across North Africa and the Middle East in 2010.

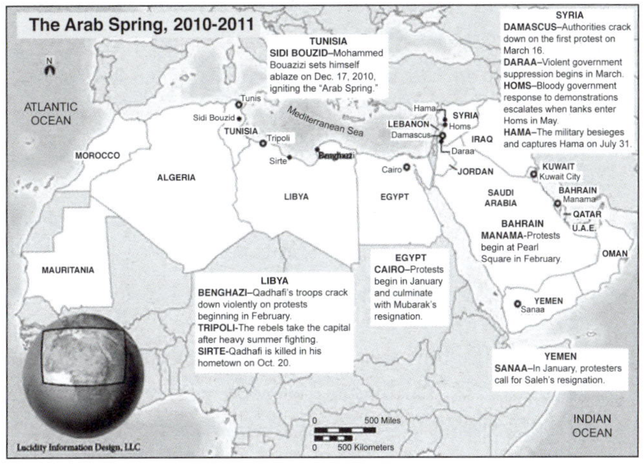

- **Cause:** Arab countries were suffering from oppressive authoritarian regimes and low standards of living. They wanted more democratic governments.
- When people in these countries tried demonstrating, the government reacted violently to stop them.
- Social media, such as Twitter and Facebook, were used to organize demonstrations and spread the Arab peoples' cause to the entire world.

Conflict: Countries rebel against their leaders in the Arab Spring.

Power: Rebels try to remove the leader from power.

EdBoosters™

The Arab Spring in Africa and Middle Eastern countries

Let me take you on a tour of the countries involved in the Arab Spring. Be prepared for serious violence. By the way, you should know the basic idea of what happened, but don't waste your brain space memorizing all these details (unless you're bored ☺).

- The Arab Spring started in Tunisia, Africa, in 2010. It spread quickly to Libya, Egypt, Yemen, Syria, and other countries.
  - TUNISIA: Tunisia had an oppressive government. The people made protests and videoed and photographed the demonstrations. Then, they sent this footage all over the world via the internet. They managed to overthrow the government and instate a more moderate leader. There was tremendous conflict between the conservative Islamists and the liberals who wanted more freedom.
  - The revolt influenced people in other countries to do the same, including Libya, Egypt, Yemen, and Syria.
  - LIBYA: al-QADDAFI ran a brutal regime. The Libyans protested against the regime and Qaddafi reacted violently to the protesters. The United States got involved, until Qaddafi fled. Currently, chaos reigns in Libya.
  - SYRIA: People protested against the government. The government responded with massacres and chemical weapons! Syria is populated by different religious groups and terror organizations, which makes peace very difficult to achieve.
    - ISIS (Islamic state in Iraq and Syria) is a terrorist opposition group in Syria (and Iraq). They spread their terror all over the world, killing people without rhyme or reason. The violence has forced millions of Syrians to flee.
- The Arab Spring has caused much chaos and violence in the Middle East and Africa, but has not been too successful in achieving peace and prosperity.

Modernization vs. Traditionalism in the Middle East

Traditional Muslim Culture:

- Tradition is very important to Muslims.
- Women are secondary to men and are expected to be modest and secluded in their homes. The women wear traditional dress, including headscarves, robes, or full burqas.
- Islamic fundamentalists are anti-Western.

Think Ataturk in Turkey, and Pahlavi and Khomeini in Iran.

Modernization:

Sometimes, modernizing and Westernizing conflicts with Muslim traditions. This major clash between culture and religions creates real tension.

Traditionalism vs. Modernization in Arab Countries:

- Iran rejects Western values, but not Western technology.
- Some Muslims want to abolish democratic political systems and return to Islamic fundamentalism.
- In Saudi Arabia, people moved to the cities to work in the oil industry. This caused many Saudis to modernize, in terms of the way women dress and in terms of people's exposure to Western influences, such as internet and TV. Saudi leaders are opposed to this Westernization and are trying to stop it.
- In Egypt, many people have moved from rural to urban areas. Muslim reformers are trying to impose Islamic law and customs on the people. They have created their own schools, social services, and medical centers.
- In some Islamic countries, women are gaining more rights. Many countries recently allowed women the right to vote. In 2018, Saudi women gained the right to drive.

Conflict/Ideas and Beliefs: Traditionalism vs. Modernization

Check off the boxes you know well. Whatever you don't know well (yet!), go back and review now!

- ☐ Oil in the Middle East (OPEC)
- ☐ Iraq's wars
  - Iran-Iraq War
  - Persian Gulf War
  - US-Iraq War
- ☐ Iranian leaders
  - Shah Pahlavi (modernization)
  - Ayatollah Khomeini and the Iranian Revolution (Islamic fundamentalism)
  - Ahmadinejad
- ☐ Afghanistan (Osama bin Laden and 9/11)
- ☐ Zionism (Theodor Herzl)
- ☐ Balfour Declaration
- ☐ Israeli/Arab Wars
  - War of Independence
  - Six Day War
  - Yom Kippur War
- ☐ PLO and Yasir Arafat
- ☐ Intifada and terrorism
- ☐ Camp David Accords and Oslo Accords
- ☐ Arab Spring
- ☐ Modernization vs. Traditionalism

Enduring Issues Essay Topics That Came Up in This Unit:

- **Environmental Impact:** Oil in the Middle East has a significant effect on world politics. Many wars have been fought over oil.

- **Conflict:**
  - Jews vs. Arabs over Israel
  - Arab Spring
  - Traditionalism vs. Modernization (Ataturk, Pahlavi, Khomeini)

- **Ideas and Beliefs:**
  - Zionism
  - Terrorism
  - Traditionalism vs. Modernization

- **Human Rights Violation:** Arab terrorism against Israeli Jews

Regents Question Time!

Now it's time to test how well you know your stuff.

Have fun!

Regents Question Time!

Source: Kevin Kallaugher, *The Economist*, February 14, 2004 (adapted)

18 Which leader's political legacy most directly influenced the situation shown in this 2004 cartoon?

(1) Ayatollah Khomeini
(2) Slobodan Milošević
(3) Augusto Pinochet
(4) Kemal Atatürk

Answer: ___

1

No title here. Move on.

Even though Iran officially became a democracy, it is experiencing conflict between the old ways and democracy. Notice that the ballot has only one choice. Doesn't look like such a democracy! The leader is trying to fit theocracy (a government where the leader rules in the name of God) into democracy.

4

2

Source: Kevin Kallaugher, *The Economist*, February 14, 2004 (adapted)

3

Who is the leader here? If you don't recognize him, you have enough other clues!

18 Which leader's political legacy most directly influenced the situation shown in this 2004 cartoon?

(1) Ayatollah Khomeini
(2) Slobodan Milošević
(3) Augusto Pinochet
(4) Kemal Atatürk

Regents Question Time!

Source: Kevin Kallaugher, *The Economist*, February 14, 2004 (adapted)

19 What is the main idea of this 2004 cartoon?

(1) Iran continues to build its modern infrastructure.
(2) Iran is experiencing tensions between tradition and modernity.
(3) Extensive ballot choices have weakened democracy in Iran.
(4) Theocracy is the best form of government for Iran to adopt.

Answer: ___

1

No title here. Move on.

Even though Iran officially became a democracy, it is experiencing conflict between the old ways and democracy.

2

Source: Kevin Kallaugher, *The Economist*, February 14, 2004 (adapted)

3

19 What is the main idea of this 2004 cartoon?

(1) Iran continues to build its modern infrastructure.
(2) Iran is experiencing tensions between tradition and modernity.
(3) Extensive ballot choices have weakened democracy in Iran.
(4) Theocracy is the best form of government for Iran to adopt.

4

Regents Question Time!

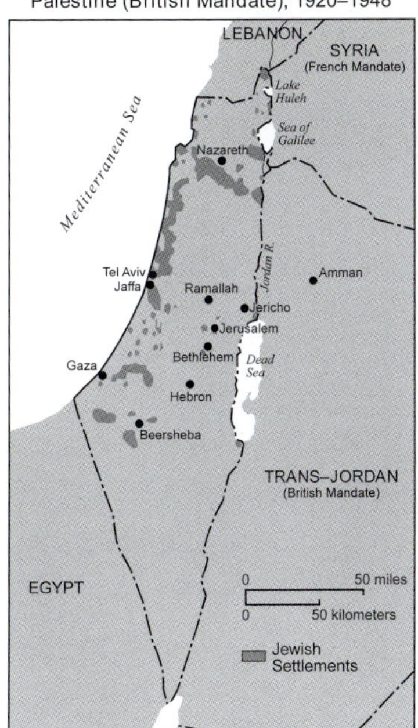

Source: Perry-Castañeda Library Map Collection, University of Texas at Austin (adapted)

Source: Peter N. Stearns, et al., World Civilizations: The Global Experience, Pearson Longman, 2005 (adapted)

14 What would be the best use for this pair of maps?

(1) to explain why European powers used the mandate system

(2) to examine the relationship between fresh water and Arab settlement patterns

(3) to understand a reason used to establish boundaries for partition

(4) to illustrate the advantages Palestinian Arabs have over Arabs living in Egypt

Answer: ___

1

Palestine (British Mandate), 1920–1948

United Nations' Partition Plan, 1947

One map shows the boundaries of Palestine under the British Mandate. The other map shows the boundaries of the United Nations' Partition Plan of 1947.

The first map shows Jewish settlements scattered throughout. The second map shows a clear partition between the Arab areas and the areas of the Jewish state.

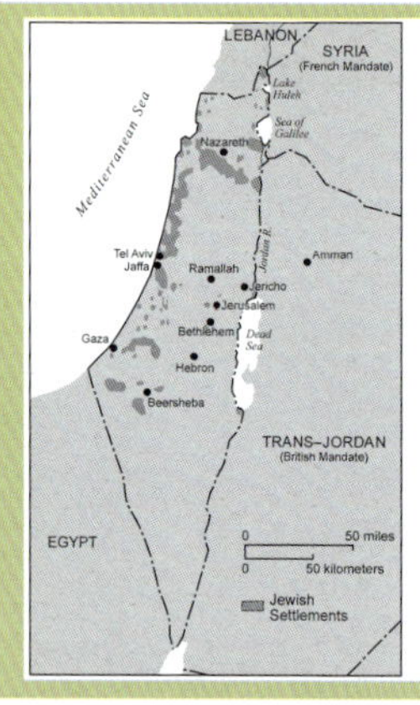

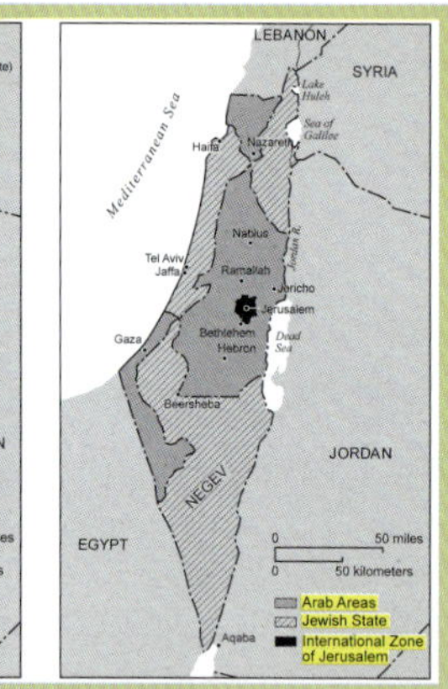

4

2

Source: Perry-Castañeda Library Map Collection, University of Texas at Austin (adapted)

Source: Peter N. Stearns, et al., World Civilizations: The Global Experience, Pearson Longman, 2005 (adapted)

3

14 What would be the best use for this pair of maps?

(1) to explain why European powers used the mandate system

(2) to examine the relationship between fresh water and Arab settlement patterns

(3) to understand a reason used to establish boundaries for partition

(4) to illustrate the advantages Palestinian Arabs have over Arabs living in Egypt

Regents Question Time!

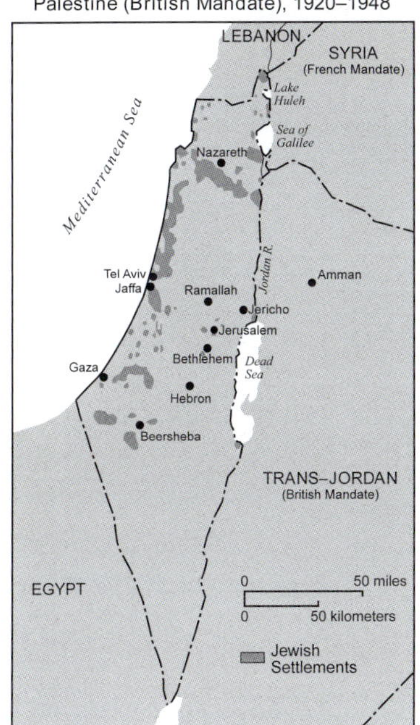

Source: Perry-Castañeda Library Map Collection, University of Texas at Austin (adapted)

United Nations' Partition Plan, 1947

Source: Peter N. Stearns, et al., World Civilizations: The Global Experience, Pearson Longman, 2005 (adapted)

15 Which situation was a contributing factor in the decision to partition British Palestine as shown on the 1947 map?

(1) mass migrations following the Holocaust
(2) decolonization from French rule
(3) capture of the Suez Canal
(4) formation of the Warsaw Pact

Answer: ___

1

Palestine (British Mandate), 1920–1948 **United Nations' Partition Plan, 1947**

One map shows the boundaries of Palestine under the British Mandate. The other map shows the boundaries of the United Nations' Partition Plan of 1947.

2

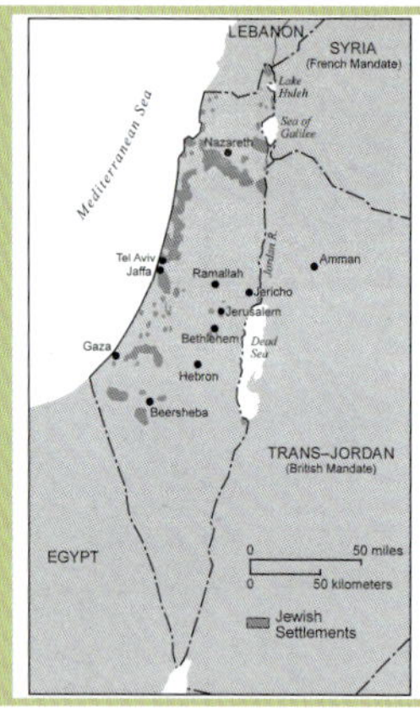

Source: Perry-Castañeda Library Map Collection, University of Texas at Austin (adapted)

Source: Peter N. Stearns, et al., World Civilizations: The Global Experience, Pearson Longman, 2005 (adapted)

4

The first map shows Jewish settlements scattered throughout. The second map shows a clear partition between the Arab areas and the areas of the Jewish state.

3

What caused the United Nations to partition British Palestine into a Jewish state and an Arab area?

15 Which situation was a contributing factor in the decision to partition British Palestine as shown on the 1947 map?

(1) mass migrations following the Holocaust
(2) decolonization from French rule
(3) capture of the Suez Canal
(4) formation of the Warsaw Pact

UNIT 16

MODERN DAY AFRICA

Geography of Africa

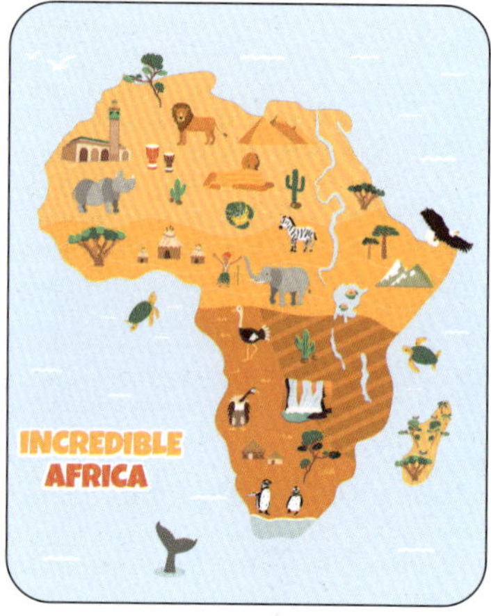

Africa has many different geographic barriers (such as mountains, deserts, and rainforests). Therefore, many different cultures, tribes, and ethnic groups have emerged.
Africa has different terrains (land features):

1. SAVANNA: grassy plains with good soil and rain, for farming This is a densely populated area.

2. SAHARA DESERT: extremely hot and barren land

3. RAINFOREST: dense forest, rich in biodiversity

Environmental Impact: Africa's geographical barriers led to the emergence of different cultures, tribes, and ethnic groups.

Pan-Africanism

Background: European powers imperialized Africa. Remember the scramble for Africa in the 1800s?

PAN-AFRICANISM:

In the mid-1900s, the Africans began a nationalistic movement to unite African people all over the world. This would begin "decolonization" (an end to imperialism) in Africa!

- This movement used civil disobedience to bring positive changes for the Africans.
- But the movement never fully succeeded, because of Africa's political corruption. When the European powers left Africa and decolonization finally happened, the Africans had no idea how to set up a solid government.

Interconnectedness: Pan-Africanism – movement to unite African people all over the world

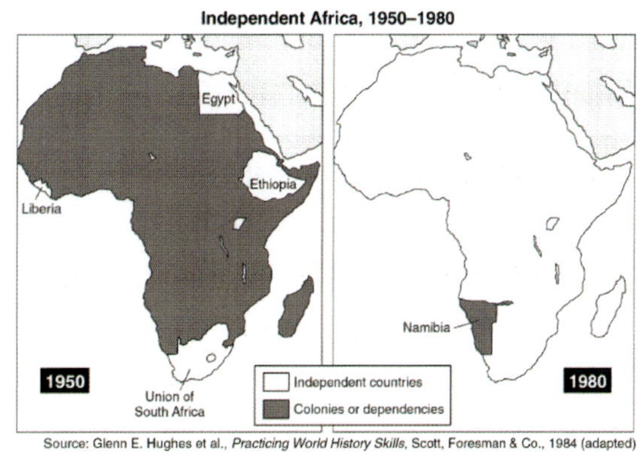

Decolonization in Africa

Nationalistic Leaders Help Gain Independence

Nationalistic leaders in Africa worked to gain independence from Great Britain for their countries.

1. KWAME NKRUMAH gained independence for GHANA (1957).

2. JOMO KENYATTA gained independence for KENYA (1964).

Nkrumah

Cause and effect: Nationalism ➲ Africa is imperialized by Great Britain ➲ Nkrumah and Kenyatta gain independence for Ghana and Kenya.

Conflict/Power: Nationalistic leaders in Africa worked to gain independence from Great Britain for their countries.

HINT: Kenyatta got independence for Kenya.

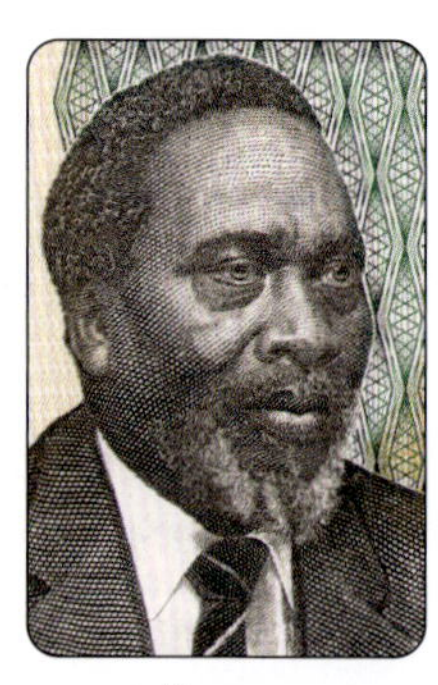

Kenyatta

Genocide in Africa

TRIBALISM: loyalty to individual tribes, and harsh feelings toward others
Tribalism causes much conflict in Africa until today.

HUTUS AND TUTSIS: 1994, in RWANDA, two tribes called the HUTUS and TUTSIS had tremendous tribal rivalries, which led to major violence and civil war. In 1994, Hutu extremists committed genocide on the Tutsis and hundreds of thousands of people died on both sides.

- The world acted as bystanders by failing to step in and stop this genocide.
- The UN eventually set up the International Criminal Tribunal for Rwanda to hold criminals responsible.
- Unfortunately, these peace attempts have been unsuccessful and the fighting continues until today.

African tribal masks

This is an example of genocide, ethnic cleansing (mass killing of people from an unwanted ethnic group), and human rights violations.

Common Regents question

Cultural Diversity in Africa

- Africa has much cultural diversity (unique and different cultures), which often leads to conflict.

Genocide in Darfur, Africa:

In 2003 non-Arab groups accused the Sudanese government of unfair treatment. The government fought back by supporting armed militias that destroyed villages, killed thousands, and forced millions to flee their homes.

Many ended up in overcrowded refugee camps in Chad, where food and resources were so scarce that people faced starvation.

Chad Refugee Camp

R There are many Regents questions on this topic. Other examples of genocide include the Armenian Massacre, the Holocaust, Pol Pot and the Killing Fields, and Rwanda.

E **Conflict/Human Rights Violations:** Genocide in Africa

South Africa

<u>Background</u>: The Boers/Afrikaners were Dutch settlers who lived in South Africa. During the Boer Wars, the British won control over South Africa. They ruled South Africa for hundreds of years!

Then, in 1910, South Africa gained its independence and became known as the REPUBLIC OF SOUTH AFRICA.
But the Europeans still controlled the South African government.

- This is an example of MINORITY RULE – the whites (minority) ruled the blacks (majority).

The European rulers in South Africa created a policy called APARTHEID – separation of blacks and whites (1948).

HINT:
<u>Apart</u>heid: <u>apart</u> – The whites and blacks had to remain <u>apart</u>.

Apartheid Laws

The Europeans controlling South Africa passed laws to separate the blacks and the whites.

- GROUP AREAS ACT: Black people had to live in specific areas.
- Public transportation and facilities were SEGREGATED (separated). Blacks were not allowed to sit in the same seats or use the same facilities as the whites.
- PASS LAWS: Blacks had to carry a pass with them. If they didn't have the pass, they were arrested.

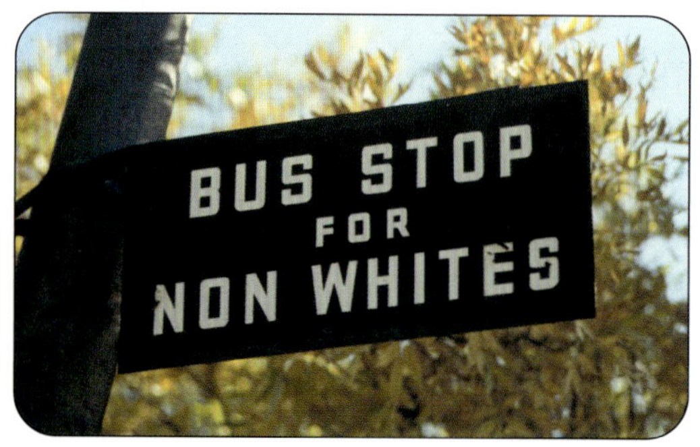

Apartheid sign

Ⓡ Common Regents questions

Ⓡ The Nuremberg Laws of the 1930s discriminated against the Jews, while the apartheid laws discriminated against black people.

Human Rights Violations/Inequality/Conflict/Power: Apartheid

Leaders Who Ended Apartheid

In 1912, anti-apartheid Africans started the AFRICAN NATIONAL CONGRESS (ANC), an organization that used violence, boycotts, and civil disobedience to stop apartheid.

Anti-Apartheid Leaders Associated with the Africa National Congress:

1. NELSON MANDELA:
   He spoke out and encouraged protests against apartheid. So, he was sent to jail for 27 years! When he was freed, South Africa held its first democratic elections and he became the president.
   R There are many Regents questions about Nelson Mandela.

2. DESMOND TUTU:
   He used civil disobedience and encouraged other countries to boycott South African goods to end apartheid.

3. F.W. de KLERK:
   He got rid of segregation laws.

Nelson Mandela

Apartheid ended in 1994!

R **Cause and effect:** Apartheid ➲ Anti-apartheid leader ➲ Apartheid ends!

E **Ideas and beliefs:** These African leaders believed that apartheid was terrible and worked to reverse it.

R **Connections:** Desmond Tutu and Gandhi both used civil disobedience.

Current Issues in Africa

1. Africa suffers from tribalism, ethnic cleansing, genocide, and terrorism, because of cultural differences. Keep in mind, when the imperialists drew the borders, they did not take the warring tribes and cultural differences into account. This contributes to the ongoing tribalism until today.
2. Thousands of Africans are suffering from AIDS, a disease that lowers the body's resistance to illness. They also suffer from many other diseases.
3. Many African countries suffer from unstable governments, corrupt dictators, and military rule, and are constantly fighting civil wars.
4. Some countries are moving towards democracy.
5. Africa suffers economically because they are so dependent on goods from European countries. Economic opportunities are not equal for everyone.
6. DEFORESTATION: Forests are being cut down.
   Rainforests in Africa, which contain biodiversity (many different types of species), are being destroyed. Plants and animals are losing their natural habitats. We are losing valuable resources found in plants and animals.

R **Cause and effect:** When Africa decolonized, they experienced scarcity. There is not enough medication to treat AIDS, Ebola, and other illnesses.

E **Scarcity:** Rainforests are being cut down.

E **Environmental Impact:** People are destroying the rainforests, which contain valuable natural resources.

Check off the boxes you know well. Whatever you don't know well (yet!), go back and review now!

- ☐ Pan Africanism
- ☐ Tribalism – Hutus and Tutsis in Rwanda
- ☐ Ethnic tension in Darfur between Arab Muslims and Black Muslims
- ☐ Nkrumah and Kenyatta help countries gain independence.
- ☐ Apartheid
- ☐ African National Congress
- ☐ Nelson Mandela
- ☐ Desmond Tutu
- ☐ F.W. de Klerk
- ☐ Current issues in Africa

Enduring Issues Essay Topics That Came Up in This Unit:

- **Environmental Impact:**
  - Africa's geographical barriers led to the emergence of different cultures, tribes, and ethnic groups.
  - People are destroying the rainforests, which contain valuable natural resources.
- **Scarcity:** There is not enough medication to treat AIDS and other illnesses.
- **Scarcity:** Rainforests are being destroyed.
- **Interconnectedness:** Pan-Africanism – movement to unite African people all over the world
- **Conflict/Power:** Nationalistic leaders in Africa worked to gain independence from Great Britain for their countries.
- **Human Rights Violations/Inequality/Conflict/Power:**
  - Genocide, tribal tensions, Rwanda
  - Apartheid
- **Ideas and beliefs:** African leaders believed that apartheid was terrible and worked to reverse it.

Regents Question Time!

Now it's time to test how well you know your stuff.

Have fun!

Regents Question Time!

The genius of apartheid was convincing people who were the overwhelming majority to turn on each other. Apart hate, is what it was. You separate people into groups and make them hate one another so you can run them all.

At the time, black South Africans outnumbered white South Africans nearly five to one, yet we were divided into different tribes with different languages: Zulu, Xhosa, Tswana, Sotho, Venda, Ndebele, Tsonga, Pedi, and more. Long before apartheid existed these tribal factions clashed and warred with one another. Then white rule used that animosity [hatred] to divide and conquer. All nonwhites were systematically classified into various groups and subgroups. Then these groups were given differing levels of rights and privileges in order to keep them at odds. . . .

— Trevor Noah, *Born a Crime: Stories from a South African Childhood*, Spiegel & Grau, 2016

27 According to this author, how did the minority white population maintain control over the majority black population in South Africa?

(1) through military conscription of black South Africans
(2) through divide and conquer techniques that kept tribes at odds
(3) by enforcing the use of tribal languages so that tribes could not communicate
(4) by allowing democracy within localized areas in the black South African community

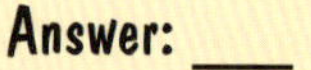

Answer: ___

1

No title here. Move on.

The genius of apartheid was convincing people who were the overwhelming majority to turn on each other. Apart hate, is what it was. You separate people into groups and make them hate one another so you can run them all.

At the time, black South Africans outnumbered white South Africans nearly five to one, yet we were divided into different tribes with different languages: Zulu, Xhosa, Tswana, Sotho, Venda, Ndebele, Tsonga, Pedi, and more. Long before apartheid existed these tribal factions clashed and warred with one another. Then white rule used that animosity [hatred] to divide and conquer. All nonwhites were systematically classified into various groups and subgroups. Then these groups were given differing levels of rights and privileges in order to keep them at odds. . . .

4

2

— Trevor Noah, *Born a Crime: Stories from a South African Childhood*, Spiegel & Grau, 2016

3

27 According to this author, how did the minority white population maintain control over the majority black population in South Africa?

(1) through military conscription of black South Africans
(2) through divide and conquer techniques that kept tribes at odds
(3) by enforcing the use of tribal languages so that tribes could not communicate
(4) by allowing democracy within localized areas in the black South African community

Regents Question Time!

> The genius of apartheid was convincing people who were the overwhelming majority to turn on each other. Apart hate, is what it was. You separate people into groups and make them hate one another so you can run them all.
>
> At the time, black South Africans outnumbered white South Africans nearly five to one, yet we were divided into different tribes with different languages: Zulu, Xhosa, Tswana, Sotho, Venda, Ndebele, Tsonga, Pedi, and more. Long before apartheid existed these tribal factions clashed and warred with one another. Then white rule used that animosity [hatred] to divide and conquer. All nonwhites were systematically classified into various groups and subgroups. Then these groups were given differing levels of rights and privileges in order to keep them at odds. . . .

— Trevor Noah, *Born a Crime: Stories from a South African Childhood*, Spiegel & Grau, 2016

28 Since the end of apartheid, which problem continues to exist in South Africa?

(1) inability of nonwhites to vote in elections
(2) restricting educational instruction to Afrikaans
(3) monopolizing of political power by white South Africans
(4) persistence of segregation as a result of economic inequalities

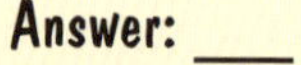

Answer: ___

1

No title here. Move on.

The genius of apartheid was convincing people who were the overwhelming majority to turn on each other. Apart hate, is what it was. You separate people into groups and make them hate one another so you can run them all.

At the time, black South Africans outnumbered white South Africans nearly five to one, yet we were divided into different tribes with different languages: Zulu, Xhosa, Tswana, Sotho, Venda, Ndebele, Tsonga, Pedi, and more. Long before apartheid existed these tribal factions clashed and warred with one another. Then white rule used that animosity [hatred] to divide and conquer. All nonwhites were systematically classified into various groups and subgroups. Then these groups were given differing levels of rights and privileges in order to keep them at odds. . . .

4

2

— Trevor Noah, *Born a Crime: Stories from a South African Childhood*, Spiegel & Grau, 2016

3

28 Since the end of apartheid, which problem continues to exist in South Africa?

(1) inability of nonwhites to vote in elections
(2) restricting educational instruction to Afrikaans
(3) monopolizing of political power by white South Africans
(4) persistence of segregation as a result of economic inequalities

This question needed to be answered with your head, not the document.

UNIT 17

MODERN DAY RUSSIA, EUROPE & LATIN AMERICA

Russia

After the Soviet Union collapsed, BORIS YELTSIN became the president of Russia (1990s).

- He faced a major struggle in changing the economy from command economy to market economy.
- There were major food shortages, unemployment and corruption.

VLADIMIR PUTIN became president in 2000.

- Putin helped rebuild the economy.
- He established ties with the West and signed a nuclear arms reduction agreement with the United States.
- Human rights organizations accuse Putin of persecuting political critics.

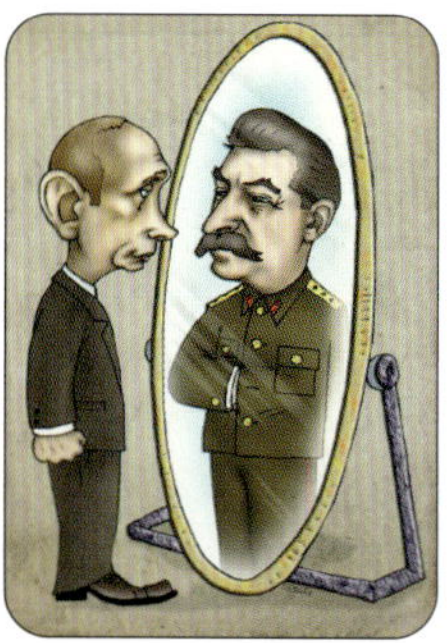

How are Putin and Stalin similar?

Vladimir Putin

- Putin ran without an opponent in the last election. Doesn't that sound like dictator-style behavior? Reminds me of some earlier Communist dictators!
- There is tension between Russia, NATO, countries in Europe, and the US because Russia supports the Syrian government.

Guess who won the elections? You are so smart!!

R Putin is on a mission to restore Russia to its previous glory. Therefore, he annexed Georgia, Crimea, and is at war with Ukraine. The Regents asks a lot of questions about Russia.

E **Innovation:** Putin rebuilt the economy and established ties with the West.

E **Human Rights Violation:** Putin persecutes political critics.

The Chechnya-Russia Conflict

Russia controls Chechnya.

Chechnya (inhabited by Muslims) wants independence from Russia. The Chechens use terrorism and military force (including massive weaponry and their air force) to try to gain independence. They are also well-known for kidnappings.

Map of Chechnya and Russia

Russia refuses to grant them independence because their territory is a major source of oil.

Intense tension between the Russians and Chechens persist until today.

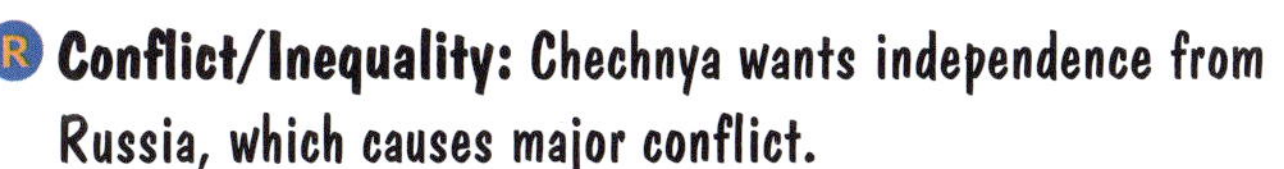

- **Conflict/Inequality:** Chechnya wants independence from Russia, which causes major conflict.
- **Human Rights Violations:** Chechnya uses terrorism, weapons, and kidnappings.

Ukraine, Europe

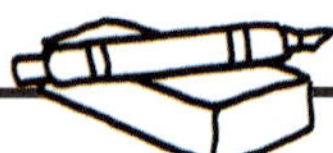

- Russia enforced communism on Ukraine, and Stalin's Holodomor genocide was his brutal tool to maintain control. The result? Millions tragically starved to death.
- The Chernobyl Nuclear Power Plant, located in Chernobyl, Ukraine, held USSR designed nuclear reactors. In 1986, the Chernobyl power plant exploded, becoming possibly the worst nuclear accident in history. Many people died from radiation exposure.
- After the Soviet Union collapsed, Ukraine finally became an independent country (1991)!
- Ukraine is the poorest country in Europe.
- The country is filled with corruption.
- Ukraine and Russia are in the midst of a territorial conflict.

Yugoslavia (in the Balkans, Europe)

YUGOSLAVIA:

- This area was home to numerous diverse ethnic groups.
- When communism collapsed, many regions declared their independence in 1991. Tensions flared.

SLOBODAN MILOSEVIC, The Serbian leader of the Yugoslavian government, organized a massive ethnic cleansing (a mass killing of a certain ethnic group) against non-Serbians (1992-1995).

- The Serbs killed more than 200,000 people!
- Milosevic was nicknamed the "**Butcher of the Balkans.**"
- Genocide alert!
- The UN held trials in Yugoslavia to hold the perpetrators accountable for their atrocities (similar to the Nuremberg trials). Milosevic was arrested and tried. He died in jail before the verdict.

Slobodan Milosevic

In 1992, Yugoslavia dissolved into smaller states. It no longer exists today.

R Common Regents question: Ethnic cleansing/genocide in Bosnia and Herzegovina
Other examples of genocide in history include the Armenian Massacre, the Holocaust, Pol Pot and the "Killing Fields," tribalism in Rwanda.

E **Human Rights Violations/Inequality/Conflict:** The Serbs performed ethnic cleansing on non-Serbs.

E **Interconnectedness:** NATO and the UN arrested the Serbian leader and tried him.

Latin America

Background: Many Latin American countries won their independence from European colonial powers in the 1800s but were unable to establish stable governments.

Many Latin American countries ended up with authoritarian leaders. Today, many Latin American countries are moving towards democracy.

The Catholic Church made major social reforms in Latin America. It protested oppressive rulership and built schools, churches, and hospitals for the poor.

Map of Latin America

Let's explore some Latin American countries. Don't memorize. Just try to get the gist of what's happening in the Latin American region.

Argentina (in Latin America)

Mothers of the Plaza de Mayo

In 1976, a military government took control in a coup.

The Dirty War (1976-1983)

- The government conducted a program of state terrorism against guerilla groups.
- They tortured and killed approximately 30,000 people.
- They brutally kidnapped approximately 20,000 people, many of them young, and made them "disappear."

  Their mothers, who became known as MOTHERS OF THE PLAZA DE MAYO, held protests demanding information about where their children were. They marched silently every week for over thirty years, holding pictures of their missing children and wearing diapers as headscarves with their children's names embroidered on them. These protests gained worldwide attention. Years later, some remains of dead bodies were found.
- In response to the Mothers of the Plaza de Mayo, over 700 people were tried and convicted for the genocide committed during the Dirty War.

Brazil (in Latin America)

Under military rule, Brazil's economy flourished due to:

- foreign investment
- exploitation (taking advantage of) of the Amazon rainforest
- hydroelectric plants to decrease the need for oil

Brazil's wealth leads to problems:

- Some Brazilians became extremely wealthy, while the working class lived in extreme poverty.
- Then, the country became democratic, and more economic problems arose.
- Reforms and new policies helped get Brazil back on its feet, but the country still suffers from political corruption and is struggling for democracy until today.

Street child in Brazil

Chile (in Latin America)

In 1973, AUGUST PINOCHET led a coup d'état (a sudden and violent government takeover). He then ruled Chile for 17 years. He established a dictatorship that violated human rights:

- He conducted mass murder against those who opposed his rule.
- Those who opposed him mysteriously disappeared, or were tortured or killed.
- In 2000, he was prosecuted for human rights violations.

August Pinochet

- Today, Chile is a democracy.

Human Rights Violation: Pinochet tortured and killed his opposers.

HINT: August (when it's hot) doesn't belong in Chile (chilly)! August Pinochet does not belong as a leader in Chile.

Cuba (in Latin America)

- (1898) Cuba gained independence from Spain.
- (1959) FIDEL CASTRO seized power and brought Communism to Cuba.
- (1961) The United States tried to invade Cuba at the Bay of Pigs. The invasion was a failure.
- (1962) Cuban Missile Crisis: Cuba was at risk of a nuclear war with Russia. Luckily, the crisis was averted.
- (1960s) United States banned trade with Cuba.

Fidel Castro

<u>Cuba Today</u>:
Cuba's economic situation is horrible. Some economic and personal reforms have recently been instated.

Current Issues in Latin America

1. International drug trade: Latin American countries are involved in selling drugs to countries all over the world.
2. Uneven economy: Some people in Latin America are extremely wealthy, while others are extremely poor.
3. Latin America suffers from crime, corruption, and pollution.
4. Mexicans are entering America illegally. The United States is working to stop this and deport illegal immigrants back to Mexico. President Trump wants to enforce tough border patrol and build a wall at the Mexico/U.S. border.

- **Conflict:** International drug trade, crime and corruption
- **Scarcity:** Poverty
- **Power:** There is much corruption among Latin American governments.
- Environmental Impact: Pollution (which causes many illnesses, including lung cancer and asthma)
- **Interconnectedness:** The United States is working to secure the Mexico/U.S. border.

Check off the boxes you know well. Whatever you don't know well (yet!), go back and review now!

- ☐ RUSSIA: Putin rebuilt the economy, but acts like a dictator.
- ☐ CHECHNYA: in conflict with Russia
- ☐ UKRAINE: anti-Westernization, conflict
- ☐ IRELAND: Southern Ireland achieved independence from the British, while Northern Ireland is still under British rule.
- ☐ YUGOSLAVIA: In BOSNIA and HERZEGOVINA, the Serbs performed ethnic cleansing on non-Serbs.
- ☐ LATIN AMERICA: Many countries gained independence, but were unable to establish stable governments. These countries struggle with poverty, corruption, crime, and drug trade.

Enduring Issues Essay Topics That Came Up in This Unit:

- **Scarcity:** Poverty in Latin American countries
- **Innovation/Power:** Putin rebuilt the Russian economy and established ties with the United States.
- **Human Rights Violations/Inequality/Conflict:**
  - Putin persecutes political critics.
  - Chechnya uses terrorism, weapons, and kidnappings.
  - The Serbs performed ethnic cleansing on non-Serbs.
- **Power:** There is much corruption among Latin American governments.
- **Interconnectedness:** The United States is working to secure the Mexico/U.S. border.

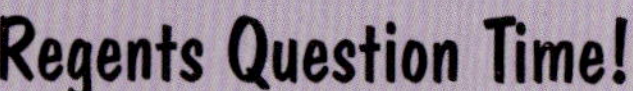

Now it's time to test how well you know your stuff.

Have fun!

Regents Question Time!

A Stadium With a Bloody Past

Chile: For weeks after the coup, the military rounded up political and social activists and suspected supporters of the former president, Salvador Allende, and brought them to the concrete edifice [structure], which opened in 1938 and hosted matches at the 1962 World Cup. . . .

Source: David Waldstein, "In Chile's National Stadium, Dark Past Shadows Copa América Matches," *New York Times*, June 17, 2015 (adapted)

The "Dirty War"

Argentina: The Mothers of the Plaza de Mayo. According to a report published in 1986, almost 9,000 Argentines disappeared during the "dirty war."

Source: Gofen and Jermyn, *Argentina*, Marshall Cavendish, 2002 (adapted)

23 Based on these photographs, which action taken by the governments of Chile and Argentina violated the principles of the Universal Declaration of Human Rights?

(1) conducting trials by juries
(2) blowing up factories
(3) arresting known criminals
(4) kidnapping political opponents

Answer: ____

A Stadium With a Bloody Past

The "Dirty War"

The military did some dirty stuff to their opponents.

Chile: For weeks after the coup, the military rounded up political and social activists and suspected supporters of the former president, Salvador Allende, and brought them to the concrete edifice [structure], which opened in 1938 and hosted matches at the 1962 World Cup. . . .

Argentina: The Mothers of the Plaza de Mayo. According to a report published in 1986, almost 9,000 Argentines disappeared during the "dirty war."

Source: David Waldstein, "In Chile's National Stadium, Dark Past Shadows Copa América Matches," *New York Times*, June 17, 2015 (adapted)

Source: Gofen and Jermyn, *Argentina*, Marshall Cavendish, 2002 (adapted)

23 Based on these photographs, which action taken by the governments of Chile and Argentina violated the principles of the Universal Declaration of Human Rights?

(1) conducting trials by juries
(2) blowing up factories
(3) arresting known criminals
(4) kidnapping political opponents

Regents Question Time!

Source: Adam Zyglis, *New York Times Upfront*, October 10, 2016

. . ."Putin sincerely believes that the end of the Cold War was a source of humiliation and misery for Russia and that the duty of any Russian leader is to erase that humiliation and restore Russia to some of the superpower glory of the Soviet Union," says Leon Aron, Director of Russian Studies at the American Enterprise Institute in Washington, D.C. . . .

— Carl Stoffers, "Are We Heading Toward a New Cold War?," *New York Times Upfront*, October 10, 2016

25 This cartoonist is comparing Vladimir Putin to

(1) Czar Nicholas II
(2) Joseph Stalin
(3) Mikhail Gorbachev
(4) Boris Yeltsin

Answer: ____

1

No title here. Move on.

In the cartoon, the "Russian doll" shows Stalin inside Putin. The document is saying that Putin feels the end of the Cold War was a bad thing.

4

. . ."Putin sincerely believes that the end of the Cold War was a source of humiliation and misery for Russia and that the duty of any Russian leader is to erase that humiliation and restore Russia to some of the superpower glory of the Soviet Union," says Leon Aron, Director of Russian Studies at the American Enterprise Institute in Washington, D.C. . . .

2

Source: Adam Zyglis, *New York Times Upfront*, October 10, 2016

— Carl Stoffers, "Are We Heading Toward a New Cold War?," *New York Times Upfront*, October 10, 2016

3

25 This cartoonist is comparing Vladimir Putin to

(1) Czar Nicholas II
(2) Joseph Stalin
(3) Mikhail Gorbachev
(4) Boris Yeltsin

Regents Question Time!

Source: Adam Zyglis, *New York Times Upfront*, October 10, 2016

. . ."Putin sincerely believes that the end of the Cold War was a source of humiliation and misery for Russia and that the duty of any Russian leader is to erase that humiliation and restore Russia to some of the superpower glory of the Soviet Union," says Leon Aron, Director of Russian Studies at the American Enterprise Institute in Washington, D.C. . . .

— Carl Stoffers, "Are We Heading Toward a New Cold War?," *New York Times Upfront*, October 10, 2016

26 Which earlier historical development best reflects Putin's strategy for rebuilding Russia's prestige in the world?

(1) granting of independence to former Soviet republics
(2) removal of Soviet troops from Afghanistan
(3) lifting of the Berlin blockade
(4) installation of communist regimes throughout Europe

Answer: ___

1

No title here. Move on.

In the cartoon, the "Russian doll" shows Stalin inside Putin. The document is saying that Putin feels the end of the Cold War was a bad thing.

Source: Adam Zyglis, *New York Times Upfront*, October 10, 2016

. . ."Putin sincerely believes that the end of the Cold War was a source of humiliation and misery for Russia and that the duty of any Russian leader is to erase that humiliation and restore Russia to some of the superpower glory of the Soviet Union," says Leon Aron, Director of Russian Studies at the American Enterprise Institute in Washington, D.C. . . .

— Carl Stoffers, "Are We Heading Toward a New Cold War?," *New York Times Upfront*, October 10, 2016

2

4

3

26 Which earlier historical development best reflects Putin's strategy for rebuilding Russia's prestige in the world?

Putin perceives communism as the source of Russia's prestige and is therefore trying to promote communism. Which choice matches best?

(1) granting of independence to former Soviet republics
(2) removal of Soviet troops from Afghanistan
(3) lifting of the Berlin blockade
(4) installation of communist regimes throughout Europe

UNIT 18

THE WORLD TODAY – ADVANCEMENTS & ENDURING ISSUES

Part 1: Economic Trends

Globalization

GLOBALIZATION: Each country is dependent on other countries all over the world. What happens in one country has a global impact.

- **GLOBAL TRADE:** Since so much trade takes place between countries, what happens economically in one part of the world affects the rest of the world.

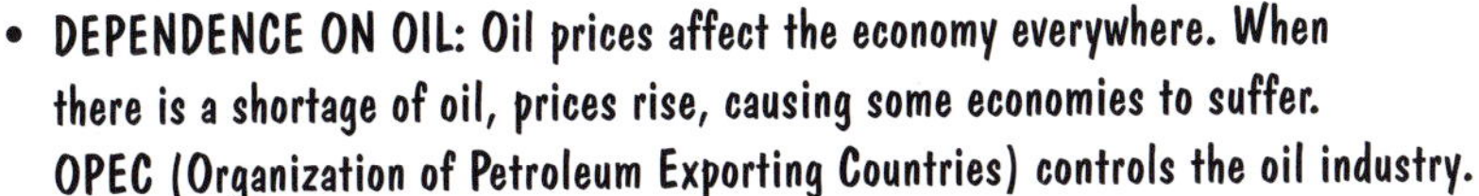

ex The rise or fall of stock markets in one country can have an impact on countries all over the world.

- **DEPENDENCE ON OIL:** Oil prices affect the economy everywhere. When there is a shortage of oil, prices rise, causing some economies to suffer. OPEC (Organization of Petroleum Exporting Countries) controls the oil industry.
- **GLOBAL BANKING** is when countries provide financial services and products to governments, corporates, and institutions worldwide. Developed countries loaned money to underdeveloped countries to help them modernize. Now the developed countries are left with huge debt.
- **MULTINATIONAL CORPORATIONS:** Many businesses started operating in numerous countries.

R **Cause and effect:** Global trade and interdependence ➲ Cultural diffusion

E **Interconnectedness:** Global interdependence

E **Environmental Impact:** Countries all over the world are dependent on oil-rich countries for fuel.

To stay or to go?

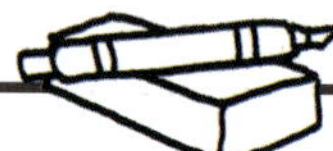

OK, we're not just talking about pizza here.
We're talking about the economy in general.
Should countries focus on trading with other countries? Or should countries trade within their own borders? Let's explore the pros and cons of each.

- Free market/export-oriented economies engage in global trade – trade between countries around the world.

+ Allows access to cheaper goods and services (think AliExpress!)
+ Gives people in poor countries job opportunities
– Exploitation (taking advantage of) of workers in poor countries. The average wage in China is under $1.60 per hour!
– Buying and selling to other countries can hurt the local economy by taking away jobs. (Are we printing books at our local printer or in another country, where it's cheaper?)
– Shipping across countries causes environmental damage. Think about all the fuel used in boats and planes.

- Local economies buy from and sell to local sellers.

+ Boosts the country's economy by supporting local sellers and helping the government earn more tax dollars
– Can be more expensive
– Less products available to buy

Guess where the Global Boosters™ are printed?

China and World Trade

China has a mixed economy – there's some capitalism, but it's mostly controlled by the communist government.

Let's examine the pros and cons of China's global trading:

+ China provides cheaper products for countries around the world.

– The Chinese government overproduces some products, which lowers prices worldwide, making it difficult for other countries to compete.

– Chinese workers are often overworked and underpaid.

– Chinese global trade threatens local businesses elsewhere and has caused many to shut down.

Economic Organizations

Several non-governmental organizations (NGOs) work to address economic issues.
Spoiler alert: They each have issues!

1. **WORLD TRADE ORGANIZATION (started in 1955):**
    - **Goal:** To promote global trade by reducing trade restrictions and resolving trade disputes
    - In other words, they're there to remove international trade "red tape" and break up fights.
    - **Issue:** Since they back free trade, they can cause wealthy countries to become wealthier and poor countries to become poorer.
2. **WORLD BANK (started in 1944):**
    - **Goal:** To fight poverty by providing loans to countries
      They provide funding for roads, education, disease prevention, etc.
    - **Issue:** Their projects can damage the environment and local culture.
3. **INTERNATIONAL MONEY FUND (started in 1945):**
    - **Goal:** To stabilize countries' economies by promoting stable currency exchange rates
    - **Issue:** Their conditions are strict and are influenced by wealthy countries, not always to the benefit of developing countries.

In addition to the organizations, let's discuss **MICROFINANCE INSTITUTIONS:**

- **Goal:** To provide loans to low-income clients who lack access to financing from banks
- **Issue:** They charge high interest rates and don't provide business training to borrowers.

Ethnic Diversity or Everyone Similar?

+ Ethnic diversity means that each country has its unique culture, fashion, media, architecture, etc. This creates a unique flavor for each country.

– Globalization causes countries to become interconnected and therefore influenced by other countries. One global style may replace the traits that make each society unique.
  - We call this HOMOGENIZATION (making things similar).
  - Think same stores, fast-food franchises, languages, etc. around the world.

International Economic Organizations

- EUROPEAN UNION (EU): an organization that was started to regulate Europe's steel and coal production. More countries joined, and the EU became a free trade association that lowered tariffs between members. (The EU also works to promote world peace and improve environmental protection.)
  - Goal: to improve European economies by developing the economic system, encouraging technological developments, and increase trade
  - The disadvantage of this and other trade associations is that the cultures and languages of smaller countries (like Belgium) are dominated by strong countries (like Germany).
  - In 2020, the United Kingdom withdrew itself from the EU. This became known as BREXIT.

- NAFTA (North American Free Trade Agreement): The US, Mexico, and Canada agreed to free trade between themselves. This helped lower international taxes between these countries.

Interconnectedness/Cooperation: Economies of countries throughout the world are linked through the EU and NAFTA.

Underdeveloped Countries

UNDERDEVELOPED/DEVELOPING COUNTRIES are countries that are very poor and whose residents live in primitive conditions.

ex Afghanistan, Rwanda, Uganda, Yemen

These countries are sometimes called **THIRD WORLD NATIONS.**

FYI: **DEVELOPED NATIONS** are the opposite of underdeveloped or developing nations. They are countries that have modern agriculture, industry, technology, and education (for example, USA, Japan, European countries).

Poverty in Underdeveloped Countries

What causes poverty in underdeveloped countries?

- **GEOGRAPHY:** lack of natural resources and rain, geographic barriers, natural disasters
- **OVERPOPULATION:** Scientists say that since these countries have so many inhabitants, there isn't enough food, housing, and medical care for everyone.
- **POLITICAL INSTABILITY:** Governments of underdeveloped countries are often unstable, and they spend too much money on warfare instead of education and health care.
- **ECONOMIC DEPENDENCE:** Underdeveloped countries depend on other countries for manufactured goods and technology, while they provide the raw materials.
    - **TRADE DEFICIT:** when a nation imports more than it exports (so it loses money). These countries typically have trade deficits.
    - They borrow a lot money from foreign banks, leaving them with huge debts.
    - Underdeveloped countries typically have a **CASH CROP ECONOMY** – they grow agricultural crops to sell for profit. If the crops fail, they are in trouble.
- **ECONOMIC INEQUALITY:** Some people lack basic necessities, such as water, food, and basic healthcare.

Environmental Impact: Geography can impact a country's economy and development.

Scarcity: If there are not enough raw materials, or if a country imports more than it exports, its economy will suffer. Underdeveloped countries typically suffer from overcrowding and lack of housing, food, and medical care.

Types of Economies Around the World

There are different types of economies around the world:

1. CAPITALISM (Market Economy)
   - Private ownership (free enterprise)
   - Based on supply and demand
   - Laissez-faire (The government has very little involvement in the economy.)
   - Most democratic countries are capitalist.

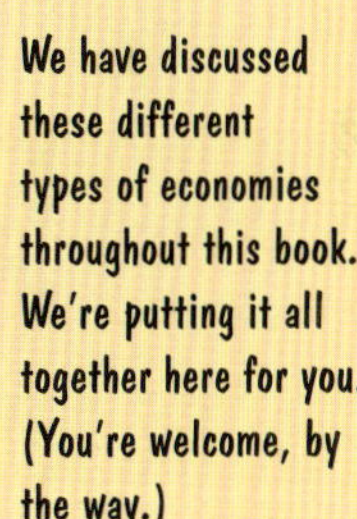

ex USA and Great Britain

2. COMMAND ECONOMY: The government controls economic decisions.
   - Many communist countries have command economies.

ex Cuba and North Korea

3. SOCIALIST ECONOMY: Market economy with public ownership and state-owned businesses

4. MIXED ECONOMY
   - A mixed economy has a mix of privately and publicly owned businesses.

ex China and Africa

Part 2: Conflict & Peace Efforts

Terrorism

TERRORISM: Unpredictable violence, such as bombings, kidnappings, suicide attacks, and hijackings against civilians to exact revenge or attain political goals.

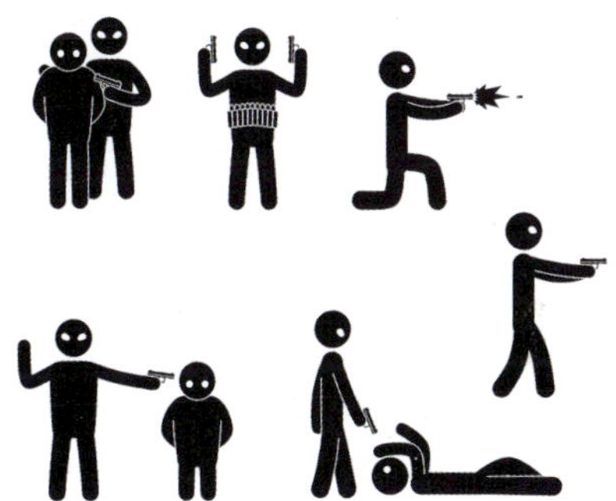

Terrorism Around the World:

- **SEPTEMBER 11, 2001 (9/11):** Al Qaeda extremists wanted to fight against modern Western society. They attacked the Twin Towers in New York City and the Pentagon in Washington, D.C., killing thousands of Americans.
- Palestinian Arabs use terrorism against Israelis in order to gain land.
- The Chechens use terrorism against the Russians to gain their independence.
- ISIS is an anti-Western terrorist organization that conducts attacks all over the world.
- International weapon trade
- **CYBER WARFARE:** A country attacks another country's computer network.

Human Rights Violations/Conflict: Terrorist attacks on innocent civilians

Nuclear Proliferation

NUCLEAR PROLIFERATION: the spread of nuclear energy and nuclear weapons

Problems:

1. Nuclear weapons are a major threat to the environment and human life. They cause much more destruction than conventional weapons.
2. Nuclear waste produced from weapon production causes high levels of radiation, which is extremely harmful to humans.
3. Nuclear energy is a "cleaner" source of energy than oil, but can cause real human and environmental damage when accidents happen in the power plant.

Nuclear technology has caused destruction around the world:

- The atom bombs dropped at the end of World War II in the Japanese cities **HIROSHIMA** and **NAGASAKI** killed thousands of people, and many children born after the bomb were severely deformed.
- In **CHERNOBYL**, Ukraine, an accident happened in the nuclear power plant in 1986, exposing people and crops to deadly radiation. This influenced countries to limit their nuclear power programs.
- In Japan in 2011, an earthquake caused a tsunami, which damaged nuclear plants. It can take over 30 years to clean up this radiation.

Nuclear Threats

<u>Current Nuclear Threat:</u>

Many countries own nuclear weapons, so there is danger of a nuclear war. North Korea and Iran have created advanced nuclear weapons arsenals. There is a real tension and fear that they will actually use these weapons and cause massive destruction in the world.

<u>Solutions to Nuclear Proliferation:</u>

- Countries are banning the disposal of nuclear waste (from the creation of nuclear weapons) into the seas to avoid contaminating the water.
- Countries are limiting their nuclear programs and working on safety measures to prevent similar accidents in the future.
- Since the 1960s, world leaders have been attempting to sign treaties limiting nuclear proliferation.

Environmental Impact: Nuclear weapons cause environmental damage.

Innovation: Nuclear weapons caused millions of deaths and threatens lives.

International Drug Trade

Countries in Latin America, Asia, and Africa are involved in trading illegal drugs around the world.

- Western countries prohibit most addictive drugs and punish drug smugglers harshly.
- The use of drugs has been linked to an increase in violent crime.
- Recently, Mexico came under the spotlight for smuggling drugs into the United States at unprotected borders.

Interconnectedness: Unprotected borders bring problems from one country to the next.

International Organizations to Promote World Peace

Globalization can lead to either world conflict or world cooperation.

Several bodies were founded to promote world peace. Examples:

1. **United Nations (UN)**
2. **North Atlantic Treaty Organization (NATO)**
3. **Nongovernmental organizations (NGOs)**

Let's explore each organization and evaluate if it was successful or not.

The United Nations (UN)

During World War II, countries all over the world were involved in a devastating international conflict.

(1948) After World War II, countries from all over the world got together to create the UNITED NATIONS – an organization that was meant to prevent such a disaster from happening again.

The UN's goal is to promote world peace and security and economic and social wellbeing.

Close to 200 countries are now members of the United Nations.

Here are some of the roles of the United Nations:

1. Makes military and economic efforts to bring peace worldwide
2. Protects human rights: The UN adopted the UNIVERSAL DECLARATION OF HUMAN RIGHTS, which is a document that declares all people's equality and entitlement to human dignity and rights.
3. Judges international disputes
4. Provides disaster relief: When countries experience disasters such as famine, tsunamis, earthquakes, or the like, the UN sends aid.

The UN has helped end devastating civil wars in some countries, such as Cambodia, but failed to prevent genocide in other places, such as Rwanda and Bosnia.

E **Interconnectedness/Cooperation:** The UN is an organization of representatives of countries all over the world who work together to promote world peace and help other countries in times of disaster.

E **Human Rights Violations/Conflict:** The UN works to prevent human rights violations and conflict.

North Atlantic Treaty Organization (NATO)

A security alliance of 30 countries in North America and Europe.

- If one allied country is attacked, the other countries will defend it.

- NATO was started in 1949 to defend countries from the Soviet threat.

- Once the Soviet Union fell (1991), NATO expanded to globalized peacekeeping. Its activities include:

+ Working to improve Middle Eastern conflicts, including Saddam Hussein in Iraq, Iranian terrorism, and the Israeli-Arab conflict.
+ Attacking Al Qaeda in Afghanistan after 9/11
+ Fighting cybersecurity threats

– NATO was unable to stop long-term terrorism in Afghanistan or to maintain peace in Libya, and it has a problematic relationship with Russia.

Nongovernmental Organizations (NGOs)

Some nongovernmental organizations promote international cooperation and peace.

GREENPEACE was founded in 1971 and grew into an international agency.

- **Goal:** To battle deforestation, desertification, global climate change, overfishing, hunting endangered whales
- **Efforts:** lobbying, education, and actively stopping the above activities

For example, Greenpeace might confront a whaling boat in the ocean or occupy a coal-fueled power plant to stop activities that harm the environment.

Issues with this agency:

- Using false claims in campaigns against businesses they say are hurting the environment
- Running campaigns that harm the environment(!) by damaging conservation sites to capture good pictures
- Increasing pollution with excessive air travel

Part 3: Social Patterns and Changes

Modernization vs. Tradition

Many societies are torn between their age-old tradition and modernization.

- Some countries view modernization as a change from a traditional rural (countryside), agrarian (agricultural) condition to a secular, urban (city), industrial condition.
- Others see modernization as a threat to their traditions.
- Developing countries are trying to find the balance between preserving traditions and religion while embracing modern technology and government.

Japan, Iran, Turkey, and Egypt struggle with the modernization vs. traditional clash.

Innovation: New Western ideas and technology often clash with traditional cultures and religions.

Overpopulation

OVERPOPULATION: There are too many people living in a place that doesn't have enough natural resources for them.

Causes of Overpopulation:

- Lower infant death rate
- Longer life spans due to improved medical care
- Steady food supply

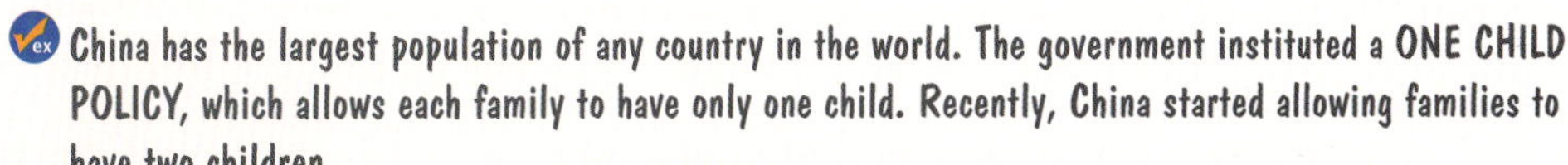

China has the largest population of any country in the world. The government instituted a ONE CHILD POLICY, which allows each family to have only one child. Recently, China started allowing families to have two children.

Much controversy surrounds this issue. Many disagree with this approach.

R Common Regents question

E **Scarcity/Environmental Impact:** People who live in overpopulated areas suffer from insufficient natural resources.

The Green Revolutions

THE GREEN REVOLUTIONS: In the 1960s, scientists began using technology to increase food production. New technologies were developed over time.

Technology Used in the Green Revolution:

- **IRRIGATION:** Pumps bring water up from below the earth's surface.
- **MACHINERY:** Machines increase production.
- **FERTILIZERS:** Chemicals make the crops grow faster and better.
- **PESTICIDES:** Chemicals kill insects that attack crops.
- **GENETICALLY MODIFIED ORGANISMS (GMOs):** Scientists modify the genes of foods to improve and increase the supply.

Some developing countries used these technologies very successfully.
For instance, India and Indonesia doubled their output with these new technologies!

Problems with the Green Revolution:

- New technology and machinery are expensive, and poor farmers cannot afford it.
- Countries need an adequate water supply for irrigation.
- GMO's may pose health concerns.

R Common Regents question

E **Environmental Impact:** The Green Revolution changed the way farming is done. Pesticides can harm the environment.

E **Innovation:** New technology is used to increase food production.

HINT: The Green Revolution – "greens" means produce. During the Green Revolution, people managed to increase produce.

Urbanization

URBANIZATION: movement of people to cities

Causes of Urbanization:

- **INDUSTRIALIZATION:** Goods started being produced by machinery. People moved to the cities to be near the factories.
- Job opportunities
- Better health care and education
- Better stores

Results of Urbanization (in Latin America, Africa, and Southeast Asia):

- Traditions have weakened.

The Caste system is weaker in urban areas in India.

- Women have more opportunity.
- **SLUMS:** Many people cannot afford city housing prices, so they live in crowded, poor-quality homes that lack sewage systems and electricity. People in slums typically suffer from disease, severe pollution, and crime.

Solutions to Urbanization Issues:

- Improve healthcare in crowded areas.
- Make education available to everyone.
- Groups can form relief agencies.

Urbanization Trends

As time goes on, more and more people are moving to urban areas.
Notice how the percentage of people living in urban areas increases with time.

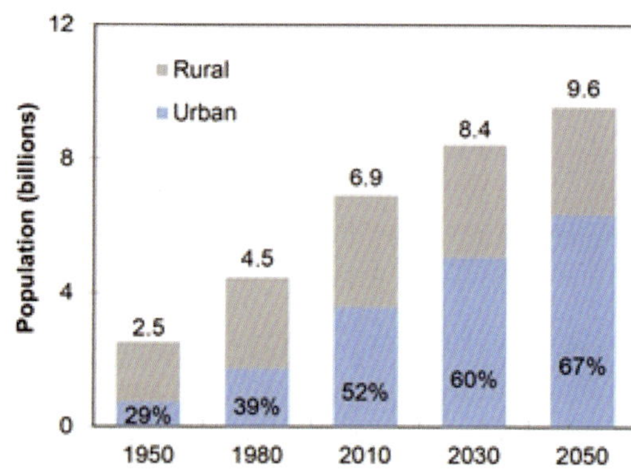

Center for Sustainable Systems, University of Michigan. 2018. "Social Development Indicators Factsheet." Pub. No. CSS08-15

- **Cause and effect:** Cities grow (because of better jobs, healthcare, stores) ➲ Slums and crime increases, and traditions are weakened
- **Environmental Impact:** People move to cities for more opportunity, which increases pollution.
- **Scarcity:** People move away from rural areas because there aren't enough jobs or opportunities.
- **Conflict:** Urbanization often weakens traditions, which brings on the traditionalism vs. modernization conflict.

How Urbanization Changed Life

Urbanization and industrialization totally changed many aspects of life, including:

- **Family**: Families started to work in different locations and were consistently apart for long periods of time.
- **Religion**: As people moved to cities and became more exposed to secular ideas, they became less religious.
- **Education**: People moved to cities with proper educational infrastructure.
- **Government**: Some urbanized countries adapted a more Western-style government.

R The Regents is sending us on a tour of parts of Africa, Latin America, and Asia to see how this plays out.

Urbanization in Nigeria, Africa

Starting from the 1970s, millions of people in Nigeria moved to cities to get a share of the wealth gained from oil sales. But the authorities managed the cities' expansion poorly, which resulted in:

- Overcrowded cities – over 15 million people live in one city (named Lagos)!
- Cities lack proper electric, water, and sanitary services.
- Primitive housing – think sheds and homemade structures
- High rates of crime and disease

Overcrowding in Nigeria

Let's explore how urbanization affected the lives of Nigerians:

- **Family:** In traditional rural settings, extended families lived together. Think Grandma and Grandpa, and dozens of aunts, uncles, and cousins. Sounds exciting (and noisy)!
  When families moved to the cities, space was limited, and only one nuclear family could live together.
- **Religion:** Many people switched from traditional African faiths to Muslim and Christian beliefs.
- **Education:** Most of Nigeria lacks proper educational opportunities – less than half of Nigerians are literate.

+ But the literacy rate of urban children is much higher (45%) than that of the rural children (19%).

- **Government:** When the Nigerian government modernized, they did not manage the cities' expansion well, and terrible urban conditions developed. A terrorist group called Boko Haram arose to abolish Westernization.

Urbanization in Brazil, Latin America

In the 1960s, Brazil's economy changed from agricultural to industrial, and millions of people flocked to the cities to get jobs. The largest city, Sao Paulo, is home to 12 million people!

- Competition for space led to a housing crisis. The middle class lives in tiny apartments in high-rise buildings, while the lower class lives in informal dwellings of cardboard and plywood, in slums called favelas.
- These slums have limited access to electricity, modern plumbing, and healthcare.

Urbanization in Brazil

Let's explore how urbanization affected the lives of Brazilians:

- **Family:** The average family size shrank, which is a typical effect of urbanization.
- **Religion:** As urbanization occurred, people became more secular and less religious.
- **Education:** Brazil's urban educational system is slowly improving, but low-income children often drop out of school, which stunts their economic opportunities. This widens the economic gap between Brazil's rich and poor.
- **Government:** Brazil went from military, authoritarian rule to democracy. The government failed to manage the cities' expansions properly.

Urbanization in South Korea, Asia

Millions of South Koreans escaped rural poverty and migrated to the cities in the mid-1900s.

This country did a superb job responding to and coordinating the rapid growth of the cities. This helped South Korea become a leading world economy.

South Korean Urbanization

Let's explore how urbanization affected the lives of South Koreans:

- **Government:** The South Korean government effectively modernized and developed the growing cities by improving education, transportation, and industry.
  - The South Korean government changed from authoritarian to democratic as the economy grew.
- **Family:** The average family size shrank, which is a typical effect of urbanization.
- **Religion:** South Koreans practiced Confucianism, whose values promoted modernization.
- **Education:** Education was always an important value in South Korea (based on Confucian tradition). This traditional value helped encourage modernization.

Opposite alert! South Korea's traditional religion worked well with modernization.

Women's Status

CHADOR

In the West:

In the 1900s, the status of women changed:

- Women gained the right to vote.
- Women joined the work force.

In the Middle East:

In most Middle Eastern countries, women are gaining rights. Other countries are lagging.

- Turkey, Syria, Egypt: Some women stopped wearing the CHADOR (robe that covers the whole body and part of the face).
- Saudi Arabia: Women are expected to wear a hijab that covers their entire body, except their eyes and hands (in most areas). Only recently, it became legal for women to drive.
- Afghanistan: Most women are illiterate and face forced marriages. Nearly 90% of Afghan women experience domestic abuse!

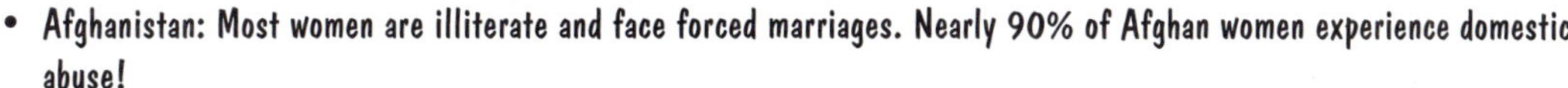

- Iran: Iran limits women's access to divorce, employment, equal inheritance, and politics.
- Israel: Women are part of society and the military.

In Africa:

Women have the right to vote, but their status is still inferior. They face disproportionate levels of poverty, education, poor health, lack of political power, gender-based violence, and child marriages.

Inequality: In the past, women in many societies had a lower status and limited rights. That's changing in some places.

Innovation/Ideas and Beliefs: Women's rights and roles

Global Migrations

GLOBAL MIGRATIONS: "Migration" means moving. In recent years, large numbers of people have moved to Europe and the United States.

Causes of Global Migrations:

- To escape persecution

  ex Muslim refugees are escaping Arab countries.

  Millions of Syrians are escaping persecution by ISIS. They are migrating to the United States, Europe, and other parts of the world.

- Many people move from poor countries to wealthier countries for economic opportunities.

Problems with Global Migrations:

When numerous people move to a new place, it creates a strain on the resources of that new place, resulting in:

- Housing shortages
- Inadequate services (schools, hospitals, government programs)

The arrival of immigrants also raises fear that terrorists will enter the country posing as immigrants.

E Connectedness: Immigrants move to new countries and bring along their culture, language, and issues!

E Scarcity: When there aren't enough jobs or resources, people migrate to other places. Immigrants can drain a country's resources.

E Conflict: Populations escape persecution and migrate.

Is it fair for the natives (people living there originally) to suffer because of immigrants? What do you think?

Part 4: Science and Technology

Global Communication

Once upon a time, if someone wanted to spread a message, he had to write a letter to a newspaper, stamp and address the envelope, and send it off via snail mail. After a few days, weeks, or months, the newspaper would choose whether to publish the message. Local people who purchased the newspaper may have seen his message.

Now, if someone wants to spread a message, he can whip his phone out of his pocket, take one minute to type a message, and post it to millions of people around the world!

Life will never be the same...

- Now, people around the world can create instant connections and new networks regardless of distance and time differences.
- GLOBALIZATION: Information is now accessed and shared on a global scale.

The Information Age

COMPUTER REVOLUTION:

Computers and digital devices have made a major impact on history. Computer technology:

- Creates new jobs
- Helps businesses
- Makes information available quickly and easily

INTERNET/INFORMATION REVOLUTION:

The internet makes information more readily available and connects countries and businesses around the world.

- Business can be performed faster.
- Businesses can outsource their work to countries all over the world.
- Countries around the world can do business with each other.
- Public health agencies can gather data and share important information to stop infectious diseases.

LITERACY and EDUCATION:

Jobs have shifted from farming to business. Therefore, people need to be more educated and familiar with technology. Most countries require education until at least age 14.

Innovation: Computer Revolution and the Internet/Information Revolution

Interconnectedness/Globalization: People around the world can communicate, do business together, and learn from each other through the internet.

Global Communication Affects Governments

Technology affects the interactions between people and their governments. Now, the president can send you instant notifications on your phone! And you can post a comment that may be seen by a government member. Internet sites and social media platforms, such as Twitter and Facebook, opened a new world in politics.

Sometimes, global communication is super beneficial:

- Governments are more aware of people's views and needs and can respond more effectively.
- Protesters against government misconduct can organize more powerfully.

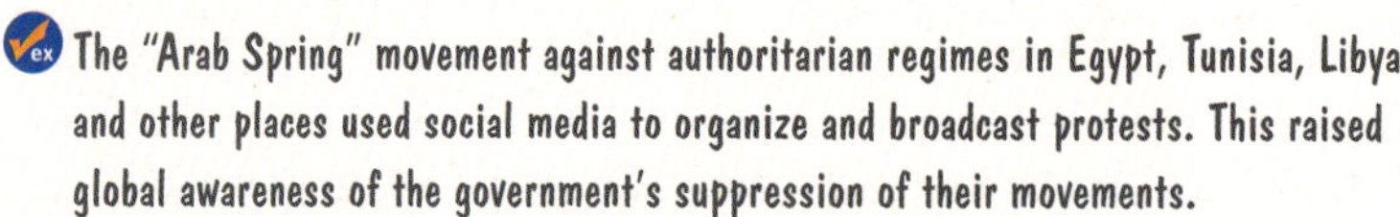

The "Arab Spring" movement against authoritarian regimes in Egypt, Tunisia, Libya, and other places used social media to organize and broadcast protests. This raised global awareness of the government's suppression of their movements.

Other times, global communication is negative:

- Some countries, such as China and North Korea, censor the information shared to control negative content about their country.
- Some governments use the internet and social media to tamper with other countries' elections. For example, some people claim that Russia spread fake and divisive stories on the internet to influence USA's elections.
- Terrorist groups, such as Al Qaeda and ISIS, use social media to promote their anti-Western agenda, recruit

Medical Technology

Medical advancements help people to live longer and reduce the number of infant deaths.

<u>Examples of Medical Advancements</u>:

- Antibiotics treat bacterial illnesses.
- Vaccines prevent viral diseases (such as polio).
- Organ transplants are available.
- Laser surgery is a non-invasive type of surgery that uses beams of light to repair body tissue.

R Cause and Effect: New medical advancements ➲ Increased lifespan ➲ Population increase

E Innovation: Medical advancements

- With global communication, public health agencies, including the CDC and WHO can collect, analyze, and provide solutions for infectious diseases.

ex During the 2015 Zika virus, the CDC and WHO gathered information and provided solutions to combat the Zika outbreak.

Medical Challenges

- New diseases:
  - AIDS damages the body's ability to fight diseases. Millions die of AIDS every year.
  - EBOLA is a virus that has killed thousands of people in Africa.
- COVID-19 is a virus that affects the lungs, heart, smell, and taste. Although the cause is unknown, COVID probably originated from an animal (such as a bat). The disease spread like wildfire, becoming a worldwide pandemic. Millions of people were infected with this disease, governments issued lock-downs for extended periods, and over 6 million people died of this disease. Vaccines were produced to prevent COVID infection and medications were found to treat the disease.

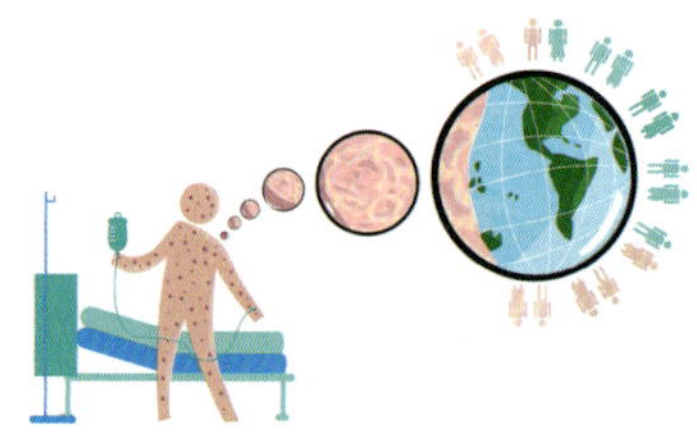

- GENETIC ENGINEERING:
  Scientists are working on cloning animals and organs, which poses many ethical questions.
- POLLUTION causes lung disease and cancers.
- DEFORESTATION: Cutting down forests makes the air more polluted, which causes illnesses. Tropical rainforests are also a source of medicines. When trees are cut down, these resources are depleted (used up).

Environmental Impact/Scarcity: Deforestation

Part 5: The Environment

Population Growth Affects the Environment

Population growth, industrialization, and urbanization

Depletes natural resources and strains the environment

Overcrowded urban areas

Spacious rural areas

- Due to the trend of people flocking to live in cities, cities are overcrowded, while the population in the countryside is often sparse.
- Overcrowding in cities causes a strain on the environment.
- New agricultural technologies help increase food production. (Think Green Revolution!)

Pollution

POLLUTION: substances that harm and contaminate the environment (air, water, and soil)

- Pollution has been a world issue since the Industrial Revolution in the 1700s.
- Factories and cars release gas and soot, causing respiratory diseases such as lung disease, asthma, and cancer.
- Water gets polluted by garbage, chemical, and pesticides, causing cancer and death.

Countries are passing laws and making efforts to lessen the environmental damage and health risks.

Innovation/Environmental Impact: Factories and vehicles emit lots of pollution, which harms the environment.

Acid Rain

ACID RAIN: When FOSSIL FUELS (coal, oil, and natural gases) are heated in cars, factories, and machinery, they release chemicals that rise through the atmosphere and settle on the bottom of the clouds. These chemicals mix into the rain and cause damage on earth.

The polluted (acid) rain causes damage to people, animals, forests, streams, and farms.

- R Cause and Effect: Modern technology ➲ Pollution and acid rain ➲ Damage to humans, plants, and wildlife
- E Environmental Impact: Acid rain

Ozone Layer Depletion

OZONE LAYER: a layer of gas surrounding the earth that protects it from dangerous sun rays

Chemicals (such as those found in aerosol spray cans) deplete the ozone layer.

Now that the ozone layer has holes in it, the harmful rays of the sun can enter and cause skin cancer.

Countries are working on limiting chemical pollutants.

Environmental Impact: Ozone layer depletion

OZONE DEPLETION

Climate Change

We are seeing extreme temperature changes, with some periods that are unusually cold and other periods that are unusually hot.

GLOBAL WARMING: Scientists say that carbon dioxide created by burning fossil fuels (coal, oil, gas) in cars, machinery, and factories is making the earth warmer. Scientists are concerned that if the earth becomes too warm, the GLACIERS (massive ice structures near the North and South Poles) will melt and flood the world.

Environmental Impact: Scientists say that pollution is affecting climate changes.

Deforestation

DEFORESTATION: destruction of forests

<u>Causes of Deforestation</u>:
- People need places to live and build factories.
- People need wood for homes, furniture, and paper.

<u>Effects of Deforestation</u>:
- Trees "eat up" carbon dioxide and release fresh oxygen into the air. When we cut down trees, there's more carbon dioxide in the air, which causes diseases.
- Plants and animals become extinct because their homes were destroyed.

<u>Solutions for Deforestation</u>:
- New trees can be planted to replace the ones that are cut down.
- Many forests are located in developing countries that cut them down for profit. These countries should be educated about the danger of deforestation and be given support to develop other means of income.

Environmental Impact: Deforestation negatively affects the environment.
Cooperation: Countries need to address and correct the deforestation issue.

HINT: Deforestation – de-forest: 'De' means removing. Deforestation means removing forests.

Endangered Species

ENDANGERED SPECIES: a species that is dwindling and is at risk of becoming **EXTINCT** (gone) in the near future

ex: Black Rhino, Asian Elephant, and Blue Whale

Causes of Endangered Species:

- Deforestation makes animals lose their natural habitats (their homes).
- People pollute the earth and water, which kills the animals that live there.
- Hunting

Why are endangered species a problem?

- These animals provide precious food and medicine resources. If they die out, we will lose out.
- The balance of the ecosystem (relationship between the environment and various animal species) will be disturbed. For example, other animals may lose their food sources and then they may die out.

Solutions:

- Many countries have banned the sale of endangered animals and animal products.
- Organizations are dedicated to preserving the habitats of these animals.
  Example: UN and Wildlife Conservation Society (The Bronx Zoo, Queens Zoo, and NY Aquarium are part of this organization and are dedicated to protecting endangered species.)

Environmental Impact: Destroying natural habitats endangers species and disrupts ecosystems.

Cooperation/Interconnectedness: Countries need to address and correct this issue or we'll have to say goodbye to some animals forever!

Desertification

DESERTIFICATION: When farmable and fertile land turns into desert land

Cause of Desertification:

- **OVER-FARMING:** planting the same crop many times on the same piece of land depletes the land's resources
- **OVERGRAZING:** allowing animals to graze on the same plot of land ruins the soil

Effect of Desertification:

Famine

This is occurring today in many areas in Africa, near the Sahara Desert.

Solution for Desertification:

- Stop over-farming and overgrazing.
- Plant new trees.

Environmental Impact: Desertification

Cooperation: Countries need to address and correct this issue.

Water Scarcity

Growing up as we do in a developed country with clean, running water in our sinks, showers, and toilets, it's hard to imagine life without it.
But let's face reality. Over two and a half billion people around the word lack clean water and toilets!

This causes major issues:

- People must walk miles and miles to collect water. This stops them from pursuing employment.
- Children miss school and playtime, as they're also responsible for collecting water.
- Often, the water is unclean and carries bacteria and disease.
  Around the world, 4,000 children die DAILY from drinking dirty water.

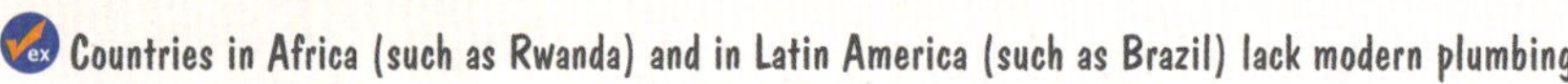

Countries in Africa (such as Rwanda) and in Latin America (such as Brazil) lack modern plumbing.

Other water issues:

- Some governments control the water supply and restrict its access!
- Droughts take place where the weather is hot and dry and the area doesn't receive enough rainfall to sustain life.
- Factories dump industrial waste into the water because it's an easy and cheap way to get rid of their garbage.

Solutions:

- Worldwide organizations should work to establish fresh water sources in countries that lack them.
- Governments should pass laws banning factories from dumping their waste into water.
- People should reduce their use of water.

Scarcity: Water scarcity is of the most serious world crises.

Efforts to Reduce Environmental Damage

Some countries are working together to provide solutions for environmental issues.

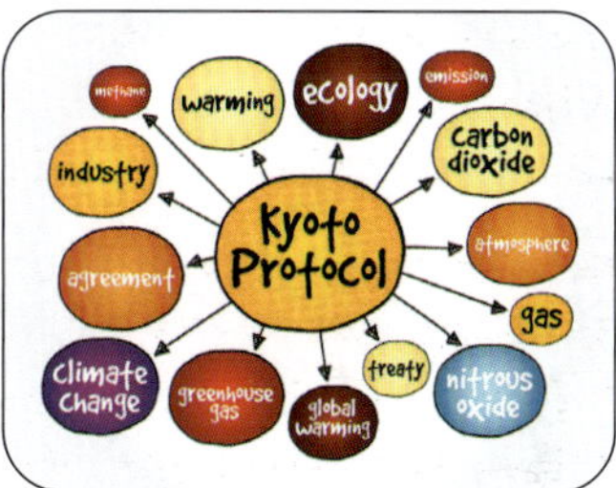

1. KYOTO PROTOCOL: In 1997, 191 developed countries signed this agreement to aim to reduce greenhouse gases (carbon dioxide and methane that people produce and may harm the environment). The United States did not sign.

2. GREENPEACE: In 1971, this international nongovernmental organization began to battle deforestation, desertification, global climate change, hunting endangered whales, and overfishing.

Cooperation/Interconnectedness: Countries are joining together to solve the worldwide issue of pollution.

Yup, we met this organization earlier on!

Quick Review

Check off the boxes you know well. Whatever you don't know well (yet!), go back and review now!

- ☐ Economic interdependence
- ☐ European Union
- ☐ NAFTA
- ☐ Poverty in developing countries
- ☐ Capitalism, command economy, mixed economy, socialist economy
- ☐ Terrorism
- ☐ United Nations
- ☐ Modernization vs. tradition
- ☐ Overpopulation
- ☐ Urbanization
- ☐ Women's status
- ☐ Global migrations
- ☐ Green Revolution
- ☐ Information age, space age
- ☐ Medical advancements
- ☐ Environmental issues: pollution, acid rain, ozone layer depletion, climate changes, global warming, deforestation, endangered species, desertification, nuclear proliferation, nuclear weapons

Enduring Issues Essay Topics That Came Up in This Unit:

- **Interconnectedness/Cooperation:**
  - Global interdependence
  - Economies of countries throughout the world are linked through the EU and NAFTA.
  - The UN is an organization of representatives from all over the world who work together to promote world peace and help other countries in times of disaster.
  - Immigrants move to new countries and bring along their culture, language, and issues!
  - People around the world can communicate, do business together, and learn ideas about each other through the internet.
- **Scarcity:**
  - Some third world countries lack natural resources which limits their economic opportunities.
  - Overpopulation
  - People move away from rural areas because there aren't enough jobs or opportunities.
- **Environmental Impact:**
  - Countries depend on oil, which affects world politics.
  - Some Third World Countries lack natural resources, which harms their economy.
  - The Green Revolution
  - Environmental issues: Pollution, acid rain, ozone layer depletion, climate changes, deforestation, endangered species, desertification, nuclear weapons, urbanization and overpopulation (which causes pollution)

More Enduring Issues Essay Topics That Came Up in This Unit:

- **Cooperation:** Countries should work together to solve the environmental issues (Kyoto Protocol, Climate Change Conference)
- **Human Rights Violations:** Terrorist attacks on innocent civilians
- **Conflict:** Urbanization often weakens traditions, which brings on the traditionalism vs. modernization conflict.
- **Inequality:** In the past, women often had a lower status and limited rights. That's changing.
- **Ideas and Beliefs:** Women's rights and roles
- **Innovation:** The Green Revolution, Computer/Internet Revolution, the Space Age, medical advancements

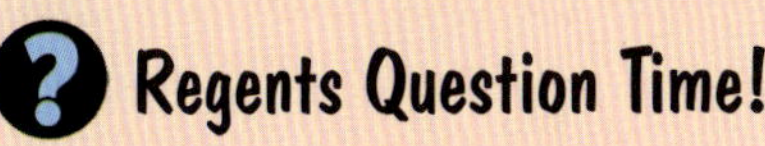

> . . . One of the most important effects on the environment is indirect, and therefore less obvious: Industrial meat production is a key factor behind deforestation of the Amazon and other tropical rain forests. They're being cleared to create fields to grow the feed needed for all those cows, especially corn and soy, which the cows eat instead of the grass they'd munch on if they were grazing in fields as they used to do.
>
> In fact, most of the corn and soy grown today goes to feed cattle, pigs, and chickens, not people. And all that grain requires vast quantities of chemical fertilizer, which in turn takes vast quantities of oil—1.2 gallons to create the fertilizer for every bushel. Finally, cutting down rain forests, which are full of carbon-absorbing trees, further exacerbates [worsens] climate change by reducing the planet's ability to soak up carbon. . . .

— Elisabeth Rosenthal, *New York Times Upfront,* January 18, 2010

27 Which issue is most closely associated with the concerns raised in this passage?

(1) drought
(2) climate change
(3) migration
(4) widespread famine

Answer: ____

1

No title here. Move on.

. . . One of the most important effects on the environment is indirect, and therefore less obvious: Industrial meat production is a key factor behind deforestation of the Amazon and other tropical rain forests. They're being cleared to create fields to grow the feed needed for all those cows, especially corn and soy, which the cows eat instead of the grass they'd munch on if they were grazing in fields as they used to do.

In fact, most of the corn and soy grown today goes to feed cattle, pigs, and chickens, not people. And all that grain requires vast quantities of chemical fertilizer, which in turn takes vast quantities of oil—1.2 gallons to create the fertilizer for every bushel. Finally, cutting down rain forests, which are full of carbon-absorbing trees, further exacerbates [worsens] climate change by reducing the planet's ability to soak up carbon. . . .

4

2

— Elisabeth Rosenthal, *New York Times Upfront*, January 18, 2010

3

27 Which issue is most closely associated with the concerns raised in this passage?

(1) drought
(2) climate change
(3) migration
(4) widespread famine

This question was really straightforward. The document told us the answer!

Regents Question Time!

> . . . One of the most important effects on the environment is indirect, and therefore less obvious: Industrial meat production is a key factor behind deforestation of the Amazon and other tropical rain forests. They're being cleared to create fields to grow the feed needed for all those cows, especially corn and soy, which the cows eat instead of the grass they'd munch on if they were grazing in fields as they used to do.
>
> In fact, most of the corn and soy grown today goes to feed cattle, pigs, and chickens, not people. And all that grain requires vast quantities of chemical fertilizer, which in turn takes vast quantities of oil—1.2 gallons to create the fertilizer for every bushel. Finally, cutting down rain forests, which are full of carbon-absorbing trees, further exacerbates [worsens] climate change by reducing the planet's ability to soak up carbon. . . .

— Elisabeth Rosenthal, *New York Times Upfront,* January 18, 2010

28 In which way have many countries joined together to address the problems described in this passage?

(1) signing international environmental agreements
(2) supporting the exportation of surplus corn and soy
(3) genetically modifying crops to increase production
(4) increasing the amount of land under cultivation

Answer: ___

1

No title here. Move on.

The world is struggling with deforestation, wasting oil, use of food to feed animals instead of people, and climate change.

. . . One of the most important effects on the environment is indirect, and therefore less obvious: Industrial meat production is a key factor behind deforestation of the Amazon and other tropical rain forests. They're being cleared to create fields to grow the feed needed for all those cows, especially corn and soy, which the cows eat instead of the grass they'd munch on if they were grazing in fields as they used to do.

In fact, most of the corn and soy grown today goes to feed cattle, pigs, and chickens, not people. And all that grain requires vast quantities of chemical fertilizer, which in turn takes vast quantities of oil—1.2 gallons to create the fertilizer for every bushel. Finally, cutting down rain forests, which are full of carbon-absorbing trees, further exacerbates [worsens] climate change by reducing the planet's ability to soak up carbon. . . .

4

2

— Elisabeth Rosenthal, *New York Times Upfront,* January 18, 2010

3

28 In which way have many countries joined together to address the problems described in this passage?

(1) signing international environmental agreements
(2) supporting the exportation of surplus corn and soy
(3) genetically modifying crops to increase production
(4) increasing the amount of land under cultivation

Regents Question Time!

Source: KAL, The Economist, November 19, 2009

23 What is the cartoonist suggesting will result if delays in reaching an international agreement to control greenhouse gases continue?

(1) preservation of endangered species
(2) heightened threat for severe glacial melting and continental flooding
(3) reduction in the impact of climate change
(4) increased availability of fresh water supplies

Answer: ___

1

No title here. Move on.

The cartoon shows a Climate Change Summit in 2040. The world is flooded, and people need to be atop Mt. Everest in an ark to avoid drowning! The cartoon is poking fun at the decision makers for taking so long to come up with an agreement.

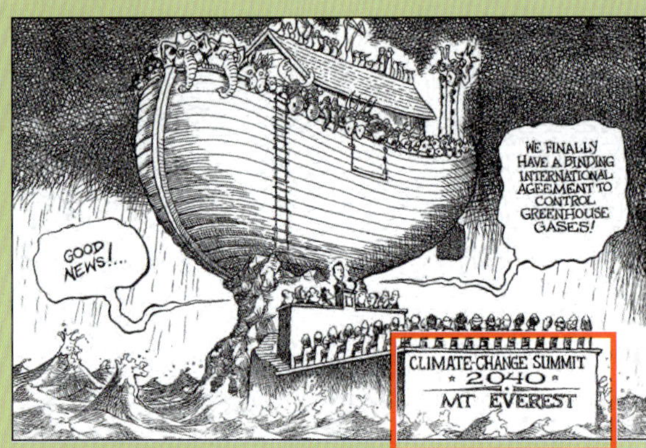

4

2

Source: KAL, The Economist, November 19, 2009

3

23 What is the cartoonist suggesting will result if delays in reaching an international agreement to control greenhouse gases continue?

(1) preservation of endangered species
(2) heightened threat for severe glacial melting and continental flooding
(3) reduction in the impact of climate change
(4) increased availability of fresh water supplies

Regents Question Time!

A World Distorted by HIV/AIDS

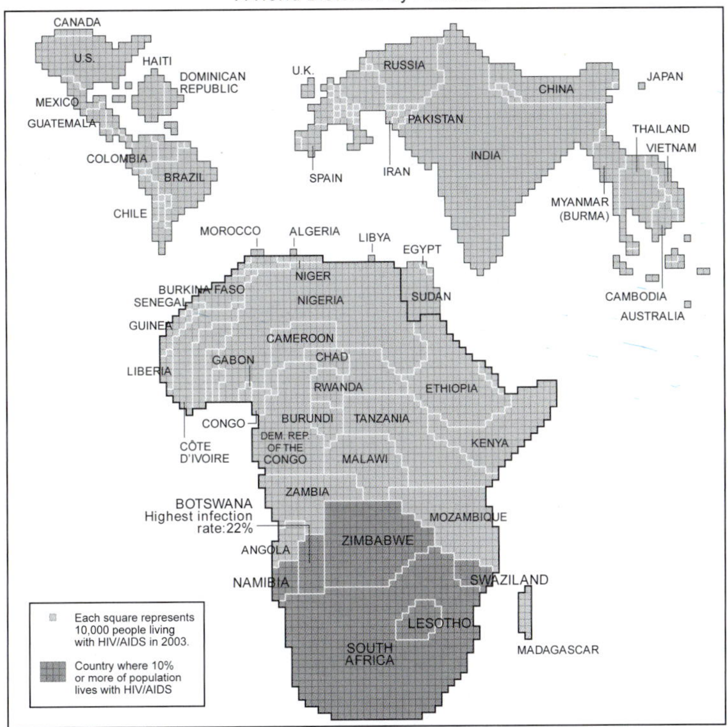

Source: "Living with AIDS," National Geographic, September 2005 (adapted)

25 Which conclusion can best be supported based on the 2003 data shown on this map?

(1) The Western Hemisphere has been hardest hit by the HIV/AIDS crisis.
(2) China and Japan have more people living with HIV/AIDS than India and Thailand.
(3) The number of people living with HIV/AIDS in the Middle East is declining.
(4) Southern Africa faces serious population issues due to the number of people living with HIV/AIDS.

Answer: ____

A World Distorted by HIV/AIDS

AIDS is a serious health issue around the world. In southern Africa, 10% or more of the population is living with AIDS. (See map key on bottom left.)

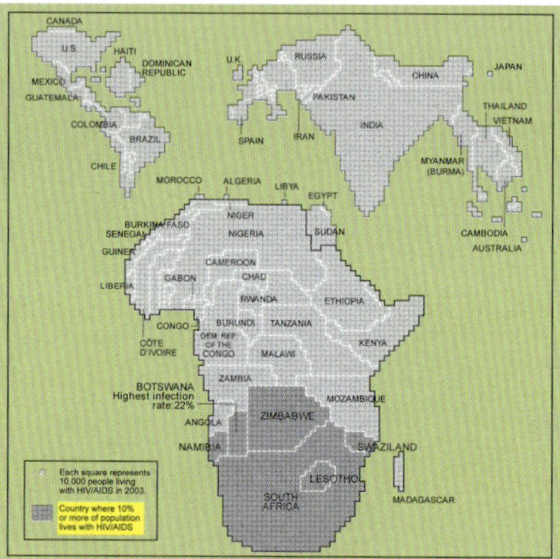

4

2

Source: "Living with AIDS," National Geographic, September 2005 (adapted)

3

25 Which conclusion can best be supported based on the 2003 data shown on this map?

(1) The Western Hemisphere has been hardest hit by the HIV/AIDS crisis.
(2) China and Japan have more people living with HIV/AIDS than India and Thailand.
(3) The number of people living with HIV/AIDS in the Middle East is declining.
(4) Southern Africa faces serious population issues due to the number of people living with HIV/AIDS.

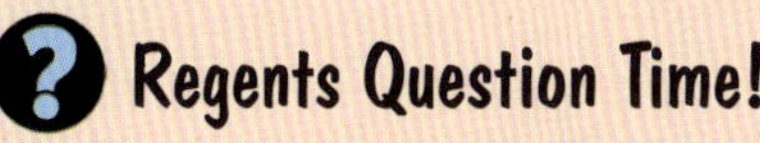

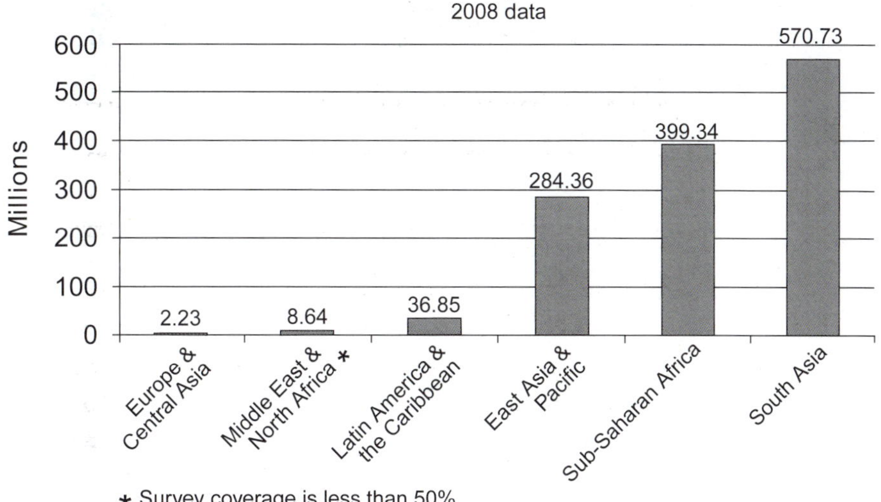

26 Which statement is best supported by the 2008 data provided by this graph?

(1) More people in the Middle East and North Africa earn less than $1.25 per day than people in Latin America and the Caribbean.
(2) Most people from East Asia and the Pacific are in debt.
(3) More South Asians struggle with extreme poverty than people from any other region.
(4) More than 100 million people in Europe and Central Asia earn less than $1.25 per day.

Answer: ___

1

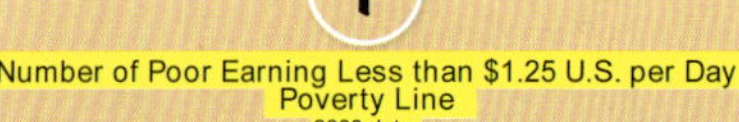

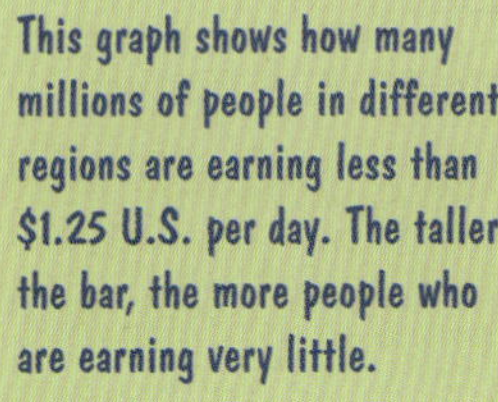

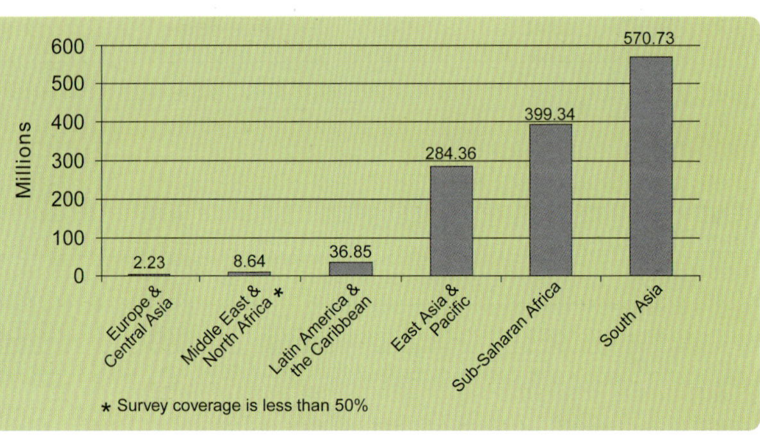

4

2

Source: World Bank (adapted)

3

26 Which statement is best supported by the 2008 data provided by this graph?

(1) More people in the Middle East and North Africa earn less than $1.25 per day than people in Latin America and the Caribbean.
(2) Most people from East Asia and the Pacific are in debt.
(3) More South Asians struggle with extreme poverty than people from any other region.
(4) More than 100 million people in Europe and Central Asia earn less than $1.25 per day.

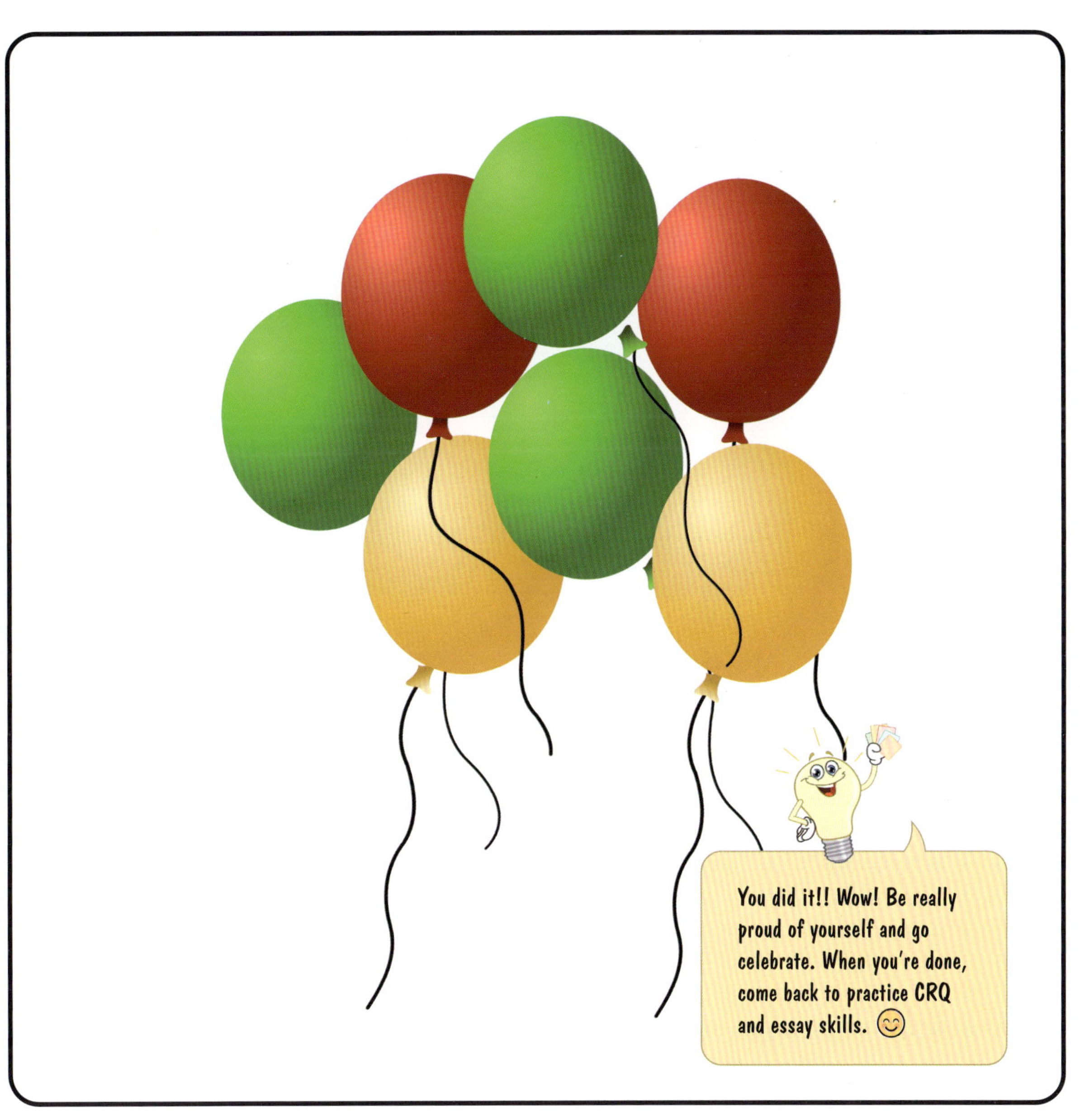
You did it!! Wow! Be really proud of yourself and go celebrate. When you're done, come back to practice CRQ and essay skills. 😊

UNIT 19

REGENTS QUESTIONS ZONE – MULTIPLE CHOICE & CRQ TRICKS

OK Global Genius! You've now mastered the history facts and you should be really proud of yourself!

Once you know the info so well, you might as well ace your Regents. This section will tell you exactly what to expect on the Regents and teach you the skills you need to know, step by step. Let's jump into it, Global genius!

Global II Regents Format

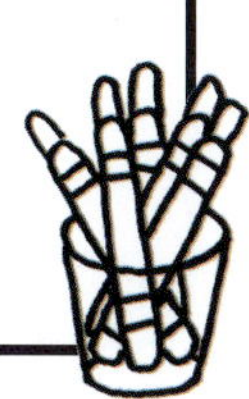

So Mr. Boosters, what's my Regents going to look like?
Great question!

PART 1: 28 MULTIPLE CHOICE QUESTIONS

To make life fun, each multiple choice question will be based on a stimulus. A stimulus is a fancy word for a text, map, graph, cartoon, chart, or picture. They'll give you a cool (or not so cool) stimulus and then 2 to 3 questions based on the stimulus. You'll use the stimulus to help you answer the questions.

PART 2: Two sets of 3 CRQ questions

What does CRQ stand for? Cool and Rocking Questions? Not quite!
It stands for Constructed Response Questions.
What's that?

- The Regents will give you two sets of questions. Each set contains 3 to 4 questions based on documents.
- Basically, they give you documents and questions and you write out the answers. Simple enough, no?
- The good news is that CRQ questions always follow a specific format, so we know exactly what to expect. We'll talk details soon.

PART 3: ENDURING ISSUES ESSAY

- The Regents will give you five documents. You will write an essay based on the documents and on your own genius knowledge.
- Great news! The essay will always be about enduring issues. So we can be totally prepared for this section after we go through all the enduring issues out there!

How much is each question worth?

Section	How many questions?	How many points?
PART 1: MULTIPLE CHOICE	28 questions	54% of Regents grade
PART 2: CRQ	2 sets of 3 questions (One question will have 2 parts.)	17% of Regents grade
PART 3: ESSAY	1 essay based on 5 documents	29% of Regents grade

Now that we know what's on the Regents, let's discuss how to ace each section.

Multiple Choice Questions Tricks

The trick in this section is to learn the skill of analyzing a document and answering the questions based on it.

You may look at a doc (document) and say, "Huh? What's going on over here? I have no idea what this picture, cartoon, map, or text is talking about!" My dear friend, something is about to change. From now on, think about analyzing documents like cracking a secret code. Let's look for clues and hints that will help us figure it out.

This section makes up 54% of your grade. So let's get this right.

The Boosters Multiple Choice Magic Technique trains your brain to take the doc apart, look out for clues and crack the question! Get out your highlighter and colorful pens to gather the clues you're about to find.

<u>Here's how the Boosters Multiple Choice Magic Technique works:</u>

1. Find the title. This will guide your brain to the main topic.
2. Find the source. This is usually found on the bottom of the doc. These tiny letters can be a huge help! The source often states the year or a key name or location.
3. Now let's look at the question. What do they want to know? This will guide us to what we are looking for.
4. Finally, we look at the actual document. Highlight, circle, sit with it and try to crack it! What's it trying to show?
5. Now that you cracked all the codes, you can go back to the question and answer it in peace and confidence!

Boosters Multiple Choice Magic Example

To make Global super clear, the Boosters magic technique uses fun colors and numbers to guide you. Here's a sample question.

First look at the title (1), then at the source (2), then at the question (3), then at the doc (4). Now go back to the question. The dark blue text is Mr. Boosters speaking out his analysis so that you can hear it and train yourself to do it, too. So first try the questions yourself and then you can check yourself using the explanation page.

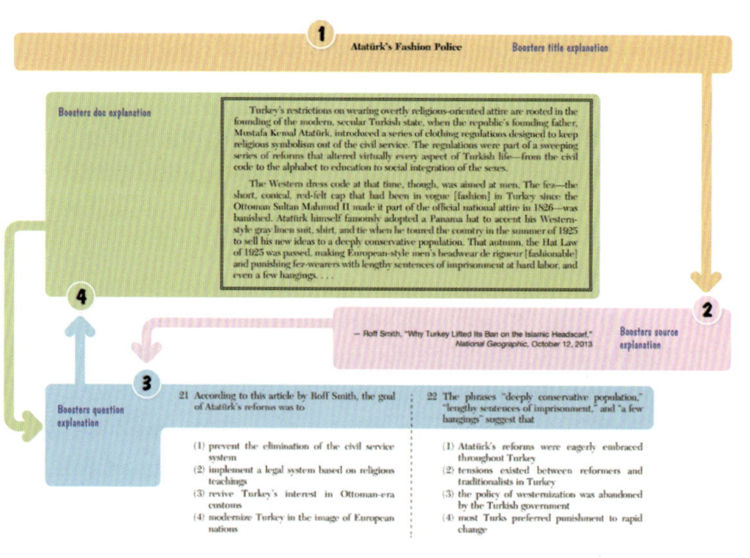

Atatürk's Fashion Police

Turkey's restrictions on wearing overtly religious-oriented attire are rooted in the founding of the modern, secular Turkish state, when the republic's founding father, Mustafa Kemal Atatürk, introduced a series of clothing regulations designed to keep religious symbolism out of the civil service. The regulations were part of a sweeping series of reforms that altered virtually every aspect of Turkish life—from the civil code to the alphabet to education to social integration of the sexes.

The Western dress code at that time, though, was aimed at men. The fez—the short, conical, red-felt cap that had been in vogue [fashion] in Turkey since the Ottoman Sultan Mahmud II made it part of the official national attire in 1826—was banished. Atatürk himself famously adopted a Panama hat to accent his Western-style gray linen suit, shirt, and tie when he toured the country in the summer of 1925 to sell his new ideas to a deeply conservative population. That autumn, the Hat Law of 1925 was passed, making European-style men's headwear de rigueur [fashionable] and punishing fez-wearers with lengthy sentences of imprisonment at hard labor, and even a few hangings. . . .

— Roff Smith, "Why Turkey Lifted Its Ban on the Islamic Headscarf," *National Geographic*, October 12, 2013

21 According to this article by Roff Smith, the goal of Atatürk's reforms was to

(1) prevent the elimination of the civil service system
(2) implement a legal system based on religious teachings
(3) revive Turkey's interest in Ottoman-era customs
(4) modernize Turkey in the image of European nations

22 The phrases "deeply conservative population," "lengthy sentences of imprisonment," and "a few hangings" suggest that

(1) Atatürk's reforms were eagerly embraced throughout Turkey
(2) tensions existed between reformers and traditionalists in Turkey
(3) the policy of westernization was abandoned by the Turkish government
(4) most Turks preferred punishment to rapid change

More Multiple Choice Tricks

- Some documents will be missing a title or source. No problem – just look for the clues in other places.
- Don't stress if you don't "get" the document. It's meant to be a challenge. And you can do it! Just try your best to crack the code! Even if you don't understand every detail of the document, that's totally fine. As long as you're able to extract the info you need to answer the question, you're good to go.

It's a challenge and takes practice, but you're playing a game of cracking the question, so have fun! The more challenging the code, the more fun the question!

Here are some tips on choosing the right answers from the choices given:

- ☐ Highlight or circle key words, dates, or numbers in the document.
- ☐ Highlight key words in the question. Pay attention: what is the question asking?
- ☐ When you're ready to choose the answer, read every choice separately.
  Here's a very helpful trick to those who have difficulty with multiple choice questions. Take two blank papers. Cover the text above and below one choice, so only that choice shows. Now focus on that choice. Does it answer the question correctly?
- ☐ Evaluate each choice separately. Make a check mark if you think it's correct. (But still go through the other choices to make sure no other choice is more correct.) Make an "X" if you think the choice is wrong. Make a question mark if you're not sure.

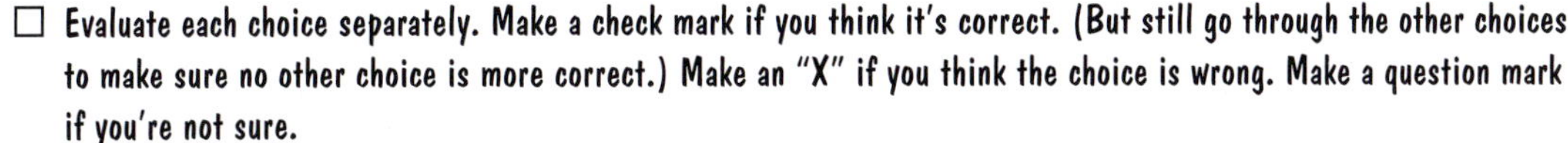

- ☐ Do NOT leave out any questions. If you guess, you still have a 25% chance of getting the correct answer. Really, really, don't leave out any questions!
- ☐ After you choose an answer, read the question and your choice again to make sure your choice answers the question being asked.

CRQ- Constructed Response Questions Section

First, the big question. What exactly are CRQ questions? In this section, you will be writing out answers to approximately 7 questions. They will always follow a specific format.

There will be 2 sets of questions.

- Each set will include 3-4 questions:
  1. Question 1 will show Document 1 and ask for a written answer based on the document.
  2. Question 2 will show Document 2 and ask for a written answer based on the document.
  3. Question 3 will ask you about the relationship between Documents 1 and 2. Sometimes this question will have 2 parts.

Here's a snapshot of the August 2019 Regents CRQ section:

Short-Answer CRQ Set 1 Structure

- Question 29 uses Document 1 (Context)
- Question 30 uses Document 2 (Source)
- Question 31 uses Documents 1 and 2 (Relationship between documents)

Short-Answer CRQ Set 2 Structure

- Question 32 uses Document 1 (Context)
- Question 33 uses Document 2 (Source)
- Questions 34a and 34b use Documents 1 and 2 (Relationship between documents)

Now that you're such an expert on multiple choice questions, you'll have no problem with the CRQ section.

Good news! (Yes, there is some!) The Regents will always ask the same types of questions, so we can totally prepare for them.

Question #1 in the CRQ Section

The first question in each set will always be based on the first document.
The question will always be based on historical or geographic info.
P.S. The Regents calls this "historical context" or "geographic context."

Now listen closely because I'm about to tell you exactly what the first CRQ question will ask.

The first question will always ask either one of these questions:

- What was the historical context that led to the development in this document?
- What was the geographic context of this document?

So what should you answer?

- If they ask you for the historical context of the document:
  Just explain what was going on at this time period that led to this idea or event.
- If they ask you for the geographic context of the document:
  Just explain where this event happened and why it happened there.
  - The document for this type of question will usually be a map or text that discusses an event whose location is important.

Major tip: First dissect the document using the Boosters Multiple choice Magic trick. Analyze the title, then analyze the source, then read the question, then read the document. Then go on to write out your ingenious answer!

Question #1 in the CRQ Section Example – Historical Context

Document 1

Source: Mrs. Ernest Ames, *An ABC for Baby Patriots,* Dean & Sons, 1898 (adapted)

29 Explain the historical circumstances that led to British attitudes about their empire as shown in this excerpt from *An ABC for Baby Patriots*. [1]

____

____

____

Score

1

No title here. Move on.

Great Britain is basically bragging about how great it is and about how many colonies it has.

B, b.

B stands for Battles
By which England's name
Has for ever been covered
With glory and fame.

C is for Colonies.
Rightly we boast.
That of all the great nations
Great Britain has most.

C, c.

E is our Empire
Where sun never sets;
The larger we make it
The bigger it gets.

E, e.

2

Source: Mrs. Ernest Ames, *An ABC for Baby Patriots,* Dean & Sons, 1898 (adapted)

3

29 Explain the historical circumstances that led to British attitudes about their empire as shown in this excerpt from *An ABC for Baby Patriots*. [1]

4

Which historical circumstances led to British attitudes?

Now, let's tackle the question:

What was going on during this period that led to Britain feeling so great about itself and imperializing?

Basically, what led to imperialism?

Jog your memory for the causes of imperialism. Hint: NEW

Here are some acceptable answers:

- Nationalism/Social Darwinism: Stronger countries felt they had the right to control weaker countries.
- Economic reasons: Imperialists needed raw materials and places to sell their goods.
- White Man's Burden: Imperialists felt they had a responsibility to educate weaker countries.

Question #1 in the CRQ Section Example – Geographic Context

Document 1

Peep Under the Iron Curtain

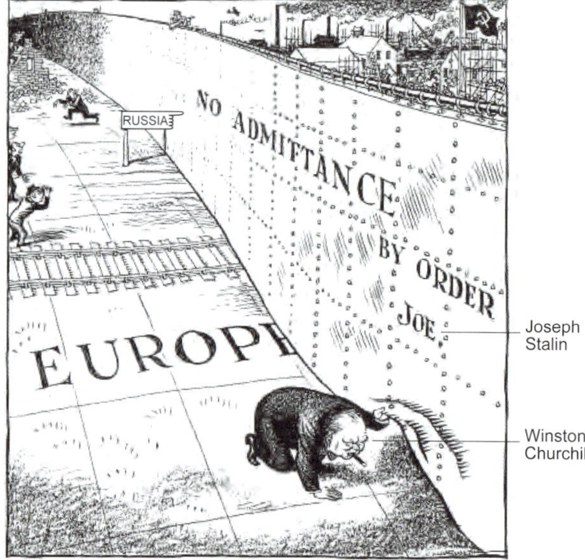

Source: Leslie Gilbert Illingworth, Daily Mail, March 6, 1946 (adapted)

Geographic Context—refers to where this historical development/event is taking place and why it is taking place there.

32 Explain the geographic context for the historical development/event shown in this 1946 cartoon. [1]

____

____

____

Score

1

Peep Under the Iron Curtain

Document: An "iron curtain" is separating Russia from the rest of Europe, symbolizing the division between communism and democracy.

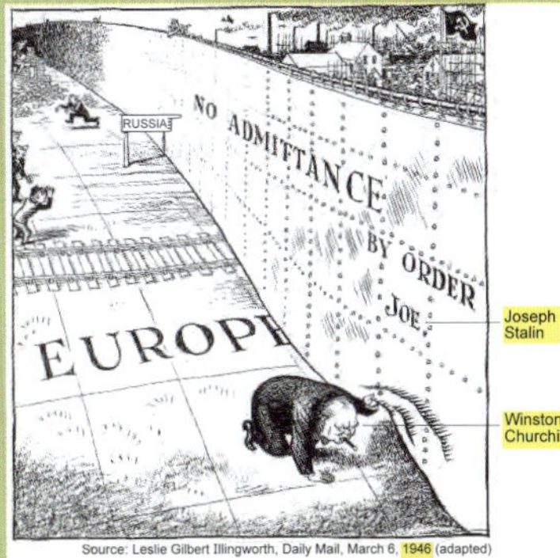

Source: Leslie Gilbert Illingworth, Daily Mail, March 6, 1946 (adapted)

Geographic Context—refers to where this historical development/event is taking place and why it is taking place there.

4

2

Source: Leslie Gilbert Illingworth, Daily Mail, March 6, 1946 (adapted)

3

Where is this taking place and why is it taking place there?

32 Explain the geographic context for the historical development/event shown in this 1946 cartoon. [1]

Good news! The Regents will remind you what "geographic context" is. Here's a snapshot of what they'll write:

Geographic Context—refers to where this historical development/event is taking place and why it is taking place there.

Now just answer where this took place and why it's taking place there.

Make sure you answer both questions or you'll get this question wrong!

Acceptable answers:

- Europe was divided after World War II into communist and non-communist countries.
- After World War II, Europe was divided during the Yalta Conference.
- The Iron Curtain split Europe into two.

EdBoosters™

Question #2 in the CRQ Section

The second question in each set will always be based on the second document. The source will usually be a primary source (original source such as a diary, artifact, or autobiography).

The second question will always ask you about the sourcing. They will ask you one of these 4 questions:

1. BIAS: Is the document a one-sided opinion?
2. AUDIENCE: Who was this document made for?
3. POINT OF VIEW: What's the author/illustrator's opinion in this document? What was their attitude?
4. PURPOSE: Why was this document printed? What point is it trying to make?

HINT: BAPP – bias, audience, point of view, purpose

Great news! Since the Regents-making committee loves you so much, they give a little intro to the document, which is super helpful. There are serious clues in there, so pay attention to it.

Then look at the source, the question, and the document. And then go ahead and answer the question. Have fun!

Don't bother memorizing each type of question! I'm just giving you a heads up on what to expect.

Question #2 in the CRQ Section Example – Source

Document 2

This excerpt is taken from John Fielden's, *The Curse of the Factory System*. This work was originally published in London in 1836. John Fielden was a Lancashire textile owner who was deeply committed to the cause of social reform. He discusses the problems faced by businessmen like himself, who were trying to make a profit and protect their workers at the same time.

> . . . Here, then, is the "curse" of our factory-system: as improvements in machinery have gone on, the "avarice [self-interest] of masters" has prompted many to exact more labour from their hands than they were fitted by nature to perform, and those who have wished for the hours of labour to be less for all ages than the legislature would even yet sanction [approve], have had no alternative but to conform more or less to the prevailing practice, or abandon the trade altogether. This has been the case with regard to myself and my partners. We had never worked more than *seventy-one* hours a week before Sir JOHN HOBHOUSE'S Act was passed. We then came down to *sixty-nine*; and, since Lord ALTHORP'S Act was passed, in 1833, we have reduced the time of adults to *sixty-seven and a half hours* a week, and that of children under thirteen years of age to *forty-eight* hours in the week, though to do this latter, has, I must admit, subjected us to much inconvenience, but the elder hands to more, inasmuch as the relief given to the child is in some measure imposed on the adult. But the overworking does not apply to children only; the adults are also overworked. The increased speed given to machinery within the last thirty years, has, in very many instances, doubled the labour of both. Mr. Longston's evidence before Mr. SADLER'S Committee establishes this fact beyond dispute, and my own knowledge of the subject requires that I should confirm, as I do, the truth of his statement. . . .

Source: John Fielden, *The Curse of the Factory System,* Second Edition, Augustus M. Kelley Publishers, 1969

30 Based on this excerpt, identify John Fielden's point of view concerning the factory system's impact on laborers. [1]

____

____

____

Score

1

This excerpt is taken from John Fielden's, *The Curse of the Factory System*. This work was originally published in London in 1836. John Fielden was a Lancashire textile owner who was deeply committed to the cause of social reform. He discusses the problems faced by businessmen like himself, who were trying to make a profit and protect their workers at the same time.

This isn't exactly a title. It's the intro to the document. "The Curse of the Factory System" gives us a hint to what Fielden thinks of the factory system.

Fielden describes how overworked the factory owners were. Make sure to focus on what the question is asking and highlight only those points. There's plenty of irrelevant information in this document and you don't want to get sidetracked.
The most important thing is to make sure you answer what the question is asking. What's Fielden's opinion about the factory's effect on laborers (workers)?

. . . Here, then, is the "curse" of our factory-system: as improvements in machinery have gone on, the "avarice [self-interest] of masters" has prompted many to exact more labour from their hands than they were fitted by nature to perform, and those who have wished for the hours of labour to be less for all ages than the legislature would even yet sanction [approve], have had no alternative but to conform more or less to the prevailing practice, or abandon the trade altogether. This has been the case with regard to myself and my partners. We had never worked more than *seventy-one* hours a week before Sir JOHN HOBHOUSE'S Act was passed. We then came down to *sixty-nine*; and, since Lord ALTHORP'S Act was passed, in 1833, we have reduced the time of adults to *sixty-seven and a half hours* a week, and that of children under thirteen years of age to *forty-eight* hours in the week, though to do this latter, has, I must admit, subjected us to much inconvenience, but the elder hands to more, inasmuch as the relief given to the child is in some measure imposed on the adult. But the overworking does not apply to children only; the adults are also overworked. The increased speed given to machinery within the last thirty years, has, in very many instances, doubled the labour of both. Mr. Longston's evidence before Mr. SADLER'S Committee establishes this fact beyond dispute, and my own knowledge of the subject requires that I should confirm, as I do, the truth of his statement. . . .

4

2

Source: John Fielden, *The Curse of the Factory System,* Second Edition, Augustus M. Kelley Publishers, 1969

3

30 Based on this excerpt, identify John Fielden's point of view concerning the factory system's impact on laborers. [1]

Acceptable answers:

- The factory system led to long working hours.
- The improved machinery in factories caused the factory workers to work harder.
- The factory system was bad/unfair.
- Adults/children were overworked in the factory system.
- The working conditions in the factory needed to change.

If you write anything regarding improvement in the treatment of workers or the acts passed to improve factory conditions, your answer will be incorrect ☹. The question is asking for Fielden's point of view – his opinion on how the factory system affected workers. Focus on answering the question asked.

By the way, you should make sure you answered the question being asked 😉. I know I just said that, but I really want you to remember that!

Question #2 in the CRQ Section Example – Source

Document 2

Deng Xiaoping was the most powerful leader in China from December 1978 until he stepped down in 1992. In early 1992, Deng Xiaoping visited and gave talks in some southern Chinese cities.

> . . . The reason some people hesitate to carry out the reform and the open policy and dare not break new ground is, in essence, that they're afraid it would mean introducing too many elements of capitalism and, indeed, taking the capitalist road. The crux of the matter is whether the road is capitalist or socialist. The chief criterion for making that judgement should be whether it promotes the growth of the productive forces in a socialist society, increases the overall strength of the socialist state and raises living standards. As for building special economic zones, some people disagreed with the idea right from the start, wondering whether it would not mean introducing capitalism. The achievements in the construction of Shenzhen have given these people a definite answer: special economic zones are socialist, not capitalist. In the case of Shenzhen, the publicly owned sector is the mainstay of the economy, while the foreign-invested sector accounts for only a quarter. And even in that sector, we benefit from taxes and employment opportunities. We should have more of the three kinds of foreign-invested ventures [joint, cooperative and foreign-owned]. There is no reason to be afraid of them. So long as we keep level-headed, there is no cause for alarm. We have our advantages: we have the large and medium-sized state-owned enterprises and the rural enterprises. More important, political power is in our hands.
>
> Some people argue that the more foreign investment flows in and the more ventures of the three kinds are established, the more elements of capitalism will be introduced and the more capitalism will expand in China. These people lack basic knowledge. At the current stage, foreign-funded enterprises in China are allowed to make some money in accordance with existing laws and policies. But the government levies taxes on those enterprises, workers get wages from them, and we learn technology and managerial skills. In addition, we can get information from them that will help us open more markets. Therefore, subject to the constraints of China's overall political and economic conditions, foreign-funded enterprises are useful supplements to the socialist economy, and in the final analysis they are good for socialism. . . .

Source: Deng Xiaoping, "Excerpts from Talks Given in Wuchang, Shenzhen, Zhuhai, and Shanghai," January 18–February 21, 1992, China Through A Lens online

33 Based on this excerpt, explain the purpose of Deng Xiaoping's speech which addresses reform and the open policy in China. [1]

____

____

____

Score ☐

Deng Xiaoping was the most powerful leader in China from December 1978 until he stepped down in 1992. In early 1992, Deng Xiaoping visited and gave talks in some southern Chinese cities.

This is an intro, rather than a title.

Xiaoping explains why reform and open policy are good for China and why China shouldn't be scared that this will interfere with socialism.

. . . The reason some people hesitate to carry out the reform and the open policy and dare not break new ground is, in essence, that they're afraid it would mean introducing too many elements of capitalism and, indeed, taking the capitalist road. The crux of the matter is whether the road is capitalist or socialist. The chief criterion for making that judgement should be whether it promotes the growth of the productive forces in a socialist society, increases the overall strength of the socialist state and raises living standards. As for building special economic zones, some people disagreed with the idea right from the start, wondering whether it would not mean introducing capitalism. The achievements in the construction of Shenzhen have given these people a definite answer: special economic zones are socialist, not capitalist. In the case of Shenzhen, the publicly owned sector is the mainstay of the economy, while the foreign-invested sector accounts for only a quarter. And even in that sector, we benefit from taxes and employment opportunities. We should have more of the three kinds of foreign-invested ventures [joint, cooperative and foreign-owned]. There is no reason to be afraid of them. So long as we keep level-headed, there is no cause for alarm. We have our advantages: we have the large and medium-sized state-owned enterprises and the rural enterprises. More important, political power is in our hands.

Some people argue that the more foreign investment flows in and the more ventures of the three kinds are established, the more elements of capitalism will be introduced and the more capitalism will expand in China. These people lack basic knowledge. At the current stage, foreign-funded enterprises in China are allowed to make some money in accordance with existing laws and policies. But the government levies taxes on those enterprises, workers get wages from them, and we learn technology and managerial skills. In addition, we can get information from them that will help us open more markets. Therefore, subject to the constraints of China's overall political and economic conditions, foreign-funded enterprises are useful supplements to the socialist economy, and in the final analysis they are good for socialism. . . .

4

Source: Deng Xiaoping, "Excerpts from Talks Given in Wuchang, Shenzhen, Zhuhai, and Shanghai," January 18–February 21, 1992, China Through A Lens online

3

33 Based on this excerpt, explain the purpose of Deng Xiaoping's speech which addresses reform and the open policy in China. [1]

What was the point of Xiaoping's speech on reform and open policy in China?

Acceptable answers:

- The purpose of Deng Xiaoping's speech was to stress the benefits and importance of economic development.
- The purpose of Deng Xiaoping's speech was to explain how China benefits from economic reforms. (Feel free to give examples from the document.)
- The purpose of Deng Xiaoping's speech was to convince the Chinese people that foreign businesses wouldn't interfere with socialism, but would help it.

Here's a great tip for the CRQ questions. Start the answer by repeating part of the question. For example, "The purpose of Deng Xiaoping's speech...." This will help you focus on answering what the question is asking you.

P.S. Did I ever tell you to make sure to answer the question being asked? 

Question #2 in the CRQ Section Example – Source

Document 2

The Discovery of India was written by Jawaharlal Nehru during his imprisonment at Ahmadnagar Fort in British India from April to September 1944. Nehru was a leader in the Indian National Congress.

> The Chief business of the East India Company in its early period, the very object for which it was started, was to carry Indian manufactured goods—textiles, etc., as well as spices and the like—from the East to Europe, where there was a great demand for these articles. With the developments in industrial techniques in England a new class of industrial capitalists rose there demanding a change in this policy. The British market was to be closed to Indian products and the Indian market opened to British manufactures. The British parliament, influenced by this new class, began to take a greater interest in India and the working of the East India Company. To begin with, Indian goods were excluded from Britain by legislation, and as the company held a monopoly in the Indian export business, this exclusion influenced other foreign markets also. This was followed by vigorous attempts to restrict and crush Indian manufactures by various measures and internal duties which prevented the flow of Indian goods within the country itself. British goods meanwhile had free entry. The Indian textile industry collapsed, affecting vast numbers of weavers and artisans. The process was rapid in Bengal and Bihar; elsewhere it spread gradually with the expansion of British rule and the building of railways. It continued throughout the nineteenth century, breaking up other old industries also, shipbuilding, metalwork, glass, paper, and many crafts.
>
> To some extent this was inevitable as the older manufacturing came into conflict with the new industrial technique. But it was hastened by political and economic pressure, and no attempt was made to apply the new techniques to India. Indeed every attempt was made to prevent this happening, and thus the economic development of India was arrested [stopped] and the growth of the new industry prevented. Machinery could not be imported into India. A vacuum was created in India which could only be filled by British goods, and which also led to rapidly increasing unemployment and poverty. The classic type of modern colonial economy was built up, India becoming an agricultural colony of industrial England, supplying raw materials and providing markets for England's industrial goods. . . .

Source: Jawaharlal Nehru, *Thc Discovery of India*, The John Day Company, 1946

30 Identify Jawaharlal Nehru's point of view concerning British colonialism in India based on this excerpt. [1]

____

____

____

Score ☐

1

The Discovery of India was written by Jawaharlal Nehru during his imprisonment at Ahmadnagar Fort in British India from April to September 1944. Nehru was a leader in the Indian National Congress.

Britain imperialized India and took advantage of it by taking their raw materials and using India as a market for its own products. This hurt India's economy, increasing unemployment and poverty.

The Chief business of the East India Company in its early period, the very object for which it was started, was to carry Indian manufactured goods—textiles, etc., as well as spices and the like—from the East to Europe, where there was a great demand for these articles. With the developments in industrial techniques in England a new class of industrial capitalists rose there demanding a change in this policy. The British market was to be closed to Indian products and the Indian market opened to British manufactures. The British parliament, influenced by this new class, began to take a greater interest in India and the working of the East India Company. To begin with, Indian goods were excluded from Britain by legislation, and as the company held a monopoly in the Indian export business, this exclusion influenced other foreign markets also. This was followed by vigorous attempts to restrict and crush Indian manufactures by various measures and internal duties which prevented the flow of Indian goods within the country itself. British goods meanwhile had free entry. The Indian textile industry collapsed, affecting vast numbers of weavers and artisans. The process was rapid in Bengal and Bihar; elsewhere it spread gradually with the expansion of British rule and the building of railways. It continued throughout the nineteenth century, breaking up other old industries also, shipbuilding, metalwork, glass, paper, and many crafts.

To some extent this was inevitable as the older manufacturing came into conflict with the new industrial technique. But it was hastened by political and economic pressure, and no attempt was made to apply the new techniques to India. Indeed every attempt was made to prevent this happening, and thus the economic development of India was arrested [stopped] and the growth of the new industry prevented. Machinery could not be imported into India. A vacuum was created in India which could only be filled by British goods, and which also led to rapidly increasing unemployment and poverty. The classic type of modern colonial economy was built up, India becoming an agricultural colony of industrial England, supplying raw materials and providing markets for England's industrial goods. . . .

4

2

Source: Jawaharlal Nehru, *The Discovery of India*, The John Day Company, 1946

3

30 Identify Jawaharlal Nehru's point of view concerning British colonialism in India based on this excerpt. [1]

Remember: point of view means opinion. What was Nehru's opinion about British colonialism in India?

Acceptable answers:

- India's economy/industries were damaged by Britain's colonialism/imperialism.
- British imperialism caused high unemployment and poverty in India.
- Britain took advantage of the Indian people (by taking India's raw goods and using India as its market).

Question #3 in the CRQ Section

Now that we've mastered the first two CRQ questions, let's jump into the last type of question (the one that's the most fun 😉!).

The third question in each CRQ will ask you about the relationship between the two documents in question one and question two.

Here's a snapshot of a typical Regents. Notice that the third question in each CRQ is based on the relationship between Document 1 and Document 2.

Short-Answer CRQ Set 1 Structure

- Question 29 uses Document 1 (Context)
- Question 30 uses Document 2 (Source)
- Question 31 uses Documents 1 and 2 (Relationship between documents)

Short-Answer CRQ Set 2 Structure

- Question 32 uses Document 1 (Context)
- Question 33 uses Document 2 (Source)
- Questions 34a and 34b use Documents 1 and 2 (Relationship between documents)

There are 3 types of questions the Regents can ask you based on the connection between the documents:

1. **CAUSE-AND-EFFECT** relationship: One document shows the cause and the other document shows the effect.
   - The first CRQ set will always include a cause-and-effect question.
2. **TURNING POINT** relationship between the 2 documents
3. **SIMILARITY** or **DIFFERENCE** between the 2 documents
   - The second CRQ set will always include a turning point or similarity/difference question.

By the way, the third question will sometimes have two parts to it.
Let's explore the 3 types of questions so that we can ace this section!

Question #3 in the CRQ Section – Cause and Effect

You will be asked to identify and explain the cause-and-effect relationship between the events or ideas described in the first 2 documents.

In case you don't know what cause and effect means, the Regents will tell you.

Here's a snapshot from a typical cause-and-effect Question #3 :

> **Cause**—refers to something that contributes to the occurrence of an event, the rise of an idea, or the bringing about of a development.
>
> **Effect**—refers to what happens as a consequence (result, impact, outcome) of an event, an idea, or a development.

Here's how you answer this type of question:

1. Write down the main idea/event described in each document.
2. Which idea/event led to the other? Fill it out:

> ______________ led to ______________.
> (Cause) (Effect)

Sometimes the idea/event described in Document 1 led to the idea/event described Document 2. And sometimes the idea/event described in Document 2 led to the idea/even described in Document 1

Question #3 in the CRQ Section – Cause and Effect Example

See documents on the following 2 pages.

Base your answer to question 31 on ***both*** Documents 1 and 2 and on your knowledge of social studies.

Cause—refers to something that contributes to the occurrence of an event, the rise of an idea, or the bringing about of a development.

Effect—refers to what happens as a consequence (result, impact, outcome) of an event, an idea, or a development.

31 Identify ***and*** explain a cause-and-effect relationship associated with the historical developments in documents 1 and 2. Be sure to use evidence from ***both*** documents 1 and 2 in your response. [1]

Score

Question #3 in the CRQ Section – Cause-and-Effect Example

Document 1

B, b.

B stands for Battles
By which England's name
Has for ever been covered
With glory and fame.

C is for Colonies.
Rightly we boast,
That of all the great nations
Great Britain has most.

E is our Empire
Where sun never sets;
The larger we make it
The bigger it gets.

E, e.

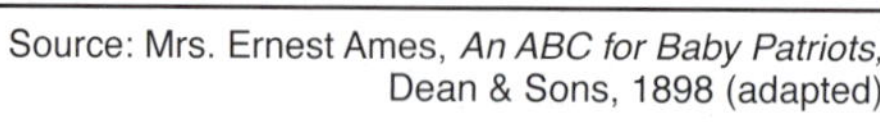

Source: Mrs. Ernest Ames, *An ABC for Baby Patriots*, Dean & Sons, 1898 (adapted)

Question #3 in the CRQ Section – Cause-and-Effect Example

Document 2

The Discovery of India was written by Jawaharlal Nehru during his imprisonment at Ahmadnagar Fort in British India from April to September 1944. Nehru was a leader in the Indian National Congress.

> The Chief business of the East India Company in its early period, the very object for which it was started, was to carry Indian manufactured goods—textiles, etc., as well as spices and the like—from the East to Europe, where there was a great demand for these articles. With the developments in industrial techniques in England a new class of industrial capitalists rose there demanding a change in this policy. The British market was to be closed to Indian products and the Indian market opened to British manufactures. The British parliament, influenced by this new class, began to take a greater interest in India and the working of the East India Company. To begin with, Indian goods were excluded from Britain by legislation, and as the company held a monopoly in the Indian export business, this exclusion influenced other foreign markets also. This was followed by vigorous attempts to restrict and crush Indian manufactures by various measures and internal duties which prevented the flow of Indian goods within the country itself. British goods meanwhile had free entry. The Indian textile industry collapsed, affecting vast numbers of weavers and artisans. The process was rapid in Bengal and Bihar; elsewhere it spread gradually with the expansion of British rule and the building of railways. It continued throughout the nineteenth century, breaking up other old industries also, shipbuilding, metalwork, glass, paper, and many crafts.
>
> To some extent this was inevitable as the older manufacturing came into conflict with the new industrial technique. But it was hastened by political and economic pressure, and no attempt was made to apply the new techniques to India. Indeed every attempt was made to prevent this happening, and thus the economic development of India was arrested [stopped] and the growth of the new industry prevented. Machinery could not be imported into India. A vacuum was created in India which could only be filled by British goods, and which also led to rapidly increasing unemployment and poverty. The classic type of modern colonial economy was built up, India becoming an agricultural colony of industrial England, supplying raw materials and providing markets for England's industrial goods. . . .

Source: Jawaharlal Nehru, *The Discovery of India*, The John Day Company, 1946

Question #3 in the CRQ Section – Cause-and-Effect Example Answer

1. Write down the main idea of each document.
   Document 1: Britain imperialized colonies.
   Document 2: Britain took advantage of India and ruined its economy.
2. Now decide which idea/event led to the other and fill it in:

_______________ led to _______________.
(CAUSE) (EFFECT)

Answer:

- Britain's imperialization led to Britain's taking advantage of India and its economy.
  (Cause) (Effect)

Notice how we showed that Document 1 (the cause) led to Document 2 (the effect). You must include information from each document and show how one led to the other.

Other acceptable answers:

- British imperialism led to the collapse of India's native industries.
- Britain's desire for raw materials led to the exploitation of India's raw materials.
- Britain's imperialism led to Nehru's opposition.

Cause and Effect Illustration

This page is dedicated to the visual learners out there!
This shows you how the concept in one document leads to the concept in the next document.

Source: Mrs. Ernest Ames, *An ABC for Baby Patriots,* Dean & Sons, 1898 (adapted)

Document 1: Britain imperialized colonies.

The Discovery of India was written by Jawaharlal Nehru during his imprisonment at Ahmadnagar Fort in British India from April to September 1944. Nehru was a leader in the Indian National Congress.

The Chief business of the East India Company in its early period, the very object for which it was started, was to carry Indian manufactured goods—textiles, etc., as well as spices and the like—from the East to Europe, where there was a great demand for these articles. With the developments in industrial techniques in England a new class of industrial capitalists rose there demanding a change in this policy. The British market was to be closed to Indian products and the Indian market opened to British manufactures. The British parliament, influenced by this new class, began to take a greater interest in India and the working of the East India Company. To begin with, Indian goods were excluded from Britain by legislation, and as the company held a monopoly in the Indian export business, this exclusion influenced other foreign markets also. This was followed by vigorous attempts to restrict and crush Indian manufactures by various measures and internal duties which prevented the flow of Indian goods within the country itself. British goods meanwhile had free entry. The Indian textile industry collapsed, affecting vast numbers of weavers and artisans. The process was rapid in Bengal and Bihar; elsewhere it spread gradually with the expansion of British rule and the building of railways. It continued throughout the nineteenth century, breaking up other old industries also, shipbuilding, metalwork, glass, paper, and many crafts.

To some extent this was inevitable as the older manufacturing came into conflict with the new industrial technique. But it was hastened by political and economic pressure, and no attempt was made to apply the new techniques to India. Indeed every attempt was made to prevent this happening, and thus the economic development of India was arrested [stopped] and the growth of the new industry prevented. Machinery could not be imported into India. A vacuum was created in India which could only be filled by British goods, and which also led to rapidly increasing unemployment and poverty. The classic type of modern colonial economy was built up, India becoming an agricultural colony of industrial England, supplying raw materials and providing markets for England's industrial goods. . . .

Source: Jawaharlal Nehru, *The Discovery of India,* The John Day Company, 1946

Document 2: Britain took advantage of India and ruined their economy.

Question #3 in the CRQ Section – Turning Point

This is the second type of question the Regents can ask in the third question of the CRQ.
This type of question has 2 parts.
Here's a snapshot of a typical Turning Point question from the Regents:

> **Turning point**—is a major event, idea, or historical development that brings about significant change. It can be local, regional, national, or global.
>
> 34a–34b Using evidence from ***both*** Documents 1 and 2 and your knowledge of social studies:
>
> a) Identify a turning point associated with the historical developments related to both Documents 1 ***and*** 2. [1]
>
> b) Explain why the historical developments associated with these documents are considered a turning point. Be sure to use evidence from both Documents 1 ***and*** 2 in your response. [1]

In short, this is what you have to do:
Part a: Write down a turning point (a major change that happened in history) from the document. Don't bother wasting your ink on any details here. Save that for the next part!

Part b: Explain how the turning point in one document led to the idea/event in the next document.
A turning point basically means a major development that led to other events or ideas. You can use this sentence to help you again:

> ________________ led to ________________.
> (TURNING POINT) (RESULT/EFFECT)

Question #3 in the CRQ Section – Turning Point Example

34a–34b Using evidence from ***both*** Documents 1 and 2 and your knowledge of social studies:

a) Identify a turning point associated with the historical developments related to both Documents 1 ***and*** 2. [1]

b) Explain why the historical developments associated with these documents are considered a turning point. Be sure to use evidence from both Documents 1 ***and*** 2 in your response. [1]

34a Score

34b Score

On the Regents, you'll have to flip back to find the documents. But here, we spoil you a bit. On the following 2 pages, we'll show you the documents. You're welcome, by the way 😉.

Question #3 in the CRQ Section – Turning Point Example

Document 1

Peep Under the Iron Curtain

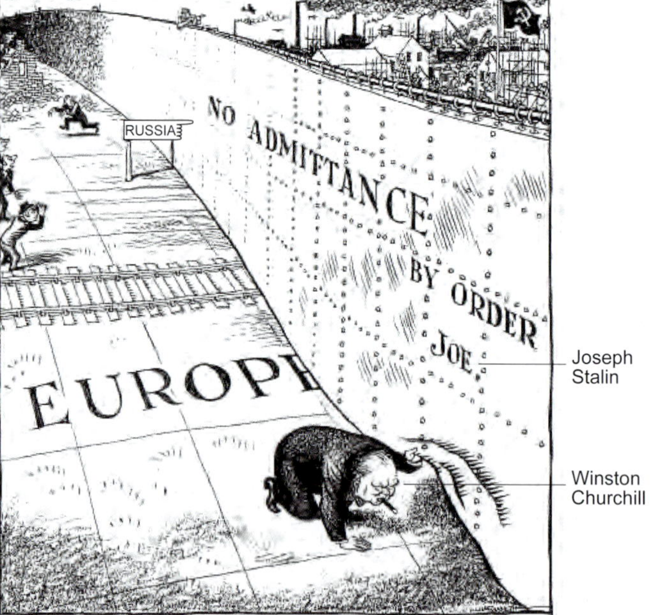

Source: Leslie Gilbert Illingworth, Daily Mail, March 6, 1946 (adapted)

Question #3 in the CRQ Section – Turning Point Example

Document 2

United States President George H. W. Bush and Russian President Boris Yeltsin met at Camp David at a United States–Russian Summit. They issued a Joint Declaration on February 1, 1992.

At the conclusion of this meeting between an American President and the President of a new and democratic Russia, we, the leaders of two great peoples and nations, are agreed that a number of principles should guide relations between Russia and America.

1. Russia and the United States do not regard each other as potential adversaries. From now on the relationship will be characterized by friendship and partnership founded on mutual trust and respect and a common commitment to democracy and economic freedom.
2. We will work to remove any remnants of cold war hostility, including taking steps to reduce our strategic arsenals.
3. We will do all we can to promote a mutual well-being of our peoples and to expand as widely as possible the ties that now bind our peoples. Openness and tolerance should be the hallmark of relations between our peoples and governments.
4. We will actively promote free trade, investment and economic cooperation between our two countries.
5. We will make every effort to support the promotion of our shared values for democracy, the rule of law, respect for human rights, including minority rights, respect for borders and peaceful change around the globe.
6. We will work actively together to:

– Prevent the proliferation of weapons of mass destruction and associated technology, and curb the spread of advanced conventional arms on the basis of principles to be agreed upon.

– Settle regional conflicts peacefully.

– Counter terrorism, halt drug trafficking and forestall [prevent] environmental degradation.

In adopting these principles, the United States and Russia today launch a new era in our relationship. In this new era, we seek a peace, an enduring peace that rests on lasting common values. This can be an era of peace and friendship that offers hope not only to our peoples, but to the peoples of the world. . . .

Source: "Joint Declaration," U.S.–Russian Summit, Camp David, February 1, 1992
Berlin Information Center for Transatlantic Security online

Question #3 in the CRQ Section – Turning Point Example Answer

The answer to part a, which asks you to identify a turning point associated with the developments related to both documents, is:

Fall of the Iron Curtain/fall of communism/end of the Cold War

We analyzed Document 1, which shows Churchill peeking under the Iron Curtain. This symbolizes the fall of the Iron Curtain.

In part b, you are asked why the historical developments associated with these documents are considered a turning point.

The fall of the Iron Curtain led to better relationships between Russia and the US.
(TURNING POINT) Doc 1 — (RESULT/EFFECT) Doc 2

Other acceptable answers:

- When the Iron Curtain came down, political relationships improved/diplomacy opened.
- The United States and its allies were enemies of the Soviet Union, and when the Cold War ended, the United States and Russia worked together to fight dangers/terrorism.
- Document 1 shows Europe divided by communism/the Cold War and Document 2 shows a major change between the United States and Russia in which Cold War hostilities ended.
- Document 1 shows Stalin/the Soviets not wanting to admit people into Eastern Europe and Document 2 shows that openness became a hallmark of relations between the Soviet Union and the United States.

Part b must include information from both documents to get full credit.

Question #3 in the CRQ Section – Similarity/Difference

This is the third type of question the Regents can ask you in the third question of the CRQ.
This type of question will have 2 parts.

Here's a snapshot from a recent Regents:

> **Similarity**—tells how something is alike or the same as something else.
>
> **Difference**—tells how something is not alike or not the same as something else.
>
> 34a-34b Using evidence from ***both*** Documents 1 and 2 and your knowledge of social studies:
>
> a) Identify a similarity ***or*** a difference between the economic development policies of Mao Zedong and those of Deng Xiaoping. [1]
>
> b) Explain the similarity ***or*** difference you identified using evidence from both documents. [1]

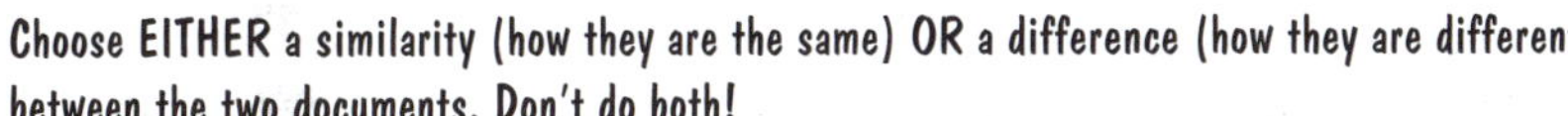

Choose EITHER a similarity (how they are the same) OR a difference (how they are different) between the two documents. Don't do both!
Now answer both parts of the question using the similarity OR difference that you chose.

Part a: State a similarity OR difference between the topics they gave you.
Don't waste your ink explaining. Save that for the next part!

Part b: Explain the similarity or difference that you chose.
To get full credit, make sure you use information from BOTH documents.

Question #3 in the CRQ Section – Similarity/Difference Example

Similarity—tells how something is alike or the same as something else.

Difference—tells how something is not alike or not the same as something else.

34a-34b Using evidence from ***both*** Documents 1 and 2 and your knowledge of social studies:

a) Identify a similarity ***or*** a difference between the economic development policies of Mao Zedong and those of Deng Xiaoping. [1]

b) Explain the similarity ***or*** difference you identified using evidence from both documents. [1]

____

____

____

____

____

____

34a Score ☐

34b Score ☐

On the Regents, you'll have to flip back to find the documents. But here, we'll spoil you again. On the following 2 pages, we'll show you the documents. You're welcome again, by the way 😉

Question #3 in the CRQ Section – Similarity/Difference Example

Document 1

Economic development has played a role in China's efforts to establish its identity and to maintain its security at different times in its history. Economic development policies have affected China's relationship with foreigners. This excerpt focuses on economic development in China before Mao Zedong came to power and during the time Mao was in power.

> . . . Chinese economic and technological systems were backward compared to those of the West. This sense of vulnerability created the dominating issue of modern Chinese politics, the search for wealth and power. Left unsolved by previous governments, the problem remained to be addressed by the People's Republic when it came to power [on October 1, 1949].
>
> To develop without relying on foreign powers, Mao Zedong and his colleagues devised a system modeled on Stalinism but with a number of unique features. They collectivized the land and organized the peasants into communes. The party-state extracted capital from agriculture, used it to build state-owned industry, and returned the profits to more industrial investment. This led to rapid industrial growth in the 1950s, although growth slowed later under the impact of the Great Leap Forward and the Cultural Revolution. In three decades China made itself self-sufficient in nearly all resources and technologies.
>
> However, by the end of Mao's life in 1976 China's economy was stagnant [not advancing], and technology lagged twenty to thirty years behind world standards and most Chinese lived in cramped quarters with poor food and clothing, few comforts, and no freedoms. Much of Asia and the world had raced beyond China toward technical and social modernity. . . .

Source: "China's Foreign Policy: The Historical Legacy and the Current Challenge," Asia for Educators online, Columbia University, 2009

Question #3 in the CRQ Section – Similarity/Difference Example

Document 2

Deng Xiaoping was the most powerful leader in China from December 1978 until he stepped down in 1992. In early 1992, Deng Xiaoping visited and gave talks in some southern Chinese cities.

> . . . The reason some people hesitate to carry out the reform and the open policy and dare not break new ground is, in essence, that they're afraid it would mean introducing too many elements of capitalism and, indeed, taking the capitalist road. The crux of the matter is whether the road is capitalist or socialist. The chief criterion for making that judgement should be whether it promotes the growth of the productive forces in a socialist society, increases the overall strength of the socialist state and raises living standards. As for building special economic zones, some people disagreed with the idea right from the start, wondering whether it would not mean introducing capitalism. The achievements in the construction of Shenzhen have given these people a definite answer: special economic zones are socialist, not capitalist. In the case of Shenzhen, the publicly owned sector is the mainstay of the economy, while the foreign-invested sector accounts for only a quarter. And even in that sector, we benefit from taxes and employment opportunities. We should have more of the three kinds of foreign-invested ventures [joint, cooperative and foreign-owned]. There is no reason to be afraid of them. So long as we keep level-headed, there is no cause for alarm. We have our advantages: we have the large and medium-sized state-owned enterprises and the rural enterprises. More important, political power is in our hands.
>
> Some people argue that the more foreign investment flows in and the more ventures of the three kinds are established, the more elements of capitalism will be introduced and the more capitalism will expand in China. These people lack basic knowledge. At the current stage, foreign-funded enterprises in China are allowed to make some money in accordance with existing laws and policies. But the government levies taxes on those enterprises, workers get wages from them, and we learn technology and managerial skills. In addition, we can get information from them that will help us open more markets. Therefore, subject to the constraints of China's overall political and economic conditions, foreign-funded enterprises are useful supplements to the socialist economy, and in the final analysis they are good for socialism. . . .

Source: Deng Xiaoping, "Excerpts from Talks Given in Wuchang, Shenzhen, Zhuhai, and Shanghai," January 18–February 21, 1992, China Through A Lens online

Question #3 in the CRQ Section – Similarity/Difference Example Answer

First, let's dissect the documents to figure out what's going on. It's a good idea to summarize the documents for yourself so that you can pull out a similarity or a difference easily.

Document 1 Summary: Mao Zedong developed the Chinese economy based on Stalinism, but with new features, including collectivized land and communes. Mao did not rely on foreign powers. The economy grew rapidly until later in Mao's life when it stagnated (stopped developing).

Document 2 Summary: Deng Xiaoping encouraged foreign investment to improve the economy. He built special economic zones for publicly owned businesses and foreign investment. He invited Western economic ideas into China.

Part a: Just state the similarity or difference. Don't expound. Save that for Part b.

Question #3 in the CRQ Section – Similarity/ Difference Example Answer

<u>Acceptable answers:</u>

Similarities:

- Both Mao Zedong and Deng Xiaoping controlled/encouraged economic development.
- Both maintained state-owned industries within China.
- Both used government-led policies to promote development. / Both made reforms.

Differences:

- Mao Zedong and Deng Xiaoping had different perspectives on the role of foreigners in economic development.
- They differed in how they viewed communist economic theory.
  They looked to different sources for economic development.
- They focused on different sectors of the economy.
- The end results of Mao's and Deng's programs were different.
- Mao and Deng used different ideologies to form their economic policies.
- Mao's and Deng's reforms led to different economic/social results

- The answer must show how Mao and Deng's economic policies were the same or different. Do not write: "They were similar" or "They were different." Also do not write: "Moa and Deng were the same" or "Mao and Deng were different."
- Just write one similarity or difference. The answers listed above are possible examples of correct answers.

Question #3 in the CRQ Section – Similarity/Difference Example Answer

Part b: Now you need to explain your answer in Part a. Pretend you're the teacher, and just talk it out.

Acceptable answers:

Similarities:

- Mao and Deng were similar in that they both maintained state-owned industries within China to encourage economic development.
- They were similar because they both used government-led policies to promote development, as Mao used collectivization and communes and Deng used special economic zones.

Differences:

- Mao wanted China to develop without relying on foreign powers while Deng wanted to open China to foreign investment.
- They were different in how they viewed communist economic theory, as Mao modeled his economic policy on Stalinism with some unique features while Deng introduced some elements of capitalism to supplement the socialist economy.
- Mao stressed self-sufficiency whereas Deng stressed foreign investment.
- Mao encouraged the growth of China through agricultural policies whereas Deng focused on growth through urban industrial policies.
- The end results of Mao's and Deng's programs were different, as Mao's Great Leap Forward/Cultural Revolution led to stagnation in China and Deng's reforms led to growth in China.

- Make sure you explained whatever you wrote in Part a in detail. Don't restate what you wrote in Part a. Expound, discuss, and explain it.
- Make sure you mentioned information from both Document 1 and Document 2!

CRQ Summary

Okay, CRQ genius! Here's a summary of what we just said: There are 2 sets of CRQ questions. Each set contains 3 questions (with one including 2 parts).

Types of CRQ questions:

1. Question 1: Historical or geographical context
2. Question 2: Sourcing (BAPP – bias, audience, point of view, or purpose)
3. Question 3: This always asks about the relationship between Documents 1 and 2. They can ask 3 different types of questions:
   a) Cause and effect
   b) Turning point (identify + explain)
   c) Similarity/difference between ideas/events in the 2 documents (identify + explain)

Keep in mind, my dear friend, that all the info in this section is here to help you, not to make you do more work. Do not memorize the different types of questions. Just know the skills to help you answer each question when you get to it.

Award Time!

All you have left is one essay!
(Start ordering pizza.)

You've just completed the multiple choice question and CRQ skill sections. Woohoo! Here's a huge medal!

UNIT 20

ESSAY ZONE

Essay Time!

Now that you're a pro at Global info, multiple choice and CRQ skills, let's dive in to learn how to write a smashing essay! There is only one essay on the Global II Regents, and I'll walk you through each step so that you'll know exactly how to write that killer essay. Get ready to shock your teacher and markers!

This essay, the last section of the Regents (yay!), is super important because it makes up 29% of your Regents grade!

Your essay will be marked based on the Global II Scoring Rubric. You can receive a score of zero to five. Flip to the end of the book to find the scoring rubric.

An essay that addresses all aspects of the task and given guidelines, analyzes information, and is well organized wins you a score of five, which means you get full credit! That's our goal.

Of course, this would never happen, but if you leave out parts of the task or guidelines, fail to analyze information, or don't organize information properly, your score will be lower.

The best part of this essay section is that the essay topic will always be about "Enduring Issues."

What are Enduring Issues?

An Enduring Issue is:

- Enduring: It has long-lasting effects.
- An Issue: An important topic or problem that society faces/faced and discussed that affects/affected a lot of people.

The Regents will give you 5 documents. You get to choose one Enduring Issue present in at least 3 of those documents. You will then go on to write a fabulous essay about that issue, using those 3 documents and your own knowledge !

How will you know which issue to choose?
Well, either you can just use your brain and find a broad issue with the requirements listed above that includes concepts from 3 of the documents they give you.

Or you can come along as I spoil you and give you the Boosters Enduring Issues Tricks.

The 9-Trick

There are dozens and dozens of enduring issues that you can write about. You are welcome to familiarize yourself with all of them. But if you're like most high school kids, you're probably not interested in memorizing fifty issues. (You're probably busy enough with your own issues.)

Here's the Boosters way: Become super familiar with these 9 broad issues that can be used on any Regents.

The Magic Nine:

1. Inequality/Human Rights Violations
2. Innovation
3. Scarcity
4. Power
5. Environmental impact
6. Conflict
7. Ideas and beliefs
8. Interconnectedness
9. Cooperation

Still don't know how you'll remember all that? Just memorize these 2 words and you're good to go!

This is an acronym for Inequality/Human Rights Violation, Innovation (the "2" indicates 2 words that start with "In"), Scarcity, Power, Environmental impact, Conflict, Ideas and beliefs, (F is for fun because we're having fun 😊 – no, that's not an enduring issue!), Interconnectedness, Cooperation.

Exploring the 9 Issues

Now let's explore each issue. After all, you'll be writing a full analytical essay on the topic!

For each issue, we'll:

1. Explore the issue
   (Get out the tissues.)
2. Explore historical examples associated with that issue

- Heads up! Sometimes the content of the document will be based on something you've learned about. That's fun, because you have that info in your pocket to expand on.
- Other times, the content of the document looks like Chinese to you. That's fun too, because you can interpret the document, figure out which issue it falls under, and then expand on it by comparing it to similar events or ideas in history that you are familiar with.
- Keep in mind that these 9 issues are broad and include ("nest") other issues. For example, "conflict" can include war and terrorism. You can choose to write about conflict or any issue that falls under conflict, such as war or terrorism.
- PS: This section includes a brief summary of historical examples of each issue. The full content is included in the first part of the book.

Enjoy the issues! (Is that an oxymoron?)

Inequality/Human Rights Violation

What's the issue?

Inequality means that one person or group of people has control and power over another.

Human Rights are rights and freedoms that every person is entitled to, according to the United Nations. Human Rights Violations are violations of those basic human rights.

Let's discuss it! (Feel free to use this content in your essay!)

Sometimes people feel superior (better than) others because of wealth, power, or advancements. They may scorn (look down at) people who they consider inferior (lesser). Since they consider themselves superior, they may feel justified in violating (abusing) the human rights of those they consider inferior. The United Nations compiled a list of basic human rights, which includes freedom of thought, freedom of expression, the right to education, and the right to ownership, marriage and family, among many others.

- Genocide is the act of deliberately killing a large group of people, usually from a particular ethnic group. This is often associated with human rights violations.

Why it's significant:

The issue affects many people: This issue has affected millions of people around the world. (Specifics are coming soon.)

Everlasting issue: Despite continued attempts by the United Nations and other organizations, human rights continue to be violated around the world.

Historical Examples of Inequality/ Human Rights Violations

Here are some examples of how this issue has played out in history.

1. **Imperialism** created a sense of inequality between the mother countries and the colonized countries. Often, the colonies' rights were violated.
   - Think British imperialism in India, China, and Africa and how Britain took advantage of these colonies.
2. **Armenian Massacre** (early 1900s): Over 1.5 million Christian Armenians living in Turkey (a Muslim country) were murdered because of their religion. (This is an example of genocide, or mass murder.)

3. The **Holocaust** (during World War II): The Nazis violated the rights of European Jews and sought to exterminate them. Adolf Hitler led this movement and wrote Mein Kampf to spread his anti-Semitic ideas. The Nazis killed over 6 million Jews because of their religion – large-scale genocide.
4. **Pol Pot and the Khmer Rouge** regime (1970s): They set up "killing fields" in Cambodia to kill anyone opposed to their communist ideas.
5. **Anti-apartheid movements in South Africa** (1980s and 1990s): Black Africans resisted their mistreatment and fought for equality and freedom.
6. **Rwanda, Africa** (1994): Tribal boundary conflicts led to severe human rights violations, as the Hutus and Tutsis committed mass murder against each other.

Innovation

What's the issue?

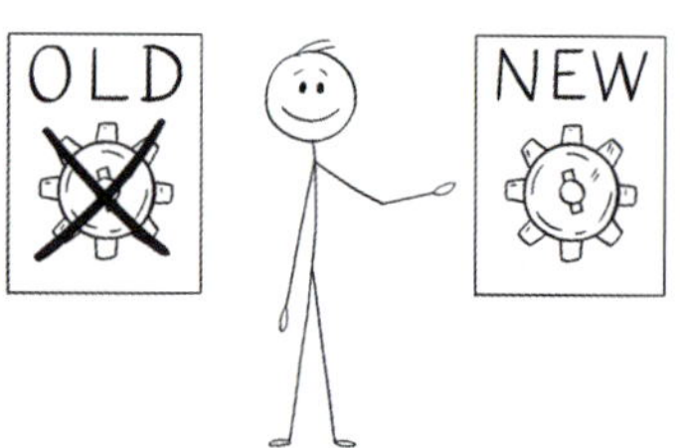

An innovation is a new idea, a change, or a new way of doing things.

Let's discuss it! (Feel free to use this content in your essay!)

Innovations can have positive or negative impacts.

Innovations have brought tremendous advancements and conveniences to society. As technology advances, more innovations impact the world. Sometimes, these innovations are extremely beneficial to society. Other times, the innovations lead to serious environmental issues and dangerous conflict.

Why it's significant:

The issue affects many people: Innovations throughout history have affected every person on planet earth.

Everlasting issue: As technology advances and more innovations happen, the world suffers from their negative impacts.

Historical Examples of Innovation

Here are some examples of how this issue played out in history.

1. **Agrarian Revolution** (1700s and early 1800s): Technological improvements in farming
2. **Industrial Revolution** (1700s-1800s): Innovations were made in the way goods were produced. Originally, goods were produced at home, by hand. During the Industrial Revolution, goods started being mass-produced in factories, by machinery.
   - Positive impacts: mass production of goods, greater production, development of capitalism
   - Negative impacts: abuse of natural resources, pollution, bad conditions, child labor
3. **Meiji Restoration** in Japan (1800s): Meiji opened Japan's doors to foreign trade and modernized Japan.
4. **World War I** (1914-1918): Technological innovations – such as submarine warfare, trench warfare, and poison gas – made this a much more dangerous war with a high death toll.
5. **Urbanization:** People move to cities to gain access to jobs and shopping. This causes serious pollution that harms the environment.
6. **Modern technology:** Computers, internet, and social media boost the economy and connect people in countries around the world. However, digital communication has also enabled the quick spread of dangerous ideas and hate, which led to conflicts, such as the Arab Spring.

Scarcity

What's the issue?

Scarcity means not having enough of something. When a country does not have enough of important materials, they may trade with other countries or fight wars to get what they need.

Let's discuss it! (Feel free to use this content in your essay!)

Natural resources are materials that occur in nature and can be used for economic gain. Examples of natural resources include minerals, forests, water, rubber, oil, food crops, and gold. Some countries are missing natural resources, which leads them to seek those resources in other places. Sometimes, people die from hunger and drought due to lack of resources.

Why it's significant:

The issue affects many people: Throughout history, nations have suffered from scarcity of different materials.

Everlasting issue: Some countries, such as some African nations, don't have enough food or medicine, and people are starving, suffering, and dying as a result. Some countries exploit the resources of other countries for economic gain, which causes serious ongoing conflict. This issue persists until today.

Historical Examples of Scarcity

Here are some examples of how this issue played out in history.

1. **Irish Potato Famine** (1845): Great Britain imperialized Ireland and exported much of its produce. The Irish had to live off their potato crop. In the mid-1800s, a million Irish people died from starvation when the potato crop failed. Millions of Irish people migrated to the United States to escape the famine.

2. **Japan after the Meiji Restoration** (1850s): Japan had to acquire natural resources from other countries, as it suffered from a scarcity of natural resources.
3. **Imperialism:** European nations imperialized India, China, and Africa to gain their natural resources for economic gain. Imperialism drained the colonies of their resources.
4. **Oil in the Middle East:** Oil (petroleum) is the primary energy source used around the world. The Middle East contains stores of oil and Middle Eastern countries fight over these precious oil fields. For example, Sandam Hussein invaded Kuwait to gain access to its oil fields. Countries around the world are dependent on the Middle East's oil. Countries established an organization called OPEC (Organization of Petroleum Exporting Countries) to control the oil industry by setting prices and production levels.
5. **Drought/lack of water in desert areas:** Pakistan and India are at conflict over the water resources in Kashmir. There are many other countries around the world who face controversy over water sources.

Power

What's the issue?

Power is the ability of people or a nation to control or influence others.

Let's discuss it! (Feel free to use this content in your essay!)

People or groups seek power for economic, political, or religious reasons. Power can be used positively, to influence and help others. However, when those in power are focused on personal economic gain and honor, they often pursue these goals at the expense of others and end up violating other people's basic rights. They often feel superior to others and abuse the groups they view as inferior.

Why it's significant:

The issue affects many people: Throughout history, people from all over the world have suffered from brutal leaders or ruling parties who abused their control and terrorized people.

Everlasting issue: Despite continued attempts by the United Nations and other organizations, leaders and ruling parties in some countries continue to abuse their power.

Historical Examples of Power

Here are some examples of how this issue has played out in history.

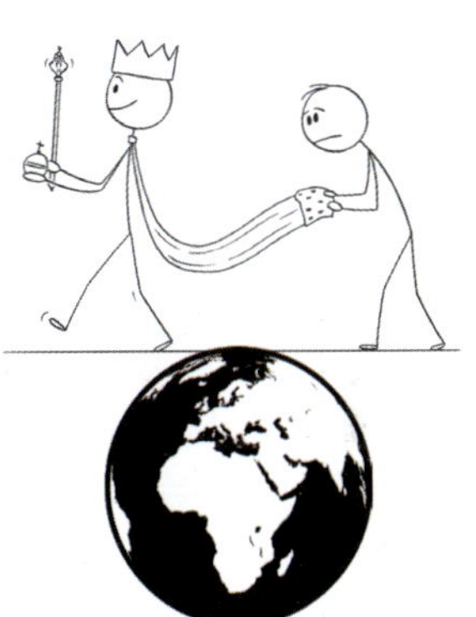

1. **French Revolution** (1789): Power was unfairly divided in the French government. The First and Second Estates (clergy and nobles) had special rights, lots of money, and didn't pay taxes. The Third Estate (middle and lower classes) had to pay most taxes and had no rights, so they revolted against the French monarchy.
2. **Imperialism** (1870-1914): Stronger nations had the power to colonize weaker nations and exploit their natural resources.
3. **Hitler and the Holocaust**: (1914-1918) Hitler used his power as Fuhrer (leader) to discriminate against and massacre millions of Jews.
4. **Stalin and communism** (early 1900s): Stalin terrorized and penalized anyone opposed to communist ideas.
5. **Cold War** (1947-1991): The United States and USSR abused their power by investing millions of dollars to advance themselves in the Arms Race and Space Race.

Environmental Impact

What's the issue?
Our environment is the area around us (the city, mountains, air...). We are affected by the environment, and the environment is affected by us.

Let's discuss it! (Feel free to use this content in your essay!)
People have a responsibility to keep the environment clean and pure. Unfortunately, pollution has become a major issue in industrialized areas, as harmful gases released by factories cause diseases, such as asthma and lung cancer, and may have contributed to global warming, which increases the risk that melting glaciers can flood the earth.
The environment contains precious natural resources, materials that occur in nature and can be used for economic gain. Examples of natural resources include minerals, forests, water, rubber, oil, food crops, and gold. Some countries are missing natural resources, which leads them to seek access to these resources in other places. Sometimes, people die from hunger and drought because they cannot access the necessary resources.

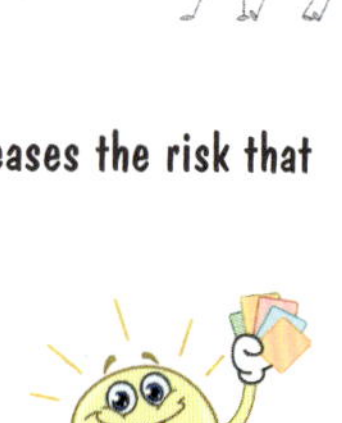

Yes, this issue overlaps with "scarcity."

Why it's significant:

The issue affects many people: Pollution and pursuit of natural resources are issues for billions of people across planet earth.

Everlasting issue: Pollution and exploitation (taking advantage) of natural resources remains an everlasting issue.

Historical Examples of Environmental Impact

Here are some examples of how this issue has played out in history.

1. **Industrial Revolution** (1760): Factories polluted the water and air terribly, causing diseases and death. The crowded slums and lack of sanitation harmed the environment.
2. **Deforestation:** People chop down forests to gather wood to use or sell for profit. Sometimes, forests are cut down to accommodate new homes, factories, and shops. Deforestation leads to increased carbon dioxide in the air, which causes disease and environmental damage. Environmentalists are concerned that the increase in carbon dioxide is increasing earth's temperature, which can cause glaciers to melt and flood the world.
3. **Urbanization:** When people move to cities, the environment is affected. More homes, factories, and shops are erected, which causes air and water pollution, which can lead to disease, global warming, and acid rain.

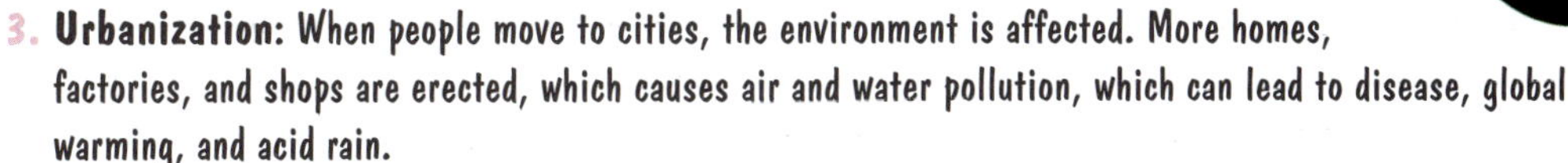

4. **Monsoons** in Southeast Asia cause flooding, damage, and deaths.
5. **Natural disasters**, such as hurricanes, volcanoes, and tsunamis can cause serious environmental damage, which can affect the economic state of the region.
6. Countries' **environmental factors** affect their history:
   - Africa has many natural barriers, which limits cultural diffusion.
   - Great Britain was able to start the Industrial Revolution because of its close proximity to water.
   - Russia has fought many wars to gain access to warm water ports.

Conflict

[What's the issue?]

Conflict means serious disagreement or argument. Conflict can be between individuals, groups, or nations.

Let's discuss it! (Feel free to use this content in your essay!)

Conflict can happen in the form of wars (foreign and civil), political revolutions, or tension between the forces of tradition and modernization. Conflict can stem from inequality, political disagreement, or a desire to gain land or natural resources. Nationalism around the world has led to many conflicts throughout history. Often, conflict leads to human rights violations, killing, and economic ruin. When disagreement arises, serious efforts should be made to reach a peaceful solution and avoid conflict and its horrendous effects.

Why it's significant:

The issue affects many people: Throughout history, wars, revolutions, and ethnic conflict have caused many millions of deaths.

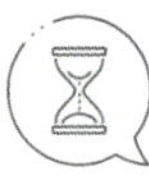

Everlasting issue: Although much effort is invested into maintaining world peace, conflict persists around the world.

Historical Examples of Conflict

Here are some examples of how this issue has played out in history.

1. **French Revolution** (1789-1799): The French monarchy abused the French people's natural rights, so they revolted (made a revolution).
2. **Latin American Revolutions** (1800s): Latin American colonies revolted to gain independence from their mother countries.
3. **Imperialism:** Major conflicts erupted between the colonies and their mother countries.
4. **World War I** (1914-1918): This war was considered a total war because it affected countries to an unprecedented extent. In this war, new military technologies were used, which increased the war's death toll considerably.
5. **World War II** (1939-1945): Hitler led the Nazi party to power in Germany, and the Nazis then exterminated millions of people whom they considered inferior, including genocide of six million Jews.
6. **Cold War** (1947-1991): The USSR believed in spreading communism, while the United States tried to contain communism. Although this wasn't a typical war with guns and bombs, it involved a major military threat.
7. **Terrorism in the Middle East:** Radical Palestinian Arabs wage attacks against Israel's Jewish population in an effort to gain more land.

Ideas and Beliefs

What's the issue?

Ideas and beliefs are the way people view government, religion, and society.
Ideas and beliefs can be positive or negative.

Let's discuss it! (Feel free to use this content in your essay!)

Our ideas and beliefs are shaped by the environment we live in, our families, our education, and the press. Positive ideas and beliefs have enhanced the world over the generations. Many innovative ideas have brought social and economic gain to society. At times, however, harmful ideas are spread, which can lead to inequality, human rights violations, and serious conflicts.

Why it's significant:

The issue affects many people: Throughout history, dangerous ideas have been spread that led to revolutions, wars, serious conflicts, and human rights violations.

Everlasting issue: As the world becomes more interconnected and technology helps ideas spread quickly, toxic ideas can spread like wildfire and cause serious damage.

Historical Examples of Ideas and Beliefs

Here are some examples of how this issue played out in history.

1. The **Enlightenment** (1700s): New ideas and beliefs spread regarding how governments should treat their people and how people's rights should be guaranteed. This led to many revolutions and independence movements worldwide.
2. **Nationalism:** Pride in one's nation can lead to discrimination against other nations. Nationalism has led to imperialism, revolutions and wars.
3. **Imperialism:** Stronger countries have often sought to control weaker countries. Kipling wrote a poem entitled "The White Man's Burden" (1899) to justify imperialism. He explained that the white man has a responsibility to educate and control colonies. The colonies were often uninterested in the white man's ideas, however.
4. **Communism versus Capitalism:** During the Cold War (1945-1990), the USSR and the United States had a major clash of ideas and beliefs regarding how the government and economy should run.
5. **Westernization versus Tradition:** In Turkey, India, and Japan, Western ideas met with resistance from those who wanted to remain more traditional.
6. **Arab Spring/Terrorism:** Incitement and hate are spread via technology. People act on this incitement and resort to violence and killing.

Interconnectedness

Huh? What's that?

What's the issue?

People and countries grow more connected though trade, cultural diffusion, and better communication.

Let's discuss it! (Feel free to use this content in your essay!)

Long ago, countries distant from one another had almost no interactions with one another. As travel via ships, cars, and planes developed, people have begun to interact much more with others around the world. Moreover, as technology has advanced and the internet and social media have flourished, the world has become closely connected. This impacts trade and international economics and promotes cultural diffusion. Increased communications can have positive effects, such as economic growth, the spread of capitalism, and the spread of technology. But interconnectedness can also lead to the spread of hate, the spread of disease, and international conflict or wars.

 HINT:

Interconnectedness: Countries are very connected with each other.

Why it's significant:

The issue affects many people: Billions of individuals are connected throughout the world by travel, internet, and social media.

Everlasting issue: As society develops better communication tools, countries are becoming more and more interconnected. Since countries are so connected, conflict and disease spread at lightning speed.

Historical Examples of Interconnectedness

Here are some examples of how this issue has played out in history.

1. **The French Revolution** (1789-1799): The revolution in France led to other revolutions around the world, including the Latin American Revolutions.
2. **Imperialism**: Mother countries and colonies became connected, which led to cultural diffusion. For example, Great Britain spread Western ideas to India, China, and Africa.
3. **Industrial Revolution** (1760): New technologies and economic ideas that developed in Britain spread all over Europe, then around the world.
4. **World War I** and **World War II**: European countries made alliances with each other, promising to help each other if a member of the alliance was attacked. Because the alliance system caused so many countries to be interconnected, conflicts between two countries escalated into world wars.
5. **Terrorism** often connects nations. For example, Arab terrorists in the Middle East are interconnected, which has led to brutal outcomes, such as the September 11 attacks on the World Trade Center in New York.
6. **Spread of disease**: Diseases that originate in distant countries are easily spread throughout the world by travelers. For example, the deadly Ebola virus that originated in Africa has spread to many other continents.
7. **Modern economy**: Economies are extremely interconnected. Businesses often outsource production and customer service to utilize available resources and manpower abroad.

Cooperation

What's the issue?

Cooperation means working together to reach a common goal. Nations often work together to solve mutual problems.

Let's discuss it! (Feel free to use this content in your essay!)

Many issues that countries face are not limited to their region, but affect other countries as well. Therefore, when countries cooperate with each other and work together to solve issues, the results can be very successful. Sometimes, however, countries team up to achieve an unfavorable common goal, such as conflict against another country, which can lead to devastating results. Teamwork yields powerful results, sometimes positive and sometimes negative.

Why it's significant:

The issue affects many people: Countries around the world have been and continue to be involved in pacts and international organizations, which affect billions of people. Additionally, when countries team up together to fight, the casualties can be devastating.

Everlasting issue: Pacts and international organizations have been around for many years. Until today, these pacts and organizations have major impacts on world events.

Historical Examples of Cooperation

Here are some examples of how this issue has played out in history.

1. The **Enlightenment** (1715): Philosophers agreed that the government must respect the basic rights and freedoms of the people. This had a positive effect, as many countries achieved independence, including France and Latin America.
2. **Scramble for Africa** (late 1800s): During the Age of Imperialism, the European nations cooperated during the Berlin Conference to colonize Africa. They split the map of Africa among themselves. These countries shared the common goal of imperialism.

3. **Warsaw Pact** and **NATO** (mid-1900s):
   - The Warsaw Pact was a result of cooperation between Communist countries, including the USSR, Poland, and Germany. They joined as allies promising to protect each other if anyone attacked.
   - NATO (North Atlantic Treaty Organization) was a result of cooperation between democratic countries, including the United States, France, and Great Britain. They joined as allies promising to protect each other if anyone attacked.
4. **League of Nations** (after World War I): This international organization was founded with the goal of maintaining world peace. Unfortunately, it was not able to achievel this goal.
5. **United Nations** (after World War II): This intergovernmental organization is responsible for maintaining peace and security between countries.
6. **OPEC**: The Organization of the Petroleum Exporting Countries regulates the oil market's supply and pricing.

Essay Guidelines – Regents Language

Now that you're an expert on the Magic 9 Enduring Issues, let's look at what the Regents wants from us in the essay section.

Great news! The task will always be the same. So let's figure out how to do this once, and then we'll be good to go with whatever the Regents throws at us!

Here's a snapshot of the task. The task will always be shown on the Regents.

***Directions*:** Read and analyze each of the five documents and write a well-organized essay that includes an introduction, several paragraphs, and a conclusion. Support your response with relevant facts, examples, and details based on your knowledge of social studies and evidence from the documents.

An enduring issue is a challenge or problem that has been debated or discussed across time. An enduring issue is one that many societies have attempted to address with varying degrees of success.

Task:

- Identify ***and*** define an enduring issue raised by this set of documents
- Argue why the issue you selected is significant ***and*** how it has endured across time

In your essay, be sure to

- Identify the enduring issue based on a historically accurate interpretation of *at least* ***three*** documents
- Define the issue using relevant evidence from *at least* ***three*** documents
- Argue that this is a significant issue that has endured by showing:
  - How the issue has affected people or has been affected by people
  - How the issue has continued to be an issue or has changed over time
- Include relevant outside information from your knowledge of social studies

In developing your answer to Part III, be sure to keep these explanations in mind:

Identify—means to put a name to or to name.

Define—means to explain features of a thing or concept so that it can be understood.

Argue—means to provide a series of statements that provide evidence and reasons to support a conclusion.

Essay Guidelines – Boosters Language

Bottom line, what do they want from me?

1. Read through and analyze the 5 given documents (which may be a text, a political cartoon, or a map).
2. Then, find a common Enduring Issue in 3 of those documents.
3. Next, plan and write an essay about the Enduring Issue you chose that addresses the tasks above:
   - ☐ State and explain the Enduring Issue you chose.
   - ☐ Show how this issue is important and has endured over time.
   - ☐ Use 3 documents to show how the Enduring Issue has played out in history.
   - ☐ Show that this issue is important because it has affected people or has been affected by people.
   - ☐ Show how this issue has continued over time or has changed over time.
   - ☐ Include outside information relevant to the topic.

Don't memorize this list! I'm just rephrasing the tasks, which you'll get on your Regents.

Great news! We're about to share with you the secret Boosters Essay Magic Method.

We'll take you through the process of writing an essay step by step with loads of tricks along the way. Hang on, you can do this!

Step 1: Read and Analyze 5 Documents

Since you did such an awesome job "cracking" the documents in the other sections, you now have the opportunity to use that skill again!
Tackle one document at a time. Spend time with it. Get to know it.

1. Use the Boosters Multiple Choice Magic technique to "crack" the document.
2. Underline and circle key pieces of information. Then, on the side of the document, jot down the main idea of the document.
   Warning! You will be coming back to the documents many, many times. Save yourself the bother of having to refigure out the main idea each time. Just jot down the main idea on the side of the document.
3. On the other side of the document, write a list of possible enduring issues.

Then repeat this process for the other 4 documents.

Good news! What if you just don't "get" one of the documents? Try. But if you still don't get it, skip it! You don't have to use all 5 documents in your essay.

HINT: When you are going through each document, focus on figuring out which Enduring Issues are being presented.

Go Global Essay Pro!

Step 2: Find a Common Enduring Issue In 3 Documents

Choosing the Enduring Issue:

After you finish analyzing each of the 5 documents, find 3 documents that have a common Enduring Issue.

There are several Enduring Issues topics that you can choose based on each set of documents. There are many possibilities. Choose the one you are most comfortable and familiar with and the one that has 3 documents that support it well.

Step 3: Planning the Essay

Now that you have chosen your main topic, let's discuss how to put together a killer essay!

The tasks on the Regents are very specific and you need to make sure to cover each aspect somewhere in your essay. There are many, many ways that you can structure your essay to get the top score of 5.

The Boosters Essay Magic Method uses a format that works well with Enduring Issues across the board. Try it!

Every essay must contain 3 parts:

1. Introduction
2. Body Paragraphs
3. Conclusion

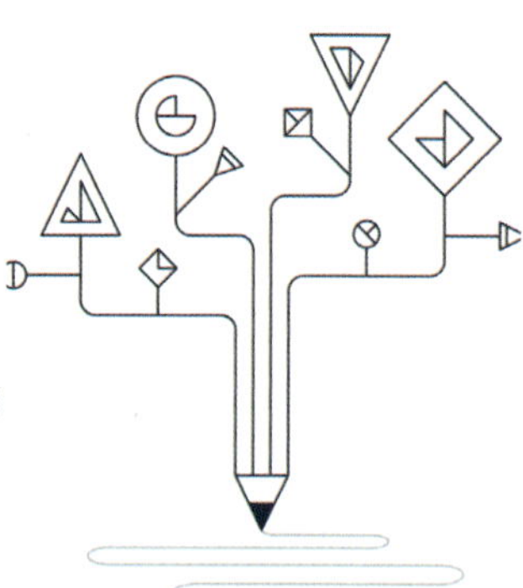

Now let's incorporate each part of the task into the 3 parts of the essay.

Let's set up an essay planner. Don't skip this! It will help you organize your thoughts and write a well-organized essay that includes all the requirements of the assigned tasks.
This will help us plan the 3 essay parts and address each task somewhere in the essay.

Notice how each part of the essay planning chart corresponds to a part of the task. If you forget how to set up the chart, go back to the task to help you remember.

Boosters Magic Essay Planner

Intro: Enduring Issue: ____________________ Why it's significant:		
3 Body Paragraphs: Write about the events or ideas described in 3 of the documents that discuss the Enduring Issue.		
Topic/ Document number	Document info	Outside info
1)		
2)		
3)		
Conclusion: How the issue has affected people or been affected by people: How this issue has persisted or changed over time:		

How to Fill Out the Essay Planner

1. Orange section: Fill in the Enduring Issue you chose.

2. Green section: You chose 3 documents that support the Enduring Issue. For each document, write the document number, the main information that you plan on including from the document, and outside information you know about that topic.

3. Blue section: Answer the 2 questions asked.
   Don't memorize these questions. They are taken from the list of tasks that the Regents will provide. (See the second-to-last bullet in the list of tasks.)
   You may include this information in the body if you wish.

Next Step: Writing the Essay

Yay! The moment we've been waiting for has finally arrived!

If you've spent time analyzing each document and filling out the essay planner, the next part will be much smoother.

Now let's discuss how to write the perfect:

1. Intro
2. Body Paragraphs
3. Conclusion

Have fun!

Analyzing How to Analyze!

If you write the perfect essay, but omit analysis, your essay grade can go from a 5 to a 3 or a 2!
The essay needs to be analytical, not just descriptive.
So what does "analyze" mean?

Analyze means to study something carefully and then explain and interpret it.
In practical terms, it means taking raw facts and information, turning it around in your brain, and then spitting out an interpretation of the facts.

Pretend you're the teacher and you're explaining what a big issue this topic is. Put on your brainy philosopher hat. Just spit out brainy, conceptual, broad comments.

You also want to include as much relevant details as possible.

Raw Information Versus Analysis

Raw information: paraphrasing the document (saying the same thing in other words), or just stating facts

Analysis: taking the information from the document or your brain and interpreting it into a broader concept or deeper idea

Raw information: The Khmer Rouge funded their civil war with profits from timber resources.

Analysis: As many communist groups have done, the brutal Khmer Rouge regime advanced their political goals at the expense of Cambodia's native citizens and precious natural resources. They exploited the country's timber resources and used the funds to finance a conflict that led to over a million deaths. The deforestation wreaked havoc on the environment...

You see the difference? The raw information version spit out bare facts. The analysis version expounded, gave a lot of detail, and, most importantly, interpreted the concept.

Tips to Get Your Brain Spinning with Analysis

- The Magic WHY question:
  Ask yourself why a specific event occurred. Your answer will most likely be an analysis!
- Ask yourself when, where, who, what, and how. What caused something to happen? What were the effects of this development? These questions will help you give over relevant details and dig deeper than the basic information.

- Explain the meaning/main idea of the topic.
- Compare the topic to something relevant.
  This is also a very helpful tool for inserting outside information. Then, it's simple to make a broad statement about events and ideas.
- Evaluate the subject by providing an opinion.
- Make generalized comments about concepts and issues.
- Use this sentence to help you brainstorm an analysis:
  Since I know ________________ (information), I can figure out ________________________(analysis).

How to Write the Perfect Introduction Paragraph:

At the start of your essay, you want to introduce the topic, establish the organization of the essay, and wow your marker.

All you need are these four steps and you get a 5!

1. **State the Enduring Issue you chose.**
   Cheat first sentence: Throughout history, around the world, nations have struggled with _______________ (state Enduring Issue).

> ex Throughout history, around the world, leaders and groups have abused their power and used their authority to oppress weaker people.

Don't write: "My enduring issue is..." or "In this essay, I will...". Avoid using the words "me, my or I" in your Global essay.

2. **Analyze/Explain/Expound/Talk out the issue.**
   Let's go, stick on your brainy philosopher hat. Think why. Make broad statements...

> ex Individuals in the position of power have the ability to influence the behavior of others and the course of events. When those in power are focused on personal economic gain and honor, they often pursue these goals at the expense of others.

How to Write the Perfect Introduction Paragraph (Continued):

3. **Explain why this issue is significant (important).**
   Cheat first sentence: ___________ is a significant Enduring Issue, as it has had lasting effects on society for generations.
   In this sentence try to include:
   a) How the issue has affected many people
   b) How the issue has lasted over a long period of time

   Abuse of power is a significant Enduring Issue, as it has had lasting effects on society for generations.

4. Last sentence: **State 3 examples of the Enduring Issue** that you will explore in your 3 body paragraphs.
   Cheat first sentence: Some examples that illustrate this trend include ___________, ___________, and ___________.

   Some examples that illustrate the trend of abuse of power include Britain's exploitation of the Indian economy, European powers' abuse of African people, and the Khmer Rouge's oppression of the Cambodians.

HINT: Write the intro with EASE –

1. **E**nduring Issue (state it)
2. **A**nalyze (the Enduring Issue)
3. **S**ignificant (Explain why the issue is significant.)
4. **E**xamples (State the 3 examples.)

Check out the green section in your Regents planner to guide you to find the three main ideas you will use as your body paragraphs.

All done! These 4 sentences are the perfect intro!

Intro Example

Throughout history, around the world, leaders and groups have abused their power and used their authority to oppress weaker people.[1] Individuals in the position of power have the ability to influence the behavior of others and the course of events. When those in power are focused on personal economic gain and honor, they often pursue these goals at the expense of others.[2] Abuse of power is a significant enduring issue, as it has had lasting effects on society for generations.[3] Some examples that illustrate this trend include Britain's exploitation of the Indian economy, European powers' abuse of Africans, and the Khmer Rouge's oppression of the Cambodians.[4]

1 Enduring Issue
2 Analyze Enduring Issue
3 Significance
4 Examples

How to Write the Perfect Body Paragraph:

Next step: Write 3 body paragraphs using the 3 examples from the 3 documents.

- It's possible to write an essay using 2 body paragraphs or 4 or more. However, the Boosters Essay party (yes, it's a party!) recommends 3 body paragraphs – to keep you on task and to help you include everything you need in that essay. Also, remember that there are tons of acceptable ways to structure your essay. We are presenting the Boosters Essay Magic Method.

HINT: Think of it as body building. You are building up the body of your essay.

Zip back to your essay planner to find the 3 events/ideas from the 3 documents. This will form the basis of your 3 body paragraphs!

Body paragraph 1	Main ideas from Example 1
Body paragraph 2	Main ideas from Example 2
Body paragraph 3	Main ideas from Example 3

How to Write the Perfect Body Paragraph (Topic Sentence):

1. **Topic sentence:** State the first example and connect it to the Enduring Issue. Your topic sentence will usually be the main idea of each example and not the specific example from the document.

- Use linking words in the second and third topic sentences to help your essay flow well.
- Align your topic sentence with the last sentence in your intro.

Last sentence in intro: Some examples that illustrate this trend include Britain's exploitation of the Indian economy, European powers' abuse of Africans, and the Khmer Rouge's oppression of the Cambodians.

The 3 topic sentences in my essay will align with this last sentence, as follows:

1. **Topic sentence – paragraph 1:** Great Britain was one country that took advantage of its power by imperializing India, forcing the Indians to work for them, and exploiting India's natural resources.
2. **Topic sentence – paragraph 2:** Similarly, in Africa, imperialists abused the African people for economic gain.
3. **Topic sentence – paragraph 3:** The Khmer Rouge regime in Cambodia is another example of abuse of power.

How to Write the Perfect Body Paragraph (Inside & Outside Info):

2. **Rephrase information from the document** and write it in your own words. Do not copy word for word from the document. Say it in your own words and... give your analysis on it. Make yourself sound smart. Don't just state plain facts. Write a brainy comment about the facts.
   - There are two ways to cite information from the document:
     a. You can either include the document number in the sentence:

        ex "Document 1 states..."

     b. OR you can place the citation in parentheses at the end of the sentence.

        ex Eventually the muslin industry in India closed down due to lack of profit (doc 2).

3. **Include outside information.** Write down anything you know about this topic that is not included in the document. But remember to stay on topic.
   Outside information is information from your brain. Yes, there's lots in there! Just dig it up!
   Tip: Compare this event/idea to a similar event/idea in history that you're familiar with.
   If you cannot remember outside information on this topic, simply use your brain to elaborate on the information from the documents, and make sure you insert plenty of outside info in the other paragraphs!

How to Write the Perfect Body Paragraph (Analyze):

4. **Analyze.** This is a sophisticated game of "show and tell"! Discuss the topic. State your analysis.

This is a statement: Britain exploited India's natural resources for its own profit.
This is an analysis: Although the natural resources originated in India, the Indian people saw no gain from it, and they became dependent on Britain's goods.

Suggestions:

- Discuss the importance of this event/idea and its effects.
- Compare this event/idea to similar events/ideas in history.
- Explore why it happened.
- Explain how many people it affected and how long it lasted.

How to Write the Perfect Body Paragraph (Concluding Sentence):

5. **Concluding Sentence:** Summarize the main idea and connect it to your Enduring Issue.

ex: Britain's abuse of India's natural resources caused lasting economic damage to the Indian economy.

More tips on writing an excellent body paragraph:
Be detailed. The more relevant information you include, the better you'll do. Most importantly, make sure to "talk out" and analyze the information you presented. Put on that brainy philosopher hat and write down your brilliant insights!
Now repeat this process for the next two examples.

You will be flipping back to the documents at each step to gain more information.... At least there'll be some action during a quiet Regents!

Body Paragraph Example

Great Britain was one country that took advantage of its power by imperializing India, forcing the Indians to work for the British, and exploiting India's natural resources.[1] As with all mother countries in the Imperialistic era, Britain controlled India for economic motives – to gain raw materials and to use the colony as a market for its manufactured goods. India was known as the "crown jewel" of the British empire because of its valuable raw materials, which the British exported and sold for a huge profit. Even though these natural resources originated in India, the Indian people saw no gain from them, and became dependent on Britain's goods.[2] Muslin, a type of handwoven cotton fabric, was one example of India's most valuable resources. Originally, the Indian people made a handsome profit selling this expensive textile. Then, the British East India Company, followed by the British government itself, forced Indian farmers and weavers to produce the beautiful cloth, which they then sold to other Europeans for profit. Later, the British exported the raw materials to Britain, produced the muslin cloth using their machinery, and then sold the muslin to the Indian market. Eventually the muslin industry in India closed down due to lack of profit [3] (doc 2)[4]. In the 1900s, Mohandas Gandhi led a movement to help India gain independence from Britain and stop the British from abusing India's natural resources and people. His main method was boycotting British goods so that Indians would become less dependent on Britain. He initiated the Homespun Clothing Movement, in which he encouraged people to spin their clothing at home. He also led the Salt March, in which a group of Indian nationalists marched for hundreds of miles to produce salt from seawater instead of buying it from Britain and paying taxes on it. After many years of protest, India eventually gained freedom from British control, but was left economically ruined.[5] Britain's abuse of India's natural resources left lasting economical damage on the Indian economy.[6]

1 Topic sentence includes example and connection to Enduring Issue
2 Outside information and analysis

3 Rephrase information from the document
4 Cite document
5 Outside information and analysis
6 Concluding Sentence

How to Write the Perfect Conclusion

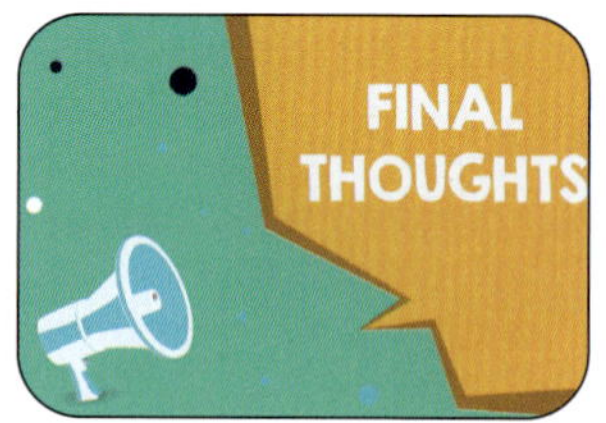

1. Restate the Enduring Issue, its significance, and the examples you used. You can take all this info from the intro and reword it.

   Exploitation of natural resources is a serious enduring issue that has had devastating impacts across the world. This exploitation has led to enduring conflict, wars, and environmental damage. This trend can be seen in Britain's exploitation of India's natural resources, European powers abusing Africa's resources, and Cambodia's use of its timber to fund its civil war.

2. How did the issue continue to be an issue or how has it changed over time?

   Although the age of imperialism is over, the damage caused by mother countries' exploitation of their colonies' resources is everlasting. Many of India's native industries have closed down, which has affected its economy. Africa's boundaries, determined by greedy imperialists, continue to cause serious tribal conflict, resulting in hundreds of thousands of deaths. Cambodia's civil war, funded by timber gathered through deforestation, has wreaked havoc on local economies and the environment. The world is still suffering from the aftereffects of these terrible affairs.

3. Explain why the issue is long lasting and significant.
4. Stick in some brainy analysis somewhere.

Conclusion Example

Abuse of political power is a serious enduring issue that has caused much devastation and death across the world. This trend was demonstrated in Britain's exploitation of the Indian economy, European powers' abuse of Africans, and the Khmer Rouge's oppression of the Cambodian people.[1] Powerful groups that pursue personal economic and political gains often trample on other peoples' basic human rights in the process.[2] Although the age of imperialism is over, the damage caused by mother countries' exploitation of their colonies' resources and people endures. Many of India's native industries have been closed, which has affected its economy. Africa's unnatural boundaries, determined by greedy imperialists, continue to cause serious tribal conflict, resulting in hundreds of thousands of deaths. Additionally, the Cambodians remain in serious conflict until today. Although groups and organizations are working to stop the human rights violations caused by groups abusing their power, the issue persists worldwide.[3]

---

1 Restate the Enduring Issue, its significance, and the examples used.

2 Analysis

3 Issue changed over time, how it lasted, its significance

Enduring Issues Essay Example

Now let's practice it!

Directions: Read and analyze each of the five documents and write a well-organized essay that includes an introduction, several paragraphs, and a conclusion. Support your response with relevant facts, examples, and details based on your knowledge of social studies and evidence from the documents.

An enduring issue is a challenge or problem that has been debated or discussed across time. An enduring issue is one that many societies have attempted to address with varying degrees of success.

Task:

- Identify ***and*** define an enduring issue raised by this set of documents
- Argue why the issue you selected is significant ***and*** how it has endured across time

In your essay, be sure to

- Identify the enduring issue based on a historically accurate interpretation of *at least* ***three*** documents
- Define the issue using relevant evidence from *at least* ***three*** documents
- Argue that this is a significant issue that has endured by showing:
  - How the issue has affected people or has been affected by people
  - How the issue has continued to be an issue or has changed over time
- Include relevant outside information from your knowledge of social studies

In developing your answer to Part III, be sure to keep these explanations in mind:

Identify—means to put a name to or to name.

Define—means to explain features of a thing or concept so that it can be understood.

Argue—means to provide a series of statements that provide evidence and reasons to support a conclusion.

The next 5 pages will show the five documents, and the following page will show the Optional Regents Planning Page.

Enduring Issues Essay Example

Document 1

This excerpt is from the United Nations Press Release of UN Secretary-General Ban Ki-moon's message on the International Day for Preventing Exploitation of the Environment in War and Armed Conflict commemorated on November 6, 2012.

> . . .We must also acknowledge that durable peace and post-conflict development depend on environmental protection and good governance of natural resources. There can be no peace if the resource base that people depend on for sustenance and income is damaged or destroyed—or if illegal exploitation finances or causes conflict.
>
> Since 1990, at least 18 violent conflicts have been fuelled by the exploitation of natural resources such as timber, minerals, oil and gas. Sometimes this is caused by environmental damage and the marginalization [making powerless] of local populations who fail to benefit economically from natural resource exploitation. More often it is caused by greed. . . .
>
> To date, six United Nations peacekeeping missions have been mandated to support the host country's ability to re-establish control over its resource base and stop illicit [unlawful] extraction by armed groups. However, we need a greater international focus on the role of natural resource management in conflict prevention, peacekeeping and peacebuilding. . . .

Source: UN Press Release, SG/SM/14615-OBV/1156, November 1, 2012
United Nations online

Enduring Issues Essay Example

Document 2

Muslin was a type of handwoven cotton fabric fit for emperors produced in Dacca (Dhaka), a part of India before the arrival of Europeans. Muslin today is a lightweight inexpensive machine-made cotton fabric.

> . . .Dhaka's Muslin was felled [demolished] by colonialism's potent mix of the Industrial Revolution and the Maxim gun. Before that fall, though, there was another rise. Europeans came to India at the beginning of the 16th century and were astonished not only at the quality and volume of its cotton textiles, but also by its extensive, far-flung trade. Soon Indian cotton textiles were exported more than ever to Europe, in exponentially increasing volumes, with Bengal taking the lion's share. Fortunes were made. As the economist K. N. Chaudhuri noted, from the earliest times "exports from eastern India . . . were a perennial [endless] source of prosperity to merchants of every nation." . . .
>
> But muslin's days were numbered. The British colonial apparatus, whether in the form of the East India Company or as direct rule by the Crown, was a vast extractive machine. So too had been the Mughal state, which had herded the weavers into designated workshops called *kothis* to labor in harsh, even punitive, conditions. But compared to the pitiless operations of the British, the Mughals were models of mercy. On one side, both Company and Crown squeezed the farmers and the weavers until nothing was left, then squeezed some more. On the other, a factory-produced, mass-product "muslin" rolled off the newly invented power looms in Lancashire cotton mills. Aided by a raft [large number] of tariffs, duties and taxes, British cotton textiles flooded not only the European markets, but the Indian ones as well, bringing Bengal's handloom cotton industry, and muslin, to its knees. . . .

Source: Khademul Islam, "Our Story of Dhaka Muslin," *AramcoWorld,* May/June 2016

 Enduring Issues Essay Example

Document 3

This 1906 cartoon depicting King Leopold II of Belgium as a snake appeared in the British magazine, *Punch*.

IN THE RUBBER COILS.

SCENE—*The Congo "Free" State.*

Source: Linley Sambourne, Punch, November 28, 1906

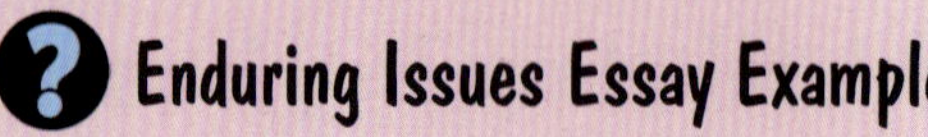

Enduring Issues Essay Example

Document 4

This is an excerpt from a case study lesson on the timber conflict in Cambodia.

> The civil war from 1970 to 1975, the Khmer Rouge regime from 1975 to 1979, and the Cambodia-Vietnam War from 1978 to 1979 virtually destroyed Cambodia's economy. Although rice is Cambodia's most important crop and a staple of the Khmer diet, by 1974, under wartime conditions, rice had to be imported, and production of Cambodia's most profitable export crop, rubber, fell off sharply. Between 1976 and 1978, hundreds of thousands of people died from malnutrition, overwork, and mistreated or misdiagnosed diseases. . . .
>
> Both sides in the Cambodian civil war, the Government and the Khmer Rouge, used timber to fund their war efforts. Global Witness estimated the value of the Thai-Cambodian cross-border timber trade to the Khmer Rouge was approximately $10-$20 million per month in 1995. Conflict over timber resources has led to mass torture, exploitation, and forced displacement in Cambodia. In addition, timber exploitation has wreaked havoc on the environment and local economies. Extensive deforestation has had severe repercussions for indigenous populations, exacerbating [aggravating] the grievances which lead to rebellion and conflict. . . .

Source: Timber Conflict Case Study: Cambodia, Global Witness: "Summary of the Cambodia Campaign: The Forestry Reform Process"

Enduring Issues Essay Example

Document 5

Blood diamond, also called conflict diamond as defined by the United Nations (UN), is any diamond that is mined in areas controlled by forces opposed to the legitimate, internationally recognized government of a country and that is sold to fund military action against that government.

Diamonds for Weapons Trade – near the end of the 20th century

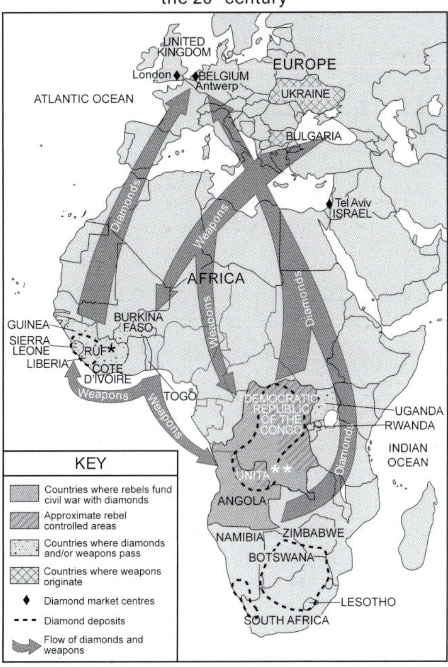

Source: "Blood Diamond," Encyclopaedia Britannica, November 28, 2016 (adapted)

* RUF, Revolutionary United Front is a guerilla unit whose actions led to civil war in Sierra Leone.

** UNITA, National Union for Total Independence of Angola was a political party that saw itself as part of a guerilla movement fighting for independence from Portugal. It fought in the Angola civil war once independence was achieved.

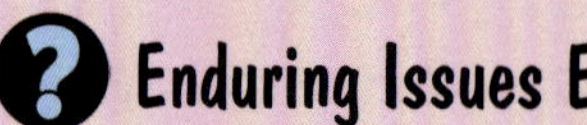

Enduring Issues Essay Example

OPTIONAL PLANNING PAGE

Enduring Issues Essay

You may use the Planning Page organizer to plan your response if you wish, but do NOT write your essay response on this page. Writing on this Planning Page will **NOT** count toward your final score.

My Enduring Issue is:____

Essay Requirements	Yes	Circle documents that apply	One or two possible ideas for outside information
Is this an issue supported by *at least* ***three*** documents? Which documents support this issue?		1 2 3 4 5	
Which documents can be used to develop the definition for this issue?		1 2 3 4 5	
Has this issue significantly affected people or been affected by people? In which document or documents do you see this?		1 2 3 4 5	
Has this issue endured across time or changed over time? In which document or documents do you see this?		1 2 3 4 5	

This page is optional. If you think it'll help you organize your thoughts, go ahead and use it! If not, skip it.

Refer back to page 24 to review the task.

Write your essay on the lined pages in the essay booklet.

Good luck!
♥, Mr. Boosters

Hope you're doing well!
♥, Mr. Boosters

Enduring Issues Answer

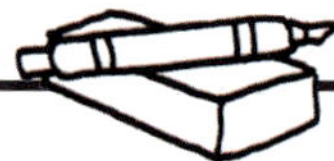

Hi there! It's been a while. I missed you!
I'm sure you wrote the most amazing essay ever and I'm super proud of you, hard worker.

Now it's my turn to write the essay and I'll let you snoop and watch how I did it.
Please keep in mind that there are many different ways you could have gone with this. I'm just giving you one example.

Step 1: Read and analyze the documents.

Come along as I "crack" each document and look out for the Enduring Issues.

Document 1 Analysis

Document 1

This excerpt is from the United Nations Press Release of UN Secretary-General Ban Ki-moon's message on the International Day for Preventing Exploitation of the Environment in War and Armed Conflict commemorated on November 6, 2012.

> . . .We must also acknowledge that durable peace and post-conflict development depend on environmental protection and good governance of natural resources. There can be no peace if the resource base that people depend on for sustenance and income is damaged or destroyed—or if illegal exploitation finances or causes conflict.
>
> Since 1990, at least 18 violent conflicts have been fuelled by the exploitation of natural resources such as timber, minerals, oil and gas. Sometimes this is caused by environmental damage and the marginalization [making powerless] of local populations who fail to benefit economically from natural resource exploitation. More often it is caused by greed. . . .
>
> To date, six United Nations peacekeeping missions have been mandated to support the host country's ability to re-establish control over its resource base and stop illicit [unlawful] extraction by armed groups. However, we need a greater international focus on the role of natural resource management in conflict prevention, peacekeeping and peacebuilding. . . .

Source: UN Press Release, SG/SM/14615-OBV/1156, November 1, 2012
United Nations online

Summary: The United Nations has taken measures to assist nations in reestablishing control over their resources and preventing illegal exploitation. Exploitation of natural resources (such as timber, minerals, oil, and gas) can lead to environmental damage, marginalization of the local population, greed, and violent conflicts.

Enduring Issues:

a) Conflict
b) Human Rights Violations
c) Environmental Impact
d) Scarcity (Groups start wars to gain natural resources that they're missing.)

Document 2 Analysis

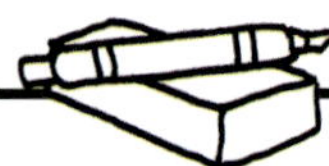

Document 2

Muslin was a type of handwoven cotton fabric fit for emperors produced in Dacca (Dhaka), a part of India before the arrival of Europeans. Muslin today is a lightweight inexpensive machine-made cotton fabric.

> . . .Dhaka's Muslin was felled [demolished] by colonialism's potent mix of the Industrial Revolution and the Maxim gun. Before that fall, though, there was another rise. Europeans came to India at the beginning of the 16th century and were astonished not only at the quality and volume of its cotton textiles, but also by its extensive, far-flung trade. Soon Indian cotton textiles were exported more than ever to Europe, in exponentially increasing volumes, with Bengal taking the lion's share. Fortunes were made. As the economist K. N. Chaudhuri noted, from the earliest times "exports from eastern India . . . were a perennial [endless] source of prosperity to merchants of every nation." . . .
>
> But muslin's days were numbered. The British colonial apparatus, whether in the form of the East India Company or as direct rule by the Crown, was a vast extractive machine. So too had been the Mughal state, which had herded the weavers into designated workshops called *kothis* to labor in harsh, even punitive, conditions. But compared to the pitiless operations of the British, the Mughals were models of mercy. On one side, both Company and Crown squeezed the farmers and the weavers until nothing was left, then squeezed some more. On the other, a factory-produced, mass-product "muslin" rolled off the newly invented power looms in Lancashire cotton mills. Aided by a raft [large number] of tariffs, duties and taxes, British cotton textiles flooded not only the European markets, but the Indian ones as well, bringing Bengal's handloom cotton industry, and muslin, to its knees. . . .

Source: Khademul Islam, "Our Story of Dhaka Muslin," *AramcoWorld*, May/June 2016

Summary: In India, the Mughal Empire, and later the British Empire, produced muslin fabric as cheaply as possible for profit at the expense of Indian laborers working in poor conditions. When the British industrialized and created factories, they displaced the need for Indian handmade muslin cloth at home and overseas.

Enduring Issues:

a) Human Rights Violations

b) Environmental Impact

c) Scarcity (Countries imperialized to gain access to natural resources they were lacking.)

Document 3 Analysis

Document 3

This 1906 cartoon depicting King Leopold II of Belgium as a snake appeared in the British magazine, *Punch*.

Source: Linley Sambourne, Punch, November 28, 1906

Summary: In the Congo Free State (Africa), King Leopold II forced Africans to extract rubber for the benefit of Belgium.

Enduring Issues:

a) Environmental Impact

b) Scarcity (Countries imperialized to gain access to natural resources they were lacking.)

If you didn't "get" this political cartoon, you have plenty of other documents to use.

Document 4 Analysis

Document 4

This is an excerpt from a case study lesson on the timber conflict in Cambodia.

> The civil war from 1970 to 1975, the Khmer Rouge regime from 1975 to 1979, and the Cambodia-Vietnam War from 1978 to 1979 virtually destroyed Cambodia's economy. Although rice is Cambodia's most important crop and a staple of the Khmer diet, by 1974, under wartime conditions, rice had to be imported, and production of Cambodia's most profitable export crop, rubber, fell off sharply. Between 1976 and 1978, hundreds of thousands of people died from malnutrition, overwork, and mistreated or misdiagnosed diseases. . . .
>
> Both sides in the Cambodian civil war, the Government and the Khmer Rouge, used timber to fund their war efforts. Global Witness estimated the value of the Thai-Cambodian cross-border timber trade to the Khmer Rouge was approximately $10-$20 million per month in 1995. Conflict over timber resources has led to mass torture, exploitation, and forced displacement in Cambodia. In addition, timber exploitation has wreaked havoc on the environment and local economies. Extensive deforestation has had severe repercussions for indigenous populations, exacerbating [aggravating] the grievances which lead to rebellion and conflict. . . .

Source: Timber Conflict Case Study: Cambodia, Global Witness: "Summary of the Cambodia Campaign: The Forestry Reform Process"

Summary: In Cambodia, timber resources helped pay for the war between the government and the Khmer Rouge. The wealth generated by selling timber led to increased conflict, damage to the environment, and torture, exploitation, and forced displacement of Cambodians.

Enduring Issues:

a) Environmental Impact
b) Human Rights Violations
c) Power

Document 5 Analysis

Document 5

Blood diamond, also called conflict diamond as defined by the United Nations (UN), is any diamond that is mined in areas controlled by forces opposed to the legitimate, internationally recognized government of a country and that is sold to fund military action against that government.

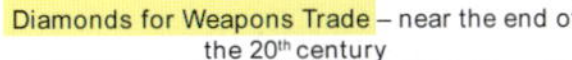

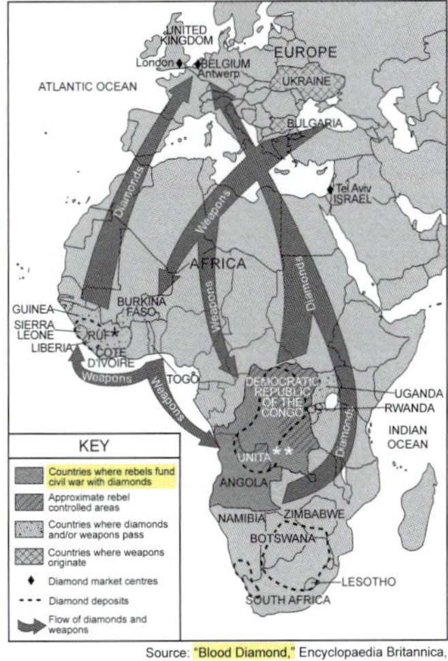

Source: "Blood Diamond," Encyclopaedia Britannica, November 28, 2016 (adapted)

* RUF, Revolutionary United Front is a guerilla unit whose actions led to civil war in Sierra Leone.

** UNITA, National Union for Total Independence of Angola was a political party that saw itself as part of a guerilla movement fighting for independence from Portugal. It fought in the Angola civil war once independence was achieved.

Summary: In Africa, exploitation of the diamond industry helped fund militias that challenged existing governments. Diamonds were often traded for weapons, while preventing legitimate governments from profiting from their sale. Exploitation of the diamond industry created conflicts/wars within Africa while Europeans benefited economically from receiving diamonds and selling weapons.

Enduring Issues:

a) Environmental Impact
b) Human Rights Violations
c) Conflict
d) Power

Step 2: Essay Planning

Now that we figured out the main idea and some possible Enduring Issues topics, let's choose 3 documents that have a common theme and fill out the essay planner.

Intro: **Enduring Issue:** Abusing power **Why it's significant:** leads to serious conflicts, harms many people, and lasts over a long period of time		
3 Body Paragraphs: **Write about the events or ideas described in 3 of the documents that discuss the Enduring Issue.**		
Topic/ Document number	**Document info**	**Outside info**
1) Britain exploited Indian economy/ Doc 2	Britain exploited India's muslin industry	Imperialism and economic motives, Gandhi's boycotts
2) European powers abuse Africans/Doc 3	Belgian king abuses Africans to gain rubber	Berlin conference splits Africa without taking tribal boundaries into account, Rwanda, segregation
3) Khmer Rouge oppress Cambodians/ Doc 4	Cambodian civil war is funded by timber	Pol Pot and "killing fields" Other communist leaders – Stalin of USSR & Mao Zedong of China
Conclusion: **How the issue has affected people or been affected by people** Led to wars and ruined economies and the environment **How this issue has persisted or changed over time** Imperialism ended, but its effects of economic ruin and tribal ethnic conflict continued. Cambodia's abuse of power continues. The issue continues today.		

Intro:

Throughout history, around the world, leaders and groups have abused their power and used their authority to oppress weaker people.[1] Individuals in the position of power have the ability to influence the behavior of others and the course of events. When those in power are focused on personal economic gain and honor, they often pursue these goals at the expense of others.[2] Abuse of power is a significant enduring issue, as it has lasting effects on society for generations.[3] Some examples that illustrate this trend include Britain's exploitation of the Indian economy, European powers' abuse of Africans, and the Khmer Rouge's oppression of the Cambodians[4].

You may recognize parts of my essay from different places in this chapter where it appeared. Now we'll put everything together to give you a clear picture.

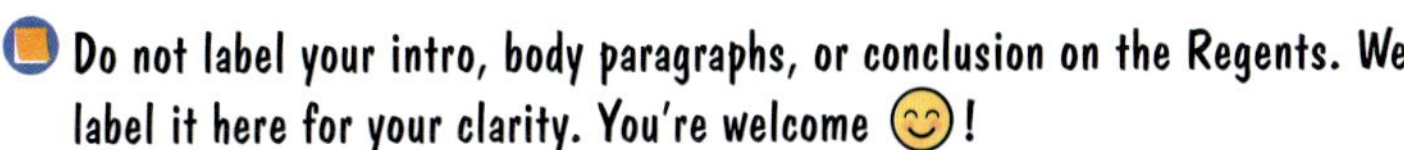

Do not label your intro, body paragraphs, or conclusion on the Regents. We label it here for your clarity. You're welcome 😊!

You'll notice that I wrote using different color inks. Look at the key on the bottom to learn what each color represents.

1 Enduring Issue
2 Analyze Enduring Issue
3 Significance
4 Examples

Body Paragraph 1:

Great Britain was one country that took advantage of its power by imperializing India, forcing the Indians to work for them, and exploiting India natural resources.[1] As with all mother countries in the Imperialistic era, Britain controlled India for economic motives – to gain raw materials and to use the colony as a market for its manufactured goods. India was known as the "crown jewel" of the British Empire because of its valuable raw materials, which the British exported and sold for a huge profit. Although the natural resources originated in India, the Indian people saw no gain from it, and they became dependent on Britain's goods.[2] Muslin, a type of handwoven cotton fabric, was one example of a valuable Indian resources. Originally, the Indian people made a handsome profit selling this expensive textile. Then, the British East India Company, followed by the British government itself, forced Indian farmers and weavers to produce the beautiful cloth, which they then sold to other Europeans for profit. Later, the British exported the raw materials to Britain, produced the muslin cloth using their machinery, and then sold the muslin to the Indian market. Eventually the muslin industry in India closed down due to lack of profit[3] (doc 2).[4] In the 1900's Mohandas Gandhi headed a movement to help India gain independence from Britain and stop the British from abusing India's natural resources and people. His main method was boycotting British goods so that the Indians would become less dependent on Britain. He initiated the Homespun Clothing Movement, in which he encouraged people to spin their clothing at home. He also led the Salt March, in which a group of Indian nationalists marched for hundreds of miles to produce salt from seawater instead of buying it from Britain and paying taxes on it. After many years of protest, India eventually gained freedom from British control, but was left economically ruined.[5] Britain's abuse of India's natural resources left lasting economical damage on the Indian economy.[6]

---

1 Topic sentence includes example and connection to Enduring Issue

2 Outside information and analysis

3 Rephrase information from the document.

4 Cite document.

5 Outside information and analysis

6 Concluding Sentence

Body Paragraph 2:

Similarly, in Africa, imperialists abused the African people for economic gain.[1] Powerful European imperialists scrambled to control parts of Africa in order to utilize its rich natural resources, which included gold, copper, rubber and ivory. During the Berlin Conference, Europeans leaders took a map of Africa and divided it among themselves. They paid no attention to tribal boundaries, breaking up some tribes, while grouping opposing tribes together, which led to serious ongoing ethnic conflict. The European powers' only concern was economic gain. They paid no attention to the African people's rights and needs. The British went as far as instituting segregation rules to separate the native African blacks from the European whites and discriminating against them in many ways. The Europeans decreed that Africans may sit only on separate benches, visit select parks, and use separate facilities. They abused the black African people and forced them to labor for Europe's benefit.[2] For example, Belgian King Leopold II forced the Africans to extract rubber for Belgium's benefit. Document 3[3] depicts King Leopold II of Belgium as a rubber snake wrapped around an African man, symbolizing his abuse of the Africans.[4] Many years later, the Europeans gave up their control of Africa, but the unnatural tribal boundaries that they established continue to cause serious conflict and war until today. Notably, in Rwanda, the Hutu and Tutsis tribes are constantly at war with each other, resulting in hundreds of thousands of deaths.[5] European imperialists exploited their power for their own greedy economic motives, causing lasting damage and hundreds of thousands of deaths in tribal boundary wars that persist until today.[6]

1 Topic sentence includes example and connection to Enduring Issue.
2 Outside information and analysis
3 Cite document.
4 Rephrase information from the document.
5 Outside information and analysis
6 Concluding Sentence

Body Paragraph 3:

The Khmer Rouge regime in Cambodia is another example of abuse of power.[1] During the Cambodian Civil War, the Khmer Rouge and the government used timber resources to finance their conflict. This had serious consequences on the natives in the region. Many Cambodians faced mass torture, exploitation, and forced displacement as a result of their desire for power [2] (document 4)[3]. The Khmer Rouge won the conflict, with Pol Pot as their ruthless leader. They murdered over a million people in places named "killing fields," in an effort to remove Western influences. Although the civil war officially ended, fighting continues until today. Other communist leaders similarly massacred those who opposed their political views, including Stalin of the USSR and Mao Zedong of China.[4] These powerful communist leaders killed millions of people in order to enforce their control.[5]

---

1 Topic sentence includes example and connection to Enduring Issue.

2 Rephrase information from the document.

3 Cite document.

4 Outside information and analysis

5 Concluding Sentence

Conclusion:

Abusing political power is a serious enduring issue that has caused devastating results and deaths across the world. This trend was demonstrated in Britain's exploitation of the Indian economy, European powers' abuse of Africans, and the Khmer Rouge's oppression of the Cambodians.[1] Powerful groups that pursue economic and political gains often trample on other peoples' basic human rights in the process.[2] Although the age of imperialism is over, the damage caused by mother countries' exploitation of their colonies' resources and people endures. Many of India's native industries have been closed down, which has affected its economy. Africa's unnatural boundaries, determined by greedy imperialists, continue to cause serious tribal conflict, resulting in hundreds of thousands of deaths. Additionally, the Cambodians remain in serious conflict until today. Although groups and organizations work to stop human rights violations caused by groups abusing their power, the issue persists worldwide.[3]

---

1 Restate Enduring Issue, its significance, and the examples used.

2 Analysis

3 Issue changed over time, how it lasted, its significance

Checking myself

Let me go back to the task and make sure I completed each piece.

Task:

- Identify ***and*** define an enduring issue raised by this set of documents
- Argue why the issue you selected is significant ***and*** how it has endured across time

In your essay, be sure to

- Identify the enduring issue based on a historically accurate interpretation of *at least* ***three*** documents
- Define the issue using relevant evidence from *at least* ***three*** documents
- Argue that this is a significant issue that has endured by showing:
  - How the issue has affected people or has been affected by people
  - How the issue has continued to be an issue or has changed over time
- Include relevant outside information from your knowledge of social studies

Read through the list of tasks again.

Ask yourself: Did I...

- ☐ Identify and define an enduring issue?
- ☐ Argue why it's significant?
- ☐ Explain how it endured over time?
- ☐ Choose an enduring issue based on at least 3 documents?
- ☐ Explain (show examples of) the enduring issue using at least 3 documents?
- ☐ Show how it affected people or how people were affected by it?
- ☐ Show how the issue has persisted or changed over time?
- ☐ Insert outside relevant information from history?
- ☐ Did I analyze?!!!

Other Issues

As we mentioned, you had many options for essay topics.
Here's a brief list of some other issues you could have written this essay about.

ENDURING ISSUE	DOCUMENTS ASSOCIATED WITH ENDURING ISSUE
Inequality/Human Rights Violations	2, 3, 4
Environmental Impact	1, 2, 3, 4, 5
Power	1, 3, 4, 5
Conflict	1, 2, 3, 4, 5

How Your Essay is Scored

Here's how the marker decides how to rate your essay:

Score of 5:

- Clearly identifies and accurately defines *one* enduring issue raised in *at least three* documents
- Develops an even, thoughtful, and in-depth argument about how an enduring issue has affected people *or* has been affected by them and how the issue continues to be an issue *or* has changed over time
- Is more analytical than descriptive (analyzes, evaluates, and/or creates* information)
- Richly supports the task by incorporating relevant evidence that includes facts, examples, and details from *at least three* documents
- Richly supports the task by incorporating substantial relevant outside information that includes facts, examples, and details
- Demonstrates a logical and clear plan of organization; includes an introduction and a conclusion

Score of 4:

- Identifies and accurately defines *one* enduring issue raised in *at least three* documents
- Develops a thoughtful argument in some depth about how an enduring issue has affected people *or* has been affected by them and how the issue continues to be an issue *or* has changed over time OR develops the argument somewhat unevenly by discussing one aspect of the argument more thoroughly than the other
- Is both descriptive and analytical (applies, analyzes, evaluates, and/or creates* information)
- Supports the task by incorporating relevant evidence that includes facts, examples, and details from *at least three* documents
- Supports the task by incorporating relevant outside information that includes facts, examples, and details
- Demonstrates a logical and clear plan of organization; includes an introduction and a conclusion

How Your Essay is Scored (continued):

Score of 3:

- Identifies and defines *one* enduring issue raised in the set of five documents; may include minor inaccuracies
- Develops both aspects of the argument in little depth *or* develops only one aspect of the argument with some depth
- Is more descriptive than analytical (applies, may analyze and/or evaluate information)
- Incorporates some relevant evidence that includes facts, examples, and details from the documents; may include some minor inaccuracies
- Incorporates limited relevant outside information that includes facts, examples, and details; may include some minor inaccuracies
- Demonstrates a satisfactory plan of organization; includes an introduction and a conclusion

Score of 2:

- Identifies, but does not clearly define, *one* enduring issue raised in the set of documents; may contain errors
- Minimally develops both aspects of the argument or develops one aspect of the argument in little depth
- Is primarily descriptive; may include faulty, weak, or isolated application or analysis
- Includes few relevant facts, examples, and details from the documents or consists primarily of relevant information copied from the documents; may include some inaccuracies
- Presents little or no relevant outside information; may include some inaccuracies
- Demonstrates a general plan of organization; may lack focus; may contain digressions; may lack an introduction or a conclusion

How Your Essay is Scored (continued):

Score of 1:

- Identifies, but does not define, *one* enduring issue raised in the documents
- Minimally develops one aspect of the argument
- Is descriptive; may lack understanding, application, or analysis
- Makes some vague, unclear references to the documents and includes minimal relevant fact, example, and details copied from the documents: may include some inaccuracies
- Presents no relevant outside information
- May demonstrate a weakness in organization; may lack focus; may contain digressions; may lack an introduction and a conclusion

Score of 0:

Fails to develop the task or may only refer to the issue in a general way; *OR* includes no relevant facts, examples, or details; *OR* includes only evidence copied from the documents; *OR* includes only entire documents copied from the test booklet; *OR* is illegible; *OR* is a blank paper

This is not happening to the Boosters Pals!

Global Genius, you did it!
It was a total blast studying with you. I'm sure you'll do amazing.
Keep in touch!

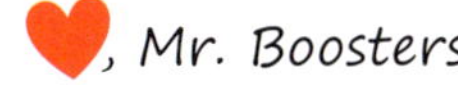
, Mr. Boosters

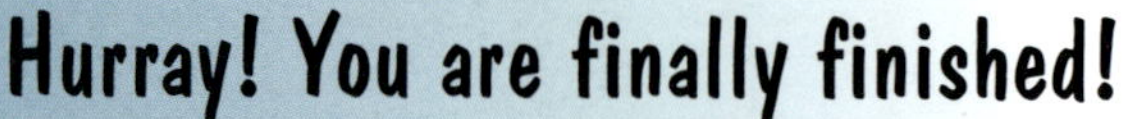

Now make sure to do a lot of practice questions to test your knowledge and get used to the questions.

For orders and comments, please email us at info@regentsboosters.com or visit us at www.EdBoosters.com.